SALISBURY
The Houses of the Close

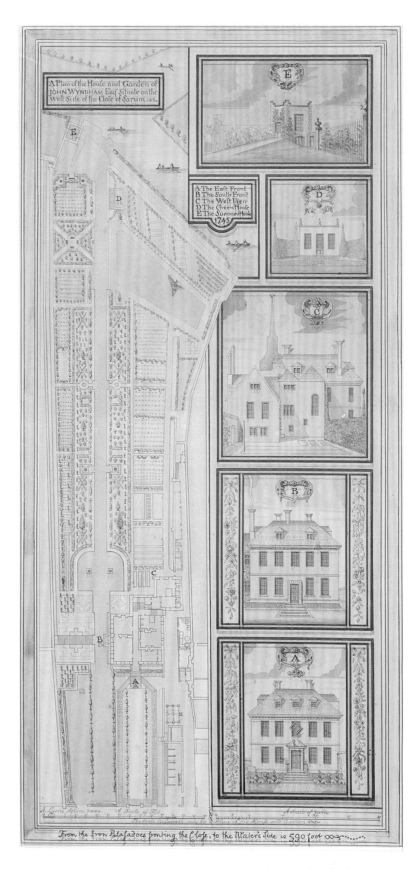

Arundells, 59 The Close, survey of 1745, by J Lyons, of house and garden layout designed c 1720

ROYAL COMMISSION ON THE HISTORICAL MONUMENTS OF ENGLAND

SALISBURY

The Houses of the Close

LONDON: HMSO

© Crown copyright 1993
First published 1993

ISBN 0 11 300017 0

British Library Cataloguing in Publication Data
A CIP catalogue record for this book is
available from the British Library

HMSO publications are available from:

HMSO Publications Centre
(Mail, fax and telephone orders only)
PO Box 276, London, SW8 5DT
Telephone orders 071-873 9090
General enquiries 071-873 0011
(queuing system in operation for both numbers)
Fax orders 071-873 8200

HMSO Bookshops
49 High Holborn, London, WC1V 6HB
(counter service only)
071-873 0011   Fax 071-873 8200
258 Broad Street, Birmingham, B1 2HE
021-643 3740   Fax 021-643 6510
Southey House, 33 Wine Street, Bristol, BS1 2BQ
0272 264306   Fax 0272 294515
9-21 Princess Street, Manchester, M60 8AS
061-834 7201   Fax 061-833 0634
16 Arthur Street, Belfast, BT1 4GD
0232 238451   Fax 0232 235401
71 Lothian Road, Edinburgh, EH3 9AZ
031-228 4181   Fax 031-229 2734

HMSO's Accredited Agents
(see Yellow Pages)

and through good booksellers

Printed in the United Kingdom for HMSO
Dd295267   5/93   C15 488 20249

Contents

Commissioners

Chairman's Foreword

Since the publication in 1980 of the Royal Commission's first volume on the *City of Salisbury*, work has proceeded on the *Cathedral* and the *Houses of the Close*. The Close at Salisbury may be regarded as one of the most beautiful as well as the largest in England. Here, Daniel Defoe noted in his *Tour Through the Whole Island of Great Britain (1724–6)*, 'the families of the prebendaries and commons, and others of the clergy belonging to the cathedral have their houses...These are so considerable here, and the place so large, that it is...like another city.' This volume is devoted to a detailed analysis of these houses.

Many changes in the staff of the Commission have occurred during our long period of involvement with the buildings of Salisbury and Commissioners wish to acknowledge the various contributions. For investigation of the buildings and preparation of the text, thanks are due primarily to Nicholas Moore and also to John Reeves and the late Norman Drinkwater. Dr Bridgett Jones carried out documentary research; Peter Spencer drew the main plans and sections and Nigel Fradgley the reconstructed plans and perspective views. Photography was carried out by Ron Parsons, Tony Rumsey, Sid Barker, Peter Williams and the late John Bassham. The former principal investigator, John T Smith, advised on the work and successive heads of the Salisbury office, Dr Spencer Corbett and Desmond Bonney, guided and encouraged the project. Veronica Smith was responsible for word processing and Jane Butcher, Lizbeth Gale and Kate Owen provided editorial guidance. For their work over the last two years in preparing this volume, especially the introduction, Commissioners wish to thank particularly Mrs Helen Bonney and Dr Thomas Cocke and, outside the Commission, Susan Leiper for her final editing of the text.

Commissioners are grateful to successive bishops of Salisbury, the dean and chapter and staff of the chapter office, and successive Cathedral chancellors, especially Canon I G D Dunlop; the Cathedral librarian and keeper of the muniments, Miss Suzanne Eward; the archivists of the former Diocesan Record Office in the Wren Hall, especially Miss P Stewart and Miss P Rundle; the Cathedral clerk of the works, Mr R O C Spring and successive Close architects from the Sarum Partnership; the principals and bursars of the Salisbury and Wells Theological College and the former Diocesan Training College; the head teachers and bursars of the Cathedral School, Bishop Wordsworth's School and the Leadenhall School; the curators and staff of the Salisbury and South Wiltshire Museum and the Museum of the Duke of Edinburgh's Royal Regiment; and the National Trust (Wessex Region).

Further afield, our thanks are also due to the following bodies, which have given every assistance to the project: the Diocesan and County Record Office, County Hall, Trowbridge; the Wiltshire Archaeological and Natural History Society, Devizes Museum, in particular their librarian, Mrs P Coleman; and the Wiltshire County Library Service.

Finally, we owe an especial debt to all the owners and occupants, both past and present, of the Close houses, without whose ready co-operation over the years this survey would have been impossible.

PARK OF MONMOUTH

Editor's Preface

The architectural investigation of Salisbury Close was begun in 1970 and since that time, not without interruptions, all the buildings have been visited, recorded and researched in detail. The dean and chapter's archives, now kept at the Chapter Office, 6 The Close, the records of the vicars choral and those of the bishop, at the Wiltshire Record Office, have all been studied to good effect.

Although most of the buildings in the Close have been listed by the Department of the Environment and are well known to visitors, none of them, before this survey, had been analysed and published, still less studied as a whole with their documentation. These supportive documents add immeasurably to the interest of the houses, although at times there are conflicts between them. For example, at Hemingsby, there is a magnificent late medieval hall, and the Chapter Act Books repeatedly stress in the late 14th and early 15th century that Canon Loring is to have certain privileges and exemptions because he has so extensively rebuilt and extended this house, and yet the hall has the entirely exceptional feature of a succeeding canon's name carved upon the cornices, and little if anything can be attributed to Loring. The Chapter Act Books include grants of houses to canons and also minutes of discussions in chapter concerning their properties, while lease books record post-medieval grants to lay people. The vicars' lease books survive only from the Restoration, and information both on their earlier grants to lay people, and on the houses occupied by their own members, is generally obtained indirectly from other documents. In general the exact location of every statement based on the dean and chapter's archives is not given on each occasion in the text in the interest of brevity, except when direct quotations are made, but transcripts of the evidence used exist in the RCHME's archives. Where examples of house inventories are given, some have been simplified and put into modern spelling. They are not to be taken as exact transcripts of the original documents. No attempt has been made to standardise the spelling of proper names, but some variations are given in the Index. No useful information is at present available from excavations and little from early topographical drawings which, apart from a very few by William Twopeny of the former Palace and Deanery, consist of a number by John Buckler (in Devizes Museum), one of the North Canonry by Bray, an otherwise unknown artist, and the plan of the house and garden at Arundells drawn by John Lyons in 1745.

The complete archive of material on the buildings is available for consultation at the National Monuments Record, RCHME, 23 Savile Row, London W1X 2JQ.

Notes on the Text

Scales and conventions

All houses that have Post Office numbers are designated by those numbers throughout this volume. There are some anomalies, eg there is no No. 61, and No. 49 is the upper part of North Gate.

Only a very few houses were deemed too recent to be included, eg Nos 28 and 30.

All plans are oriented with N to the top of the page except those of Nos 62 and 65 (Old Deanery and King's House) which have W to the top of the page, as dictated by the format.

All date-hatched plans and the majority of reconstructed plans are published at a uniform scale of 1 inch to 24 feet (1:288), unless otherwise indicated. Sections through buildings are at 1 inch to 12 feet (1:144) and those through the Close Wall at 1 inch to 6 feet (1:72). Details (windows, balusters etc) are, with some exceptions, at 1 inch to 3 feet (1:36) or 1 inch to 1 foot (1:12). On sections, details and dated plans, dotted lines are used to indicate features now gone or, where a separate reconstructed plan seems unwarranted, any that are conjectural. Additionally, on sections and details, wooden mouldings are represented by oblique hatching and stone by a fine stipple. Neither is indicative of date. On reconstructed plans, dotted lines always indicate conjectural features. The use of pecked lines on any drawing represents features that are concealed, or not in the plane of the illustration.

Documentary sources

The text includes numerous references to manuscript material amongst the archives of the dean and chapter, now in the care of the Cathedral Librarian and Keeper of the Muniments (Chapter Office, 6 The Close). Such references are abbreviated as D and C Muns, D and C Leases etc. This material includes Chapter Act Books and Lease Books, Vicars Choral Lease Books, Communars Accounts etc and an extensive series of notebooks compiled by C R Everett in the 1930s and 1940s (referred to in the text as Everett A, B, C, etc).

It was the custom to title each of the Chapter Act Books by the name of the notary who held the office of chapter clerk during the time, or for a part of the time of its compilation, eg Bergh, Draper, Hutchins, Frome and Prince, Penruddock. Only the earliest volume, Heminsgby's Register (1329–48), which contains no surveys of houses, has been published [Chew 1963].

All references in our text to surveys of houses datable 1649/50 are to the Parliamentary Survey (see p 26 and n. 6) unless otherwise stated.

The following 15th-century surveys of houses have been extracted from the Chapter Act Books. They are referred to from time to time in this volume, particularly in the introductory section pp 13–14. The surveys were carried out room by room, except for the seven on f 25 of the book for 1440–47, which are short inventories of fittings.

Extracts from the Chapter Act Books

Date of Act Book	Folio number	Name of occupant	Name of house where known – suggested identifications are in brackets	Date of survey
1402–5	f 3	John Norton, chancellor	(S Canonry)	1402
	f 16v–17	John Searle, canon	—	1403
1408–13	f 36	Master Edward Prentys	—	1409
1413–18	f 32	Master Richard Pittes	—	1415
1419–32	f 87v	Sir George Louthorp, treasurer	(S Canonry)	1427
1440–47	f 25	7 short inventories of fittings:		1440
		Edward Prentys, precentor	(S Canonry)	
		Gilbert Kymer, treasurer	(No. 68)	
		John Chedworth	—	
		—	Aula le Stage	
		Master Nicholas Upton	—	
		Walter Hende	—	
		William Swyft	—	
	*f 27	Master Dean	The Deanery	1440
	f 70	John Cariter	(No. 69)	1443
	f 77	Bluntesden's Chantry	(site N of No. 65)	1443–4
	f 91	Master William Swifte	—	1445
1447–57	f 41	Walter Hende	—	1449
	f 95	Richard Langryssh	—	1454
	f 121	Master John Simondesburgh	(No. 7)	1454–5
1468–75	f 40–1	John Stokes, precentor	(S Canonry)	1470

*transcribed in full as Appendix to No. 62

Maps

Details of the maps referred to in the text are as follows:

Naish 1716   *Map of the City of Salisbury...surveyed by William Naish 1716* [RCHM 1980, Plate 16]

Bothams 1860   J C Bothams, City Surveyor, *Plan of the Borough of Salisbury, 1860*

OS 1880   Ordnance Survey, town plan of Salisbury, scale 1:500, surveyed 1879, published 1880

Illustrations

The Royal Commission is grateful to the various institutions and individuals who permitted the photographing of topographical material in their care and the reproduction of copyright material.

Sources of illustrations, other than photographs or line drawings prepared by Royal Commission staff, are as follows:

The Trustees of the British Museum, Plates 27 and 162; the dean and chapter of Salisbury Cathedral, Plates 105 and 144 (and Frontispiece); Mr Godfrey Meynell, Plate 151; Traffic Technology Limited, Skyscan Balloon System, Plates 30, 57 and 149; Wiltshire Archaeological and Natural History Society, Plates 3, 9, 10, 17, 18, 19, 22, 25, 28, 88, 134, 155, 160, 166, 167, 168 and 182; and the Wiltshire Record Office, Plate 23.

Every effort has been made to trace copyright holders; the Royal Commission wishes to apologise to any who may have been inadvertently omitted from the above list.

The Houses of the Close

History and foundation of the Close

The Norman foundation at Old Sarum

The serene aspect of Salisbury Close today, with genteel houses overlooking long vistas and level lawns, is largely a 17th- and 18th-century creation, but the generous scale and spacious layout belong to the grandiose scheme whereby, in the early 13th century, a new cathedral, close and town were built on this low-lying site in the meadows beside the River Avon. However, the ecclesiastical community for which all this was to provide a perfect setting owed its form and organisation to the late 11th century, to Osmund, Bishop of Salisbury (1078–99).

As a consequence of the Council of London (1075), which had decreed that the seats of certain bishops should be transferred from villages to towns, that of the bishop of the combined dioceses of Sherborne and Ramsbury, brought together as recently as 1058, was moved to Old Sarum, or rather to the Borough of Salisbury as it would have been known at the time. The transfer to Salisbury took place under Bishop Herman, but the construction of the cathedral, consecrated in 1092, was largely the work of his successor, Bishop Osmund. Osmund endowed his cathedral with episcopal lands, and was the only Norman bishop to give the chapter – the corporate body serving the cathedral – a written constitution. This, his 'Institution' of 1091, was used as a precedent by other English cathedral chapters and thus became a source of great prestige to Salisbury. It was also a main source of the 'four-square' constitution characteristic of the English secular cathedrals, based on the four great dignitaries, Dean, Precentor, Chancellor and Treasurer, with their stalls at the four corners of the choir [VCH 1956, 156].

Salisbury was one of the nine medieval cathedrals in England served by secular canons, the others being Chichester, Exeter, Hereford, Lichfield, Lincoln, London (St Paul's), Wells and York. Their canons did not live like monks in a communal dwelling; each occupied a house of his own and could hold personal property and possessions, as well as one or more of the estates or 'prebends' belonging to chapter. At Salisbury more than thirty 'prebendaries' were supported by the estates given by Bishop Osmund, and by 1217 this number had been increased to fifty-two or fifty-three by later gifts, particularly during the reign of Henry I [VCH 1956, 160]. This community was to find its quarters at Old Sarum increasingly cramped and uncomfortable.

The Iron Age hill-fort at Old Sarum, which the Romans had called Sorviodunum [RCHM 1980, where all the remains at Old Sarum are fully described], was already occupied before the Norman Conquest as a borough under royal control. The castle founded by William I became the sheriff's headquarters and was visited frequently by the early Norman kings, not least for the great gathering in 1086 when Domesday Book was accepted as a true 'extent' or survey of the kingdom. Bishop Osmund had acted as one of the commissioners for the survey in the midlands and this may account for the presence of North and South Grantham amongst the prebendal estates of the cathedral [Jones 1879, 40; VCH 1956, 157]. He had acquired his skill as an administrator in the service of the royal household, becoming the king's chancellor or 'Chief of the Royal Chaplains' [Torrance 1978, 11–12].

The cathedral at Old Sarum was sited outside the castle defences but within the northwest quadrant of the hill-fort, an area which was levelled up to receive it and which appears to have been developed as an ecclesiastical precinct. Bishop Roger (1107–39), the rich and powerful minister of Henry I, planned to rebuild the entire church on a grander scale. He finished the east end, the transepts and the crossing, but after his disgrace in 1139, no further work was undertaken on the cathedral for the rest of the century and the old nave remained standing. Roger also obtained custody of the castle, probably soon after 1130, and is said to have surrounded it with a wall, probably the unfinished stone wall of which foundations remain on the line of the inner rampart of the hill-fort. This effectively enlarged the castle to include the ecclesiastical precinct, an act which was to prove a recurrent source of trouble. Friction between the clergy and the castle occurred sufficiently often thereafter to be claimed as a valid reason for removing the cathedral and close to a new site on ecclesiastical land.

The site of New Salisbury

Stretching on either side of the royal stronghold at Old Sarum, to north and south along the Avon valley, lay a

1

large estate, nearly nine miles in extent, belonging to the bishop. The central part had developed into a manor and parish around the settlement of Stratford, a name descriptive of a position at or close to the point where the Roman road to the southwest crossed the Avon [RCHM 1980, p xxx, map]. The borough at Old Sarum lay within this part of the estate and had acquired certain of its lands, probably during the 11th century. The remainder of the bishop's estate, the parish of St Martin, lay to the south and east between the Avon and the Bourne. It too was a separate manor and from the early 14th century onwards was usually known as the manor of Milford, but it was also known as the manor of Salisbury at least until the late 14th century. The chief settlement of the manor, sometimes referred to as 'the old town', lay close to St Martin's Church, with a second settlement, Milford itself, on either side of an important crossing-point of the River Bourne. A third settlement may well have existed on the west side of the manor, close to the bishop's mill, beside the River Avon. The founding of New Salisbury disrupted the existing pattern. St Martin's Church and the old settlement around it were left on the very edge of the new town and soon became a form of extramural suburb; any settlement which might have existed beside the bishop's mill would have been absorbed into the town itself.

The idea of removing the cathedral establishment from Old Sarum to the site by the Avon appears to have been approved during the episcopate of Herbert Poore (1194–1217) and was effected during that of his brother and successor Richard Poore (1217–28), which allowed plenty of time for the layout of this, the most successful of the many new towns of the early 13th century, to be carefully planned, taking into account the contours of the site and the presence of existing settlements, routes and river-crossings. The papal bull of Honorius III, granting permission for the move, listed chapter's complaints about Old Sarum, emphasising among other inconveniences that the inhabitants were 'forced to buy water, at as great a price as would purchase the common drink of the country', and that the accommodation available for the canons was inadequate: 'as you have not dwellings sufficient for yourselves, you are compelled to rent houses of the laity' [Dodsworth 1814, 110]. Priority was therefore given on the new site to the need for an ecclesiastical precinct giving both space and privacy, and to the need for an ample water supply for the whole urban area. Less obtrusive was the wish to establish a new town in the fashion of the time, in which the privileges granted to the inhabitants would provide increased incentive to trade, and where tolls would make a welcome addition to the revenue. In 1219 a licence to hold a market was obtained and in 1221 the grant of an annual fair; both were confirmed in the royal charter of 1227, which emphasised the ecclesiastical

nature of the foundation and granted the bishop and his successors the right to hold the city as their demesne in perpetuity. By 1400 New Salisbury had become one of the half dozen most prosperous towns in England, and ranked third on at least one occasion during the 15th century [VCH 1962, 129].

The Close, the new precinct of the bishop and clergy, was to occupy much of the lower-lying southern part of the site and stood physically separate from the town and largely independent of it. It was bounded on the west and south by the Avon and on the north and east by the Close Ditch, a deep wet ditch which provided drainage for the houses of those canons whose tenements backed on to it and which also helped to drain the Close as a whole. During the first century of its existence it probably also provided the precinct with a measure of defence or protection, until it was supplemented by the building of the Close Wall (see p 38).

The new town

In 1225 Bishop Poore set out the conditions of tenure within his city. The citizens of New Salisbury were to hold their tenements by what amounted to burgage tenure. The standard plot was to be seven by three perches, or about 115 ft by 50 ft – an ample size, in keeping with the character of the whole scheme – and the standard ground-rent was to be 12d a year. Tenants who held more or less land than that were to pay more or less rent accordingly, so it is evident that from the very outset the tenements were expected to vary in size. However, the plan of streets and chequers was in part laid out to accommodate standard plots. New Street, undoubtedly one of the earliest streets, was laid out parallel with the north side of the Close and approximately the length of a burgage plot from it. The name Novus Vicus was originally used of the whole street-line, now bearing six names, which extends from Lower Fisherton Bridge on the west to the town boundary at the top of Payne's Hill on the east.

The grid-iron town plan, so characteristic of new towns of the period, was affected by certain pre-existing features, in particular routeways. A major road linking Winchester and Wilton descended Milford Hill and proceeded west to a crossing of the Avon, presumably a ford on or near the site of Upper Fisherton Bridge; the alignment of Milford (formerly Winchester) Street probably follows it closely. A road from north to south passed by way of Old Sarum towards a crossing of the Avon near Ayleswade Bridge; Castle Street and High Street mark its approximate line and the continuation of the latter southwards through the Close may have had some influence on the position of the Cathedral, the west front of which abuts it. In the northeast angle of the intersection of these two routes the large market place of the new town was laid out, and almost at the crossing the first parish church within the town, St Thomas's, was built.

Of the pre-existing settlements, the one at St Martin's was probably the most important, concentrated along the way which leads southeast towards the church, now known as St Martin's Church Street. The presence of this street may well have caused St Ann's Street, which meets its northwest end, to deviate from an original planned line parallel to New Street; it is noticeable that the west part of St Ann's Street is parallel to New Street (Ivy Street) and that a continuation of this alignment would have led straight to St Martin's Church.

The decision to provide the town with a supply of water running in shallow channels down the centres of most of its streets must have been taken at an early stage and was probably the most important single consideration in the actual siting of the town. It required a large, nearly flat area close to, but above, water level and for the most part above the level of regular flooding. Within the whole extent of the bishop's Salisbury manors only one such area, that within the bend of the Avon, east of its confluence with the Nadder, met that requirement. Here, in addition, the leat or stream supplying the bishop's mill (on the site of the present Town Mill, just north of Fisherton Bridge) constituted a ready source of water at the correct height above river level to feed the system of street channels, which were designed to provide water for both household and industrial use. Since the channels ran along the centres of the streets, it was essential that the latter should be carefully aligned, to respect the contours and to ensure a gentle gradient for the water all the way from the mill-stream on the northwest to the meadows at Bugmore. Water entered the system from the mill-stream by means of two inlets controlled by sluices, one (a) west of Castle Gate, the other (b) further south, to the west of Scot's Lane (map, p 4). Water at the level of the mill-stream could be made to flow in surface channels to a point (c) a short distance east of Endless Street on the north, and as far as the south side of St Edmund's churchyard (d) on the northeast. From this crucial latter point the water was taken south at the foot of the rising ground along the line marked by St Edmund's Church Street and Gigant Street. That this constituted its absolute eastward limit is indicated by the fact that the alignment of these streets tends to follow the contour rather than a straight line. (It is noticeable that the next street up the slope to the east, where no water channel had to be accommodated, is markedly straight.) In all, four streets on the east side of the town run parallel, or very nearly so, to this most easterly water channel. The interval between them is, understandably, the approximate length of two burgage plots, and they are the most obvious manifestation in the town plan of an attempt at a regular layout. To accommodate the most westerly of these streets it was necessary to impinge on the northeast corner of the Close. Their divergence from the old line of Castle Street and High Street to the west, however, left an irregular area between and prevented a true grid plan overall. A truly rectangular pattern of streets was achieved only in the most northerly chequers. Further south the rectangularity is broken by Winchester Street, the direction of which was probably determined by the slope of the ground and the resultant necessary alignment of the water channel along it.

There were also two much deeper watercourses, the Town Ditch (also called New Canal) and the Close Ditch. These took water from the River Avon below the bishop's mill and therefore flowed at a considerably lower level than the street channels. The Close Ditch was carefully positioned to collect water which passed under the easternmost arch of Lower Fisherton (Crane) Bridge, while the Town Ditch similarly collected water at Upper Fisherton Bridge. This it carried southwards for a short distance, to maintain the flow, before turning sharply to the east. The Town Ditch defined the south side of the Market Place, at its fullest extent, and acted as a main drain in that area. Its existence accounts for the notably oblique alignment of the north side of New Street Chequer. Beyond the Market Place, in Milford Street, the Town Ditch turned south through Trinity Chequer and Marsh Chequer, where for the whole of its length it served as a property boundary. South of St Ann's Street it turned east to flow past the Friary precinct and thence to the Avon once more; it also joined the ditches draining Bugmore.

The historical context

The foundation of a new town was an enterprise very much in the fashion of the time, not least in this part of England. In 1194 Richard I himself had founded Portsmouth, or had given borough status to the nascent settlement, where in 1189 he landed on his accession [*VCH* 1973, 186; Beresford 1967, 380, 447].

In 1190 Richard I gave his friend William Brewer, one of the four justices left in charge of the kingdom while he was on crusade, the manor of King's Somborne. In the northwest corner of the parish, 'apud le Strete', a market was confirmed in 1200 and the town of Stockbridge grew up on either side of a causeway carrying the Winchester to Salisbury road, where before there had been merely a ford. Henceforth the old river-crossing on the line of the Roman road, three miles to the south, fell gradually into disuse. Like Salisbury, Stockbridge made good use of a riverside site, the burgage plots being defined at least in part by the River Test, here divided into seven streams [Beresford 1967, 449]. William Brewer was to prosper further under King John, acting as one of the executors of his will in

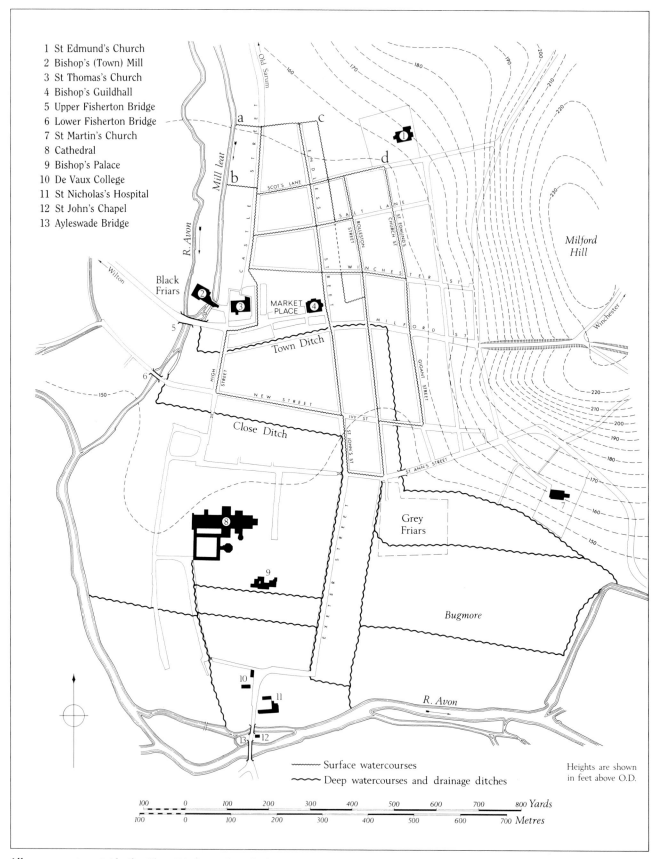

1 St Edmund's Church
2 Bishop's (Town) Mill
3 St Thomas's Church
4 Bishop's Guildhall
5 Upper Fisherton Bridge
6 Lower Fisherton Bridge
7 St Martin's Church
8 Cathedral
9 Bishop's Palace
10 De Vaux College
11 St Nicholas's Hospital
12 St John's Chapel
13 Ayleswade Bridge

Surface watercourses
Deep watercourses and drainage ditches

Heights are shown
in feet above O.D.

100   0   100   200   300   400   500   600   700   800 *Yards*
100   0   100   200   300   400   500   600   700 *Metres*

All monuments outside the Close Ditch are described in RCHM 1980.

1216 [Powicke 1962, 3; *DNB*]. Amongst the many offices held by him was that of Sheriff of Wiltshire and Castellan of Old Sarum from 1209 to 1211 [Benson and Hatcher 1843, 704]. In 1201 he founded Mottisfont Abbey a few miles downstream of Stockbridge and in 1220 his gift of a silver-gilt pyx to the new Cathedral at Salisbury made him the first of its many benefactors [Jones 1884, 13].

On the road leading to Salisbury from the south the Bishop of Winchester, Peter des Roches, founded in 1208 a new borough across the River Avon from the old castle and village of Downton, one of six new towns sited on manors of Winchester during the early 13th century [Beresford 1959, 187]. Perhaps he and William Brewer were both aware of the plan to move Salisbury to a new site and hoped to benefit from the increase in traffic, but their new boroughs were small and simple compared with the new city.

Certain events during the reigns of Henry II and his sons provide a backcloth to the founding of New Salisbury. Henry II (1154–89) was the first of the Angevin kings to make the royal residence at Clarendon, situated in the forest less than three miles east of Salisbury, into more than a hunting lodge. The chapel there was served from the first year of his reign by the nearby priory of Ivychurch, probably founded for the purpose [RCHM 1987, 149]. During the 1170s and 1180s lavish expenditure included the building of a great hall 82 ft by 52 ft [James and Robinson 1988, 5]. The new status of the place was already demonstrated by the signing there in 1164 of the Constitutions of Clarendon. The Constitutions, which were, of course, resisted by the Archbishop of Canterbury, Thomas Becket, led to his martyrdom in 1170, and to the resulting cult of St Thomas which sprang up immediately. Eight miles north of Salisbury was the great nunnery at Amesbury, refounded by Henry II with nuns from Fontevrault, one of the three religious houses with which he expiated his responsibility for the murder of Becket [RCHM 1987, 103, 233].

There were to be further links between Canterbury and the new Salisbury. Becket had been consecrated Archbishop on 3 June 1162, the Sunday next after Pentecost, and had ordained that in England thereafter the feast of Holy Trinity should be held on that Sunday; this English usage was extended to the whole Western Church by Pope

John XXII in 1333 [Cheney 1961, 62; Poole 1955, 200]. It seems more than a coincidence that Trinity Sunday was to be chosen as a significant day on several occasions during the building of Salisbury Cathedral. Also the first new parish church in the town was to be dedicated to St Thomas Becket [RCHM 1980, 24].

Hubert Walter

After Bishop Jocelin of Salisbury, who had been closely involved in the whole Becket controversy [Benson and Hatcher 1843, 33], died in 1184, the see remained vacant for five years until the appointment of Hubert Walter, then Dean of York. A secular-minded ecclesiastic, he was to spend little time in Salisbury and after three years' absence on the Third Crusade, this trusted administrator of Richard I was appointed Archbishop of Canterbury. However, the Salisbury scheme was certainly approved during the 1190s and the grandiose scale of the project may owe as much to Hubert Walter as to his successors. As archbishop his support was essential for the scheme and it may have been the case that 'the sanction of the King was obtained by Hubert, Archbishop of Canterbury, who had shared with him the dangers of the Crusade, and was honoured with the highest proofs of his confidence and favour' [Benson and Hatcher 1843, 37]. Hubert was promoting other grandiose schemes during the later 1190s: the great hall which he began at Canterbury, superseding that of Lanfranc [Tatton-Brown 1982; Rady, Tatton-Brown and Bowen 1991], and the abortive college of secular canons at Lambeth [Cheney 1967, 137–57].

Herbert and Richard Poore

The archbishop was succeeded at Salisbury by Herbert Poore (1194–1217) who had been an administrator of the see during the previous vacancy from 1185 to 1188. His brother Richard Poore, appointed dean in 1199, was to succeed him as bishop and was to achieve the foundation of the new Cathedral after a delay of over twenty years. These events are recorded in a reminiscent but near-contemporary account [Jones 1884, translated from the Latin in Dodsworth 1814, 107–21] which is generally accepted to have been written by William de Wanda (precentor 1218, dean 1220–36); his account begins as follows:

> In the time of Herbert, of happy memory, bishop of Sarum, the canons of the church held frequent consultations, relative to its translation to a more free and convenient place. For, as it was surrounded by the walls of the king's fortifications, it was exposed to various troubles, and continually laboured under the most grievous injuries and oppressions. By the diligence of this bishop, who was a person of great sagacity and able in temporal matters, the affair was so far advanced, that a plot of ground was

Watercourses and ditches (from RCHM 1980, xxxix)
The map shows watercourses and drainage ditches in relation to physical topography and the city streets. Contours based on OS spot heights which often represent modern surfaces cannot be precisely those of the 13th century, but relative heights probably are not much distorted. The watercourses are as on Naish's map (1716 edition), except for a conjectural stretch in Three Swans Chequer which presumably linked the known channels of Gores and Cross Keys Chequers.

selected, with general approbation, as a more commodious situation for the church, and as affording each of the canons a proper space for the erection of a dwelling-house. The design was favoured by the illustrious king of England, Richard, who freely gave his assent. But afterwards, the bishop having computed the charges of finishing so great a work, and maturely considered his own ability to defray the expense, concluded that it would far exceed his utmost means, although he was rich and careful. Hence he proceeded no farther in the project. Afterwards in the reign of the most cruel king John, he suffered great losses in his goods and possessions; being stript by confiscations, of what he had devoted to so pious a purpose.

This implies that the long delay of over twenty years between the first discussions of the project and the laying of the foundation stones of the Cathedral in 1220 was largely a matter of lack of money, exacerbated by the turmoil in church and state affairs under King John (1199–1216).

In 1205 the death of Hubert Walter, Archbishop of Canterbury, was followed by the disputed election of Stephen Langton to the see, which resulted in the papal interdict of 1208, King John's excommunication and his confiscation of church property [Poole 1955, 448]. Many of the bishops and other clergy retired to France to share Langton's exile. Of special interest amongst this company, because of his later involvement with Salisbury, is Master Elias de Dereham (see p 8). When Archbishop Langton returned to England in 1213, Elias appears to have acted as his steward. He also acted as steward for Jocelyn, Bishop of Bath and Wells, whom he had accompanied for some of the sojourn in France, and he probably held a prebend at Wells from as early as 1206 [Thompson 1941, 4–5].

Archbishop Langton was in the forefront of the negotiations between King John and the barons before their meeting at Runnymede in June 1215. After the signing of Magna Carta, Elias de Dereham was appointed one of the commissioners for the distribution of copies of the great charter [Thompson 1941, 6], one of which still remains in the care of Salisbury Cathedral. King John, by submitting to the Pope, ensured papal support in the ensuing civil war, which ended only with his death in 1216. Negotiations for peace were delayed for a while by the papal legate's refusal to include Elias de Dereham and three other clerics in the general pardon, on the grounds that they had stayed with the rebellious barons in London, and had preached at St Paul's in favour of the short-lived invasion by Prince Louis of France [Powicke 1962, 8, 12].

Throughout these troubled years, Herbert Poore and his brother Richard appear to have remained as much as possible at Salisbury, which had suffered less than some bishoprics [Poole 1955, 446]. They had not succeeded in moving to the new site, but it can be presumed that they

continued to make active preparations. Richard Poore was clearly a man of distinction; in 1205 he was in Rome as one of the two candidates in the disputed election for the bishopric of Winchester, competing unsuccessfully with Peter des Roches [DNB]. He was to remain dean of Salisbury for another ten years before being appointed bishop of Chichester in 1215, a position he held until 1217. In 1213, as dean, he presided over preliminary discussions in chapter concerning a reformed version of the Institution of St Osmund, the Nova Constitutio of 1215 [Jones 1883, 275]. Also in 1213, chapter appears to have discussed the layout of the canons' houses in the proposed new close [Jones 1879, 241; see also p 8].

As bishop of Chichester, Richard Poore acted as one of the executors of King John's will, and so became automatically one of the group who formed a council for the young King Henry III [Powicke 1962, 3]. William de Wanda said that his appointment to the see of Salisbury in 1217 'was approved by the whole nation, which had found him a loyal and excellent champion against Lewis, son of the king of France, and his frenchmen, who, at that time, were come over to take possession of the kingdom' [Dodsworth 1814, 109].

As bishop of Salisbury, Richard Poore was able to bring the proposed move to a successful conclusion. The speed with which the final arrangements were made from 1217 to 1219 and with which the cathedral building, once started, was raised, is evidence of thorough planning beforehand. On 29 March 1219 Pope Honorius issued the bull authorising the transfer [RCHM 1980, 16].

Foundation of the Close

The first recorded building on the site was the bishop's own house: on 28 June 1218 Richard Poore dated a charter 'ad Novum Locum apud Veteres Sarisbirias' [Jones 1891, 82; VCH 1956, 165] (from his new place at Old Salisbury), on this occasion using the earlier name of the settlement. A wooden chapel was begun on the Monday after Easter 1219, and here on Trinity Sunday, Bishop Poore celebrated divine service for the first time, and consecrated a graveyard. The canons promised to 'assist in the building of the new fabric according to their prebendal estates, continually for seven years' [Dodsworth 1814, 111–12]. The urgent need for funds for the new church was to be a recurring theme of later chapter decrees, while many gifts and seven-year covenants were donated by the clergy and nobility who attended when the foundation stones were laid in April 1220, and when the first three altars were consecrated at Michaelmas 1225.

On the first of these two great occasions, Bishop Poore 'prepared a solemn entertainment, at a great expense, for all who should appear' [Dodsworth 1814, 114]. Whether his house was large enough for this is not known, but it was certainly being enlarged or rebuilt in 1221, when Henry III gave timber couples for the bishop's hall and chamber [Wordsworth 1891, 166–9]. It was presumably finished in time for the festivities of 1225, when the first altars were consecrated in the presence of the archbishops of Dublin and Canterbury (Langton) and thirty-six of the canons, who now included Elias de Dereham in their number: 'after some hours spent in prayer in the new church, they went down, with many nobles, to the house of the bishop, who generously entertained the numerous company during the whole week' [Dodsworth 1814, 118].

The Bishop's Palace is the most important building described in this volume. A considerable portion survives amongst additions and alterations from the 15th century and every century since. In scale, the surviving 13th-century fragment, with its vaulted undercroft and grand upper rooms (remodelled in the 18th century), is comparable with the royal private apartments which Henry III was to build at Clarendon a few years later. The vaulting can be compared with that at Mottisfont Abbey, built soon after 1201. It may be assumed that a great aisled hall, similar to that of the Norman bishops at Old Sarum [RCHM 1980, 21] or that of Henry II at Clarendon, was either attached to the east of the surviving wing or linked to it by pentices, but any evidence has disappeared under later buildings.

The supervision of the simultaneous building of the Cathedral and Close was too complex a task for Richard Poore alone. By the 1220s the administration appears to have been entrusted to Elias de Dereham. He was acting as the bishop's steward soon after 1220, had become a canon of Salisbury by 1222, communar or keeper of the common fund of the canons by 1224, and keeper of the fabric fund of the Cathedral at least by 1225 although possibly soon after 1220 [Thompson 1941, 7–12]. On the Sunday following the consecration in 1225, Bishop Poore obtained leave to appropriate to the fabric fund all the offerings made in the next seven years at the main altar of the Holy Trinity and All Saints, when the daily mass of the Virgin was sung; these 'he committed to the custody of Elias de Dereham, having at that time no confidence in the trustworthiness of any other person' [VCH 1956, 166].

Elias de Dereham's role as financial supervisor is clear, but the extent and nature of his involvement in architectural design are difficult to determine [Harvey 1987, 81]. He was already famous for the part he had played in the setting up of the new shrine of St Thomas at Canterbury in 1220, an event in which Bishop Poore also took part. On 7 July, Archbishop Langton, assisted by Bishop Poore [Fletcher 1939, 492], had moved the saint's relics from the crypt to the Trinity Chapel, to the shrine contrived by, according to Matthew Paris, 'the incomparable artificers, Master Walter of Colchester, sacrist of St Albans, and Master Elyas of Dereham, canon of Salisbury,

by whose advice and ingenuity all things needful for the artificial working of the shrine and its elevation and translation were got ready' [Thompson 1941, 7]. William de Wanda illuminates the contemporary view, in Salisbury, of the importance of this occasion when he remarks that the year 1220 was notable for three events: the laying of the foundation stones of the Cathedral, the coronation of the king (the official coronation by Archbishop Langton at Westminster as opposed to the first hasty crowning of Henry III in 1216 by the Bishop of Winchester at Gloucester), and the translation of the body of St Thomas at Canterbury [Jones 1884, 14].

The removal from Old Sarum was symbolically completed in 1226 when the remains of Bishops Osmund, Roger and Jocelin were brought to the new Cathedral on Trinity Sunday, for reburial in the Trinity Chapel. Bishop Poore hoped to arrange before long the canonisation of Osmund. By 1228, documents supporting the canonisation were ready to be sent off to Rome, when circumstances changed: Archbishop Langton died, and Bishop Poore was transferred to the see of Durham, while Elias de Dereham was required to administer the will of the one and the vacant see of the other. Before his departure to the north, the bishop wrote to the dean and chapter urging them to persevere with the canonisation but it was allowed to lapse for almost two hundred years; it was finally achieved by Bishop Beauchamp in 1457.

The plot of ground selected in the time of Bishop Herbert Poore for the new Cathedral and Close was said to afford 'each of the canons a proper space for the erection of a dwelling-house' [Dodsworth 1814, 108], and the size of the site was certainly unusually generous compared with that of other cathedral precincts which had to be developed within existing towns. The Close occupies 83 of the 260 acres given to New Salisbury and it is clear that the layout was planned methodically, although the plots were not of equal size, and some discrepancies have been exaggerated by early amalgamations (Fig 2). Apart from the Bishop's Palace which, together with the meadow on the south, occupied about 7½ acres, the largest site was Coldharbour, occupying 3¾ acres. Along the western side there were probably intended to be another fourteen large plots, each of about 1½ acres; in this way fifteen canonical sites took up about half the 50 acres available for residential purposes. The Leadenhall and the canonry to the south both occupied double sites. The next largest sites were the four fronting what is now Bishop's Walk on the east, each of about one acre. The remainder, in the northern part of the Close, varied considerably, none being much more than half an acre and many very much less. Also in the northern part are two large houses built on small sites: Aula le Stage and the house that later became the Vicars' Hall. This highly unequal distribution reflects a division which was already admitted to exist, despite the ultimate ideal of the common life, between wealthy canons who wished to reside in the Close and dispense hospitality and therefore needed substantial houses, and others who did not have the means. This situation already pertained before 1200 when the scholar Peter de Blois, secretary to Archbishop Hubert Walter [Cheney 1967, 159], had refused to reside, declaring that the income (5 marks) from the prebend which he held would not even pay for his journey to Salisbury, and that 'the constitutions of Osmund and Jocelin were designed for those rich prebendaries who could afford to build houses and easily procure what they required for residence' [Edwards 1939, 65–6; VCH 1956, 165].

Chapter decreed in about 1213, when Richard Poore was still dean, that the canons should build 'fair houses of stone, near the wall of the close, or the river that compasses the close, and two stone walls to enclose the ground assigned to them' [Jones 1879, 241].[1] Stone was an expensive and prestigious material at this period, when most domestic buildings were of timber. Fragments of the boundary walls remain, of flint rubble and stone, up to ten or eleven feet high. Some have been incorporated into later houses but two notable survivors are the north and south boundary walls of No. 59, Arundells. The west wall of Coldharbour was said to be 12 ft high in 1649, when it was to be reduced to 7 ft [Malden 1893–4, 138].

The Cathedral graveyard too, in the mid 13th century, was surrounded by a wall about 9 ft high, built of stone, including some fragments from Old Sarum (see p 45). It was reduced in height to about 5 ft in 1342, to provide extra material for the Close Wall, which was only then under construction (although apparently envisaged as early as 1213).

By August 1219 the canons were considering when they should move to their new houses; it was decreed 'that the translation from the old place to that of the new fabric should be made on the Feast of All Saints [1 November] next following, by those who were willing and able' [Dodsworth 1814, 114], or in other words had adequate houses ready for occupation. Others in the meantime were intending to build: 'aliis interim intendentibus aedificationi' [Jones 1884, 12]. It seems that some were hesitant, possibly on grounds of expense. By 1222 the need for the canons to build was becoming pressing, and on 15 August chapter decreed that 'everyone who has a site must begin to build to some purpose by Whitsuntide next ensuing, or failing this, the bishop shall dispose of his site' [Edwards 1939, 63; Jones 1884, 18–21].

Elias de Dereham and the Leadenhall

Of the first houses only fragments have survived into the 20th century. These include a portion of Elias de Dereham's own house, the Leadenhall (No. 70), which stood, albeit precariously, until 1915. Photographs taken before demolition in that year have made possible the partial reconstruction of the house in this book (Plates 183–6). Built of flint rubble and stone, with tall windows, painted interior decoration and a roof presumably covered with lead, the Leadenhall was both stylish and expensive. Three deeds drawn up in 1232 [Wordsworth 1917, 440] record that Elias donated the house into the bishop's gift, declaring that he had built it as an example for other canons to follow and in honour of the Virgin Mary. In consideration of the enormous expense, he expected his successor to make payments to his executors and to the Cathedral fabric fund, to observe his obit and to entertain each year on the day of his death one hundred poor persons [Jones 1891, 204]. These expectations are some indication of his high personal standing, to which could be added the fact that after his death, his prebend, the rich estate of Lavington and Potterne, near Devizes, was first seized by the legate for the use of the papacy and then, in 1254 by special sanction of Pope Alexander IV, became the bishop's own prebend [Jones 1879, 409–10; Fletcher 1939, 497].

The career of Elias de Dereham was unusual in many respects, not least in his involvement in architectural matters. *Magister* was habitually prefixed to his name, which implies that he held a university degree, probably in law [Thompson 1941, 23]. As a protégé of Hubert Walter, whose native place, Dereham in Norfolk, he shared, he would have received a thorough training in the skills of administration. As a young man, he had witnessed the foundation deed of the Premonstratensian Abbey at West Dereham, founded in 1188 by his patron, then dean of York. Elias's whereabouts during the 1190s are not known, but it can be assumed that he was aware of the great works then under construction at Canterbury: the rebuilding of the cathedral choir, the new Trinity Chapel and 'corona' built above the tomb of St Thomas (later the setting for the shrine which was to bring Elias fame) and Hubert Walter's huge great hall. When the archbishop died in 1205, Elias was appointed one of the executors of his will, and was one of those entrusted with the temporalities of the see of Canterbury during the ensuing vacancy.

During the latter part of his life (he died in April 1245), Elias presumably continued to be in charge of the work on Salisbury Cathedral but was also much involved in the construction, alteration and decoration of secular buildings. Henry III required him to supervise work at Winchester and at Clarendon (where King John had made only minor additions, rebuilding instead his hunting lodge at Cranborne (1207–8), thirteen miles southwest of Salisbury) [RCHM 1975, 7–12]. At Winchester the royal castle had been badly damaged in 1216, when it was besieged by Prince Louis, a fate which might well have befallen Old Sarum but for the brief defection of the castellan, William Longspee, Earl of Salisbury, to the French side [*HKW* 1963, 826]. Rebuilding of the great hall at Winchester had begun in 1222 and Elias de Dereham was in charge for several years from 1233 [*HKW* 1963, 859]. New royal apartments were added to Clarendon Palace, which became a favourite residence. Here, in the mid 1230s, Elias remodelled the windows of Henry II's great hall and supervised the building of Henry III's new chapel, a first-floor room 50 ft by 20 ft, elaborately decorated with paintings, sculpture, gilding and a circular tiled floor [James and Robinson 1988, 15–16].

From 1237 to 1238 Elias acted again as an executor of the wills of two bishops, Peter des Roches of Winchester and Richard Poore of Durham. Bishop Poore was buried at Tarrant Crawford in Dorset, where he is said to have been born and to have refounded the nunnery there under Cistercian rule [Jones 1891, 269]; nothing now remains of the church [RCHM 1972, 86]. When the king's sister, Queen Joan of Scotland, died the same year she too was buried at Tarrant, under a tomb of Purbeck marble which the king had asked Elias de Dereham to erect [*HKW* 1963, 478]. In 1239 Elias was at Canterbury, where Archbishop Edmund Rich, who had been Treasurer of Salisbury from 1222 to 1233, intended to build a new collegiate church and required advice in marking out the site for the church, and plots for the canons' houses [*HKW* 1963, 100], but this project came to nothing when the archbishop died in France the following year. In 1241 Elias was still supervising work at Winchester, but his last documented task was in 1244, when the king gave him 30 marks for the making of a cup for the reserved sacrament over the high altar in Salisbury Cathedral.

The Close completed

The new Cathedral was consecrated in 1258 and finished during the next decades together with the Bell Tower, freestanding to the northwest (Fig 91, p 144). The cloisters and chapter house and finally the spire were constructed during the remaining years of the 13th century and early 14th century.

Bishop Poore's successors also founded a group of buildings near the river to the south of the Cathedral, within the Liberty of the Close but later left outside the enclosing wall [*VCH* 1962, 71, 73]: the Hospital of St Nicholas, Ayleswade Bridge and the Chapel of St John, all founded *c* 1230–40 by Bishop Robert Bingham [RCHM 1980, xxxviii, 45, 51, 54–5], and the College of St Nicholas de Vaux founded in 1262 by Bishop Giles de Bridport [RCHM 1980, xl, 130]. In 1269 the boundaries of the three city parishes were set out when the collegiate church of St

Edmund was established [RCHM 1980, map xxxix, 36]. At this period, Salisbury was a centre of theological learning and briefly the seat of a nascent university [*VCH* 1956, 169]. Under Bishop Simon of Ghent (1297–1315), the organisation of the ecclesiastical community in the Close was reviewed, discussions were held in full chapter and the results were embodied in the Constitution of Bishop Roger Mortival (1319) which made a series of amendments to the original Constitution of St Osmund [*VCH* 1956, 173].

The building of Ayleswade Bridge to replace the ford over the Avon was an immediate benefit to the growing city, which by the mid 14th century was entering a long period of prosperity [RCHM 1980, xl]. This was a time, all over Europe, when many cathedrals and monasteries came to be at odds with the towns that surrounded them and Salisbury was no exception [Street 1915, 319–67]. The Close Wall (Plate 1), built *c* 1327–42, with its three strong gateways – North, St Ann's and Harnham Gates (Plates 5, 4, 11) – was to provide a measure of protection from any turbulence in the town, and has served over succeeding centuries to encapsulate the Close. Blocks of stone from Old Sarum were used in the construction of the wall (see p 42), as were others from the original graveyard wall which was lowered at this time to provide materials. A janitor or porter is first recorded in 1339 and thereafter his house (No. 48 The Close) was established beside the North Gate.

The occupants of the Close

The bishop

Each of the larger houses in the Close sheltered a sizeable household but there is little precise information about them. The bishop, of course, had the largest. Medieval bishops travelled constantly, in attendance on the king [Sandell 1976, 19–25] and in supervision of their dioceses, staying at their country manor houses and elsewhere; the 14th- and 15th-century communar's accounts show that the bishop never spent more than a few days in any quarter of the year at Salisbury Palace [Edwards 1949, 104–5]. However, the wealth, power and responsibility of his office required a staff of fifty to a hundred people consisting of personal servants, chaplains and clerks, who attended to his business and administered his large estates [Moorman 1945, 169–84]. The two canons who were permitted to be absent from the Cathedral on the bishop's affairs might have been members of his household first and canons second, since the power of nominating canons (except the dean) belonged to the bishop and there were obvious advantages in making appointments from among his own staff [Edwards 1949, 90–1].

At his palace, the bishop was expected to provide

generous hospitality to the clergy on great festivals and other special occasions [Thompson 1925, 165–6], and to entertain the king and other distinguished visitors, as Bishop Poore had done in 1220 and 1225.

There is no trace or record of any 14th-century alterations to the Bishop's Palace, except for general licences to crenellate issued to the bishops in 1337 and 1377; the latter can be taken as the date of construction of the surviving gatehouse in the Close Wall (Plates 19, 20).

It seems that little was done at the Palace itself until the extensive reconstruction undertaken c 1460 by Bishop Beauchamp (Fig 20; Plates 22, 26, 31). The scale and grandeur of the surviving porch tower and the two-storey range containing parlour and chamber (now chapel) are characteristic of this energetic bishop, who reasserted episcopal authority in Salisbury after his predecessor, Bishop William Aiscough, was murdered at Edington near Westbury during Cade's rebellion, by a mob including men from Salisbury in its number [VCH 1962, 102]. The rental for 1455 in Bishop Beauchamp's *Liber Niger* is one of the few surviving documents to provide a general conspectus of medieval Salisbury [Nevill 1911, 66–91].[2] Richard Beauchamp was a member of the great family of that name, the younger son of Sir Walter Beauchamp of Powyck and his second wife, Elizabeth Roche of Bromham near Devizes. He occupied the see of Salisbury for more than thirty years, from 1450 to 1481. In 1457, after a sustained effort by chapter of over sixty years, well supported in its latter stages by the new bishop, the canonisation of St Osmund was finally granted and a new shrine erected in the Cathedral [VCH 1956, 178]. William Beauchamp, Lord St Amand, the bishop's elder brother, contributed generously to the cost of the shrine but died in the same year [Fletcher 1938a, 165]. The bishop was to live for another twenty years; his will, composed in 1481 [Benson and Hatcher 1843, 541, where it is misdated 1461], made provision for a chantry in the Cathedral served by four priests, who were to live in a small house on the site of No. 11.

The chantry chapel was built during the bishop's lifetime, in the later 1470s, on the south side of the Trinity Chapel. It contained his tomb, freestanding in the centre, and two canopied monuments, probably those of his parents, in the thickness of the Trinity Chapel wall which was pierced to receive them. In the southwest corner stood the canopied tomb and effigy of Sir John Cheney (died 1509), standard-bearer to Henry Tudor at the battle of Bosworth Field. He was a benefactor of the Cathedral [Dodsworth 1814, 169], acted as one of Bishop Beauchamp's executors and had been Bailiff of the City of Salisbury since 1479 [Benson and Hatcher 1843, 698; VCH 1962, 102]. The chapel was demolished c 1790 and the fragmented monuments of Bishop Beauchamp and Sir

John Cheney removed to the nave. Today, the main memorial to Bishop Beauchamp in his own cathedral is the lierne vault over the main crossing (1479–80) which bears his arms.

Chantry chapels built for the Beauchamp family in the 15th century were amongst the most expensive and elaborate of the period, in particular, the Warwick or Beauchamp Chantry of c 1430 at Tewkesbury and the Beauchamp Chapel at Warwick, built from 1443 to 1464 and consecrated in 1475 [Cook 1948, 155]. Bishop Beauchamp's Chapel at Salisbury was equally lavish [Shortt 1970, 8–11], its east wall covered, between a pair of windows, with tiers of niches to contain figures of saints, and the ogival roof supported by a double cornice of diminutive fan vaulting, reminiscent of the small side chapel at Warwick [Cook 1948, 155, Plate 48]. The ceiling of 'curiouslie caru'd Irish wood' [Camden Miscellany 1936, 62], was much more heavily decorated than that which survives in the bishop's new chamber at the Palace, with its deep mouldings and small gilded bosses (Plate 31, Fig 22). Heavily decorated ceilings are a feature of two later Beauchamp chapels in Wiltshire, at Bromham [Cook 1948, 170, Plates 41, 47] and Devizes (St John's). The former was built by the bishop's nephew, Richard Beauchamp, Lord St Amand, and contains the tombs of his mother and of her second husband Sir Roger Tocotes (died 1492), constable of Devizes Castle and steward of all the lands in Wiltshire belonging to the Earldoms of Warwick and Salisbury and the Duchy of Lancaster. Although the identity of the builder is uncertain, the chapel at Devizes contains Beauchamp heraldry, exterior details are similar to those at Bromham, and the tall crocketed pinnacles are reminiscent of the short spire that tops the stair turret of the bishop's porch tower at Salisbury Palace (Plate 27, Fig 21).

In 1466 Bishop Beauchamp entertained his kinsman, King Edward IV, at his newly refurbished Palace. A decade later the king was to build the even larger great hall at Eltham Palace (1475–83), while the bishop was involved in another royal building scheme. In 1473 he had been appointed master and surveyor of the king's works at Windsor Castle, and was to supervise the first stage of the rebuilding of St George's Chapel [HKW 1963, 884–8]. He became dean of Windsor in 1477 and was to bequeath a Sarum missal to St George's. From as early as 1452, he had acted as Chaplain to the Order of the Garter and in 1475 he was appointed their Chancellor, an honour held until 1830 (with one long interval *temp* Edward VI to Charles II when it was held by laymen) by succeeding bishops of Salisbury [Fletcher 1938a, 166–7].

The canons

Salisbury, with Lincoln and Wells, was one of the three largest secular cathedral chapters, its prebends, with those of York and Lincoln, among the richest [Edwards 1949, 33, 40]. At the time of the transfer from Old Sarum the constitution was already established, with fifty-two canons. In one respect Salisbury was unusual: the bishop was always given one of the prebendal estates, which entitled him to a seat in chapter and a stall in choir as a canon as well as his episcopal throne. The archdeacons of Dorset, Berkshire, Sarum and Wiltshire acted as the bishop's deputies in the four subdivisions of the diocese, but these four canons were subsidiary in chapter and choir to the *quatuor personae*, the four dignitaries, of whom the foremost was the dean [Jones 1879, 214]. The second in rank was the precentor who directed the ceremonial of divine worship and was in charge of the choristers [Jones 1879, 222]. The third, the chancellor, acted as secretary to chapter, keeper of their seal and supervisor of the theological schools [Jones 1879, 225], and the fourth, the treasurer, cared for the ornaments and treasures of the church, providing all the candles at his own expense, maintaining the bells and paying the stipends of the sacrists (vergers) and altarists (servers) [Jones 1879, 231].

Few houses were tied to particular offices as they were in other cathedral closes on more confined sites. At Lincoln, for example, chapter bought up properties around the Minster for new residentiaries, and by the mid 13th century houses had been reserved for the dean, precentor, chancellor and subdean, though not for the treasurer [Major 1974, *passim*]. At Exeter, the four dignitaries, the subdean and the four archdeacons all had tied houses by the mid 14th century [Weekes 1915, *passim*] and at Chichester all four dignitaries had their residences in the close. At Salisbury only the dean had a tied house, given in 1277 by Dean Robert of Wykehampton when he became bishop. The house may indeed have been occupied by his predecessors as dean, and was held by all his successors until 1922. Much of the 13th-century house survives, restored in 1960, and the open hall provides the most complete interior of the period in the Close today, while the inventory made of the contents in 1440 is the most revealing contemporary description of a Salisbury canonry (Appendix to No. 62, p 212).

No doubt the four dignitaries maintained larger households than the other canons. The dean appears to have been the wealthiest member of Salisbury chapter and in 1440 there were nine beds available at the Deanery for servants as well as those of the steward and porter. Until 1322, when they were given one of the smaller houses (No. 54), the choristers, who numbered fourteen in 1314, were dependent on the precentor or the other canons for food and lodging [VCH 1956, 176]. The chancellor presided over much of the official and legal work of the Cathedral; until the late Middle Ages, when his work was increasingly done by lesser officials, he employed staff whom he may

have housed. He also employed the church beadle who 'lived with him as his *domesticus* and *familiaris*' [Edwards 1949, 232]. The treasurer also had deputies and assistants, in particular the sacrists whom he had to maintain at his own expense until 1634; they are first recorded as having their own houses in that year.

The resident canons likewise lived as minor magnates, each maintaining a 'competent and decent household' [Weekes 1915, 40]. At Salisbury and elsewhere canons are known to have had chaplains, chamberlains, cooks, esquires and yeomen [Edwards 1949, 61]; a 15th-century canon of St Paul's with fewer than three or four servants was considered very poor [Brooke 1957, 93].

Every canon, including the bishop, drew income from his prebendal estate, but the value of these varied and their allocation was something of a lottery. In *c* 1226, in the time of Richard Poore (1217–29), the rich prebend of Calne (Wilts) was permanently annexed to the office of treasurer, which obviously required an ample endowment [Jones 1879, 234; *VCH* 1956, 167]. Similarly, soon after 1240, the prebend of Bricklesworth (Brixworth, Northants) was permanently annexed to the office of chancellor [Jones 1879, 228; *VCH* 1956, 169] and in 1280, 'during the episcopate of Robert Wykehampton, who had himself been Dean, the prebend of Heytesbury (Wilts) was permanently annexed to the Deanery of Sarum' [Jones 1879, 217]. The precentor was endowed with the Rectory of Westbury (Wilts), but no special prebend was permanently annexed to his dignity [Jones 1879, 224].

The *communa*, or common fund, of the canons was derived from those chapter estates which were not allocated to individual prebends. It was distributed among the resident canons only and consisted of money payments, although at other secular cathedrals distributions of bread and ale were included. The fund had been swelled at Salisbury in the late 12th century by additional endowments and by the appropriation of one fifth of the prebendal income of non-residents. Only the four dignitaries were expected to reside continuously and they received double commons but it seems that there were usually about twelve canons who were spending sufficient time in residence to qualify for a share [Jones 1879, 2]. Already before 1195 the minimum time required to qualify for a share had been reduced from eight to three months of the year [*VCH* 1956, 162] but some canons resided for much more than the minimum.

The principal duties of the canons were daily attendance both in choir and in chapter. Those who were away from their cathedral for part or much of the year were employed elsewhere on royal or episcopal business or at the universities. Some were pluralists, holding prebends at more than one cathedral, while others lived on their prebendal estates. They came into residence occasionally for a few days at a time, in particular at the election, enthronement or installation of a bishop or dean, at an episcopal visitation or for a general meeting of chapter. It is not known where the non-resident canons, not all of whom had houses allocated to them, stayed on those occasions; possibly they lodged with the residentiary canons, which may account for the double set of apartments at, for example, the North Canonry (No. 60) or the (later) Vicars' Hall (Nos 12 and 13). Those who did have houses of their own presumably occupied some of the smaller ones.

Resident canons were expected to have means of their own in addition to the income derived from their prebends and the common fund, in order to maintain a suitable house and household and to provide the various forms of hospitality required of them by tradition. All Salisbury canons on admission to residence swore to offer hospitality regularly [Edwards 1949, 59]. It was of two main types. First was the more routine variety of hospitality given to junior ministers and boys serving the Church, to the poor and to strangers visiting the city [Edwards 1949, 59]. At Exeter it was said that the 'ministers and the choir-boys depend chiefly for their diet on the canons' tables' [Weekes 1915, 40]. The dignitaries also had individual extra obligations, although our knowledge of them is very limited. In the 14th century the dean was expected to feed a large number of ministers on particular feast days, and on obit days when masses were sung for the dead [Chew 1963, 165–6]; the precentor similarly provided for all the clergy involved in the services on three particular days in the year [Jones 1879, 233]. Similar if even more onerous arrangements pertained at Exeter and Lincoln [Weekes 1915, 38; Moorman 1945, 206–7].

Second was the hospitality levied upon admission to residence, when the canon had to provide a feast at his house in the Close for the bishop, canons and lesser clergy or, from the early 14th century, pay a fine of £40 to the Cathedral fabric [VCH 1956, 171]. This, and the similar arrangement which existed at other cathedrals, ensured that canons were not taking up residence merely for a share of the communal income [Moorman 1945, 169]. In 1385 a canon entering residence had to entertain his bishop for forty days, the dean for thirty and the other canons for twenty, an obligation commuted in 1428 into a cash payment of £105 for new dignitaries and £72 for other canons [Jones 1879, 244–5]. Nevertheless, in the middle and latter part of the 14th century, there were normally from eight to twelve residentiary canons [Edwards 1949, 78–9 and Appendix 2].

As the 14th century progressed, more of the canons were non-resident. Salisbury was one of the three cathedrals most affected in this manner, because its wealthy benefices tempted Pope and King to have their own

nominees appointed [Pantin 1955, 60]; in 1325, of the fifty-two members of chapter, twenty-eight were papally appointed [VCH 1956, 170] and in 1320–1, of twenty-nine non-resident canons, fourteen were cardinals or foreigners [Edwards 1949, 84–5]. Between 1297 and 1379, all six deans and four out of eight treasurers were non-resident foreigners, the precentor also was frequently an absentee, and not until the 1390s were all four dignitaries again to have English names and all to be in residence [ibid, 86]. Consequently, a smaller number of canons performed longer periods of residence than heretofore, each receiving a larger share of the income from the common fund [VCH 1956, 170–1]. There was a conscientious pattern of residence in the middle and latter part of the 14th century when eight to twelve canons were present fairly continuously right through the year; the remainder of those not permanently absent merely attended less frequently [ibid, 77–81]. When Thomas Montacute became dean in 1382 the era of foreign appointments was at an end, and by the early 15th century Salisbury chapter was conspicuous as 'one of the most distinguished ecclesiastical bodies of the later Middle Ages' [VCH 1956, 176].

The vicars choral

With the growing length and elaboration, both liturgical and musical, of the Cathedral services during the 12th century, the practice had grown up of appointing vicars choral to take the canons' parts. This was regularised by constitutions of 1214 and 1222 which laid down that every canon, resident or non-resident, must support a vicar choral to sing the daily services in the Cathedral on his behalf [VCH 1956, 164]. There were accordingly fifty-two vicars, for whom musical ability was a prerequisite of admission. Originally each of the vicars attached to a resident canon lived with his master, presumably serving as his chaplain and celebrating mass in the private chapel with which each canonry was provided (see below, p 15). There was a tendency to exploit the vicars for mundane purposes, and in 1319 Bishop Mortival forbade the canons to set them to 'catering for the household wants of their masters' [Wordsworth 1915, 219]. On the other hand, vicars sometimes converted parts of their masters' houses for their own use and it became necessary to prohibit them from making 'little chambers for themselves within the great canonries at the death of their masters, rendering them unsuitable for their successors' [Edwards 1949, 276]. Some vicars occupied canonries on behalf of masters who were permanently 'absent', but few would have had sufficient income to maintain a grand house. Some, especially the vicars of non-resident canons, held houses on their own behalf on the smaller sites. In the time of Bishop Mortival their obligation to provide hospitality was limited to entertaining vicars and other ministers only [Wordsworth

1915, 239–41]. It was the custom for the vicars of canons residentiary to invite those of the non-residentiaries to dine at their masters' tables.

Some vicars were able to supplement their stipends by accepting the chaplaincy of a chantry in the Cathedral. In 1390 only seven chantry chaplains were not also vicars choral [VCH 1956, 175]. There appears to have been a full quota of fifty-two vicars in that year [Edwards 1949, 274], and in 1395 thirty-one of them held houses in the Close, either in their own names or in those of the chantries they served [Edwards 1939, 83]. Not all the chantries provided houses for their stipendiary priests; those that are known to have done so are Henry Bluntesden's chantry (near No. 64), the two Hungerford chantries (Nos 54 and 63), the Audley chantry (No. 64) and Roger Clown's (Cloun's) which had a house on the site of the Matrons' College (Nos 39–46). Bishop Beauchamp's priests in the late 15th to early 16th century occupied a house on the site of No. 11. During the 15th century the priests of Bishop Waltham's chantry (founded 1395) were living in the town, alongside St Thomas's churchyard [RCHM 1980, 64], but none of the vicars lived outside the Close.

Although the vicars had been able to acquire and hold property in common from at least 1214, Salisbury was the last of the secular cathedrals to incorporate its vicars; a charter of 1409 granted them rights of self-governance and one of the canonries (Nos 12 and 13) as a common hall where they could live together. The inevitable disadvantage to chapter was that a number of small houses were unoccupied, but they nevertheless compounded the situation in 1442 with a statute compelling all vicars of non-resident canons to live in hall. Some of the vicars' former houses were probably acquired for chantry priests at this time. As sufficient accommodation was available, the need to found a chantry priests' college with its own hall and chapel, as was made at York in 1461 [RCHM 1981, 62–8], was never felt.

The houses of the Close

Construction and maintenance

The construction of the houses in the Close, and any later improvements, were paid for by the clergy individually, the financial burden on the canons of building their own houses while subscribing to the concurrent work on the Cathedral later being recognised by chapter in 1222 [Jones 1879, 241–2]. In the first instance the houses belonged to their builders, who were free to sell or bequeath them to their successors, but gradually, by bequest or donation, ownership passed to the bishop, the dean and chapter or to the vicars choral. Houses bequeathed to chapter or the

bishop were commonly charged with an obit rent, which the canon in possession paid annually, to be distributed among those attending masses sung for the donor's soul. Chapter allotted houses to the canons in order of seniority so that when the senior residentiary canon died or resigned every canon in turn was offered the option of moving to another house. The bishop seems to have owned the Walton Canonry (No. 69) and was given the Leadenhall (No. 70) and the Wardrobe (No. 58); any of these three could be obtained only by the bishop's gift, but their occupants were free to move into a chapter property during a general redistribution if they so wished.

Although these arrangements led to rapid changes in possession of the less popular houses, several long tenures are recorded at others: Chancellor Holes at the Leadenhall from 1445 to 1470 and Chancellor Norton at the South Canonry from c 1369 to 1402. Richard Whitby was probably more typical in occupying three or more houses during his forty-two years as a canon resident; he lived at Aula le Stage from 1452 to 1464, and moved from an unidentified house to Hemingsby, which he chose in 1474 and where he probably stayed until his death in 1494.

Chapter was concerned with the maintenance of the houses, though only rarely did it make contributions. Upon the death of a member it would appoint others to make a survey or 'schedule of dilapidations', the costs of any repairs to be borne by the executors. This procedure was also supposed to happen each time members merely exchanged houses. A number of these surveys have survived, recorded in the Chapter Act Books (see list, p x). Unfortunately not all the houses described therein can be identified with standing buildings, but nonetheless the surveys add considerably to our knowledge of the canons' houses. Some houses became so neglected that no one would willingly move into them. In the 1390s chapter offered a grant towards a repair of No. 15 to attract an occupant, but to no avail. When a similar situation occurred at Aula le Stage in the late 1440s, chapter undertook the work.

Two houses which were in continuous ownership were those which belonged to two of the monasteries holding Cathedral prebends: No. 65 belonged to the abbey of Sherborne and a smaller one (No. 23) to the priory of Loders, whose abbot and prior respectively had been canons of Salisbury since before the Cathedral was moved from Old Sarum. They were not allowed to become full residents with a share in the common fund, but they required houses in the Close for occasional use. 'Loders' was considered superfluous in 1446 as its parent priory had been suppressed, and so it was demolished by chapter and the materials salvaged. Two of the smaller houses were granted as tied houses in the mid 15th century: one, since demolished, to the subchanter in 1440, and the other, No. 18, to the subdean in 1442. Both men were officials bound to continuous residence.

Little disquiet is recorded concerning the state of the houses for the major part of the 14th century, and possibly Bishop Mortival's threat in 1319, that the ruinous state of the houses was disfiguring the Close and that those who did not take remedial action would have their prebendal income sequestrated, had had some effect [Wordsworth 1915, 179]. However, Henry Chichele, Archbishop of Canterbury from 1414 to 1443 and a former Salisbury chancellor, is said to have been 'constantly beset' as archbishop by the claims of Salisbury canons against their predecessors over the dilapidation of their houses and prebendal farms [Jacob 1947, 487]. Bishop Beauchamp condemned the 'great ruin' of the canonries in 1454 and it was stated then that the canons had not been paying their obit dues 'because of the enormous expense incumbent on them for repairs to the said houses, which are laid on them to the scandal of the church' [Act Book Bergh; Everett G, 27]. The system was therefore more onerous than at Lincoln, where canons paid rent for their official houses, but the cost of repairs could be reimbursed from the common fund [Major 1974, 27]. At Salisbury, mainten- ance of the fine houses which had been built in the 13th century as an ornament to the Church (and then, in the late medieval period, belonged to the body corporate) was becoming a burden on the individual canons who occupied them.

Canon Serle's house, for instance, needed more than £66 spending on its repair in 1403 [Acts 1402–5, ff 16v–17]. Inevitably some canons tried to evade holding a house at all, although, as they had to be reminded in 1398, this was a prerequisite of residence [Edwards 1939, 56–7]. Some canonries were allotted to minor clergy (eg Nos 5, 12 and 13, 18) but others became derelict or were pulled down, such as Copped Hall (No. 15) which was demolished in 1399 and its materials salvaged.

A house on the site of No. 16 appears to have been last occupied before 1418, Coldharbour in 1460, Simonsbury Place (No. 7) in 1476 and Crowton's (adjacent to Nos 20 and 21) in 1477, while others such as Myles Place (No. 68) and the canonry to the south of the King's House lasted until the 16th century. Another canonry, probably in North Walk, may have been taken over as the School of Theology, which existed in the 15th century, although very little is known of it [Edwards 1939, 86–7].

During the first half of the 15th century the work of the Cathedral was increasingly undertaken by a smaller number of canons who actually resided, while the contri- bution made by the others diminished. In 1447 there were said to be thirteen canonries, including the Deanery [Edwards 1939, 68], but the number of residentiaries fell thereafter and while there were still eleven in 1468, there

were only nine in 1470–1, seven in 1488, eight in 1524 and seven in 1534 [Jones 1879, 245; VCH 1956, 180]. Early 16th-century deans were consistently non-resident and other dignitaries were absent, with only one of them residing in 1534 [VCH 1956, 180], and from 1524 to 1535, for the first time, even the bishop, Cardinal Campeggio, lived abroad.

Chapter met the loss of demand for houses in the mid 15th century by admitting lay tenants, but we do not know their names or which houses they were offered. The decision had been made by bishop and chapter in about 1448 that houses other than the thirteen which were reserved for residentiaries could be let to 'honourable persons' [VCH 1956, 180]. The vicars also attempted to let their houses but Bishop Beauchamp objected in 1454 that they were letting to strangers without the consent of the dean and chapter. It may have been this admittance of lay folk that inspired the development of shops owned by chapter and the vicars at the North Gate (Nos 50–2), also condemned by Bishop Beauchamp in 1454; they were presumably leased on a commercial basis to outsiders in the 15th century, as they were in subsequent centuries.

The canons' houses

The majority of the larger houses on the west side of the Close were set well back from the graveyard wall and roadway, with forecourts flanked by ancillary buildings and entered by gatehouses. Although much of the evi- dence for forecourts, both documentary and architectural, dates from the 15th and 16th centuries, the standard rearward position of the principal ranges from the 13th century onwards suggests that subordinate buildings had always been placed at the front. By the early 19th century, most had been removed and replaced by walls or gate piers and railings. Gatehouses were demolished at the Deanery as early as c 1640 and at the King's House and the Wardrobe as late as 1804 and 1807 respectively. Parts of subsidiary ranges survive at the South Canonry and Hemingsby, and at Aula le Stage where three once enclosed an entrance courtyard; here the main part of the house was set at right angles to the North Walk and to one side of its tenement, with the gatehouse in a side alley.

One of the many uses of the outer ranges was to provide lodgings for dependants and staff. Consequently some canonries had more extensive forecourts than others according to the size of household they were to accommo- date. However, the moderately large house which later became the Vicars' Hall apparently had none, perhaps because the reconstruction and enlargement of c 1300 left no room for a normal forecourt. Another exception is the North Canonry (No. 60), which, though large, is built hard up against the road. The normal scheme appears to have been reversed, with the principal rooms along the front, facing the Cathedral, and the ancillary buildings at the rear, reached through a great gateway penetrating the main house; however, the site of any early hall at this house is uncertain.

Halls

The largest room in every canonry, in common with the houses of other prominent people, was the hall, the setting for canonical hospitality. Almost always, its position, where known, was parallel to the road and opposite the main gateway to the house, an exception being the hall of the North Canonry, a house whose plan was unusual in several respects. At Aula le Stage and the Vicars' Hall the halls were 14th-century additions which caused the blocking of upper windows in pre-existing residential ranges; in both houses, the original hall may have been smaller, or a detached building. The Deanery hall is very large, comparable in size with all but the greatest of 13th- and 14th-century unaisled halls [Wood 1965, 62–4], but the others which have survived are more modest. Much the smallest hall among the larger houses was that of the abbots of Sherborne who, as they were debarred from a share in the common fund, were not required to provide hospitality.

Although it has been claimed that 13th- and 14th-century halls were not arranged with 'high' and 'low' ends [Faulkner 1958, 112], such a distinction was certainly made in the canonries at Salisbury. At the Deanery there is evidence of a dais for the high table, which was set against a wall with painted decoration. The plain gable-end opposite supported dragon-braces. At Aula le Stage no evidence of a dais has been found, but the 'high' end of the hall is denoted by a sculptured cornice (Plate 89). The open hearth at the Deanery was set close to the dais for the comfort of the high table; originally the louvre was positioned over it but this was subsequently moved towards the lower end of the hall, perhaps because it was difficult to make it fully weatherproof, a difficulty also experienced with its modern reconstruction. Similarly, the louvre at Aula le Stage was not placed at the 'high' end. By the 15th century louvres appear to have been placed in the lowest bay, as at Hemingsby, or in the centre as at the King's House.

In one of the smaller houses, No. 10, the 14th-century side chimney in the hall is right at the 'high' end, so was intended to warm the high table rather than the whole room (Figs 36, 37).

Upper rooms

At one or both ends of the hall range were two-storey cross-wings containing apartments on the upper floor of one or more chambers each. The principal services were on the ground floor. The most common arrangement

seems to have placed the canon's own chamber(s) on the upper storey of the cross-wing at the 'high' end of the hall; there is evidence for this plan, with the cross-wing placed to north or south of the hall, at Hemingsby (south), Braybrooke (south), the Wardrobe (north), Arundells (north), the Deanery (south), the Leadenhall (south) and the South Canonry (south). In three 13th-century houses, the Deanery, Arundells and the Leadenhall, the upper storey of the cross-wing has, or had, a large traceried window in at least one gable-end which presumably lit an important room. At the Deanery, the upper storey was probably divided into two rooms, which were combined to make one in the 16th century, divided again into two in the early 19th century and made into one yet again in the 20th century. The first-floor apartment at the 'low' end certainly originated as two rooms, the inner one much the smaller (Fig 139).

At Aula le Stage, the North Canonry and the Vicars' Hall, there appears to have been only one cross-wing with chambers, and therefore the accommodation found in two units elsewhere must have been combined in one. Reconstructions of the upper floor plans suggest that at the Vicars' Hall and the North Canonry there were pairs of similar if not identical apartments, each of two rooms (Figs 44, 134), whereas at Aula le Stage there were two single chambers of different sizes (Fig 64).

The use of these upper rooms in the 13th century is difficult to reconstruct in the absence of inventories, but at least one apartment would have been the canon's private room or rooms [Faulkner 1958, 114]. At the Deanery, the first-floor entrance at the 'high' end is unexpectedly small and simple, suggesting that it was only for personal use (Plate 159). The provision of a second apartment of equal scale to the first was presumably for the accommodation of important guests, as at the Deanery where in 1586 the chamber over the services was called the king's chamber. The canon's vicar was not accommodated in such a room and perhaps not in the main house at all.

The upper chambers were no doubt served by a latrine, sometimes in a closet within the corner of the room or in a projecting building, as on the west side of the Deanery (Fig 139). At the Vicars' Hall there were probably privies between the larger and smaller rooms of each apartment and accessible from both (Fig 44). At Aula le Stage, there is a small window high up, in a corner of the larger ground-floor room, which probably lit a privy; privies attached to parlours are occasionally noted in 15th-century surveys.

Chapels

Each canonry had a chapel, and in 1324 at least one vicar's house, near No. 64 (*qv*), also had one. They were primarily for the canon's own use but could be called upon for public worship as well; for example in 1463, when the Cathedral was closed for several days after blood had been shed there, services were transferred to the chapel at Aula le Stage, probably because the occupant, Canon Whitby, was *locum tenens* for the dean at the time. Chapels were usually attached to, or part of, the cross-wings; that at Aula le Stage rose through both floors, with the altar at ground level and the canon's gallery above (Fig 62). In the 13th century the Deanery and the Leadenhall chapels seem to have been similarly arranged.

The Deanery chapel was almost certainly the largest chapel of all, measuring some 40 ft by 18 ft while that at Aula le Stage was about 19 ft 6 ins by 12 ft 3 ins. Access to the canon's gallery at Aula le Stage was from the smaller of the apartments, but at the Deanery, the South Canonry (survey of 1402) and probably the Leadenhall, the chapel was approached through the apartment at the 'high' end of the hall, which was the larger of the apartments, at least at the Deanery. Other chapels were described in surveys as being on the ground floor (Simonsbury Place, 1455) or under a separate roof (R Pittes' house, 1415, R Langrish's, 1454) (see list, p x). At the South Canonry in 1402 it was above a little chamber, and at the Vicars' Hall it was also on the upper floor.

Lower rooms

Rooms below the principal apartment at the high end of the hall are less easily understood because of their varying height and lack of original features. Some were fairly tall, for example, 10 to 12 ft at the Deanery or Vicars' Hall (Fig 41); the undercroft at the North Canonry is 8 ft high, and that below the lesser chamber at Aula le Stage, 9 ft 3 ins. At Arundells and the Leadenhall they were only about 6 ft 6 ins high and they may have been used for the storage of valued goods such as wine, as at Lincoln where canons' houses in *c* 1230 and in 1343 had their solar, or great chamber, over the cellar [Major 1974, 19, 23]. At three 13th-century houses, the Leadenhall, the Deanery and Arundells, there were external doorways to the cellars, presumably to facilitate delivery of wine barrels. A front room at the Vicars' Hall may have been a wine cellar with an external doorway (Fig 44), but it is also possible that it was a room for the porter.

However, the relative size and elaboration of some lower rooms, such as that at the Wardrobe, the large windows of which are probably original (Figs 124, 127), suggest that they were used as parlours. At the Deanery a stout wall which may be the original partition between cellar and parlour remains; a parlour described as 'old' there in 1440 (Appendix to No. 62) was possibly the 13th-century room. Those cross-wings which contained a single apartment on the upper floor probably had no

change in floor level between rooms, and the ceilings of the cellars would therefore have been the same height as the adjoining parlours, an arrangement which survived the 15th-century rebuilding at the Wardrobe. At Aula le Stage the two apartments were placed in adjacent ranges where they could be on different floor levels. Soon after 1400 there is clear evidence of the arrangement of cellar and parlour side by side at both the Deanery and the Vicars' Hall, where the parlours are denoted by chimney-pieces and (at the Deanery) larger windows and the cellars by small slit windows. At Braybrooke in 1449 the parlour and wine cellar were evidently near each other, but at Arundells there seems to have been no parlour in the 13th-century cross-wing, which has a low ceiling and no sign of either a dividing wall or a doorway leading from the hall.

Service rooms and kitchens

The 13th-century arrangement at the 'lower' end of the hall is well preserved only at the Deanery, where a triple doorway (Plate 157) led to two service rooms conventionally known as the buttery and the pantry, one on either side of a passage leading through to a detached kitchen. In the late 14th century, this kitchen was replaced by one adjoining the house (Fig 139) but, in the same period at the Vicars' Hall, a new triple doorway (Plate 59) was built, implying that the kitchen there was still a detached building (Fig 44). A 'passage from the kitchen to the hall' is named in an inventory of Braybrooke. The centre one of the triple doorways at the lower end of a medieval hall is usually assumed to have led into a passage to the kitchen, but the total enclosure of this passage would have been inconveniently dark. A careful examination of the 13th-century joists at the Deanery and of the 15th-century ones at the King's House, which are well preserved, reveals no trace of a second partition and possibly in some houses at least the 'passage' may have been no more than a space left free at the side of the pantry with a door at both ends.

At Nicholas Upton's house in 1440 [Acts 1440–7, f 25] the kitchen and pantry were next to one another, connected by a hatch. Normally the buttery and pantry were low rooms, which allowed one or more good-sized chambers to be constructed over them, either in line with the hall and under the same roof, as at the Deanery (Fig 142), or in a second cross-wing as at the Wardrobe (Fig 124). With the construction of the King's House in the 15th century, the integration of the kitchen into the main range of the house was complete, as a room with a fireplace beyond the buttery and pantry (Fig 153). The second Deanery kitchen, of shortly before 1400, was a lofty room in a projecting wing with a massive fireplace at one end; this room is still spanned by a central truss with a neatly finished stop-chamfered collar. An almost identical feature, richly smoke-blackened, was reused in an 18th-century partition at Aula le Stage.

In addition, there was usually a bakehouse close to the kitchen; evidently at Salisbury each household made its own bread, unlike at St Paul's or Exeter where bread was baked communally [Edwards 1949, 240, 245]. The South Canonry in a survey of 1402 (see list, p x) had its own brewhouse as well.

New rooms

By the 15th century, accommodation was becoming more comfortable and more varied in type; there were more rooms for the private use of the owner, more and larger windows, more fireplaces, and more latrines. There are also more documents to supplement what we know from the buildings themselves, in particular a number of surveys and inventories recorded in the Chapter Act Books (see list, p x).

The principal upper room was generally listed in the surveys as the 'great chamber' and was no longer a private room. Usually it was sited, as before, at the 'high' end of the hall, as at the South Canonry (1402) and at the houses of J Searle (1403) and R Langrish (1454), while at Simonsbury Place in 1455 it was called the 'long chamber' and was over the parlour. Elsewhere it was at the 'low' end, as at No. 69 in 1443 where it was above the chief entrance, and at the King's House, where it was a larger room than the abbot's own chamber. When situated in a cross-wing, the great chamber commonly formed a set of rooms together with a lesser chamber and latrine, as at the South Canonry, Braybrooke in 1449, and at the houses of J Searle (1403) and W Swifte (1445), while at E Prentys's house (1409) the room next to the great chamber was said to be lacking a latrine. In two of these houses the latrine was evidently appended to the 'great' or 'principal' chamber and in two others to the smaller chamber of the set. Such a pair of 15th-century chambers survives in the cross-wing at the 'upper' end of the Wardrobe (Fig 124).

The survey made of the Deanery in 1440 (see Appendix to No. 62) is informative as it not only names the rooms but illustrates their use better than any other (Fig 139). The principal chamber was more lavishly furnished than the hall, which suggests that the dean performed his more select hospitality there. There were three chambers in which people could both sleep and receive visitors. Chambers appear to have become more public, as is evidenced by the construction of a large new door to the dean's great chamber (Plate 163) and the blocking of the old one.

New private rooms were therefore needed and these were usually sited at the 'upper' end of the house. The three-storey towers containing small rooms, which were added to the Deanery c 1400 and Aula le Stage c 1440, remain the most obvious response to the new require-

ments (Plate 160, Figs 138, 139; Plate 88, Figs 62, 68, 69). The north range added subsequently to Aula le Stage, between the tower and the earlier house, and the surviving medieval range at the South Canonry probably provided each of the houses with another new chamber above a parlour. However, apart from the South Canonry (much better documented than other houses at this period), which had seven or eight chambers, only the Deanery was listed in the 15th century as having more than four.

The earliest evidence of studies occurs in the mid 15th century. Canon Langrish had not only a first-floor withdrawing ('drawghte') chamber as well as his great chamber, but also a study in which the fittings in 1454 'remain as first built', suggesting that it was new and perhaps had been set up since his appointment as a residentiary in 1447. Another study, at Simonsbury Place (No. 7) in 1455, was over a porch and there may have been others over the hall porches at Hemingsby and the Wardrobe in the 15th century, while some may have been in the towers at the Deanery and Aula le Stage.

Lodgings and outbuildings

Some members of the canon's household would have been housed in separate lodgings in subsidiary ranges by the forecourts. The only range to have survived in a recognisable form is the 15th-century gatehouse range at Aula le Stage, where there are three chambers at the head of a staircase, one rather grander than the others, and a small room or closet (Fig 60). A curious feature of the two lesser rooms here is that their partition wall goes up only to the tie-beam, with no sign of a division or ceiling above that level. However, one room had a wainscot ceiling in 1586.

The bishop had to provide the greatest number of lodgings, as he had the largest household; he not only travelled with a numerous retinue, but also needed various officials to look after the Palace in his absence. The three-storey tower built by Bishop Beauchamp in the 1460s provided an imposing entrance to his new great hall as well as increasing the number of lodgings, each room with its own fireplace and privy.

One of the bishop's senior staff presumably occupied the lodging over the 14th-century Palace Gate. Of three well furnished chambers, the largest is unheated and was perhaps the great chamber, while a second one with a fireplace and another which probably had a privy were perhaps the parlour and private chamber.

Other outbuildings are listed in the 15th-century surveys, and they may also have existed in the 13th century. In addition to stables and fuel stores, there were barns for hay and straw, granaries, poultry houses, dovecotes and even harrier kennels, while other buildings are described less informatively as gatehouses, or more enigmatically as 'a house called Hethous', 'Mempirum', or 'Dormand'.

The smaller houses

Most of the houses held by non-resident canons or vicars choral were in the northeast part of the Close (Fig 2). Only four remain (Nos 10, 18, 29, 31), none of them complete. The surviving cross-wing, which is now No. 29, provides a good picture of the scale and comfort of these dwellings (Plate 97; Figs 81, 82, 84).

Three of the four were vicars' choral property by the mid 17th century but No. 18 belonged to the dean and chapter. In 1443 it was made the subdeanery. It nicely illustrates the lack of distinction between vicars' houses and the smaller canonries since, prior to 1443, it had been occupied by canons; however, it bore the obit of a vicar, it adjoined vicars' properties, and most of the 15th-century subdeans were vicars.

All four houses are predominantly of rubble construction but also partly timber framed. Nos 10 and 29 are built adjoining the roadway, with the entrance leading into a screens passage, and any ancillary buildings would have been at the rear of the house, whereas No. 18 was set back from the street with a gatehouse in front. No. 31 was built around a small courtyard but the plan is uncertain; Fig 87 suggests two possible reconstructions. Nos 10, 18 and 29 date mainly from the 14th century and are of hall and cross-wing plan. In the smallest house, No. 10, the hall penetrates the wing (Fig 36) and the entrance is in the side wall in an alley off the street.

It is clear that these houses were as well heated as the great canonries. The hall of No. 18 had an open hearth, and at No. 10 there is a side-wall chimney of 14th-century date and the room over the parlour also had a fireplace in the medieval period. There is little doubt that the back room of No. 29 with its large hearth, smoke-bay and external doorway was a kitchen, the earliest surviving kitchen in the Close to be integrated into the main house (see above, p 16). There were two chambers with fireplaces on the upper floor of No. 29, where the arrangements reflect its original form as a suite of rooms: a larger chamber into which the stairs led, an inner room and a small porch chamber, possibly used, respectively, as great and private chambers and a study or chapel, or both.

In general these houses are comparable in size and accommodation with certain priests' houses in southwest England [Pantin 1957]. However, the way of life of a vicar choral would have been quite different from that of a country priest, and documentary sources giving any details of the vicars' households are lacking. Some of the houses may have been larger than those that remain and one, which later became the Subchantry (Fig 2), changed hands twice in the early 15th century with the first vicar in the sequence reserving two rooms to himself.

Two examples of houses held by chantry priests are Nos 63 and 64, both of which had high and low chambers in the 15th century, with the front rooms raised above cellars. No reference is made to a hall, although this could in each case have been a room at the rear (Fig 150) if the houses had side entrances, as at No. 10. Alternatively, there may never have been a ground-floor hall in either house, in which case they were similar to another probable chantry priest's house in the town, built in the later 14th century on a cramped site to the east of St Thomas's Church; there, too, the principal room, heated by a large fireplace, was on the first floor [Reeves and Bonney 1981, 100].

The Porter's Lodge (No. 48) is another 14th-century house of similar size to the vicars' houses, with a stone cross-wing and timber-framed hall. The porter appears to have been a man of higher status than the vicars [Edwards 1949, 232] and his cross-wing is built largely of squared stone which was perhaps available because the house was being built at the same time as the Close Wall. However, the single-storey hall is only two thirds of the size of the small halls at Nos 10 and 18; even if it were of two bays and not one as suggested (Fig 105), it was not only single storey but low. The anomaly seems more curious because of the quality of the parlour and great chamber, which are of good size with fireplaces. The explanation may lie in the difference in date between the cross-wing and its hall: the former may be the earlier. There is also reason to believe that the porter's status declined in the Middle Ages, his perquisites in 1451 and 1502 comparing with those of the beadle and subtreasurer [Wordsworth 1915, 33].

Building materials and details

The use of stone

The early houses were built mainly of flint rubble. Dressed stone, from the quarries at Chilmark some twelve miles west of Salisbury, was employed on the Close and graveyard walls, but, with the exception of the Porter's Lodge (No. 48), it was used on the houses only as dressing, although this might be extensive as on Bishop Beauchamp's additions to the Palace. At first, the priority given to the Cathedral may have been the reason for the limited use of dressed stone, but later the high cost was probably a sufficient deterrent. One result was the reuse of stone removed from Old Sarum, some of it carved with 12th-century designs, though such carved stones are not as prominent on the houses as they are on the Close Wall (see p 42).

Some 13th- and 14th-century masonry consists of flint

coursing neatly layered externally but heavily laced with herringbone courses of roof tiles internally (eg, the west range of Aula le Stage). Such tile courses are also common in medieval rubble externally, and the 14th-century porch at Hemingsby, especially its south wall, is largely built of them. It is a curious use of an otherwise valuable artefact, and since such tiles are much less common in the medieval city, it seems likely that the canons had access to a supply of damaged ones, presumably at Old Sarum. No doubt all rubble would have been plastered originally and the remains of possibly medieval render survive at Aula le Stage and on the chamber block at the Deanery.

Windows and doorways

The 13th-century two-light windows with trefoiled heads and quatrefoil above, which exist or did exist at the Palace, the Deanery and Arundells, occur in other buildings which were, or may have been, connected with Elias de Dereham, such as the great halls of Winchester Castle [HKW, 860] and Canterbury Palace [Tatton-Brown 1982, 117] (the latter has uncusped lights), and Bishop Jocelyn's solar at Wells [Wood 1965, fig 109 and plate LIII]. Detached oculi in gables are more unusual but they occur at the Leadenhall (two roundels), Winchester Castle (roundels), and at Wells and Canterbury palaces (quatrefoils). The possibility that the cusped oculi used at the Deanery in the early 19th century were derived from 13th-century parts of the building (Plate 155) cannot be confirmed and they were not included when the building was reconstructed.

Later in the 13th century the Vicars' Hall was well provided with cusped and moulded windows. Smaller traceried windows remain in the 14th-century porch at Hemingsby and in the parlour at Braybrooke (mutilated), and the hall window seen by Buckler at the King's House had blocked-up tracery (Plate 168); there are also 15th-century cusped windows in several of the larger houses.

In the 13th and early 14th century some windows and doorways were of depressed form, as in the parlour at the Wardrobe, the hall at Aula le Stage, and the cellar of the North Canonry. Thirteenth-century doorways are chamfered but not ornamented, with the exception of one with pyramidal stops in the cellar of the North Canonry and another with shouldered stops in the South Canonry (Plate 187). Even the doorway at the head of the stairs leading from the hall to the principal apartment of no less a person than the dean was small and plainly finished (Plate 159). Moulded arches are most common in the 14th century, especially for the main entrance to a hall, as at the Vicars' Hall (Plate 58), No. 29 and Hemingsby, and occur again in the 15th century at the Bishop's Palace and the King's House. The four-centred arch appears in the 14th-century service doors of the Vicars' Hall and, less steeply, at No. 29. In the late 14th century, at Palace Gate,

two-, three- and four-centred arches are employed contemporaneously for doorways as well as windows, which are variously chamfered, hollow chamfered or moulded. Both two- and four-centred doorways and windows also appear in the additions made by Bishop Beauchamp (1450–81) at the Palace, the largest doorways being still two centred, as are the doorways and large windows at the King's House and the hall at Hemingsby, both datable after the middle of the century. Lights with shouldered lintels occur at the Vicars' Hall, a narrow one of the 13th century and a larger one to the upper chamber added in the 14th century.

Square-headed windows are numerous in lesser buildings or rooms and also some principal ones, for example, the great chamber of the Wardrobe. They may be chamfered or hollow chamfered, but generally there is little to suggest a date for them. Those with a broader moulding and no external rebate occur in medieval contexts with which they are probably contemporary, for example, the side window of the porch at Hemingsby and a chamber added to the Vicars' Hall, both 14th-century buildings, and a triple-light in the tower at Aula le Stage. Small squat windows, much broader than tall, occur in several houses; in the 13th-century parts of the North Canonry and Aula le Stage (Plate 86) such windows probably ventilated latrines, and may have had a similar use in the 14th century at No. 18, while they also occur in vaulted cellars, perhaps of the 13th century, at the North Canonry, and in the early 15th-century tower at Aula le Stage.

Several windows retain iron grilles, in which the stanchions normally pass through rings on the external face of the saddlebars, but some 13th-century examples differ: a latrine window at Aula le Stage has internal saddlebar rings, while in a side window of the chapel the stanchion pierces the middle of the saddlebars with the glass on the exterior; at the Leadenhall the early 13th-century window has its saddlebars similarly divided, with the glass groove on their inward face.

Chimneys and fireplaces

Halls were usually heated by an open fire with louvre above (see p 15) but smaller rooms required other methods of heating. Where there were chimneys these may have been constructed within the thickness of the wall, as at No. 29, for traces of them are rarely found. The stone cap of a 13th-century chimney has been excavated at the Deanery [Drinkwater 1964, Plate XXXII]. It may be that chimneys were comparatively unusual until the 15th century as they are then mentioned several times in surveys or inventories as abutting a parlour or chamber, without any claim that they needed repair. Chimney-breasts of 14th- or 15th-century date remain at the Deanery, Porter's Lodge, Aula le Stage and No. 10, the last retaining the seating for its chimney shaft (Fig 37). Corbel-tables support 15th-century chimneys, as an original feature on the tower at Aula le Stage, and a secondary one at the Wardrobe, while another at the King's House occurs high up and was probably a decoration.

Fireplaces of the 14th century have chamfered or hollow-chamfered stone jambs and stone or timber lintels, and three had moulded stone cornices (two at No. 29, and the chamber of the Vicars' Hall). Larger chimney-pieces, of late 14th- or 15th-century date, are at Palace Gate, the South Canonry (Plate 190), the parlour at the Vicars' Hall (Plate 61), Bishop Beauchamp's chamber, and at the Deanery (Plate 162). Those in the early 15th-century tower at Aula le Stage, large and small, are simply hollow chamfered with square heads. Several tiled firebacks are probably medieval, for example, one in the hall of No. 10, two at No. 29, and one in the tower of Aula le Stage (No. 21).

The use of timber

Timber-framing was commonly used, not only for subsidiary buildings but also for the halls of smaller houses, and possibly even for certain larger halls which have disappeared, as at Arundells. Surviving timber-framing is seldom exposed, being clad generally in hung-tiles.

That at No. 10, of the early 14th century, may be the oldest in the Close and its juxtaposition with rubble for the different walls of the same room, or even for different parts of the same wall, can be paralleled in other 14th-century halls, for example, at Nos 29 and 18. A similar combination occurs in storeyed ranges: in the 14th-century chamber block at No. 18, in the 15th-century gatehouse range of Aula le Stage (No. 20) and at the three shops (Nos 50–2). Many of these buildings are, or were, originally jettied, several of them above lower storeys of rubble: the 15th-century gatehouse of Aula le Stage is jettied on both sides. Where visible the framing commonly has long curved braces, for example, at Nos 29 (Fig 82) and 51, with particularly decorative effects in the tower added in the 15th century to Aula le Stage (Fig 69). However, there is no bracing in the 15th-century stoutly framed end wall of the hall at Hemingsby, which was perhaps intended to be concealed by hangings. In several buildings which are otherwise constructed of the usual rubble, the gables alone are framed. Such gables are datable from c 1300 for the chamber range of the Vicars' Hall, to the late 14th or early 15th century for the service rooms added to the Deanery and for the great parlour and chamber at Braybrooke, with the hall at Aula le Stage and the southeast chamber at the Vicars' Hall dating from the 14th century.

In the tower at Aula le Stage the framing is infilled with mainly chalk rubble but in the north gable of the 14th-century hall of the same house and at Palace Gate and No. 31 there was wattle and daub, the staves nailed in. By the time of the early 16th-century range at No. 31, the staves were fixed top and bottom by drilled holes and a groove respectively, and a changeover to this more workmanlike practice in the 15th century may be demonstrated at Aula le Stage, where the upper walls of the gateway employ both methods. A 14th-century partition wall at No. 29 was filled with flush panels of oak, but a former partition in the north range of No. 31, perhaps datable to the late 14th century, was constructed with planks and hollow-chamfered muntins (Fig 89). In the wardrobe at Aula le Stage another partition, probably also of 14th-century date, has tiers of chamfered timber-framing but the original filling is unknown.

Oak floorboards of exceptional width are probably also medieval. In the southern part of the ground floor at the North Canonry they measure 14 ins, and on the first floor of the Porter's Lodge 12½–13 ins, both above close joisting perhaps of 14th- or 15th-century date. In certain later buildings where they also occur, they may be medieval and reset, as at No. 16 in the attic of the original range (18 ins), the eastern attics of the Leadenhall (14–15 ins), and the chamber added over the medieval kitchen at the Vicars' Hall, where 15 ins boards are mixed with narrower ones.

Several late medieval doors remain, planked and counter-planked, as in the tower at Aula le Stage and the kitchen added to the Deanery, and one in the stair turret of St Ann's Gate has an ornamental finish (Plate 8).

Roofs

Two hall roofs attributed to the 13th century were of three bays without aisles; the Deanery roof, if it dates from Wykehampton's years as dean (1258–74), is of advanced construction with base-cruck trusses supporting an upper structure of uniform scantling with crown-posts and scissor-bracing [Alcock and Barley 1972, 148], and the Wardrobe may also have had base-cruck intermediate trusses. At Arundells the roof of the demolished hall had scissor- or passing-braces.

More 13th-century roofs have survived from chambers. They have collared rafters of uniform scantling without longitudinal stiffening; those at the Palace and over the large chamber at Aula le Stage are scissor-braced, a refinement appropriate to the higher status of these houses, even though the latter roof was not visible originally (Figs 16, 65). The other two 13th-century roofs at Aula le Stage have braced collars, as did that at the Leadenhall, where the roof is only known from photographs (Plates 183–6); the tie-beams were probably an original feature, although it is doubtful whether the structure was unaltered early 13th-century work (Plate

184, Fig 165). At the Palace and the Leadenhall, it seems that the roofs were open to the apex, as there was wall plaster or windows high up in the gables above collar level, but at Aula le Stage neither occurs, which may imply that there were ceilings at this level. A late 13th-century crown-post roof over the chamber block at the Vicars' Hall has collared rafters with crown-post trusses, which may always have been concealed by a ceiling at tie-beam level since there is no sign of closures between rooms in the upper parts of the trusses (Fig 41).

The 14th-century hall roof of Aula le Stage combines individually collared rafters of uniform scantling with arch-braced collar trusses, wind-braced purlins and an ashlar-boarded cornice. One of the smaller houses, No. 29, has two chambers each spanned by a principal truss, the greater with an arch-braced collar and the lesser scissor-braced (Figs 84, 85). Both roofs are wind-braced as is another chamber roof of later 14th-century date, at No. 31 (Fig 88). Chambers added to older ranges at the Vicars' Hall and Aula le Stage, in the 14th and 15th centuries respectively, have curved timbers supported on stone corbels at upper storey level (Plate 60). In the former, the truss which spans the middle of the chamber has principals with curved feet, but in the latter the timbers are true crucks and upper crucks [Alcock 1981, 2–4].

Two of the Close gates have 14th-century roofs. At St Ann's Gate, finished shortly before 1354, there is a boldly moulded ridge-piece and two open intermediate trusses with purlins clasped on short struts and end trusses curiously shaped, perhaps to avoid the original windows (Fig 9). At the later Palace Gate, the trusses have cranked arch-braces to collars, with secret tenons between brace and principal (Fig 12).

In the 15th century roofs were commonly of arch-braced collar form with clasped purlins, and often elaborately finished as is the hall roof at Hemingsby of c 1460 (Fig 116). Ashlar-boarded cornices grace this hall and the great chambers of the King's House and the Wardrobe. Clasped and butt purlins both occur, even in the same building, in closed and open trusses respectively, as for example, at No. 51, an early 15th-century shop.

By about 1400 wind-bracing was hardly more than a decoration and was therefore omitted from the kitchen added to the Deanery and even from the rooms rebuilt at the 'upper' end of the Wardrobe, where the roof is otherwise handsomely finished. Elsewhere, much decorative use was made of this obsolescent feature, for example, in the 15th-century hall at Hemingsby (Fig 116), while inverted braces, which had been used in the early 14th-century hall at Aula le Stage, appeared at the King's House (Fig 154) and at the smaller houses, Nos 29 and 31 (Fig 88). The hall roofs at Hemingsby and the King's House, which date from the latter part of the 15th century, both

have a ridge-piece. Closed trusses commonly have tie-beams with two or three struts to cambered collars, for example, at Nos 51 and 52 and the outbuildings of the South Canonry and Hemingsby, and at the South Canonry in the chamber (but cf 15 Queen St (before 1403) [RCHM 1980, 85–7]). There are false hammer-beam trusses at the Song School (No. 5), which was reroofed c 1460 to 1470 (Fig 28), the hall at Hemingsby (Fig 116) and probably the former gatehouse chamber at Aula le Stage, now No. 20 (Fig 61); this type of construction is not uncommon in Salisbury city. The low-pitched lead roofs over Bishop Beauchamp's tower and chamber at the Palace (after 1450), on the tower at Aula le Stage (before 1440) (Fig 69), and over the North Gate were constructed on cambered tie-beams.

Painted decoration

It is clear from a photograph taken of the Leadenhall before demolition in 1915 (Plate 186) that the interior of the 13th-century building was decorated with painted walls: an upper chamber had ashlaring, partly filled with stencilled flowers of stylised design, and heavier lines and friezes of *rinceaux* emphasising such features as windows, doorways and gables (Fig 165). Painted decoration was similarly used in the inner and outer chambers at the Palace (Fig 17), in an outer chamber and other parts of the North Canonry (Plate 153), in a room described as the 'hall' at the Subchantry [Harding 1897, 96], and in the Deanery hall where, in addition to the predominantly red (and black) colouring used elsewhere, cream paint occurs in the frieze. The simpler stencilled frieze can be paralleled in the Cathedral treasury and north porch and at 86 Crane Street [RCHM 1980, Plate 43], and the flowers in the chancel of East Wellow Church [*VCH* 1911, 538]. In its simpler forms such decoration is not closely datable, the Cathedral friezes being not earlier than the mid 13th century while those at the Palace and the Leadenhall could be c 1220. The more elaborate stiff-leaf forms at the Old Deanery, however, probably date from the second quarter of the century (Plate 158). Stencilled flower decoration also occurs in a developed form in one of the smaller houses (No. 10) in the early 14th century (Plate 51).

However, not all rooms were painted; at Aula le Stage restoration has revealed that the walls of the 13th-century parlour and large upper chamber were not plastered, but instead oak battens were built into them at regular intervals. As these do not appear in areas altered in the 16th century they must be medieval, and wainscoting was possibly their original finish.

Other decorative detail

Inlaid tiles similar to those in the Cathedral muniment room and the Queen's Chamber at Clarendon Palace, paved from 1250 to 1252 [Eames 1958, 97], have been discovered at the Deanery [Drinkwater 1964, Plate xxxiii] and the Wardrobe (Plate 135, Fig 125). At the Bishop's Palace, wall-arcading on one side of the room over the undercroft still existed in 1736; possibly it was of 13th-century date and perhaps comparable with that of the outer chamber at Temple Manor, Strood, of the second quarter of the 13th century [Rigold 1966, Plate x]. Architectural elaboration is also suggested by a stiff-leaf capital and sculptured heads of a king and queen, of mid 13th-century date, discovered *ex situ* at the Deanery in 1961 [Drinkwater 1964, Plate xxxii].

The carved stones from Old Sarum

In 1219 the cathedral and close at Old Sarum were surrendered into the king's hands. Permission to rob the old work to build the new was not obtained until 1276 [HMC, Var Coll I, 362], and was renewed in 1331 [Dodsworth 1814, 146–7]. A chapel remained in use there until 1332, when the canons obtained consent to rebuild it elsewhere [RCHM 1980, 16], which suggests that by then total demolition was envisaged. Nonetheless, it is quite clear from the carved 12th-century stonework reset both in the easternmost parts of the new Cathedral and in the graveyard wall, that the old cathedral was being used as a quarry from the start [HKW ii, 826]. Although they are not easily visible in the new Cathedral, the carved stones are very prominent in the better preserved parts of the graveyard wall and in the Close Wall, where most are placed facing outwards on to Exeter Street. Some symbolic gesture of the continuity of Salisbury see from the old castle to the new Close may be implied.

Many of the carved stones come from the ornamental south and west façades of the old cathedral, begun by Bishop Roger (1107–39) after 1125. They include examples of scaled cappings from pinnacles, miniature arcading, respond capitals from small or decorative arches, leaf-frieze and stones with cabled arrises, chevron ornament, etc (Plate 3), most of which are closely paralleled by others in the *lapidarium* at Old Sarum, together with fragments of figure sculpture. There are also many stones with a face some 8 ins square which resemble ballflower, and these may have lined the jambs of doorways as on the architecturally related work on the west façade of Lincoln Cathedral [Stalley 1971, 71–81]. This type of carving is especially prominent in the Close Wall but it also occurs at the new Cathedral and elsewhere in the Close, so that no sequence can be suggested for the destruction of the old cathedral.

The Old Sarum stonework was evidently a valued commodity, which led to its being continually reset; that in the 18th-century build of Malmesbury House, for example, was derived from the Close Wall, which in turn had been built from material previously in the graveyard wall.

A collection of carved stones which have been removed from various positions in the Cathedral and from the Close Wall has been formed by the clerk of works and is at present in the masons' yard. Carved stones remain, or did until recently, in the following contexts:

Date of carved stones	Location of stones
13th century	Cathedral In the side walls internally above the vaults of the Trinity Chapel, presbytery aisles and eastern transepts; begun 1220 Footings on west of northeast transept Cloisters, south perimeter wall, east part of south face, after 1248 Pulpitum, c 1260 Graveyard wall
Later medieval	Close Wall North Gate, south face Song School (No. 5) Porter's Lodge (No. 48) Hemingsby, porch (No. 56A and B) Garden wall between Braybrooke and the Wardrobe (Nos 57/8)
Post medieval	Porter's Lodge (pillaged from Close Wall?) Arundells (No. 59), wall of staircase, c 1720 (from Close Wall?) North Canonry (No. 60), south elevation, c 1738 Palace coach-house, 1843 Vicars' Hall (No. 12), passage wall built in 1814, probably with rubble from the 14th-century hall North Canonry, removed in 1875 from an unknown position to Salisbury Museum, a finely sculpted head of Christ in Glory probably from a Cathedral doorway tympanum

The 16th and 17th centuries

The secular cathedrals were affected much less by the Reformation than were those with monastic chapters. Medieval statutes remained in force and the organisation altered little, although the numbers of clergy, especially of the humbler ranks, were reduced. At Salisbury six prebends were lost but the number of residentiaries fell only from the seven or eight usual throughout the Reformation period to the seven, or six with the dean, which became the rule from *c* 1600 until the Cathedrals Act of 1840 [*VCH* 1956, 184–5]. Most of the Cathedral treasures described in an inventory of 1536 [Dodsworth 1814, 229–32] were confiscated and the shrine of St Osmund destroyed. The chantries were dissolved in 1547–8 and thus the chantry priests disappeared from the Cathedral. With fewer services and less liturgical music the number of vicars choral was reduced, from twenty in 1552 to only seven in 1568, now assisted by seven lay vicars. The Cathedral establishment, together with the porter and the vergers,[3] continued to be provided with houses but empty houses or sites previously occupied by canons, vicars or chantry priests were leased to lay tenants, thus accelerating a trend already apparent in the 15th century to lease surplus houses to the laity. Moreover the clergy could now marry, which, despite the disapproval of Elizabeth I, led to the establishment of wives and families within the Close and a consequent change in the character of the households and in their accommodation requirements.

The yield of the common fund, from which the resident canons were paid, as listed fully for the first time in the *Valor Ecclesiasticus* of 1535, was fairly high in relation to that of other cathedrals [*VCH* 1956, 182] so there were no pressing financial reasons for the canons to neglect their duties. Elizabeth I's injunctions of 1559 to the Cathedral required canons with £10 a year to maintain a house in the Close and those with less to 'provide for themselves to be lodged within the Close' [Frere 1910, iii, 34]. The reforming Bishop Jewel (1560–71) attempted to reaffirm the rights and duties of the canons. Two of the principal issues were still residence and hospitality. Bishop Jewel ordained that the four dignitaries should be fully resident and that all the non-resident canons, or, as they were then more usually called, prebendaries, should come into residence for a term or pay fines of one fifth. These requirements, like Jewel's scheme whereby Braybrooke (No. 57) was set aside as a residential college for prebendaries coming into residence, did not prove lasting. Much more successful was his establishment of annual Pentecostal chapters, which all prebendaries were expected to attend, and an annual rota for all prebendaries to preach in the Cathedral, two reforms which long survived him. The requirements of residence were reduced so that forty days a quarter would suffice for receiving full commons. The dignitaries, except for the dean, had no rights to a canonical house or to a share in the profits of residence until 1635, when they were allowed to compete in the elections for residentiary places and were allotted single commons, rather than their traditional double share [*VCH* 1956, 187–90]. Also from 1635 two canons were to be resident each quarter, attending service daily and keeping open house.

Hospitality had been recognised as a continuing obligation in the royal injunctions of 1559 and it was emphasised by Bishop Jewel, who practised it generously himself. Poor, honest and needy persons were to be helped and especially the 'poor ministers of this church'. In 1562 it was said that the dean should hold seven feasts annually and the other dignitaries three each [Frere 1910, 395]. The duty of keeping open house (*hospitalitatem tenere*) was repeated in statutes of 1635 and 1672 (*ibid*, 415, 447). While some canons were lax, Canon Coleshill being admonished in 1568, in 1634 some were said to be neglectful but others diligent, and the newly appointed Dean Baylie was likened in 1635 to a cardinal for the lavishness of his hospitality [*VCH* 1956, 190].

Seven houses were retained as canonical residences, remaining so until after the Cathedrals Act of 1840: the Deanery (No. 62), the Leadenhall (No. 70), Aula le Stage (No. 21), Hemingsby (No. 56A and B), and the North, South and Walton Canonries (Nos 60, 71, 69). New uses were found for four of the medieval canonries. Of these, Arundells (No. 59) was leased as a private house and so was the Abbot of Sherborne's former residence (the King's House, No. 65), although ownership of the latter, as allegedly monastic property, was unsuccessfully contested by the Crown. Braybrooke (No. 57) was allotted to the master of the Choristers' School in 1559 as school and residence, which it remained until 1947, except for a brief interlude from 1562 to 1564 when it was used as a college for non-resident canons (see above). The Wardrobe (No. 58) was probably decayed in 1568 when Bishop Jewel exchanged it with chapter and it was then divided in two, with one part being leased by William Blacker, the chapter clerk, in 1569. Although Blacker was probably not at this time living in the Close, he already owned the lease of No. 54 and subsequently acquired leases of the 'little house south of the Deanery' (Fig 2), No. 63 (which at one time he occupied), certain vicars' properties on the site of the Mompesson House stables, and No. 15, then gardens with subtenants, where he appears to have built a house. He is a symbol of the new age in the Close, as the first of several people to farm its leases; another was William Barfoot, the Cathedral clerk of works in the period before the Civil War.

New houses were constructed on the Cathedral green, especially around the Bell Tower, and a shop was built in 1588 on the site of No. 38. St Ann's Chapel over the east gate was converted into a house. Although the increase in lay population was to prove permanent, at this stage it did not please all parties: Archbishop Laud at his Visitation in 1634 endorsed the margin of his report: 'Think of a course for ye present remedying of this. And for ye freeing of the churchyard and close from lay dwellers as far as may be' [*Wilts N and Q* i, for 1893, 14, 22].

Chapter's first lease book begins in 1534. The new

tenants came from every social class. Many were gentry, occupying both large and small properties. There were widows, including in time those of Cathedral clergy, merchants such as Thomas Sharpe, successively at Nos 53 and 34, clerks, physicians, lawyers and notaries. Tradesmen were encouraged in the northern part of the Close, especially in the shops at the North Gate and around the Bell Tower. Among their trades were cloth and clothing: there was a linen draper, a tailor, a weaver and a shoemaker. The building and furniture trades were represented by glaziers and a stonemason, a joiner, a turner and a 'turker', presumably a maker of turkeywork upholstery. Most of these men each held a house with a shop. They are recorded prior to a statute of 1612 which attempted to limit tradesmen in the Close to one carpenter, a glazier and a plumber, although in 1637 seven tailors still kept open shop there [Bod Lib, Rawlinson MS C 421].

Despite the upheavals of the Reformation period, work did not cease on the buildings of the Close. Already in the 1520s some pieces of Renaissance ornament were being introduced, such as the timber panels carved with profile heads in the Italian manner at Hemingsby and moulded panels at Aula le Stage (Plate 90). Of the seven canonical residences, two were refurbished in the 1540s: Aula le Stage for Dr Thomas Benet, who had been secretary to Wolsey and vicar-general for Cardinal Campeggio but survived as precentor until his death in 1558, and the North Canonry. At this latter house, Canon Robert Okyng, Archdeacon of Sarum under Edward VI but deprived by Mary, carried out extensive alterations and probably built the great bay-window which, with its polygonal angle buttresses is the most prominent piece of Tudor architecture in the Close (Plate 152). Dr Benet installed fashionable ceilings in his principal rooms at Aula le Stage, with geometrical patterns formed by moulded oak ribs (Plate 91). At both houses, large windows and internal doorways are of stone, the doorways with arched heads (Fig 68) and fine stop-chamfers (Fig 137), the windows elaborately moulded. Those at the North Canonry have arched lights and the great bay-window (heavily restored) is hollow chamfered. Brick was used at both houses for new chimneys and for minor structural work. The North Canonry retains a timber staircase of this period and several original doors, including the external ones of the carriageway and the entrance to the north wing. Other doors are of reset linenfold panelling, of which there is more at Aula le Stage, at No. 54 and also in a room at Hemingsby (Plate 128). The insertion of ceilings into upper rooms at the North Canonry created cramped attics among the roof trusses which, although difficult of access, were lit by dormer windows and fitted with floorboards; presumably they were used for storage.

Alterations were also made at the Deanery in the mid

16th century. A new fireplace and chimney were installed in the north chamber, which was heightened in stone and flint under a new, transverse roof (see p 210). Subsequently an attempt was made to update the open hall by boxing in the 13th-century trusses with round arches and carved pendants; a fragment of this scheme was discovered in 1960.

In the vicars' houses little of significance survives from this period and no documentation. At their own Hall (Nos 12 and 13) an upper chamber, added c 1550 (Fig 43), is timber framed with a brick chimney. At No. 10, a moulded timber window (Fig 39) was inserted, probably in the early part of the century. Minor timber-framed buildings of the 16th century are No. 52 and part of No. 16.

In 1562 Bishop Jewel was told at his Visitation that the canons' houses 'be all in decay through our predecessors' fault' [Wordsworth 1915, 394], and likewise the vicars' houses and the Close Wall. He ordered them to be repaired, and that in future the dean and the senior canon should visit each canonry every October, valuing any building works done in the last year so that recompense for a proportion of the expenditure could be made if the benefactor died or left within ten years [ibid, 403–5]. The desired effect was achieved and in 1593 the canons told Bishop Coldwell at his Visitation that 'the houses be now in better reparation than for years before they have been' [Chapter Acts, Penruddock, 29]; a similar comment was made to Bishop Cotton in 1607 [Everett 1943, 180].

The ways in which these medieval houses had been brought up to date are demonstrated by a series of inventories made in September 1586, which can be supplemented by the evidence of dilapidations surveys made in the same and the previous year [Chapter Acts 1563–1606].[4] Some correlate very closely one with another, others reveal that one survey of a house may contain rooms omitted from another of the same building. The houses appear to have been perambulated systematically. Gatehouses were general, except at Hemingsby and the Leadenhall. There were three or more external doorways including the main entrance, a garden door and a back or kitchen door. Each house had a hall and most had two parlours, named 'great' and 'little' or 'inner'. For service rooms a kitchen, buttery, pantry and larder were standard and only two houses, Hemingsby and the South Canonry, were not said to have a cellar. Only three chapels were listed and they lacked the size and the furnishings necessary for medieval worship but not for Protestant domestic prayer. The previous larger chapels were presumably secularised; at Aula le Stage the chamber next to the former chapel was still known as the Chapel Chamber. Most houses appear to have had four or more upper chambers, including the rooms in gatehouses and porches. Nurseries were listed at Hemingsby and at Aula le

Stage, which also had a wardrobe. This house appears to have had the most comprehensive outbuildings of any canonry, with a bakehouse, granary and dovecote. Stables were mentioned for all but three of the buildings, including, curiously, the Deanery.

The inventories list a great quantity of fittings. Much wainscot is mentioned, not only on walls but also on ceilings where it is named in parlours at the Deanery and the Leadenhall, in chambers at Aula le Stage and the North Canonry, and in the chapel at the Leadenhall; one such ceiling survives, at Aula le Stage (now covered in). There were many 'portals' (internal porches or draught lobbies), either square or round, with one, two or three doors, some rooms having more than one, and many cupboards, presses, benches and shelves, some built in, as well as obviously movable furniture which had been donated to the house by present or previous incumbents. Aula le Stage and the North Canonry, which held a large number of these fittings, also had window-shutters ('wainscot covers' or 'leaves'). At Aula le Stage most of these fittings must have been new, since the inventory of 1586 was made some seventeen months after a dilapidations survey wherein much of the joinery had been sold after the death of Canon Procter.

The open halls were furnished with one or more tables and benches or forms, and all but one had a cupboard, but they were not the most fashionable of rooms. Only that at the Leadenhall boasted a portal and that at Hemingsby wainscot. All the houses had at least one study, except the Walton Canonry, which instead had three parlours. Hemingsby and Aula le Stage had two studies, and the North Canonry three: the little study 'within' the great parlour, a 'higher' study near the canon's own chamber, and a third at the 'upper' end of the hall described as formerly a parlour. The conversion of older rooms into studies perhaps demonstrates the emphasis in the reformed Church on a learned clergy. It could also show the occupants' status, as witnessed by the elaborate fittings. At Hemingsby the little study had a turning desk in the middle, at the Deanery there were shelves, and in the garden study at Aula le Stage there was a round frame for books with four turning desks, double shelves overhead, and two hanging desks with a chair in the middle. Dean Bridges, in 1592, called his study the 'Museum' [Robertson 1969, 150]. Three houses had a gallery, probably then the usual name for a medieval pentice, that at the North Canonry being 80 ft long (in 1649) while at the Leadenhall it was 'by the garden' and at the South Canonry it adjoined the court.

An apartment unique in the Close and unusual in England [Thornton 1979, 317–21] was that arranged for Canon Colcell's steam bath at the North Canonry. It contained a stove chamber, with wainscoted walls and a portal and screen, and the stovehouse, also wainscoted with a portal, and having a lockable door, two 'fair' shelves of graduated size, the stove, a tub, and a glass lantern fixed in the wall; at the back of the stove there was a brass pump and lead trough, and there was also an inner chamber containing a cupboard. Presumably the canon undressed in the stove chamber, using the screen, and then locked himself into the stovehouse. This well-equipped canonry also had a hoist contrived in the thickness of the wall to carry items from the covered gateway to an upper chamber.

Renovations were also carried out on buildings which were once canonries but which were later leased to lay tenants. The Abbot of Sherborne's house (No. 65) has been known since the late 18th century as the King's House because a succession of improvements made it fit for the reception of James I in 1610 and in 1613. The medieval house had been refurbished already in the third quarter of the 16th century when floors and new hollow-chamfered windows were inserted in the open hall, the flint and stone rubble walls heightened and attics lit by dormers, as at the North Canonry, were created. Thomas Sadler steadily enlarged the house between 1596 and 1621 (Fig 151), adding a new cross-wing in brick with stone dressings, the brickwork diapered to the east; this was the first use of brick as a show material in the Close. Large, ovolo-moulded windows light the interior, with handsome plaster ceilings in the first-floor rooms (Plate 171), and a framed staircase (Fig 159) extends the full height of the house.

Two other former canonries, the Wardrobe and Arundells, were extensively rebuilt by new tenants. The Wardrobe was heightened, like the King's House, in flint and stone, to provide a great chamber on the first floor (Fig 129) approached by a new staircase (Plate 136). At Arundells Sir Richard Mompesson's works carried out after 1609 were much admired at the time, although little remains today. Brick was used for the new kitchen chimneys (Plate 146); at the Wardrobe it had been used for internal walling, the new north and west chimneys and relieving-arches to the windows. Although these former canonries were occupied by laymen, there was still a chapel at Arundells in 1579 and a chapel chamber at the Wardrobe in 1586.

No. 17, a smaller house built by a private leaseholder early in the 17th century, echoes the new splendour of the King's House with its brick front and stone dressings, and a first-floor great chamber fitted out with ovolo-moulded windows, a stone chimney-piece, oak wainscot and a ribbed ceiling (Plates 74, 76, 77). The gabled rear walls are timber-framed on flint and rubble plinths, with two original windows, ovolo moulded in wood. The quality of this house must always have been greatly superior to that of the other small houses of similar date which are less well preserved, such as Nos 15, 16 and 34.

Surviving timber-framed buildings of this period are minor and most of their details are concealed by later tile-hanging. They include the range adjoining St Ann's Gate on the north, reconstruction at No. 10, and the study built by Francis Parry in 1632 at Nos 34–5. The one building with its framing exposed is No. 47, constructed in the middle of the 17th century as a stable (Fig 102).

Roofs and wainscot

The roofs of the late 16th and early 17th century fall into three categories. The most primitive is that represented by the south range of the Wardrobe, probably built in 1569, with collared rafters of uniform scantling and no longitudinal stiffening (Fig 128). Another such roof, also built during the remodelling of a medieval service range, formerly existed at the Deanery; it had raking-braces from rafter to collar in addition, and dated from about the middle of the 16th century.[5]

In a second, more common type, the purlins are clasped between the principal rafters and collars and the principals are diminished in thickness above collar level. Mid 16th-century examples are the subsidiary roofs at the North Canonry, the roofs of the heightened northeast range at the King's House (third quarter of the century), and over the kitchen chambers at the Vicars' Hall and at No. 38. At this last house the walls appear to be late 17th century and so the roof may be reset. Another, over the service range at Mompesson House, is similar. Windbraces are absent, although they do occur in the 17th century, for example, at No. 17.

The most usual form of roof (in the 17th as in the 15th century) has butt purlins and collars; examples include those in two of the main ranges of the North Canonry and in the great chamber at the Wardrobe, of the mid and late 16th century respectively, in the parlour range of the King's House c 1600, and the south range at Arundells c 1610. An example of a smaller building with a butt purlin roof is the range attached to the north side of St Ann's Gate. In most of these the tie-beam carries a pair of vertical struts, which, at the North Canonry, support the collar, but in roofs of c 1600 are moved to the sides and support the principals below purlin level.

Oak wainscot remains in situ in the great chamber at No. 17, where it has moulded edges and pilasters, and in the chapel chamber at Aula le Stage, where the frames are chamfered. There are chip-carved friezes with guilloche and other conventional Elizabethan and Jacobean motifs in the Bishop's Palace, Nos 37, 48 and elsewhere. So commonly does wainscot occur reset, even in houses wholly of later date (for example, as a first-floor door at

Mompesson House, built in 1701), that much of it may derive from earlier buildings on the same site, rather than all being introduced from elsewhere in later centuries.

The Civil War and Interregnum

The period of the Civil War was one of enormous change to the institutions of the Close although few of the buildings were seriously damaged. Salisbury Close, despite its enclosing wall and river, was spared the role of stronghold suffered by Lichfield and Worcester. A Royalist attempt under a Colonel Coke to fortify it in late 1644 was thwarted [Benson and Hatcher 1843, 398]. The only military action occurred in the winter of 1644–5, when a Parliamentarian force which had occupied the Close was chased out by the Royalists, who literally smoked out the token garrison left in the Bell Tower by setting fire to the door. There was some damage later to the Cathedral cloisters from prisoners interned there, but the major threat to all the buildings was a more insidious one. During the 1640s Parliament passed acts which abolished first bishops and then deans and chapters and confiscated their property. Their ancient buildings lost their function and thus the need for maintenance.

As the Close could no longer claim a privileged position, the mayor and corporation were able to gain jurisdiction over the former Liberty in 1656. The Cathedral became a parish church and its minister was assigned a canon's residence, as were the ministers of the town churches. In 1649 the town acquired four of the canonries for £880. Damage to the buildings was relatively slight, with two exceptions. The new owners of the former Bishop's Palace exploited the rambling old-fashioned building by splitting it into several occupancies, including a tavern, and breaking its isolation by making another opening in the Close Wall, on the south side. The great hall, now quite obsolete, was largely demolished. The partial destruction of the South Canonry, the worst affected of the canonries, can be attributed to equally pragmatic motives. The Commonwealth tenant, John Trenchard, perhaps doubtful of his tenure and not bound by chapter's administrative routines, apparently preferred the profits of quick demolition to the burden of maintaining ancient fabric (see p 240).

The Parliamentary Survey

Ironically the process of confiscation which threatened to destroy the Close provided a vivid picture of it. The Parliamentary Survey conducted in 1649 of the former dean and chapter property (that of the bishop had been dealt with separately) describes all the houses, gardens and open spaces which had belonged to the canons and vicars choral in enough detail for us to reconstruct something of the appearance of the Close at that time.

The Commissioners who compiled the Survey held their meetings in the Cathedral chapter house [Dodsworth 1814, 227]. Their reports covered not only the Close but tenements and buildings in the city of Salisbury and in the suburban village of Fisherton Anger.[6]

At the time of the Survey the Deanery was occupied by William Stephens Esq, the Recorder of the City. Several canonries were inhabited by members of the new Puritan clergy: the Leadenhall by Dr Faithfull Teate, Minister of the Cathedral, the North Canonry by John Conant, Minister of St Thomas's, and Hemingsby by John Stickland, 'one of the Ministers of Salisbury'. One of the former residentiaries, Matthew Nicholas, remained at Aula le Stage, which he had leased in 1641 [Malden 1893–4], and even the former Precentor, Humphrey Henchman, a firm Royalist who aided the escape of Charles II in 1651, still resided in the Close, though he lost his canonical house, the South Canonry [Fletcher 1938b, 301]. The 'Common hall' of the vicars choral was leased to Richard Young but six lay vicars were still in occupation of their small houses in the northern part of the Close. Two vergers retained little houses between the south side of the Cathedral chancel and the wall of the bishop's orchard.

The Survey also provides a glimpse of the general appearance of the Close at this date. The grazing of the twenty-four acres of the graveyard had belonged before the Interregnum to the dean, who let it 'to whom he pleased. But nevertelesse the Priviledge and right of buryeing therein doth by Custome appertayne and belong to the Inhabitants of the Close of Sarum aforesayd And all trees groweing thereupon were reserved for the use of the Fabrick' [Malden 1893–4, 137]. There were houses in the north part of the churchyard, some built up against the Bell Tower, including one inhabited by the widow of Bishop Curle of Winchester. The pastures at the south end of the Close were used for the annual sheep and cattle fairs and were crossed by footpaths leading to the canonries. Forty trees, large and small, were growing in the three acres of Coldharbour and an avenue of sixty young elms had been planted leading to the South Canonry, presumably by the previous occupant Humphrey Henchman.

The descriptions of the houses in the Survey, where identifiable, have been transcribed or quoted in the inventory section of this volume. They are uneven in the amount of detail included. However it appears that open halls still existed in all the canonries, and the one at Aula le Stage was wainscoted. There were still chapels at Aula le Stage, the South Canonry and the Leadenhall, but the one at Hemingsby was described as 'a great decayed roome anciently a Chappell', and was presumably no longer in use. Both in the canonries, for example, Aula le Stage and the Leadenhall, and in tenanted houses, for example, the Wardrobe, and Nos 15 and 17, the wealthier inhabitants

used a large upper room as a dining room, usually a room which would have been referred to as the great chamber in the previous century. The continuing practice of clerical hospitality can be inferred from the dean's maintenance of both large and small dining rooms. Several canonries still kept their high boundary walls and were entered by 'a handsome gate into a green court'. The 'fair gate' mentioned at the Deanery may have been the existing one (Plate 164), an isolated example of the new classicism of the mid 17th century.

The Restoration

Some three months after the Restoration of Charles II in 1660, chapter resumed its meetings. The Commonwealth sales of church property and abolition of the independence of the Close were now void. Four of the residentiaries had died but the survivors, Dean Bailey, Matthew Nicholas, now Dean of St Paul's, and Humphrey Henchman, soon to succeed Duppa as bishop, responded vigorously to the need to resume the ecclesiastical life of the Close and to restore its physical fabric.

Henchman, in the less than three years he held the see before his translation to London, put the Bishop's Palace back to order. A decorative north façade was built in flint and stone chequerwork, a technique common in the locality (Plate 30), and a broad staircase with symmetrically turned balusters (Plate 33) was formed to lead up to a new chapel, created within the 15th-century first-floor chamber (Plate 32).

After his Visitation in 1661, Bishop Henchman passed a statute that all the houses in the Close must be inspected annually before Easter and any necessary repairs done within fifteen months [Wordsworth 1915, 433]. Despite the need for repairs in some buildings, others had already been rebuilt during the Interregnum. Thomas Chafyn built a new wing at No. 11 shortly after 1649; the main elevation, overlooking the garden, has well-designed chamfered quoins and square windows with gauged flat arches, but the roof is still gabled. The detailing at No. 14 (built in the 1660s) is similar, the platband matching the plane, not of quoins, but of a centrepiece (Plate 63). Francis Sambrooke, a lawyer, replaced the long-neglected canonry called Simonsbury Place with a completely new house (No. 7) before 1660. The fenestration has been changed, but the deep eaves and rusticated chimney-shafts are original, as are the raised brick quoins here and at No. 6, which was added as a service wing soon after (Plates 40, 41). No. 38, leased as 'lately erected' in 1674, was probably in part rebuilt before 1658 because it contains a wall painting attributed to Edward Pierce who died in that year (Plate 103). The house was occupied in 1640 by William Barfoot (died 1666), clerk of works to the Cathedral before and after the Interregnum, who may have still been the occupant when the staircase was built in the 1660s (Fig 98).

During the 1660s several of the smaller houses must have been rebuilt as they were described as 'newly built' in 1671 when a comprehensive survey of the properties of the vicars choral was made. Typical of these houses is No. 9 (Plate 43). It was almost certainly built by one John Holt, whose name first appears in connection with it in 1660 and who died in 1669, after which his widow Catherine probably remained there and was buried in the Cathedral three years later. It was built of brick, still in English bond, with plain projecting quoins, a broad platband, and a hipped roof on shaped modillions. Disturbed brickwork shows that the windows have been rebuilt entirely, as at No. 7, so perhaps they were originally of horizontal format. The original staircase, however, with spacious flights, heavy mouldings and jewel ornament (Plate 44), is distinctly old fashioned for its date, like other joinery in the house (Plate 45), and it was remodelled in c 1675. The contemporary carved finials and panels in the vestibule were introduced only in 1777. They had formed part of the Cathedral choir woodwork, designed in 1671 with the advice of Sir Christopher Wren.

Repair and rebuilding were also necessary at some of the canonries. John Trenchard, who held the lease of the South Canonry in 1648 'for one year', had pulled down much of the house and sold the materials. In the 1660s and 1670s it was reconstructed by successive canons at a cost of over £500 but it still fell 'far short of what it was before' [Bishop Ward's Visitation Return 1672, Diocesan Records]. At Hemingsby the hall had been floored over and the rooms to the north of it demolished. At the Leadenhall £500 was spent on repairs before 1665, at the Deanery £475. Some traditional features were maintained. Open halls remained at Aula le Stage until 1713 and at the Walton Canonry and the North Canonry perhaps until 1718 and 1739 respectively. At the Deanery the hall remained a large open room even though reduced in size. Chapels were kept up in at least some canonries, those of the Leadenhall and Aula le Stage being used for private marriage ceremonies in 1664 and 1692 respectively. The chapel at Hemingsby (not the same room as that described in the 1649 survey) survived until 1727.

The tenanted houses had not been affected in the same way by the upheavals of the Civil War. The most notable characteristic from the mid 17th to the early 19th century is the long residence of certain private families. This is more evident at the larger houses, where one generation commonly succeeded another, the Coles family, for example, occupying the Wardrobe from 1659 until 1824 and the Harris family Malmesbury House from before 1660 until 1781. As for the smaller houses, the lease of No. 63 passed by descent from John Poncherdon in 1605 through the

Roberts and Hearst families to Henry Wyndham, who gave it up in 1785, No. 17 was in the possession of the Earle, Benson Earle and Benson families between 1763 and 1862, and there were Goldwyers at No. 13 from 1699 until after 1805. In addition to long successions at the same house, there were several families whose members held different houses over a period, perhaps overlapping one another in time. During the 17th century there were sixteen members of the Royalist family of Hyde in the Close, either as private tenants (for example of the Little House south of the Deanery, see Inventory, p 202) or as officials. Apart from Alexander Hyde, residentiary and then bishop (1665–7), they included two dignitaries, a subdean and two clerks of the works, and were a dominant presence during the political ascendancy of Lord Clarendon, the head of the family, in the years immediately after the Restoration (see North Canonry, p 193).

Bishop Seth Ward

The single most significant figure, however, in the post-Restoration Close was perhaps Seth Ward, bishop from his translation from Exeter in 1667 to his death in 1689. He was a man of outstanding ability and intellectual curiosity, being one of the founder-members of the Royal Society. He generously promoted the repair and embellishment of both Cathedral and Palace, drawing on the advice of his friend and colleague in the Royal Society, Christopher Wren, who in 1668 submitted a long survey of the Cathedral and a shorter one of the Palace. At the Palace, Ward's main enterprise was the insertion of a new staircase and the rebuilding of the great hall c 1674, prompted partly perhaps by his conscientious fulfilment of his duties of hospitality to the clergy and partly by his sense of history (Fig 21, Plates 35, 36). In 1671 he reclaimed from lay hands the Bishop of Salisbury's right to the Chancellorship of the Order of the Garter.

By the time of Bishop Ward's Visitation in 1671, the canons were able to assure him that all their houses were back in good repair except for the South Canonry. The bishop himself promoted one important new building within the Close: in 1682 he founded the Matrons' College (Nos 39–46) just inside the North Gate, to accommodate the widows of clergy in the dioceses of Salisbury or Exeter (his previous bishopric). This was the first charitable foundation by a bishop of Salisbury within the Liberty of the Close since the 13th century. Its contemporary purpose, giving relief to a group unknown in pre-Reformation times, is reflected in the contemporary style of its architecture (Plates 106, 108). As in its probable model, the Matrons' College founded by Bishop Morley at Winchester in 1673, there was a deliberate emphasis on the building as a 'college' rather than the less genteel 'hospital' or almshouse. The designer of the Matrons' College is unknown although the building contract survives, the only one for the Close before 1850 (printed in full as Appendix to Nos 39–46). The traditional attribution to Wren is untenable but there may be a connection with Alexander Fort who had 'remodelled' the Cathedral choir furnishings under Wren in 1671–2 and was, just at the time of the foundation of the Matrons' College, employed as surveyor to the large almshouse and perhaps the church erected by Sir Stephen Fox at Farley only four miles to the east. The builder, Thomas Glover of Harnham, was recorded on his tombstone as an 'Architect...of many stately curious and artful edifices' and may have contributed to the design [Colvin 1978, 348].

The other significant work of the post-Reformation period is the present Theological College, No. 19, built as a house for the lawyer Francis Hill from 1677 to 1679 (Plate 80) and carefully sited with its central entrance facing down the Bishop's Walk. The plans of both ground (except for the hall) and first floor are little altered; two apartments, each of two large rooms, open off a long wide corridor, the floors being connected by a wide staircase with twisted balusters (Plate 82).

More difficult to interpret is the long south range at Nos 8 and 9 with its evenly spaced windows, which could have held a great room such as a gallery, or a sequence of perhaps three rooms (Fig 32). The façade extends beyond the gable-end, presumably for the sake of symmetry.

Roofs and joinery

Deep eaves with coved cornices or carved ogee modillions and pyramidal pendants are a feature of the late 17th century, for example at Nos 7, 8 and 9 and on Malmesbury House (No. 15). In roof construction the knee-principal was introduced, a technique in which principal rafters are cranked near their feet so as to assist the formation of overhanging eaves while transferring the weight of the roof inwards and on to the wall-head [Taylor 1982]. Examples are in the east extension of the south range at the Palace (probably after 1674) and on the front range at No. 38 (before 1674?), also over the front range of No. 25 (early 18th century) and at Arundells (c 1720). An unusual structural detail found in two roofs is that the common rafters, instead of being pegged on to the backs of the purlins, are tenoned into them at top and bottom; these occur at No. 7 (before 1660) and at the Palace (1660–2), in the roofs over Bishop Henchman's staircase and in his kitchen build and its eastern extension.

Much remains of the joinery and carpentry of the late 17th century. Three staircases of the 1660s, at Nos 14 and 38, and at the Palace, have symmetrically turned balusters, a common pattern in southeast Wiltshire and elsewhere, which was succeeded by vase shapes at the Palace (1674), the Matrons' College (1682) and No. 8 (c 1700).

Doors are commonly of butted planks, which either may meet at a moulding (No. 9) or have lapped edges with ogee mouldings. The latter persist into the early 18th century and examples may be found at Loders (c 1705) and Braybrooke (c 1710). At the Palace and Matrons' College the recessed central plank also has framing pieces at top and bottom to create an elongated panel on one face. Doors of similar pattern at No. 47 (c 1685) have shaped wooden latches operated by cords.

The Choristers' School

The Choristers' School (No. 56) provides both a postscript to the Restoration period and a foretaste of the 18th century. It was built before 1717 in a restrained but elegant style [Macartney c 1925] and survives complete with original panelling and masters' desks (Plates 130, 131, 132). It is possible that the new school was paid for by Sir Stephen Fox, the trusted servant of Charles II, who had been a chorister himself as a boy [Robertson 1938, 220]. The design has been wrongly attributed to Wren and is more likely to be the work of Thomas Naish, clerk of works to the Cathedral from 1680 to 1727, who supervised the construction. Disappointingly little is known of Naish, although there are some details recorded in the diary written by his son, also Thomas (1669–1755), subdean of Salisbury and occupant of No. 18 [Slatter 1965]. The Naish family held the lease of No. 47 Winchester St from 1671 to 1748. This is a brick building, similar to contemporary work in the Close (No. 6, for example), which was constructed from 1671 to 1673 for Giles Naish, gentleman, the uncle of the elder Thomas [RCHM 1980, 139]. As clerk of works at the Cathedral Thomas Naish had instigated a system for measuring the declination of the spire in 1681 and in 1691 made a detailed survey of the building and the necessary repairs [Chapter Archives 347, Document 1; Price 1753, 68–71]. In 1717 the elder Thomas was permitted to make his third son William his deputy and was succeeded by him in 1727, although William was an apothecary by training and mayor of the city in 1715. He was probably the William Naish who published, in 1716, the first map of Salisbury to be sufficiently detailed to show accurately the layout of the chequers and watercourses and the individual houses in the Close with their walled gardens and gatehouses [RCHM 1980, Plate 16]; a second edition was printed in 1751, with few alterations.

The 18th century

It is to the first thirty years of the 18th century that many of the Close houses owe their present air of gentility and elegance. A succession of houses was built or largely rebuilt: Mompesson House (No. 53) in 1701, Loders (No. 23) in 1703–5, Malmesbury House (No. 15) in 1705,

Braybrooke (No. 57) after 1706, Arundells (No. 59), Myles Place (No. 68) and the Leadenhall (No. 70) after 1718 (but this last was rebuilt again later in the century), No. 20, No. 55 and the Walton Canonry (No. 69), all *c* 1720, and Hemingsby (No. 56A and B) in 1727.

It was becoming the fashion for the local gentry and some professional men to have a house in Salisbury, either in the city or in the Close [RCHM 1980, xlvii–xlviii]. The Wyndham family is only one example. Arundells was rebuilt for John Wyndham of Norrington when he acquired the lease in 1718, and the survey made of it by John Lyons in 1745 presents an evocative contemporary picture of the house and its gardens (Plate 144). From 1660 to 1871 a different branch of the Wyndham family owned the College, the largest private house in Salisbury, which, as it so happens, was not in the Close but in the northeast corner of the town [RCHM 1980, 48–50]; it too was rebuilt in the first half of the 18th century.

A Member of Parliament, Charles Mompesson, built Mompesson House, a physician, George Mullens, leased and refronted No. 55, and a lawyer, William Swanton, brother of Francis Swanton, MP for Salisbury from 1714 to 1721, built Myles Place, a grand and completely new house. Swanton married Anne Hill, presumably the daughter of Francis Hill of Lincoln's Inn, builder of No. 19 a generation earlier. Intermarriages among these families were common as were marriages between them and the canons, several of whom came from aristocratic families or, thanks to traditional nepotism, were the sons or kinsmen of former bishops.

The Cathedral clergy were also active in rebuilding their houses, for example Canon Francis Eyre at the Walton Canonry and Treasurer Talbot who, when he requested chapter's permission to rebuild the Leadenhall in 1718, emphasised 'the founder's intention that the houses should be not only kept repaired but also a beauty and an ornament' to the Close [Acts 1696–1741, 16 Oct]. In his case, this antiquarian sentiment did not prevent him using an up-to-date design but Canon Coker was more conservative at Aula le Stage in 1713: he added a second gable to his south front, making it artificially tall for the sake of symmetry, but matching the flint and rubble walling and reusing an Elizabethan doorway and windows (Plates 86, 87). The eastern part of the garden and forecourt he leased to another clergyman, John Smith, who built an uncompromisingly fashionable house (No. 20) of brick and stone (Plate 85) but incorporated the medieval gatehouse range of Aula le Stage as a service wing (Plate 84, Fig 59).

A canon would apply to the dean and chapter to approve any proposed alterations and these applications provide valuable dating evidence for the houses. In 1727 chapter gave Canon Sager twelve months to rebuild

Hemingsby and in 1738, Canon Bampton three years to modify the North Canonry. By 1713 a formula had been established for a canon to be repaid by his successor for two thirds of the cost of building works sanctioned by chapter, to the value of £100. Treasurer Talbot caused them to modify this principle in 1718 so that if his works at the Leadenhall cost £800, compensation would be made according to a formula tapering from £500 after four years to nothing after twenty.

These considerations did not affect the private tenants. Their leases were granted on forty-year terms with renewals every fourteen years, although these intervals were not minutely observed; normally the rental remained at a fixed low sum, such as £1 annually, with rising premiums or 'fines' paid upon renewal. Because these were liable to be increased following improvements, a tenant who was planning renovations would be likely to renew his lease to take maximum advantage of the old terms immediately before work began, resulting in two leases being granted at short intervals; thus John Wyndham in 1718 renewed a lease of 1714 to his predecessor at Arundells and James Harris at Malmesbury House renewed his own lease of 1703 in 1705. A dispute arose in 1719 as to the terms of a further renewal, which resulted in a small rise in his fine, but it was stated then that chapter commonly did not take advantage of a tenant's improvements until the second subsequent renewal. This is borne out by a later note in a chapter estate book which states that William Coles had improved the Wardrobe since 1762 but that his fine in 1776 remained at £73 10s.

The larger houses changed hands fairly seldom, as did the tenancies of many of the smaller houses, but this seeming stability is misleading. The actual occupants are often not known; subletting was so common and so little noted in official documents that many people who are recorded on their funerary monuments or in the *Salisbury and Winchester Journal* as having been resident in the Close cannot be associated with any particular house. It was a convenient practice. The canons were often pluralists, having other preferments elsewhere, and allowed their houses to be occupied by subtenants, provided they looked after them. Precentor Whitby had had to defend the poor condition of Hemingsby at the bishop's visitation in 1683 by explaining that his tenant ignored all his orders to repair it, a neglect which perhaps explains his successor's decision in 1727 to reconstruct half the house.

For those vicars choral who lived on their cures outside Salisbury, the granting of subtenancies was a common convenience also and a means of supplementing their stipend. Subdean Naish, for example, found tenants for No. 18 once he had acquired livings elsewhere [Slatter 1965, *passim*]. Neither did the lay vicars necessarily inhabit their allotted houses [VCH 1956, 197] with the result that these were similarly available.

The complexities of private tenancy are well displayed in the activities of the Wyndham family. Between 1675 and 1881 at least twenty-one members of the family owned the leases or freeholds, or were subtenants, at ten or more houses and two of these were held twice: No. 9 from 1675 to *c* 1695 and from *c* 1738 to 1745 and No. 19 from 1768 to 1797 and again from 1828 to 1859. The methods by which they acquired them and the purpose of their ownership are typical of the period, when leases were often held as an investment. Henry Penruddock Wyndham of the College, on marrying Caroline Hearst in 1768, obtained not only the lease of her parents' house, No. 19, which he made a dower house for his father, but the freeholds of the Hungerford and Audley chantries (Nos 54 and 64), and the lease of No. 63; presumably the Hearsts had purchased the two freeholds and let or sublet them, as did Wyndham initially. George Wyndham and his successors at No. 7 were more typical in having to remain as subtenants from 1722 to 1765 before they could acquire their lease from the tenant, and Anne Wyndham similarly was a subtenant at No. 31 from 1749 to 1760, after which members of her family owned the lease and lived there until 1836. Anne was a widow and several of the later tenants were unmarried daughters.

A new type of tenant, the small private school, appeared in the Close in some numbers from the 17th century onwards. The earliest one was kept by Dorothy Langford, who was licensed by Dean Bowle in 1629 to teach English and needlework in the Close. Anne Deare, who occupied Aula le Stage between 1696 and 1713, is described on her Cathedral floorslab as 'the most Famous Mistress in the West of England for well educating and instructing young Ladys and Gentlemen'. A boarding school occupied the Hungerford Chantry between 1752 and 1800, at first under Mrs Stevens and then Mrs Ivie [Robertson 1938, 242–3, 254], in rivalry with Mrs Smith from 1762 to 1781 and Mrs Voysey from 1786 to 1793, who both kept schools in parts of the King's House [Everett Q, 33]. The Godolphin School for Girls, which is still in existence in buildings on Milford Hill, had opened at No. 25 in 1784 before moving to Arundells from 1821 to 1836, and was at the King's House from 1836 to 1847. Arundells was occupied by F N Bracher's boys' school from 1839 to 1844 and another boys' preparatory school was kept by the Misses Noyes at the Vicars' Hall from 1817 to 1845, while J T Biddlecombe, a lay vicar living at No. 30 from 1814 to 1856, improved his income by 'admitting a few pupils into his family' [*SJ*, 5 Jan 1818].

Genteel houses

The architects of the early 18th-century houses are unidentified but the Cathedral clerks of works, Thomas and William Naish and then Francis Price, as well as other local surveyors, would have been available for the supervision and design of work done on chapter properties. Such jobs could vary from routine maintenance to demolition or the execution of carefully considered façades. Price was certainly involved at Braybrooke, where he was paid £55 in 1746, and at the North Canonry, where he was employed in 1751 as 'undertaker' to remove obsolete buildings.[7]

Three of the grandest buildings, Mompesson House (1701), Malmesbury House (1705) and Arundells (*c* 1720) (Plates 110, 64, 145), each have a symmetrical elevation of stone articulated by plain windows, a pedimented doorcase, platband, and a hipped roof on a prominent eaves cornice. At Mompesson House the plan is of a type common in smaller gentry houses, with a central hall leading straight into a large two-storey staircase hall, two rooms on each side, a first-floor drawing room opening into a room on either flank and a secondary staircase to one side. The original kitchens were not, as in other contemporary houses of this type, in the basement but in a wing to the east, with a stable block of *c* 1680 beyond (Plate 111, Fig 109).

There is another group of three houses, built in the course of a decade, which share a number of features and may have had a common designer. They are Myles Place (1718), a complete three-storey house with — unique in the Close — a giant order of Doric pilasters (Plate 173), the two-storey central part (Plate 179) of the adjacent Walton Canonry (*c* 1720), and the single-storey wing (Plate 129) at Hemingsby (1727). All have a compact plan with a raised ground floor containing rooms of varied size and entered on the garden front by a central doorway. Kitchens and service rooms are in the semi-basement. The elevations are very similar, especially the main front of Walton Canonry and the garden face (Plate 174) of Myles Place, where stone pilasters upon pedestals articulate the principal storeys. All share the device of a cornice, with or without its frieze, resting directly upon the keystones of the windows. Hemingsby has channel-rusticated stonework at the angles, supporting a frieze and cornice. Each roof consists of multiple low ridges behind parapets and the lesser elevations resemble one another in the simplicity of their brick-dressed stone rubble.

A generation later, in the late 1730s and 1740s, many of these houses were brought up to date, with elaborate plasterwork installed, for example, at Malmesbury House, Mompesson House, the Wardrobe, Myles Place and, first and foremost, at the Bishop's Palace.

Bishop Sherlock

Thomas Sherlock was appointed to the see in 1734. He was a favourite of Queen Caroline and one of the most distinguished of the bishops of his time, refusing Canterbury in 1747. He carried out an extensive refurbishment of the Palace (Fig 18d) as well as initiating a programme of important repairs in the Cathedral. In both enterprises he employed Francis Price. Price, a carpenter by origin, had risen to become general builder and surveyor. He had a precocious understanding of medieval buildings and produced a detailed survey of the Cathedral fabric in 1753, the first such account to be published in England. Already by 1736 Price was designing a new roof for the 13th-century cross-wing at the Palace, where the upper room was to become the great dining room (Plate 29); he consulted John James, who was then completing Hawksmoor's west front of Westminster Abbey. The roof was executed almost exactly as planned and still survives (Fig 23). It forms an interesting comparison with the contemporary high roofs that Price was framing in the Cathedral.

Interior decoration

The most striking aspect of the work done for Bishop Sherlock at the Palace is the stucco decoration, both in the new dining room and in the refurbished 15th-century parlour. Drawings survive [WRO] of the proposals made in 1739 for the redecoration of the parlour and Bishop Ward's great hall by the Blandford carver and architect, Francis Cartwright (Plate 23). Comparisons of style between the plasterwork at the Palace and that in contemporary Close houses indicate that much of it must have been executed by a team working under his guidance.[8] Most of their commissions appear to have been for ceilings but Cartwright's drawings show walls articulated by stucco decoration, with a broad frieze of Vitruvian scroll dividing the lower storey from an upper which was arranged as a regular series of tall panels. Closely similar is the scheme chosen for the staircase at Mompesson House, which has a frieze of Vitruvian scroll (Plate 114), and for Malmesbury House (Plate 65). The plaster wall-panelling at Myles Place and the Wardrobe (Plate 139) was inserted at the same time as the ceilings there and shares the same style of mouldings.

On ceilings, the plasterwork is designed around raised panels, which commonly are disposed either one within another, filling the whole ceiling (Plate 65), or are arranged in series (Plate 116), with larger square or rectangular panels enlivened by dished corners and other shapes (Plates 29, 178). Among the principal decorative motifs are crossed branches, full-face female heads, baskets of fruit (Plate 115) and scallops, both on cartouches and mouldings. Two types of cornice were favoured, with either acanthus modillions or a cove decorated with individual acanthus leaves (Plate 114). Boldly modelled eagles with open wings form the centre-pieces in the first-floor drawing room at Mompesson

House, the grand dining room at the Palace and in the dining room at the Wardrobe (Plate 140). There are lavish cartouches, enclosing literary and allegorical motifs (Plate 65), not only on ceilings (Plate 139) but on elaborate chimney-pieces (Plate 68). When one of these new ceilings was provided for a room in which older panelling was to be retained, the timber cornice was replaced by a plaster one modelled with egg and tongue.

Similar contemporary plasterwork survives in four houses in Salisbury city, although more no doubt existed at one time: they are 47 High Street, 20 Queen Street, which has another eagle panel and a rococo overmantel, 16 Endless Street and 32 Fisherton Street [RCHM 1980, Monuments 87, 133, 391, 477; Plates 94, 95, 97]. It also occurs in several of the gentry houses close to Salisbury, for example, Little Durnford and Homington Manor, and, further afield, at Crowcombe Court, Somerset, completed in 1739 [Hussey 1955, 118], and in eastern Dorset at St Giles's House, Wimborne St Giles (1740–4), Crichel House, Moor Crichel (after 1742) [RCHM 1975, Plates 38, 39, 75, 77], the Manor House, Blandford St Mary [RCHM 1970, Plate 72] and J Bastard's house at Blandford of c 1732 [ibid, Plate 116].

The stucco decoration is generally accompanied by richly detailed joinery, to be found, for example, in the chimney-pieces and doors with their architraves at the Palace, the Wardrobe (Plate 141) and Malmesbury House (Plate 66). These may have been supplied by Cartwright, as several parallels can be made with similar joinery in houses at Blandford erected after the fire of 1731 [RCHM 1970]. Other details of early 18th-century date are staircases with panelled tread-ends at No. 20 and the Leadenhall, and doors with trellis glazing on the garden front of Myles Place and in the summerhouse at Malmesbury House, possibly removed from the house (Plate 69).

Perhaps the most memorable Georgian room in the Close is, however, in a very different style. The library at Malmesbury House (Plates 70–2) was decorated for James Harris (1708–80) in the late 1750s in a rich Gothick with crocketed ogee arches. The design has similarities to the former library at Corsham Court of c 1759, attributed to Henry Keene [Ladd 1978, 51–2]. Probably contemporary with it is the delicate rococo overmantel designed for the display of Chinese porcelain that survives in a small upper room (Plate 68).

Not all the supposed 'early Georgian' detail in the Close is truly of this period. At the Wardrobe, the architrave joinery has cable-moulded arrises carved in different techniques, much of which can be dated c 1730–40 as it matches similar detail in plaster at Malmesbury House, but other parts date from 1832. At the North Canonry at least one 'Georgian' chimney-piece (that in the library) appears to be an early 19th-century pastiche, perhaps intended to harmonise with a ceiling cornice of c 1740. The doors of the wing added to Malmesbury House c 1705 have their original configuration visible in the hall but the dining room and parlour faces have their panels quite differently arranged. A seam around the middle of these doors shows that they were reskinned when the carved door-cases of mid 18th-century design were installed in those rooms. The latter look convincing enough but it is uncertain whether the reskinning of doors was a practice of the period. Again, at the Wardrobe, some rococo decoration in the staircase hall in the style of the mid 18th century, probably made of papier mâché, lacks the cornice expected of the 18th century, and on one side the ceiling fades into the wall while on the other the ornament is partly applied to a large bent sheet of some undetermined material (Plate 137). This inferior work may have been executed by a minor member of Cartwright's team (see above, p 32 and note 8) or it may be a later concoction.

Other fittings arouse suspicion because of their crisp perfection, which may seem too exact and mechanical, or may appear not to have had two and a half centuries of wear. Alternatively, their detailing may be unlike contemporary work elsewhere in the Close or in the gentry houses of the neighbourhood. Such doubts are raised by certain carved and pedimented door-cases in Mompesson House, which seem too crisp to be authentic but which must date from at least the latter part of the 19th century as they are already present in early photographs of the interior. Several of the other fine decorative features of that house are also probably reproduction work.

The process of rebuilding or refronting the canonries continued throughout the 18th century. In 1739 Canon Bampton remodelled the south part of the main range at the North Canonry (Plate 150), in 1747 the front range of the Organist's House (No. 5) was rebuilt (Plate 39), and after 1749 Canon Moss built the east front of the South Canonry (Plate 188). When Dr Thomas Greene moved into the Deanery in 1757, he intended to rebuild it, but instead appears to have been content to 'gothicise' the main façade (Plate 155).

Several small houses were built on vacant land at Harnham Gate (Plate 191). The earliest is No. 73, datable between 1713 and 1721, followed by No. 72 in c 1754 and No. 74 in c 1769, which were both built for lay vicars by wealthier clergymen who could then rebuild in grander fashion the houses previously occupied by the vicars, Nos 36 and 26. No. 36 (Fig 95) is a handsome five-bay house, probably occupying far more ground than its predecessor and projecting forward on the west corner of North Walk. At No. 26, John Chaffey chose to lease out No. 10, his appointed residence, and build No. 74 for the tenant he was replacing, in order to build for himself and succeeding vicars choral this rather plain, tall house facing the north

side of the Cathedral. Two other houses, Nos 63 and 64, were refronted as a unified design shortly before 1785.

Brick was the everyday material in the 18th and early 19th century, although flint rubble was also used, and flint and stone were combined to produce chequerwork. Stucco was employed on the south elevation of the Palace and at the Leadenhall, to give a fashionable appearance to an older structure. Timber-framing, however, remained in occasional use for economical building. It was sometimes tile-hung, as at No. 22, c 1765, but it was more commonly hung with mathematical tiles, especially on side elevations. They appear earlier in the Close than in the town: at No. 11 they date from shortly after 1753, at No. 26 from c 1770, and at No. 33 from some time in the latter part of the century. They imitate brick closely, being normally red in colour, and in header, stretcher and Flemish bond.

From the 1760s on, the advertisements for leases now frequent in the *Salisbury Journal* give an insight into the way in which houses were used. Especially in those without a semi-basement to house the kitchen, the placing of one or more of the principal rooms on the first floor was a common practice, evident in the addition of bay-windows to the first-floor drawing rooms, for example, at Nos 13, 14 and 16, a feature popular also in the town in the 18th and early 19th century.

The advertisements also provide lists of outbuildings. In addition to the usual stables and coach-houses and a few brewhouses and laundries (including a first-floor laundry at No. 24 in 1787), Arundells and Myles Place had granaries, the latter of which survives. At the lower end of the social scale, the cottage built by Harnham Gate c 1754, No. 72, had, according to the original specification, a wash-house and brewhouse in an outshut or lean-to.

Bishop Barrington

With the arrival of Bishop Shute Barrington (1782–91), there began a decade of alteration and restoration, first at the Palace, then at the Cathedral. From 1783 to 1785 the bishop spent over £7000 on the Palace. His architect was Sir Robert Taylor, who designed a new main entrance in a rather stiff Gothic style (Plate 34) and converted the parlour into an entrance hall (Fig 18e). All the main rooms were now to be arranged on the first floor as a precaution against damp, and the open hall in the east wing was finally divided up. The great dining room of the 1750s now became the great drawing room (Plate 29); the Venetian windows were rebuilt with exterior lunettes set over them (Plates 21, 37), while the view of the Cathedral from them was improved by the demolition of intervening buildings. An interior view of the room by J Buckler, dated 1817, shows it comfortably furnished and hung, as it still is, with portraits of the bishops wearing their Garter robes (Plate 28).

The Close landscaped

The Palace was not alone in being damp at ground-floor level. Despite all the improvements made to the houses during the 18th century, the Close had not yet become the trim and tidy place that it is today. The extensive graveyard was used as a cow pasture and complaints were made at intervals about the derelict state of the medieval drainage ditches [Robertson 1938, 227–8]. When the Cathedral was restored by James Wyatt from 1789 to 1792 the opportunity was taken to landscape the whole area. Though controversial even at the time, the improvements had their apologist in William Dodsworth, who describes how the whole area was levelled and lawns were laid to set off the north and west views of the Cathedral [Dodsworth 1814, 184–5, 222]:

> ...the church yard itself was left in the most unsightly, not to say disgusting, state. The avenues were indifferent, and after heavy rains difficult to pass; for the water which was conveyed from the roofs ran along open gutters into a large ditch which traversed the church yard, where in dry seasons, it stagnated and became extremely offensive. Accordingly a new circular underground drain was formed, three feet in diameter, which runs from the west to the east end, and receives all the water from the north side of the church. The ground itself was raised and levelled, and spacious gravel walks were made to the principal entrances. As this operation rendered it necessary to cover the graves, an exact plan of the church yard, with the dates and a reference to each place of interment, is now lodged in the muniment room. The area of the cloister has been since used as a cemetery.
>
> On the north side of the church was a large, substantial, and heavy belfry. As it had been only partially applied to its original use since 1745, and as it greatly intercepted the most striking view of the structure, it was taken down, and the produce of the materials employed in making the repairs [Fig 91].[9] Thus, on entering the cemetery, the eye is enabled to catch at one view the whole of the building, which appears on this side with peculiar grandeur and effect.
>
> The prospects towards the south-west are marked by similar features; but they acquire additional beauty from picturesque groups of trees, of which the foliage is contrasted with the mellow hue of the stone.

The spire and upper part of the Bell Tower had been demolished in 1758 and six of the eight bells sold in 1762 [VCH 1956, 200]. In 1767 chapter decided against renewing the leases of the houses adjoining the Bell Tower, one of which was demolished with that building in 1790 while the other, No. 32, was retained as a verger's house to replace one on the south side of the Cathedral which was to be removed. Chapter presumably also prevented the advertised intention of a Salisbury builder to demolish the King's House in 1792 and replace it with thirty new houses. The popularity of the Close as a place of residence had not diminished and the intended development of the King's House site had been promoted as 'a great utility to the city, by affording suitable residences for genteel families, which are at present much wanted' [SJ, 11 June 1792]. The population of the Close was to increase only slowly during the succeeding century. In 1801 it was 542 and was still under 700 in 1891, whereas by then the city had more than doubled in size [VCH 1959, 356].

The 19th century

Whereas certain well-known paintings by Turner and Constable have coloured for ever our mental picture of Salisbury Cathedral and Close in the early 19th century, drawings made by John Buckler between 1804 and 1817, of which seventeen are illustrated in this volume, provide a group portrait of the Close buildings, either clad in new stucco like the Leadenhall or in a state of romantic decay like Aula le Stage. Chancellor Douglas occupied the Leadenhall from 1799 to 1819, making it Gothic outside but neo-classical within (Plates 181, 182). The revival of Gothic architecture ironically sometimes accompanied the destruction of medieval fabric, even in the same house. For example, Canon W L Bowles in c 1830 added 15th/16th-century detail to Aula le Stage and arranged a cellar room as a chapel with a medieval stained glass window, while dividing up the well-preserved 13th-century chapel into service rooms. Elsewhere, at the same time as buttresses and 'medieval' detail were being contrived on the exteriors of the Leadenhall and of the King's House (Plate 167) from 1800 to 1810, the great 16th-century bay-window of the North Canonry was being adapted to accept sash frames. At the Deanery in 1810 the open hall was finally disused and the east wing containing the former chapel demolished, while the 14th-century hall of the Vicars' Hall was also destroyed, probably in 1814.

The combination of mixed Gothic and Tudor motifs on the exterior and of neo-classical detail within developed a stage further at the Wardrobe in 1832; the house was described at the time as 'Old English', a suitably vague term as the exterior was medieval-Jacobean and the interior ranged from Gothic to Georgian and included a French room for good measure. Other attempts to introduce period detail ranged through medieval to Jacobean styles, although 'early Georgian' was an increasing influence from the 1830s onwards.

The Victorian Close

The Cathedrals Act of 1840 made drastic alterations to the traditional constitution of the chapter. Its main aim was to transfer the surplus endowments of cathedral and collegiate foundations to finance the Church's efforts in the industrial North and Midlands. The prebendaries were abolished and their estates transferred to the Ecclesiastical Commissioners; in their place were appointed honorary, unpaid canons, usually senior clergy in the diocese. The canons residentiary were reduced in number from six to four. They lost their separate estates and their right to elect their fellows, who in future were to be nominated by the bishop. Thus when the existing residentiaries died, first Hemingsby and then Aula le Stage became redundant as canonries and were let privately.

Ironically this harsh pruning of the chapter's resources came at a time when their value was declining. As they consisted largely of agricultural land and tithes rather than commercial or industrial property, revenues in general continued to fall well into the 20th century [*VCH* 1956, 200–6]. Already in the 1830s, although the dean enjoyed an annual income of over £2500, the average net yield of the common fund was little more. Further reforms, such as those of 1861 when the dean and chapter gave up their common and fabric funds in return for an annual payment of £4200, failed to solve the problem and as late as 1951 the stipend of a residentiary canon was fixed as low as £800. Thus individual dignitaries and canons were rarely able to initiate architectural improvements, unless they possessed substantial funds of their own.

However, the radical reforms of the 1840s did not, as is often alleged, galvanise an institution sunk deep in torpor, as the Victorian revival of church life had already begun. In 1836 Edward Denison, a Fellow of Merton sympathetic to the emerging Tractarian Movement, was appointed bishop, one of the youngest Salisbury has ever had, and he in turn persuaded Walter Kerr Hamilton to follow him from Oxford to be first treasurer and then precentor. On Denison's death, Hamilton succeeded him as bishop. Both men made a great impact on the worship of the Cathedral and the life of the Close. Not only were the number of services, particularly of Eucharists, increased but there was a conscious effort to make the Cathedral the focus of the diocese. The members of the chapter were encouraged to assist the bishop in educational, pastoral and charitable work.

Several diocesan institutions were now housed in the Close. The most notable of these were the Training College for Schoolmistresses, opened, with the encouragement of Bishop Denison, at No. 9 in 1841 and established from 1851 to its dissolution in 1979 in the King's House, and the Theological College founded by Bishop Kerr Hamilton at No. 19 in 1860. The Theological College occupies the late 17th-century house of Francis Hill almost unaltered except for the addition during the 1870s of students' lodgings to the rear and a chapel with a library

below to the east. The architect was William Butterfield who had built or restored several churches nearby, such as Amesbury and Landford [RCHM 1987, 72–3]. His chapel is perhaps the most characteristic Victorian contribution to the Close, its Gothic style and use of stone and flint making a deliberate contrast with neighbouring buildings. Characteristic too of Butterfield is the lack of reference between the Gothic of the chapel and that of the Cathedral it faces. The Training College extensions began more modestly with a block to the north, on the site of the Subchantry, by T H Wyatt, the diocesan architect [RCHM 1987, 72], but at the end of the century a wing was added to the west containing dining rooms and a chapel. The architect was E Doran Webb and the style Gothic. Much larger additions were planned in the 1930s and carried out in the 1950s to neo-Georgian designs by Curtis Green. These were intended to replace the Deanery, which had been in use as one of the college buildings but were resited to the east of it. Since the closure of the college they have been converted into flats.

A third educational institution was added at the end of the 19th century, again as a result of episcopal initiative. Bishop Wordsworth (1885–1911) was determined to prevent the supplanting of Church control over education in Salisbury by the establishment of non-denominational board schools, and thus created a controversy that reached Parliament and the national press. He therefore instigated in 1890 the foundation of four new schools, including one within the Close to the north of the Palace, a move not welcomed by many of the genteel inhabitants. The school, named after the bishop, is mainly accommodated in modern, utilitarian buildings but it has also absorbed No. 11. In 1947 it acquired another school as neighbour when the Choir School moved from its traditional site at Braybrooke to the Bishop's Palace. Thus despite the outward appearance of unchanging serenity and introspection, which helped to inspire the Barchester novels of Anthony Trollope, the 19th century was one of change and some difficulty.

At the Palace, Bishop Denison altered the gardens and in 1843 commissioned T H Wyatt to build a gatekeeper's lodge (p 73) and a new coach-house and stables (p 72), demolished in 1965; he reused a square wooden bell turret from the porch tower (Plates 26, 27). An ashlar bell turret with pierced quatrefoil openings, also by Wyatt, was added to the chapel by Bishop Hamilton (Plate 21). Later bishops were chiefly concerned with the practical problem of mitigating the damp, by replacing the roughcast on the walls by Portland cement and by laying asphalt floors but Bishop Wordsworth restored the 13th-century undercroft, rebuilding the windows.

In 1875 Sir Gilbert Scott (who was then in charge of the Cathedral restorations) returned the North Canonry to something of its medieval aspect, with authentic detail, and here the mastery of the experienced architect makes it hard to determine the extent of his work. In 1881 Dean Boyle borrowed £700 from Queen Anne's Bounty to pay for extensive repairs to the Deanery, including the replacement of all the chimney-stacks in brick. There were few major alterations to the remaining clerical houses, except that the size of the Victorian family – Bishop Moberly had fifteen children – and the much stricter requirements of residence often demanded the provision of more bedrooms and service rooms. The rebuilding of the South Canonry in 1890 was in part prompted by such a need; it was enlarged for Canon Bernard to designs by G R Crickmay in an undistinguished Queen Anne style (Fig 168).

The lay tenants were no more venturesome in the treatment of their houses. No. 27, having been rebuilt c 1810 by the surveyor John Peniston, was refitted at the end of the century; its neighbour, No. 28, was demolished and rebuilt in 1898. At No. 37 the main elevation was heightened and rendered and, later, a new staircase was installed. Following common practice, fittings of earlier date were also inserted, such as 17th- and 18th-century doors and panelling. Similarly Stanley Baker, the last vicar to inhabit No. 12, apparently introduced 17th-century wainscot and a late medieval traceried timber window. As late as 1919 the tenants of Hemingsby reinstated 16th-century oak panelling, with profile heads in roundels, said to have been found in the attics.

The 20th century

The Close has escaped serious damage in the 20th century. It did not suffer from enemy action, despite the number of military establishments nearby on Salisbury Plain, and it has been little affected by recent commercial redevelopment in the town. The last remaining part of Elias de Dereham's original Leadenhall, long in a decrepit condition, was demolished in 1915. In 1922 the deans exchanged their traditional residence for the smaller No. 7. After the Second World War the Old Deanery was threatened with destruction but was largely reprieved after

the significance of its 13th-century hall was recognised. However, the block of student accommodation built to the east did sever its ancient relationship with the Cathedral. The 18th- and 19th-century west wing of the Palace was removed in 1931 and the bishops ceased to reside there in 1947, moving first to Mompesson House, and latterly to the South Canonry. On the positive side many of the houses have been restored in the past thirty years, notably Mompesson House, Malmesbury House and Arundells. Others such as Aula le Stage have been divided into several dwellings. One new house has been built, next to the South Canonry.

The most significant modern development has been the growth of tourism. The Cathedral and Close have always been the resort of visitors, whether the unruly crowds of the traditional Whitsun fair (abolished in 1833) or more sedate travellers, but it was only with the coming of the railway that mass tourism began. The Cathedral now receives hundreds of thousands of visitors a year and they must all traverse the Close. Alterations to accommodate them have hitherto been confined to paving and lighting but more extensive plans have been discussed to provide a visitors' centre and increased parking. The medieval hall at the Old Deanery is frequently used for cultural activities and two of the largest houses have recently been made into museums: the Wardrobe, after a period of disuse, was adapted to house the regimental museum of the Duke of Edinburgh's Royal Regiment, and the King's House, vacant through the closure of the Training College (known latterly as Sarum St Michael), has likewise been converted to become the Salisbury and South Wiltshire Museum, founded a century before in St Ann's Street in the city. Mompesson House was presented to the National Trust in 1952 by Denis Martineau, who had acquired the freehold, and it is now open to the public.

It is a tribute to the wisdom of the founders of the Close, Bishop Richard Poore and Elias de Dereham, and of their successors, that the Close still provides a spacious and dignified setting for the great Cathedral at its heart. Nearly eight centuries after the move from Old Sarum their vision still holds true.

Notes

1 The original source of this statement has not been identified; it is quoted by Canon Jones, whose knowledge of the Cathedral records was unrivalled.

2 An earlier list of citizens made in 1399–1400 contains 997 names, under Wards [RCHM 1980, xxvi, printed in full in Chandler 1983, 262–72].

3 Until 1790 the vergers lived in two houses already considered ancient in 1634, which lay southeast of the Cathedral chancel; they were demolished by Wyatt in 1790.

4 Excerpts from the surveys are included in the inventory section of this volume and many of the room names appear on the house plans, in those cases where their identification can be suggested, eg, Fig 63 (Aula le Stage), Figs 133, 135 (North Canonry).

5 Compare also the roofs of Newhouse, Whiteparish (Wilts), a gentry house of 1605, which have scissor-braced trusses of uniform scantling without longitudinal stiffening.

6   One of the several bundles of documents which make up the Survey has been published [Malden 1893–4], and it includes most of the larger houses in the Close together with fifteen vicars' houses. Descriptions of the other Close properties are scattered throughout the remainder [Chapter archives].

7   The suggestion that Francis Price may have been the architect of the south wing of Hemingsby [Colvin 1978, 659] is unlikely, as it assumes a date 'contemporary' with his design for the west end of Ellingham Church of 1747, whereas the Hemingsby wing was rebuilt in 1727.

8   The following advertisement appeared in the *Salisbury Journal* for 19 Dec 1757, and may well identify one member of the team:

> RICHARD KEYNES, Plaisterer in Brown street hereby acquaints all Gentlemen etc. that he makes all sorts of Papier Mache, as Ceilings for Rooms, Borderings for Rooms that are hung, also Frames for Looking-Glasses and Pictures, and all other sorts of ornamental Work, in Papier Mache. He likewise works plain and ornamental Stucco, all in the neatest Manner, and in the newest Taste, on the most reasonable Terms; which, the Work and Recommendation he has had the Honour of from several Gentlemen in this City and Neighbourhood, he hopes will justify. He also does Plaistering in as neat a Manner and as cheap as any one. Such Gentlemen etc as please to favour me with their Commands may depend upon my Endeavours to please.
>
> RICHARD KEYNES
>
> Who serv'd greatest Part of his Time in Mr. Cartwright's Business in Blandford, and work'd for him some Years afterwards, and had much Practice since in London.

9   The architecture of the Bell Tower will be discussed in a forthcoming volume on the Cathedral.

Inventory of the Houses of the Close

Abbreviations used on reconstructed plans

B	Bedroom	L	Latrine	Sch	Schoolroom
Ba	Bakehouse	La	Larder	SH	Servants' hall
Brew	Brewhouse	LC	Lodging chamber	Sit	Sitting room
By	Buttery	Li	Library	Sr	Store
Ce	Cellar	Lo	Lobby	St	Study
Ch	Chamber	P	Parlour	U	Undercroft
Cl	Closet	Py	Pantry	w	Well
D	Dining room	s	Staircase	Wash	Wash-house
Drg	Drawing room	S	Store	Wood	Woodhouse
Dy	Dairy	Sc	Scullery	Yd	Yard
EH	Entrance hall				
FR	Fruit room				
G	Gallery				
H	Hall				
Ho	Housekeeper's room				
HP	Housemaid's pantry				
K	Kitchen				

Note Although the word 'chamber' had no connotations of being on an upper storey in the Middle Ages or 16th century, it is here adopted for convenience as denoting an upper room, eg 'parlour chamber' for the room over the parlour, except when quotation from a documentary source is indicated.

Room and area names on dated plans

Different typefaces have been used on the dated plans in the Inventory to distinguish the various uses and states of rooms and areas. They are as follows:

Roman capitals: PARLOUR	original use
Roman lower case: Drawing Room	intermediate use
Sans-serif lower case: Dining Room	modern use
Sans-serif capitals: COURT	unroofed areas

The Close Wall

The Close Wall is a defensive structure some 13 ft high with a walkway and battlemented parapet, lookouts and an external ditch; it has three main gatehouses, together with a private one to the former Bishop's Palace. In addition to providing protection in times of trouble, either with the townsfolk or from further afield, the wall provided a physical measure of enforcement to the sanctuary rights granted to the Close in 1317 [Coulson 1982, 97, n. 161], and its construction can also be seen as an act of pride by the clergy, displaying their status and lordship of the Close.

The wall is built mainly of squared Chilmark stone, with some sandstone from the Upper Greensand, and with rubble and brickwork in areas of reconstruction. Although continuous walls are found only on the N, E and S of the Close, the W side, flanked by the River Avon, was formerly walled also (Fig 2). Intermittent construction over a long period and extensive reconstruction have combined to give the walls their varied appearance.

Before 1327 the Cathedral precinct had been defined on N and E by the Close Ditch, a deep drain carrying water from the River Avon to E as far as Catherine Street and then turning S to rejoin the Avon some way downstream from Ayleswade Bridge (map, p 4). Between the NE corner and St Ann's Gate the E boundary of the Close is

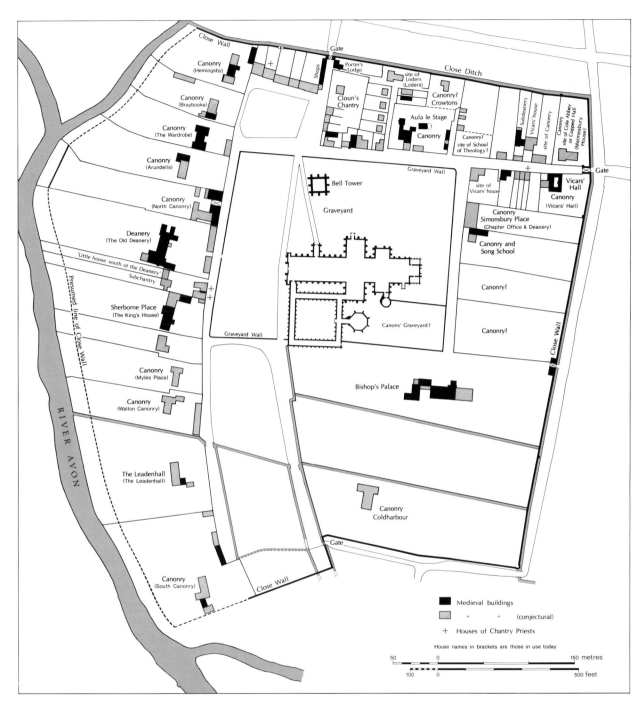

Fig 2   *Reconstructed map of the Close in the late medieval period*

deflected by the ditch from its true alignment, suggesting that the ditch is older, and indeed it is probably one of the earliest features of the new city, preparations for Salisbury's formal foundation in 1220 having begun before 1200 with the allocation of sites for canons' houses [VCH 1956, 165].

Edward III gave permission for the Close to be walled in 1327 [VCH 1962, 75], and in 1331 the dean and chapter were authorised to use the stone of the old cathedral and houses 'for the improvement of the church of New Sarum and the Close thereunto belonging' [Dodsworth 1814, 146–7]. In 1342 chapter agreed to reduce the height of the existing graveyard wall to provide stone for the Close Wall [Chew 1963, No. 171]. Two canons were appointed *magistri et ordinatores* of the work in 1345 in succession to the archdeacon of Salisbury and the keys of a 'chest relating to the same' were handed to them [*ibid*, No. 198]. Preparations began enthusiastically, Thomas de Bokton paying £5 towards the £15 he owed in 1342, the archdeacon of Dorset donating £20 in 1343 [*ibid*, 114], and in 1345 Richard de Chaddesley asked chapter to continue the work 'from whence it had last ended' and so to enclose his house (unidentified), promising to pay for his portion if others would do the same [Everett A (4), f 31 v]. In 1406 chapter agreed with Canon Harborough for it to continue opposite his house, Harborough paying £20, chapter £40 and further costs being shared [Chapter Acts, Draper, 55]. He was also allowed to build a privy on it for his own use on condition that he maintained it.

In the 16th century Leland noted that 'the Close walle was never ful finished as yn one place evidently apperith' [Toulmin Smith 1964, 267]. However, by this time repair was already the main concern: Bishop Beauchamp at his Visitation in 1475 complained that the wall threatened ruin, especially on S, but chapter replied that 'great repair' had been made the previous year [Everett M, 35], when forty-five loads of Tisbury stone had been used on the stretch to E of Harnham Gate. Repairs remained chapter's responsibility until 1562 when Bishop Jewel ordained that the canons (individually) and vicars choral should maintain the stretches abutting their properties [Wordsworth 1915, 179].

By 1678 the wall was in 'great decay'; the vicars attempted to repudiate their liability for maintenance, unsuccessfully, and chapter ordered them to reimburse Mr Gardener, their tenant at No. 55, £6 that he had spent on repairs [Chapter Acts, Frome and Prince, 43]. But in the late 17th century the prohibition on 'postern' doorways was becoming ineffectual and chapter's tenants were allowed to cut ground-floor windows in the wall at Malmesbury House. By about 1700 chapter had abandoned any attempt to preserve the wall's medieval character; in 1705 they permitted James Harris to replace the section enclosing his house so long as he maintained one of the same height, and in 1713 Canon Coker was expressly allowed to take stones from the Close Wall to repair his house, Aula le Stage, and to replace it with brick.

The W wall was being maintained in 1598 when Thomas Sadler 'set about the repairing of the main wall of the Close' at the King's House [D and C Leases, 5 Eliz – 4 James I, 5 Mar 1598/9], but by 1733 it was 'notorious' that the canons had demolished the greater part, 'converting [it] to their own private uses' [Rex v D and C; Everett B, 58]. The act books show that chapter's permission was only sought by Canon Sager at Hemingsby in 1727, and in 1757 by Archdeacon Rolleston at the Leadenhall, and by Dean Greene. Sager and the dean were both rebuilding their houses and no doubt there is a general connection between the appearance of architectural stonework along the W side of the Close and the disappearance of the wall.

The Close Ditch remained open until 1860 [*VCH* 1962, 79]. On the E side it flowed along the base of the wall in place of the footpath which now flanks the W side of Exeter Street. Stout posts which formerly separated the street from the footpath [Lovibond, 91–6] probably originated as a parapet to the ditch.

The S and E walls

The wall bounding the Palace grounds on S and E was built in the 14th century of regularly coursed ashlar and remains the best preserved stretch (Fig 1, in end-pocket). Medieval masonry remains to a height of 6 ft or more, and the wall generally retains its wall-walk and crenellated parapet (Plates 1, 2, Fig 3), although there is evidence of 18th- or 19th-century reconstruction and alterations. A large number of masons' marks occur here and elsewhere (Fig 4 and see Appendix p 44). In the S wall opposite the road to Ayleswade Bridge, some 14 ft of masonry has been wholly replaced in stone rubble, which suggests that this was the entrance opened during the Commonwealth to give access to the Palace, then used as an inn. Between here and Harnham Gate the merlons have been removed. At the SE corner an octagonal 'bastion' [OS 1880] was destroyed by a falling tree in 1896 and rebuilt as a splayed angle. Presumably the moulded string-course, shaped corbels and lion-mask bosses formed part of the 'ornamental appearance' which chapter requested be retained in the reconstruction [Chapter Acts, Nov 1896].

In the E wall, about 70 yds from the SE corner, two conspicuous vertical joints some 17 ft apart appear to illustrate the wall's erratic construction; the S one probably marks the medieval boundary between the Bishop's Palace and the former Coldharbour Canonry to S, and several other straight joints in the E wall occur mainly at property boundaries. In the build to N of these joints, for 70 yds, the crenellations are larger than to S and the ashlar of the E face is differently coursed, although masons' marks show some continuity. Further N the crenellation and walkway have been removed and there is a tiled coping of 18th-century date. Several reused stones with 12th-century ornament are seen in this part, many about 8–9·ins square with stylised flowerheads either projecting or cut into the stone in repetitive designs; they derive from Old Sarum (see p 22), and with few exceptions appear in the outward face of the wall. These carved stones were noted by Aubrey who thought they came from 'the church' at Old Sarum [Aubrey 1969, 97]. For some 60 yds S of Palace Gate the wall is thinner; it is mainly of 17th-century date and contains the blocked windows and doorways of cottages demolished probably in the late 18th century. Masons' marks and stones with 12th-century carving occur here and there. A stretch of the wall N of

Plate 1   *Close Wall from SE, with turret at A–A (see Fig 1, in end-pocket)*

Plate 2   *Close Wall from SW, with wall-walk and turret at A–A (see Fig 1, in end-pocket)*

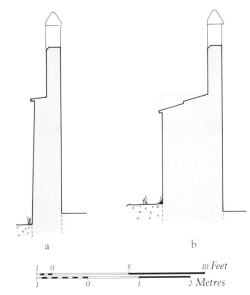

Fig 3   *Close Wall, typical sections*
a. S stretch
b. E stretch

Fig 4   *Close Wall, masons' marks (not to scale)*

Plate 3   *Close Wall, E stretch, carved stones from Old Sarum.*
J Buckler 1810

Palace Gate was rebuilt in the 19th century; it is only 6 ft high and reused stones with 12th-century designs are prominent. Masonry of the normal height, capped by crenellation, starts again about 80 yds S of St Ann's Gate and continues up to the change of alignment and building break on S of the gate. This stretch has been restored and many stones with Romanesque carving are seen, especially in the S half; three have eroded head-corbels, others have miniature arcading, rope mouldings etc (Plate 3). On the W face, seen from the garden of No 14, the walkway rests partly on rounded stone corbels, possibly the 'planks and corbel-stones' hewn for the wall by two masons in 1572 and 1573 [Fabric Rolls, Everett N, 48]. To S and on the same face is an area of heavily disturbed masonry, indicating the site of a privy which served the Vicars' Hall (No.

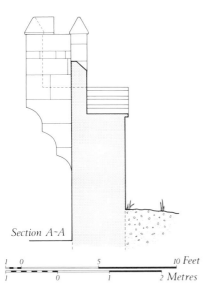

Fig 5 *Close Wall, section A–A of E stretch, with side elevation of S turret, 130 yds N of SE corner (see Fig 1, in end-pocket)*

12). It is one of at least two such privies known from 15th- and 16th-century documents, which were built to take advantage of the Close Ditch, and it remained in use until at least 1701.

Two turrets project on corbels from the E wall, one 10 yds S of St Ann's Gate, one about 130 yds N of the SE corner; they were probably built for watchmen. The S turret (Fig 5) has five separated corbels while that by St Ann's Gate is not continuously coursed with the adjoining masonry and may be an afterthought (Plate 4, Fig 6).

North of St Ann's Gate the wall forms part of the E elevation of Malmesbury House, complete with blocked embrasures. Beyond, where it bounds the garden of Malmesbury House, it is at first continuous although the walkway has been crudely removed. The adjoining section,

which is banded in stone and brick, was rebuilt by James Harris *c* 1705 only 1 ft 6 ins thick. The full width rubble base of the 14th-century wall was revealed during alterations in 1970. To N of the garden the wall is of brick and stone rubble with a tiled coping.

The N wall

At the boundary between Nos 15 and 17 a buttress-like feature projects some 2 ft 4 ins into the ditch but lacks its upper walling, and is probably the remains of a medieval privy (Fig 7). In the gardens of Nos 17 and 18 the Close Wall is of ashlar with a walkway and crenellated parapet, possibly medieval, and masons' marks are again visible; the walk rests partly on rounded corbels and retains a rebated doorway across it in the boundary wall between the two properties. At the Theological College (No. 19) the wall dates from *c* 1862, and is of flint and stone rubble interlayed with brick, rebuilt at chapter's expense by request of the college [Chapter Acts 1797–1870, 2 Apr 1862]. The wall to W is extensively rebuilt without its walkway until very near North Gate, the length at Aula le Stage substituted by Canon Coker in or after 1713 being of poor quality rubble (see p 129). There was another privy at the head of an alley running up the E side of Loders garden (No. 23) in the 16th century, the alley still 'common' in 1649.

West of North Gate the wall bounds the gardens of Mompesson House (No. 53) and the Hungerford Chantry (No. 54), where it is similarly renewed, but medieval ashlar is seen near the ground on the N side. This stretch was singled out for comment as 'much decayed especially in the foundation' at Bishop Ward's Visitation in 1671 [Chapter Acts, 3 Oct 1671]. It was already without a walkway at this date since John Stevens at the Hungerford Chantry had cut a doorway through the wall which he was

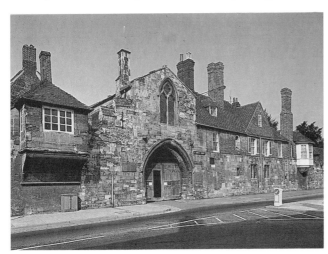

Plate 4 *St Ann's Gate from SE, with turret in Close Wall on left and Malmesbury House (No. 15) on right*

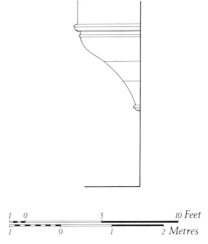

Fig 6 *Close Wall, side elevation of turret base in E stretch 10 yds S of St Ann's Gate*

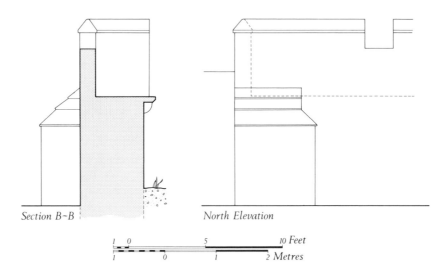

Section B–B   North Elevation

```
I   0              5           10 Feet
├───────────────────────────┤
I        0              1       2 Metres
```

Fig 7 *Close Wall, section B–B and N elevation of N stretch at boundary between Nos 15 and 17 (see Fig 1, in end-pocket)*

ordered to block in 1672 [*ibid*]; this still exists. There is a fine privy of early 18th-century date at Mompesson House, built over the ditch, entered through a doorway with classically moulded architrave. Further W, the wall forms the rear elevation of No. 55A, which is the part 'repaired' by Mr Gardener before 1678 (see p 170), and beyond it is mainly of 18th-century brick.

The W wall

The W wall is known chiefly from documents, and allusions to it in 1440 at the South Canonry and Subchantry (a small house formerly to N of the King's House) are the earliest explicit references [Chapter Acts, Hutchins, 25, 21]. The subchanter's garden was then described as extending to the Close Wall, but leases of 1547 define the gardens of the North Canonry and of a former house on S of the Deanery as 'along unto the river as well within the great wall called the Close Wall as without, between the wall and the river on the west', suggesting that the wall's defensive properties were already being compromised [Leases, 25 Henry VIII – 4 Eliz, 2 Sept]. The only part of it to survive is in the garden of the North Canonry, standing some 40 ft from the riverbank. Built mainly of squared stone rubble it is 2 ft thick at the base and about 8 ft high with a weathered stone coping but no walkway; a stone doorway with chamfered square head and jambs is of 16th-century appearance and probably dates its reconstruction.

A section of wall about 9 yds long, of rubble and brick, 4 ft thick and 8 ft high, is perhaps a vestige of the former S wall towards its presumed W end, and is aligned roughly E – W in the garden of the South Canonry. A continuation E towards No. 72 in brick-laced flint and stone rubble is possibly dated by a payment of £5 8s for 'mending the Wall

at Harnham Gate' in 1714–15 [D and C Communar Book 1690–1720, Everett J, 4].

Appendix: Masons' marks in the Close Wall

At least 130 different masons' marks occur on the Close Wall (Fig 4). Since this was built at least partly with stone from Old Sarum, the question arises as to whether the incisions were cut at Old Sarum in the 12th century or New Sarum in the 14th century. The marks are mainly straight lines forming generally simple shapes, with very few complicated ones, and are much more in the style of those at Old Sarum, both on stones *in situ* on various buildings and in the museum there, than those on the new Cathedral [Overfield 1947, figs pp 66, 68]. Marks resembling the letters N, V, Z, triangles, simple arrows and crosses are found in both locations, as well as marks 3 and 36 (*op cit*, fig p 66) which may be identical in both places.

That each mark occurs most commonly in one area of the wall, some with scatterings in other places, is consistent with their being derived from demolished buildings, although the possibility that the marks are partly of both periods cannot be ruled out; one stone indeed has two clear marks superimposed on one another, and the fact that some of the Old Sarum stone in the Close Wall had an intermediate use in the graveyard wall adds a further element of uncertainty. The most probable explanation is that the marks are of the Romanesque period and that the stones that bear them, like those carved with ornamental designs, were reset in the Close Wall as best they could be with the fairest face outwards.

The Graveyard Wall

The Graveyard Wall (Figs 1, in end-pocket, and 2) bounds the area of level grass, formerly a graveyard, which extends some 80 yds N and W and 40 yds E of the Cathedral. The wall is low, and built of random rubble capped by two courses of weathered Chilmark ashlar. Where the wall abuts the W range of the cloisters it seems clear that the Graveyard Wall is older and was made use of to buttress the cloister; consequently a mid 13th-century date may be assumed for it. In 1342 chapter decided that the wall should be 'reduced in height' to provide materials for the Close Wall [Chew 1963, 112–13] and it probably assumed its present general level of some 5 ft then; 17th- and 18th-century views show it so. In the 16th and 17th centuries it was pierced, especially opposite the canonries, by a number of 'whirlegogs' or turnstiles, whose manufacture and repair were logged in the fabric rolls.

The stretch of wall close to the Cathedral on SE is well preserved and, where aligned E–W, appears to be of the 13th century. It is 2 ft 9 ins thick, up to 9 ft high, and built of roughly coursed stone rubble, including many 12th-century carvings of wheel-like motifs, sections of chevron ornament, zigzag etc, from Old Sarum (see p 39); the wall did not then bound the Palace grounds and it is not clear why it escaped the 14th-century reduction. Its N return on to the Cathedral is of ashlar some 1 ft 9 ins thick, probably rebuilt by Wyatt c 1790 (Fig 1, in end-pocket).

The E wall, flanking Bishop's Walk, is about 4 ft high and has been rebuilt partly in 17th-century brickwork and partly in rubble of uncertain date. The N wall, mainly of rubble, is similar to the N part of the E wall; it retains a double-chamfered ashlar coping, perhaps partly original. At a point due N of the Cathedral crossing, a deep groove cut in the S side of the coping and the word 'Meridies' carefully incised in 18th-century lettering probably relate to the plumbing of the spire which was carried out in 1737 by James Mill [Price 1753, 68]. The W part of the N wall has gone; its presumed alignment corresponds with the S front of Nos 34 and 35 The Close. A short length of possibly medieval flint walling which appears in the N elevation of No. 35 must remain from some building which stood outside the graveyard. The extreme W end of the N wall, of brick and squared stone, dates from c 1680 when Sir Thomas Mompesson was given permission to rebuild it 'more firmly' as the S wall of his stable [Diocesan Records, Press 1/25], which stood there until the early 19th century.

The W wall of the graveyard, mainly of rubble, was largely rebuilt during the 19th century but the curved SW corner at 2 ft 6 ins thick and 5 ft high is probably of 13th-century origin. Similar 13th-century rubble continues in the S wall for some 30 yds from the corner; after this the wall is 19th century and contains fragments of Purbeck shafting. Near the cloisters the N face of the original wall remains, containing a 12th-century rosette, and its original thickness of 2 ft 9 ins resumes against the cloister wall; its upper part was rebuilt as a buttress when the wall was lowered in 1342, and stands adjacent to a cloister buttress which is narrower than the others below

but attains its intended width at a height of 9 ft, thus confirming the original height of the Graveyard Wall.

The Close Gates

North Gate

North Gate is the principal entrance to the Close (Plates 5, 6, Fig 8). It was probably built between 1327, when the Close Wall was licensed, and 1342 when tenements 'outside the north gate of the Close' were leased [Chew 1963, Nos 173, 174], but no doubt all the present stone gates replace earlier, less permanent ones (see St Ann's Gate). The Close porter has lived adjacent at No. 48, probably since the early 14th century, and in the 16th century the gate was considered to be part of his purlieu. In 1650 it was sold as Church property by parliamentary trustees to Alexander Hatchett, a London haberdasher [D and C Muns, Box H–L, Press 1], and recovered at the Restoration, but otherwise there is an almost complete lack of documentation.

The gate was doubtless designed for the daytime use of the porter or his employee. It comprises a carriageway, flanked by a small room on one side, whose original character has been greatly altered, and a staircase on the other leading, via a privy, to a first-floor room and formerly no doubt on to the roof. Perhaps surprisingly there is no sign of any direct access from inside the gate to the walkway of the Close Wall; access may have been gained from the porter's garden.

The gate survives substantially in its 14th-century form and is constructed partly of rubble on S and E but mainly of coursed, squared stone. The upper storey is original and on S the 14th-century niche with vaulted canopy occurs a little above three courses of reused stones carved with 12th-century decoration, presumably from Old Sarum. The doorways of this period are of chamfered stone; the door at the base of the stairs has a segmental head, while the privy door has a square head. The privy is ceiled with stone slabs and lit by a window with two-centred head.

In the latter part of the 15th century the N face was rebuilt, incorporating a portcullis (since removed), the only gate to have one, and an apt reminder of the deteriorating relations between the City and the Close during that century. The upper room was reconstructed; now known as 49 The Close, it was the guard-room from which the portcullis was operated. Also belonging to this period is the low-pitched roof resting on two equally spaced chamfered, cambered tie-beams, supporting a roll-moulded and hollow-chamfered ridge-piece, all originally covered with lead.

Plate 5   *North Gate from N*

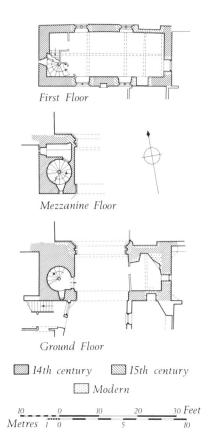

First Floor

Mezzanine Floor

Ground Floor

▨ *14th century*   ▨ *15th century*

▨ *Modern*

10   0   10   20   30 *Feet*

Metres 1   0   5   10

Fig 8   *North Gate*

Plate 6   *North Gate from S, with entrance to No. 48, the Porter's Lodge, on right*

The small ground-level room was originally lit by a chamfered, square-headed window on S, and at different times was probably the janitor's room and a prison. In the 17th century a doorway into the Porter's Lodge was knocked through beneath the window and this may be when a stone chimney-piece, now mutilated, was built across the NE corner. At that time there was an upper floor, but this has been removed and in the 18th century the partition with the carriageway was renewed in timber.

Also in the 17th century, perhaps at the Restoration, the Stuart royal arms were added to the N elevation (heavily restored) and a statue of a Stuart king placed in the niche on S; the latter, greatly decayed, was taken down and replaced in 1902 by the figure of Edward VII. The building has been repaired several times this century, and chapter minutes reveal that in 1901 the lead roof was replaced by a slatted structure and the parapets rebuilt. Buckler in 1809 had shown the S windows with square heads and the N ones all but blocked; the former had been restored with their present arched lights by about 1900 [Lovibond, 126] and the latter were reopened in 1912, when a chimney heating the upper room was also removed. The building was cleaned in 1938–9 and general repairs made, some of the stone being replaced with patches of tilework. In 1950 the upper room was the office of the Cathedral clerk of works and it remains in use as an office today (No. 49).

The gates are of oak with square-, trefoil- and ogee-headed panels, of early 18th-century design, remade in 1982 [Spring 1987, 166]. The windows of the upper chamber contain old glass brought from the Cathedral in 1950, having the inscriptions of 17th-century and later glaziers, and also a quarry painted with the initials HM in the style of *c* 1600. On the N arch there are graffiti, including '1641 IV' on the W jamb.

St Ann's Gate

St Ann's Gate (for plan, see Fig 50) was noted in its early form in 1293, when a house assigned to Nicholas of Winton was 'next to the East Gate of the Close' [Diocesan Records Press 1, 26/3]. However, the existing substantial structure (Plate 7) was in use by 1354 when an indulgence was granted to penitents visiting 'the chapel of St Anne and the Blessed Virgin, newly constructed by the chapter of Salisbury over the eastern gate...' [Cal Papal Letters, 538]. Attempts were made to endow the chapel later in the century, eg in 1363 [Wilts Inq. p.m.], and it appears to have continued in use until the Reformation; the name 'St Ann's Chapel' for the upper storey has never lapsed.

By 1611 the gate had passed into the ownership of the Vicars when they granted a lease of it to William Barnston and from about 1640 until the present century it has been held as an adjunct to Malmesbury House on N. In 1705 William Goldwyer, a surgeon living at No. 13, requested

Plate 7 *St Ann's Gate from W*

that a wicket be made in the gate for his use at night, to which he held a key for twenty-seven years, and the present gates, which are uniform with those of North Gate, incorporate a wicket as an original feature. The chapel is said to have been used in the late 18th century as a concert hall and theatre [Brodie 1848]; it is now an architect's office.

The gate is of two storeys with ashlar walls and lead-covered roofs. Perpendicular joints and variations in coursing suggest a complicated development. The E arch together with the immediate abutments of the Close Wall and its walkway date from about the time of the

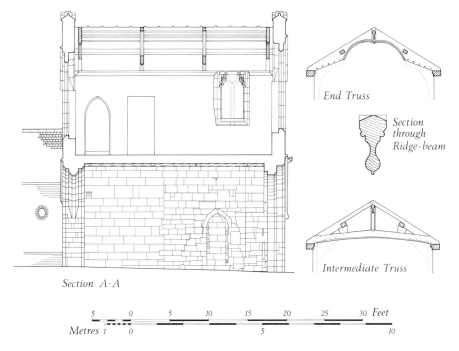

Section A-A

End Truss

Section through Ridge-beam

Intermediate Truss

Fig 9 *St Ann's Gate, long-section, with details of former roof trusses and (not to scale) ridge-beam (for plans, see Fig 50)*

Plate 8 *St Ann's Gate, doorway to stair turret*

foundation of the wall in 1327, and cambered stone joints above the arch indicate the early wall-head. The arch has a roll-moulded label retaining a headstop to S with a crown above curling hair. Stone joints near the middle of the gateway on N and S indicate the second phase (Fig 9), involving the construction of the first gatehouse which had an open platform above it, drained by eroded gargoyles on E; the approach up flights of steps from the Close Wall was protected by massive roll-moulded merlons containing a cruciform arrowslit to S, and the jamb of a corresponding arrowslit on N is evidence of the original symmetrical arrangement (Plate 4).

This arrangement was also short-lived since the gateway had been further extended to W and given its upper storey by 1354. The chapel was lit by windows to E and W, which now have tracery of 1852 [inscription], and by one to N with trefoiled ogee lights. The original entrances were a pair of chamfered doorways with two-centred heads in the side walls. The 14th-century roof had intermediate trusses with tie-beams, and end ones shaped to accommodate the window-heads (Fig 9); the king-struts and wall-plates are roll moulded and other members chamfered. Original wall-posts and braces were removed in the 18th or early 19th century when a ceiling was inserted, and the roof was dismantled and considerably altered in 1967. Below, a mason's mark which occurs repeatedly in the W

Plate 9 *St Ann's Gate from SW, before restoration. J Buckler 1803*

Plate 10 *St Ann's Gate from NE, before restoration of E window.*
J Buckler 1805

build of the gateway has not been noted elsewhere. A pair of chamfered doorways in the E part of the gateway was probably inserted *c* 1354 to facilitate access to the wall-walk via steps now gone; they have depressed two-centred, chamfered rear-arches on plain jambs.

About a century after the chapel was completed a stair turret was added on N, ascending to the chapel and to the leads. It has a moulded lower doorway (Plate 8), the door having keeled planks with shaped tops within the trefoils, a chamfered first-floor doorway and a casement-moulded window adjacent with large beast-stops; the window was given inappropriate tracery *c* 1909 of 14th-century form to replace sash frames seen in Buckler's drawing (Plate 9). The lead capping on the semi-octagonal upper stage is doubtless a renewal of the 17th century, and graffiti on the leadwork include 'GA ACT. 22 1699', '1707 CC' etc.

In about 1600 when the chapel was divided into two rooms, a stone chimney-piece with chamfered Tudor arch was built in one of them, and a floor inserted to create a garret in the roofspace; it formed part of a house which extended into a timber-framed building to N, containing three storeys of rooms, to which the 15th-century stair turret provided access. Subsequently the approach was enhanced by a single-storey brick porch with moulded strings and eaves courses and a (restored) ovolo-moulded bull's eye window, built in a mixture of English and Flemish bond; it is first named in a lease of 1677 but is likely to be of earlier date as this small dwelling had already been merged with Malmesbury House at the time of the Parliamentary Survey (1649–50).

The chapel was restored in the early 18th century by a member of the Harris family as a domestic room, when the extra storey was taken out and the present handsome doors with beaded, fielded panels installed. Buckler's drawings of ·1803–5 show the porch walled up and sash windows with segmental heads (Plates 9, 10).

Graffiti include the name 'Galeyon' scratched in cursive 16th-century writing on the N doorway of the chapel.

South or Harnham Gate

South or Harnham Gate (Fig 10) dates from the middle of the 14th century. It was built as a platform above a deep arch, perhaps originally protected by a crenellated parapet; to E this projects on spaced corbels with a double wave-moulding (not pierced as a *machicoulis*), reminiscent of a bastion on the Close Wall (Plate 11). Rainwater was channelled away through grotesque gargoyles at the angles (Plates 12–15).

The original approaches along the wall-walk have been destroyed (Plate 16). To S, a former doorway at eaves level in No. 73 occurs opposite a patched-up area in the side of the gate, showing that although access by this route was maintained when No. 73 was refronted in 1713, it had been abandoned before 1803 (Plate 17) and the wall coped with brick.

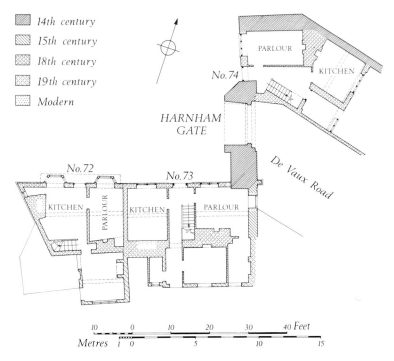

Fig 10 *Harnham Gate, with Nos 72–4*

Plate 11   *Harnham Gate from SE*

The gates, of 19th-century date, are of oak. They replace those seen by Buckler, with three tiers of nail-studded panels, perhaps of Restoration date; it was to accommodate these that the N reveal of the gate was pared back (Plate 18).

Palace Gate

Palace Gate dates from the late 14th century (Plates 19, 20, Figs 11, 12), and without much doubt results from Bishop Erghum's licence to crenellate his Palace in 1377. Its size and quality suggest that it was the residence of a senior member of the bishop's retinue, and the relatively minor nature of any later alterations indicates a subsequent decline in status.

The carriageway had gates to E only and was heated by one of the two original fireplaces (Fig 11), an unusual feature for the benefit of the gatekeeper. To N, the ground-floor room was entered from the gateway and provided access to the rooms upstairs as well as being used perhaps for storage; on the floor above a quarter-bay of the roof shows signs of having been partitioned off for the main stairs with perhaps a small closet at the W end,

Plate 12   *Harnham Gate, gargoyle at SW angle*

Plate 14   *Harnham Gate, gargoyle at SE angle*

Plate 13   *Harnham Gate, gargoyle at NW angle*

Plate 15   *Harnham Gate, gargoyle at NE angle*

Plate 16   *Harnham Gate from W, with No. 74*

Plate 17   *Harnham Gate from NW, with Nos 73 and 74. J Buckler 1803*

Plate 18   *Harnham Gate from SE. J Buckler 1805*

where a first-floor window looked into the gateway. The stairs continued upwards in a form of internal turret partly roofed with stone weatherings, through an original doorway, into the high chamber over the gateway which is lit by original windows to E and W and two small ones above the roof to S (now blocked), and heated by the other original fireplaces; it was perhaps the occupant's principal

daytime chamber. A small doorway with an opening some 4 ft 6 ins high by 1 ft 9 ins issuing within the apex of the roof to S, evidently at a staircase (or ladder), was presumably provided for emergency defensive use. To S of the gateway there is a large first-floor chamber which, although its floor level has been altered, is almost certainly original; the roof lacks the smoke-blackening which would be expected in an open hall, and it was probably a great chamber above a low storey.

The gate is built of flint, stone and tile rubble, with ashlar flanking the arch on E, and exhibits a considerable variety of detail in its stone dressings. The gateway arches are a pair, with depressed two-centred heads and hollow chamfer and ogee mouldings, and the two main internal doorways have low arches of both three-centred and four-centred forms, one chamfered; the small first-floor doorway is chamfered with a two-centred head. The upper fireplace also has hollow chamfer and ogee mouldings, and

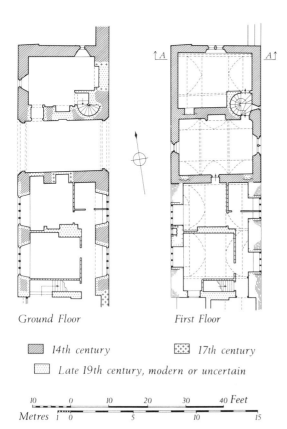

Section A-A

Ground Floor   First Floor

▨ 14th century   ▧ 17th century

▨ Late 19th century, modern or uncertain

Fig 11   Palace Gate

Plate 19   Palace Gate from NE. J Buckler c 1805

Plate 20   Palace Gate from W

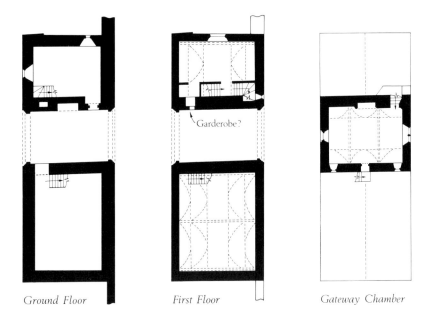

Ground Floor   First Floor   Gateway Chamber

Fig 12   *Palace Gate, reconstructed plans, as built*

a stone lintel cut with a four-centred arch, and the fireplace in the gateway (Fig 12) has a broad hollow chamfer with an arched head, mutilated at the apex. Windows are mostly chamfered with four-centred rear-arches; the largest are those to E above the gateway, which has a two-centred head (restored), and that lighting the first-floor room on N, which has lights with four-centred arches and head, and a pierced spandrel now blocked (Fig 11). The room over the gateway has a W window with three-centred head with hollow chamfer and roll mouldings, and S windows hollow chamfered with four-centred heads, and the N room on the ground floor is lit by windows with two- and four-centred heads.

The building's three roofs are similarly constructed, and all are still exposed to their rooms below collar level. They have plain collars and principals and lightly curved wind-braces (which are plain except over the gateway chamber), butt purlins and long curved arch-braces with chamfers; the latter maintain their relationship with the principals by means of short struts and secret double tenons. The exception is the quarter-bay over the stairs, which is plainly finished.

Later history

Buckler's drawing (Plate 19) shows that windows were pierced in the E wall in the 17th century and a stone doorway of the same period was discovered in the S wall of the gateway in 1982. One first-floor window on W (now blocked) indicates the former floor level on S of the gateway; it is ovolo moulded and probably of the early 17th century. In 1859 T H Wyatt proposed that the gatehouse should be 'converted' to provide two rooms for the bishop's muniments in place of the top floor of the Palace tower which was considered a fire-risk, at a cost of £450 [WRO, Bishop's Admin, 28]. The S range was then reconstructed with a taller ground floor, the wall at the S end was taken down and an extension built; the large E window was given cusped tracery, the present spiral staircase was constructed, and the eaves were partly remodelled as a parapet. Subsequently the original chimney-stack was dismantled and roofed over. Wooden gates, in the E arch only, resemble those of North and St Ann's Gates but have flush panels and date from the late 18th century. Elaborately carved graffiti in the gateway include 'M Brown 1708' and 'IH 1751'. The gate remained a document store until 1956, and now accommodates a classroom and library for the Cathedral School, and a staff cottage.

The Bishop's Palace

The former Bishop's Palace (Fig 13, in end-pocket) stands SE of the Cathedral and it is the principal of several residences in the diocese used by medieval bishops. The two approaches from N through the Close and E from Exeter Street are probably both original and the Palace was the only house with a private entrance through the Close Wall; the bishop's grounds, which were divided into N and S areas by a 'canal', draining into the Close Ditch, were so arranged that he also had a private doorway into the SE corner of the cloisters.

Bishop Poore (1217–28) founded the Palace in conjunction with the new Cathedral and work on it progressed rapidly. In 1221 King Henry III granted twenty timber couples from Gillingham Park for making the hall and ten from Melchet Wood for the chamber [Wordsworth 1891, 166–9], both of which must have been functional in September 1225 when the E part of the Cathedral was consecrated, and the bishop played host to the archbishops of Dublin and Canterbury and many nobles for a week [Jones 1884, 38–40, 43–4]. It has been suggested from a single document issued by the bishop in 1218 *'ad Novum Locum apud Veteres Sarisbirias'* [Jones 1891, 84] that the bishop had a residence called New Place by then [*VCH* 1956, 165] but this is unsubstantiated. Of the 13th-century Palace, two storeys of larger and smaller rooms at right angles to one another remain; a ground-floor hall probably lay to E or NE, but of this and any chapel etc there is now no trace.

During the 14th century Bishops Wyville in 1337 and Erghum in 1377 obtained general licences to crenellate various properties including Salisbury Palace [Peacock 1889, 128]; Erghum's permit probably resulted in the building of the present Palace Gate on to Exeter Street.

In the mid 15th century a great restoration was undertaken and Leland noted *c* 1540 that Bishop Beau-champ (1450–81) had 'made the great haulle, parler, and chaumbre of the palace' [Toulmin Smith 1964, I, 267], for which a *terminus ante quem* may be suggested in the visit of Edward IV, who stayed there in 1466. When Henry VI visited Salisbury in 1457, he stayed at the Old Deanery, perhaps because the Bishop's Palace was in some way unfit for his reception [Wheeler 1889, 11]. Beauchamp's new hall measured approximately 87 ft 6 ins by 37 ft 6 ins and was one of the largest built in the 15th century, though exceeded later by Edward IV's hall at Eltham Palace which measures 102 ft by 37 ft 3 ins. Beauchamp's chamber and parlour still exist, and originally they and the hall porch had low-pitched lead roofs; it was doubtless during the vicissitudes of the Parliamentary interregnum that these were removed, and if his hall was similarly roofed this could explain its destruction at that time. This is more than likely, as a valuation of the Palace for its building materials was made in April 1647 and the cost of demolition calculated; the lead was one of the most valuable items listed and its 32,000 lb would probably have covered the rooms as suggested [WRO, Bishop's Admin, 28].

In the 16th century Bishop Jewel (1560–71) extended the Palace grounds: in 1568 he obtained the Glasshouse tenement which stood on W of his N entrance in exchange for an episcopal canonry, the Wardrobe, and he took a ninety-nine-year lease of Coldharbour Close (which was continuously renewed until the freehold was obtained in

Plate 21 *Bishop's Palace from NW*

1827). This was some three acres in the SE corner of the Close, the site of a canonry last occupied in about 1460. The Palace chapel (*capella sive oratorio*) is first referred to in 1588 although there are references to ordinations within the Palace during the reign of Bishop Jewel [Wordsworth 1891, 170].

One of the first actions of the Parliamentary trustees after the Civil War was to dispose of the Palace; in July 1648 William and Joseph Barter paid £880 2s for it [Dodsworth 1814, 233], the early sale excluding it from the Parliamentary Survey. After passing through various hands most of Beauchamp's hall was demolished, and the remainder converted into an inn and small tenements for poor craftsmen.

At the Restoration, Bishop Henchman (1660–3) began the work of repair, creating a chapel and building other new rooms, and although Bishop Ward's apologists later complained that nothing had been done before Ward's accession in 1667, Wren alluded (rudely) to this work and Pepys noted on his visit in June 1668 'a fine palace for the Bishop' [Latham 1976, 229]. Nevertheless, Ward found the hall still in ruins, and he obtained advice on rebuilding it from his friend Wren:

> At the request of the Rt Reverend Father in God, Seth, Lord Bishop of Sarum, I have viewed the Pallace there, in wch there was an auncient Hall, about 90 foot in length, and 36 foot in breadth demolished in ye late troubles, and nothing remaining of it but a Porch, and the foundation, and a small building of meane low Roomes erected out of the ruines. And I conceive that to accommodate the house with an hall though of much less extent, and to connect together the buildings now standing, with any tolerable convenience for wholesome habitation, it will be necessary to rebuild from the ground at least 18 or 20 Squares of building of two Stories high, wch may amount to £1200 and upwards, & to finish it decently to £1500, according to the Prices of building in that place. Chr. Wren [Wren Soc 1941, 30].

This report is presumably contemporaneous with that on the Cathedral dated August 1668, and work on the Palace

Plate 22   *Bishop's Palace from N. J Buckler 1809*

was begun in December that year under the supervision of James Harris, Cathedral clerk of works [WRO, Ward, Notitiae, 44]. The resulting building is of three storeys measuring approximately 24½ squares (or one hundred square feet on plan) and cost about £1140 [ibid], the extra expense of the third storey evidently offset by utilising the ruins of Beauchamp's hall.

Ward may also have built the two pairs of square ashlar gate piers with ball finials to N of the Palace. The cost of his work other than on the hall is buried in his general expenditure of £537 on the Palace, Close Wall and Guildhall [ibid]. In his day the Palace was again fit for the reception of royalty, and in 1683 the Duke of York, later James II, stayed for three days with the Duchess and Princess Anne.

There is evidence of one or more further phases of enlargement made some time between the arrival of Bishop Ward in 1667 and Naish's map of 1716 [RCHM 1980, Plate 16], with a service court at the E end and new private rooms to W; but the stages can no longer be unravelled and these additions were mainly demolished in 1783. The grounds were also developed; the Naish map shows formal gardens with a bowling green on S of the cloisters and the Bishop's Walk to N planted as an avenue of approach.

Bishop Sherlock (1734–48) considered extensive proposals, mainly for beautifying the Palace, with Francis Price, the Cathedral clerk of works, co-ordinating the efforts of Francis Cartwright of Blandford and his stuccoists and John Soffe of Salisbury as joiner. Only one of Cartwright's letters survives, dated 13 November 1739, in which he compares his proposals for the parlour and chapel, as illustrated in his drawings [WRO, Bishop's Admin, 28]. Further designs from the same hand include alternative and unexecuted proposals for redecorating Ward's hall (Plate 23), and what is probably a rejected drawing for the dining room ceiling, as well as full-size cornice mouldings. Price had written to John James about the new roof for the then dining room as early as 1736 and it was built almost exactly as proposed, but an undated scheme to reroof Ward's hall, eliminating two valleys, was not adopted.

In the late 18th century Bishop Barrington (1782–91), who shortly afterwards employed James Wyatt at the Cathedral, engaged Sir Robert Taylor to transform the Palace, at an alleged cost of £8000 [Greig 1925, 228]. The works took about three years (1783–5) and effectively transferred all the principal rooms to the first floor as a precaution against damp, with reception rooms in the W half and bedrooms to E. In addition to imposing an up-to-date elegance on the 'gloomy' mansion with its many periods of building, he also pulled down a number of older structures which interrupted his view of the Cathe-

dral [Britton 1801, 45], including the vergers' houses. Bishop Fisher (1807–25) further improved the outlook, cutting down trees and making the grounds 'picturesque'. Within, he arranged for the collection of bishops' portraits to be displayed in the drawing room [Greig 1925, 228–30], where they can be seen in Buckler's domestic interior of 1817 (Plate 28).

Several of Fisher's 19th-century successors changed the Palace in various ways. Bishop Denison (1837–54) formed the gardens on S with a terrace and low walls of white brick, originally enclosing a fountain and parterres. The canal marked by Naish in 1716, which perpetuated the boundary between the bishop's meadow and Coldharbour, he turned into a pond of irregular shape. Elsewhere he employed T H Wyatt to build the lodge and coach-house, the position of the lodge reflecting Bishop Fisher's enlargement of the grounds northwards to the Graveyard Wall.

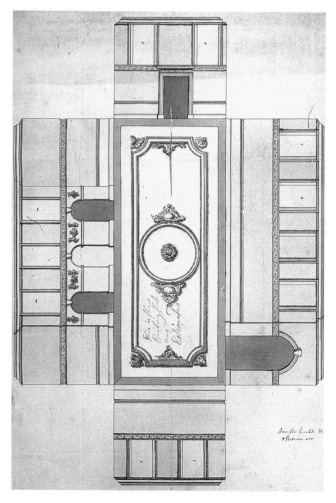

Plate 23 Bishop's Palace, design for redecoration of hall. Francis Cartwright 1739. WRO D1/31

Plate 24 *Bishop's Palace, S pier in undercroft, looking E*

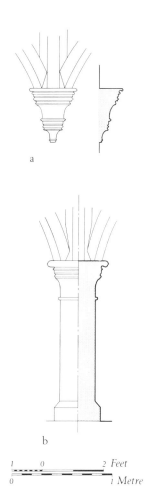

Fig 15 *Bishop's Palace, undercroft*
a. N corbel in W wall
b. N pier

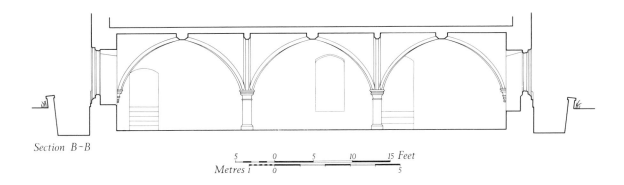

Section B–B

Fig 14 *Bishop's Palace, long-section of undercroft in solar range*

The Palace grew to its greatest post-medieval extent under Bishop Burgess (1825–37) and so remained until 1931, when Bishop Donaldson (1925–36), with the advice of H Passmore [WRO Church Commrs File 20419], demolished a large wing at the W end, which had developed by stages in the 18th and 19th centuries, and made associated alterations. Bishop Wordsworth's School had already occupied the Palace with forty-five boys from January to April 1890 until their premises were ready at No. 11 [*VCH* 1957, 366–7], and when, in 1947, Bishop Lunt moved to another house, the buildings were ceded permanently to the Cathedral School. With the help of the Historic Buildings Council, a rolling programme of repair and restoration has been initiated, including the reinstatement of the low-pitched lead roof on Beauchamp's porch.

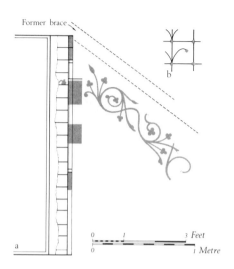

Fig 17 *Bishop's Palace, painted decoration*
a. in W chamber
b. in solar

The original Palace

Bishop Poore's buildings are of stone-dressed flint rubble with small regular quoins. There remain only a large chamber or solar, 52 ft 4 ins by 24 ft 2 ins, above a vaulted undercroft, and a short wing set at right angles containing an inner chamber 23 ft 4 ins by 19 ft 3 ins (Fig 18a) above a ground-floor room. These probably correspond to the bishop's private rooms at the 'high' end of the hall, set above rooms which were possibly a parlour and a storage place for wine and other valuable goods. Some 13th-century decoration has survived in the solar, and behind Bishop Sherlock's battens and plaster an area of painted decoration has been exposed on the W wall with black squares and red flowers (Fig 17b); elsewhere the 'high level windows and three arches on one side' seen in 1736 may also still exist [WRO, F Price to Bp, Misc Docs]. In the undercroft (Plate 24, Figs 14, 15) the vaulting, columns and corbels are original but the windows to W and S are restored; in their early form they had double-chamfered two-centred openings, segmental rear-arches and widely splayed jambs, grouped singly and in pairs; those to N are now wholly of the late 19th century [Reeve 1891, 181–2]. The original entrance was probably from E into the S bay where the mouldings of the N corbel continue in a defaced condition on the jamb of a rebuilt opening.

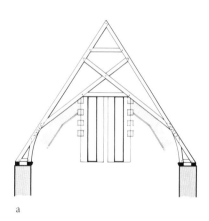

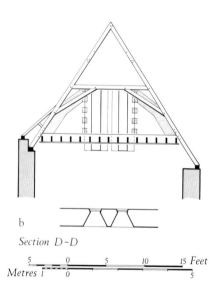

Section D–D

Fig 16 *Bishop's Palace, W chamber roof and window*
a. reconstruction as built
b. as existing

Fig 18 *Bishop's Palace, sequence of reconstructed plans, scale 1 in. to 48 ft (pp 59–62)*
a. as built for Bishop Poore
b. as altered by Bishop Beauchamp
c. as fitted up for Bishop Henchman after the Civil War
d. as enlarged for Bishop Ward, and again for Bishop Sherlock
e. as remodelled for Bishop Barrington

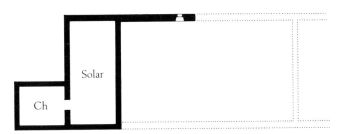

First Floor

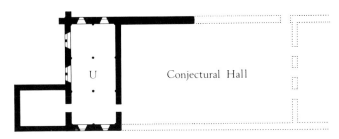

Ground Floor

a. *c*.1225

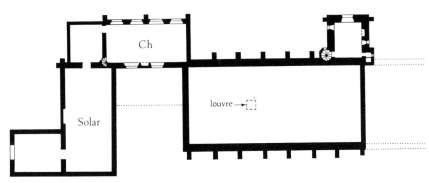

First Floor

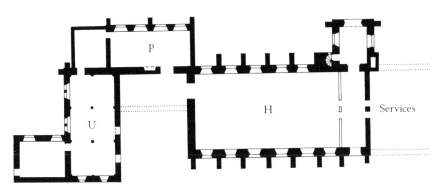

Ground Floor

b. *c*.1470

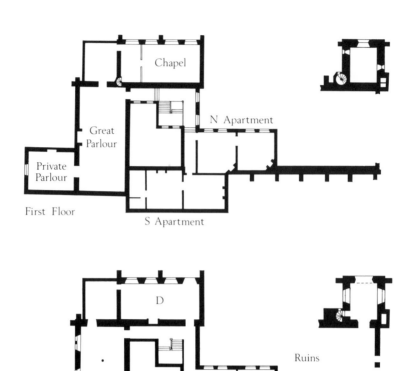

Chapel

N Apartment

Great
Parlour

Private
Parlour

First Floor

S Apartment

D

Ruins

U   Yard

K   K

Ground Floor
c. By 1663

The upper chamber to W was presumably at the same level as the solar, and the W wall has two 13th-century windows in the gable, chamfered with square heads and wide splays, the external stonework of the openings being wholly renewed. The adjacent plaster has red and black 'ashlaring' and red rectangles and scrollwork bordered in yellow ochre (Fig 17a). The roof was originally scissor braced and the plaster shows that it was open to the apex; subsequently the trusses were ceiled and the decoration below painted out. In the 15th or 16th century the roof was rebuilt in its present form, incorporating sixteen original couples of oak rafters (Figs 16, 17a).

On E of the solar a wall projects and is now part of the 15th-century parlour range; it contains a small window with diagonal tooling and stone-lintelled head, which may be 13th century, and suggests that a staircase or building of more than one storey stood in the position that the hall

would otherwise be expected to occupy.

A stone fragment noted in 1890 seems to have belonged to the original Palace. It formed part of a window with 'trefoil-headed lights with quatrefoil above, the whole being rebated outside for iron casements, while the lights were also rebated inside for wooden shutters' [Reeve 1891, 183]; this is a type associated with Elias de Dereham (see pp 8–9).

From the 15th century to the Commonwealth

Bishop Beauchamp's mid 15th-century work is characterised by its noble scale, use of two-centred arches and cinquefoil cusping for the principal doorways and windows respectively, and carved stonework, with labels having headstops, and battlemented parapets upon moulded strings with tablet flower, grotesque heads etc (Plates 26,

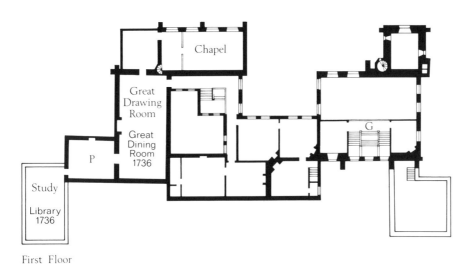

Chapel

Great
Drawing
Room

Great
Dining
Room
1736

P

Study

Library
1736

G

First Floor

D

Parlour 1736

U

Yard

K

Py

Sc

Steward

H

Yard

Wood

Brew

Wash

La La Dy

Ground Floor

■ By 1674   □ By 1716

d. Late 17th - mid 18th century

27, Figs 20, 21). Of his once magnificent hall, the porch and enough of the walling at the E end remain to show that it had a screens passage and six bays each approximately 13 ft long (Fig 18b). One three-stage ashlar buttress remains on N (Plate 26) and the footings of two more were exposed temporarily in 1973, but on S the buttresses were cut down to two stages in 1668 (Plate 25). In the rubble masonry of the S wall there are traces of the moulded plinth, parts of a sill and the jambs of two

windows, and the rear doorway to the screens passage (now blocked). In the side wall of the screens passage, now the E end wall of the Palace, the double hollow-chamfered moulding of a service doorway remains partly visible.

The hall porch is built as a three-storey tower, served by a stone newel staircase; a main alteration has been the insertion of an upper storey within the entrance, lit unobtrusively from E, in 1782. Before then the gateway formed a handsome entrance with moulded inner and

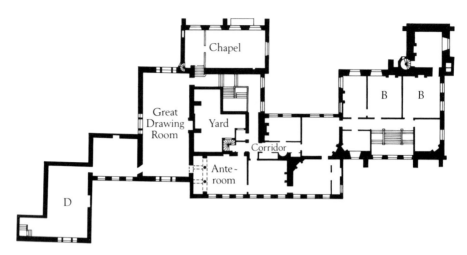

First Floor

Ground Floor

e. 1785

Plate 25   *Bishop's Palace from S. J Buckler 1803–4*

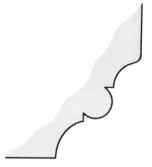

Scale: 1 inch = 1 foot

Fig 19   *Bishop's Palace, porch tower, moulding of entrance arch*

outer arches (Fig 19) lit by two-light hollow-chamfered and roll-moulded side windows. Of the upper rooms, that on the top floor is the better preserved and its main window has yellow and black stained glass in the spandrels, probably 15th century; a side window on E and the doorway are hollow chamfered with four-centred heads. It may have been heated originally and has a privy chamber, ceiled with stone slabs, which is entered through a square-headed rebated doorway. In the exposed roof, which had a pyramidal tiled structure removed and its original low-pitched lead covering restored in 1980, the ridge-piece, wall-plates and central cambered tie-beam are moulded with plain or hollow chamfers, and the supportive posts were added probably in the 17th century. In the room below (originally the lower chamber but now on the second floor), the floor was raised in 1782 and the side windows and privy door blocked, the E light having a trefoil head. The ornamental top of the stair turret, which gives access to the leads, is vaulted in eight compartments, with hollow-chamfered ribs springing from the newel and making four-centred arches.

Beauchamp's parlour and chamber (Plate 21) are built of ashlar-dressed rubble, incorporating an older wall to S. Four-centred doorways on W with external mouldings, chamfered on the ground floor, double ogee above, frame the approach to these rooms from W. The parlour windows are hollow chamfered with double ogee-moulded segmental rear-arches and similarly moulded jambs (graffiti on which include a ragged staff, 'A', 'AW 1661', 'BP 1707' and a repeated 'W' which may be a mason's mark). In the chamber, the N windows are roll moulded with trefoil-headed tracery lights and rear-arches as below, and of the windows on S (now blocked) one retains its square head and external moulded ashlar jambs. The oak roof has richly moulded cornices, cambered tie-beams and subsidiary beams, and is dotted with small carved bosses, some original, others perhaps 15th century reset (Plate 31, Fig 22); the original lead flats are now represented by a hipped roof not more than a century old, but the newel staircase to the parapet remains.

Bishop Beauchamp may also have remodelled Poore's solar. In 1966 part of the ogee-moulded and hollow-chamfered S jamb and arch of a fireplace were discovered in the W wall, supplanted by the 18th-century window. A blocked doorway leading from E into the centre bay of Poore's undercroft may also be Beauchamp's; it is hollow chamfered and integral with a ventilator above, all under a four-centred arch.

Plate 26 (top left) *Bishop's Palace, porch tower from NW*

Plate 27 *Bishop's Palace, porch tower from NW. W Twopeny 1833.*
BM S&D 1933 Vol IV b. 9

From Bishop Beauchamp's time until 1650 only minor alterations are known. The royal arms with a lion and dragon as supporters, dating from late in Henry VIII's or early in Edwards VI's reign, were added to the porch, perhaps as a symbol of allegiance by Bishop Capon (1539–57), promoted from the abbacy of Hyde near Winchester. He or a successor restored Bishop Poore's chamber wing, inserting a garden doorway on W with four-centred head and concave stop-chamfers, and a window above of horizontal format (now blocked); the latter implies a first-floor level some 1 ft 6 ins lower than the present one and may be associated with the reconstruction of Poore's original roof.

Restoration of the Palace

After the ruination of the Parliamentary interregnum, Bishop Henchman undertook elementary rehabilitation, fitting Beauchamp's chamber as a chapel (dedicated 1662) and using the parlour below as entrance and dining room [Wordsworth 1891, 170]. To divide off the W bay of the chapel he added the screen, now painted with oak graining (Plate 32); the two lower stages are closely articulated with panels and arcading, the upper stage possibly being reset or added subsequently using 17th-century parts. The stalls are perhaps made up, partly from 17th-century chip-carved panels, now oak grained. The oak staircase is also Henchman's and gave a spacious ascent from his dining room (Plate 33), the heavily bevelled panels being closely paralleled on the middle stage of the chapel screen. The staircase has rusticated wooden pillars at the base and an asymmetrical roll-topped handrail, the newel-caps being replacements.

The restoration of what is now the centre of the Palace was part of the same project, with two new two-storey ranges which, together with the staircase, enclosed a small yard. The ground floor contained chiefly service rooms,

Plate 28 *Bishop's Palace, great drawing room looking S. J Buckler 1817*

with residential apartments upstairs (Fig 18c). Henchman's main elevations, subsequently heightened, are those facing N and E (Plate 30), stately but unambitious with their stone and flint chequers and chamfered windows, while those to the yard are of brick in English bond with segmental-headed openings, bullnosed plinth, and coved eaves cornice. Joinery attributable to Henchman's period includes doors on the top floor of three planks, of which the centre one is recessed but framed at top and bottom to form a tall ogee-moulded panel, hung on original strap-hinges, and perhaps the main external door on N, of four by four nail-studded panels (cut down and reset in its present position).

Two other Restoration bishops came and went in quick succession, so that it fell to Bishop Ward (1667–89) to give the Palace a new hall. Having taken advice from Wren (p 28), he adapted the E half of the 15th-century hall, reusing the porch as his entrance. Much of the N and S

walls with their buttresses are Beauchamp's, and Ward's new exterior work was designed economically to harmonise with that already existing; so the N elevation adjoining the porch is of ashlar, its W return facing Henchman's is chequered, and the S wall is mainly of ashlar. The construction of the hall resulted in a three-sided court on N, which was made more uniform by adding on W a false wall complete with dummy windows at second-floor level, to balance the hall, while on S the attics were heightened to a full storey. A central stone doorway with cornice on scrolled brackets was inserted (which necessitated moving an internal partition), and a cartouche of royal arms dated 1674 was added above.

The new hall was grandly conceived, rising through two storeys and overlooked at first-floor level by a gallery; it was heated by a chimney on N (only remaining at roof level), and was connected by a passage beneath the gallery with Henchman's service rooms (Fig 18d). The interior

Plate 29   *Bishop's Palace, great drawing room (Bishop Barrington, c 1784) looking N*

Plate 30   *Bishop's Palace, aerial view from NE. Traffic Technology Limited, Skyscan Balloon System*

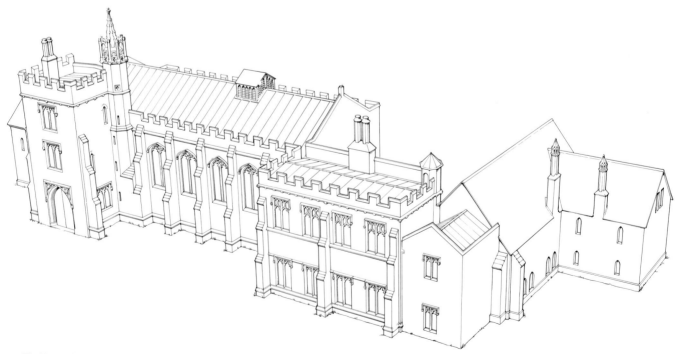

Fig 20   *Bishop's Palace, reconstructed perspective view, as in c 1470*

has been wrecked by later subdivision, but the colonnade of square oak pillars carved with plain rustication and crude Ionic capitals remains (Plate 35), together with part of an ovolo- and ogee-moulded plaster cornice under the gallery, and the main posts embedded in a later wall. The oak staircase, elegant but fairly plain (Plate 36, Fig 24), rises in twin flights and returns as one, repeating the process to the top floor. (Pillars added subsequently support the newels one upon another, displacing many of the turned pendent finials.) This grand approach suggests the importance of the rooms on the top floor, but those facing N have lost their original fittings while the smaller rooms flanking the stairs at this level and on the first floor

retain remnants of fielded, bolection- and ogee-moulded panelling, bolection chimney-pieces and double cymatium cornices. A number of bolection-moulded doors on the second floor are *ex situ*. Two rooms survive relatively intact from this period, both on the first floor of the central block, the NE room and the parlour to W, with bolection-moulded softwood joinery and heavy cornices.

It was probably Bishop Ward who enlarged Henchman's kitchen block eastwards, adding a steward's room below an extension of the S apartment, but the new roof is very similar to its predecessor: both have knee-principals cantilevered out to tie-beams to N, and the unusual feature of rafters tenoned into the purlins.

The 18th century

Further substantial additions are shown on Naish's map of Salisbury in 1716 [RCHM 1980, Plate 16] and in more detail on an 18th-century ground-floor plan of the Palace [Reeve 1891, 184] (Fig 18d). The origin of this plan has not been traced. The detail shown argues its authenticity as an 18th-century plan; however, it seems doubtful that a staircase shown projecting in the angle between the original solar and chamber ever existed. The work was

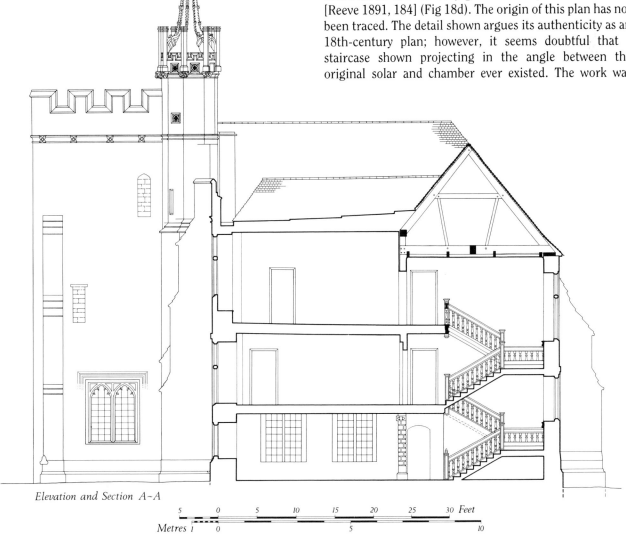

Elevation and Section A~A

5   0   5   10   15   20   25   30 *Feet*

Metres 1   0   5   10

Fig 21   *Bishop's Palace, section of hall range, with side elevation of porch tower*

Plate 31   *Bishop's Palace, chamber (now chapel) ceiling, looking W*

probably done in two phases, as indicated by different hatching on the 18th-century plan, the offices to S and E being added first and the room beneath Poore's chamber improved with mullioned and transomed wooden windows, and refaced to N in brick and stone. Subsequently the upper room at the W end was built, probably as a study, though converted by Bishop Sherlock into a library. The plan also shows opposed entrances on E and W of the court, substituted for Ward's, and the forecourt roofed in upon a colonnade.

An undated codicil to the will dated 24 October 1711 of Bishop Burnet (1689–1715) names the parlour, dining room, great drawing room, the bishop's study, the King's room and the White room within the Red room; the last three were probably in the central block, while the dining room was probably still beneath the chapel and the parlour perhaps between drawing room and study.

Burnet or one of his immediate successors added a cupola to the N parapet of Beauchamp's porch housing the bell for a clock. The cupola was originally classical with an order and is seen in the engraving by S and N Buck, *The North East Prospect of the City of Salisbury*, 1734 [RCHM 1980, dustjacket], and in Buckler's drawing of 1809 (Plate 22), but by 1833 it had been gothicised with a pair of two-centred arches and in 1843 was transferred to the stables.

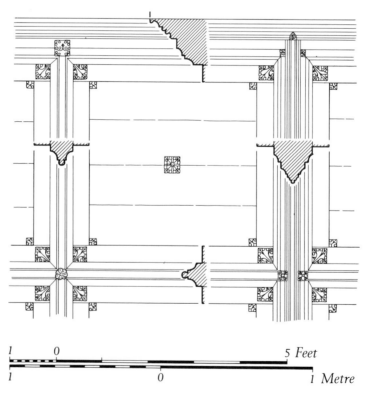

Fig 22   *Bishop's Palace, chamber (now chapel) ceiling, plan of typical panel, with sections of mouldings (cornice at top)*

Plate 32   *Bishop's Palace, chapel screen from E*

Plate 33   *Bishop's Palace, W staircase*

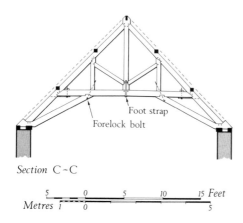

Section C – C

5   0   5   10   15 *Feet*
Metres 1   0   5

Fig 23 *Bishop's Palace, roof over great dining room (Bishop Sherlock, 1736)*

Sumptuous redecoration followed the translation of Bishop Sherlock (1734–48) (see pp 31–2), principally in the dining room which became the parlour and in the great drawing room which became a grand dining room. One design for the parlour shows it panelled, with sash windows and a pedimented door-case, but the changes effected were probably limited to the carved chimney-piece and splendid ceiling. The great drawing room was heightened as a dining room (Plate 29) and its ceiling, chimney-piece and the dado rail carved, with Vitruvian scroll installed, while the roof was reconstructed in oak with iron reinforcements (Fig 23), incorporating many members with carpenters' marks and redundant mortices probably from the original roof.

Sir Robert Taylor's work for Bishop Barrington, carried out between 1783 and 1785, touched every aspect of the Palace; it included the demolition of the office court at the E end and the shifting of the services to the centre and W part of the house (Fig 18e). Externally, the S elevation and W part of the Palace were stuccoed, lunettes were placed over the drawing room windows, and the 17th-century kitchen build was given symmetrical sashed fenestration. Within, Sherlock's parlour was converted to an entrance hall by blocking the N windows and adding the portal bearing a gartered shield of arms of the see impaling Barrington, which is an interesting example of Taylor's Gothic style (Plate 34). The lobby between hall and stairs was given a plaster groin vault, and a new entrance was made to the chapel up a steep flight of stairs from the first-floor landing. Sherlock's library at the SW angle became the dining room, with a staircase to kitchens beneath, and was fitted with a chimney-piece with garlands, jugs and other carton pierre enrichments. The drawing room (formerly Sherlock's dining room) was given four new doors (one a dummy), their frieze tablets

carved with ribband and leaf garlands, while the Venetian windows were rebuilt (Plate 37). The room to SE was made into an ante-room, the communicating door being set off-centre behind a Corinthian screen, the ceiling enriched with a plaster cornice, and the floor strengthened from below with slender stone pillars.

Outside the ante-room, a top-lit E–W corridor with plaster groin vaults and circular lanterns extended W into the kitchen yard, where it joined a new back-stair connecting all storeys, and served as an artery between day and night quarters; it destroyed the 17th-century N apartment, the E room becoming a thoroughfare, while the reduced W room was rebuilt and fitted with mahogany doors to the chimney recesses. Ward's hall and Beauchamp's porch

Plate 34 *Bishop's Palace, N portal, Sir Robert Taylor 1783–5*

Plate 35   *Bishop's Palace, pillar supporting former hall gallery*

Plate 36   *Bishop's Palace, main staircase, upper flight*

were floored over at gallery level, creating six new bed-rooms [Cassan 1824, 364–5], with panelled joinery, coved ceiling cornices and wooden chimney-pieces with den-tilled friezes. They were linked to the W part of the house by truncating the room W of Ward's stairs and cutting a doorway into the central range, and were also given direct access to the garden by making a window on the former hall stairs into a doorway, with a pair of flush-panelled oak doors. New windows were required on E, lighting the porch room, and on E and W to the base of the former hall, causing the sills of those above to be raised. The range of offices to E was demolished. The Palace as Barrington left it is seen in Buckler's drawing of 1809 (Plate 22). It now seems astonishing that Carter could still write in 1803: 'the body of this palace has been totally changed to the style of Charles the Second's reign' [Carter 1803, 642].

Barrington may also have been responsible for the inserted E window of the chapel. It is of 15th-century date with three trefoil-headed lights under vertical tracery with normal and inverted cusping, large square label-stops and double ogee-moulded two-centred rear-arch, and bears a strong resemblance to the side windows of the Hungerford Chantry Chapel demolished in 1789 [Gough 1796, Plate LXXI].

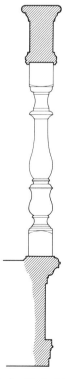

Scale: 1 inch = 1 foot

Fig 24   *Bishop's Palace, main staircase, section of balustrade*

Plate 37 *Bishop's Palace, Venetian window at S end of great drawing room (c 1784)*

The 19th and 20th centuries

In the early 19th century, perhaps for Bishop Burgess (1825–37), the three S-facing rooms of the central block were partially refitted, probably as family rooms for everyday use, with marble chimney-pieces, and a single-storey kitchen and scullery were added at the W end.

T H Wyatt, who designed the coach-house and lodge in 1843 for Bishop Denison, is presumed to have added features of medieval design to the tower, including a stone chimney with a fireplace on the third floor and false doors masking the ashlar with which Barrington had walled up Beauchamp's porch. These could have been among the improvements made by Bishop Hamilton (1854–69), who added a bell turret to the chapel [Reeve 1891, 189], and who commissioned Wyatt to make a number of alterations, mainly of a practical nature, in 1859 [WRO, Bishop's Admin, 28]. They included renewing the drainage, laying on piped water to the Palace and lodge etc, and curing the penetrating damp by replacing the external roughcast with Portland cement, and rising damp by forming the existing asphalt floors. He also suggested the insertion of many dormer windows to light the servants' attics, and proposed to cure the inconvenience of having no direct access from the garden to the dining room by building external stairs to its ante-room.

From 1885 to 1890 J Arthur Reeve restored Poore's undercroft for Bishop Wordsworth (1885–1911), rebuilding the windows, and adding detached shafts to some. He removed an inserted partition considered to be medieval, which divided off the two S bays of the undercroft [Reeve 1891, 182]. The side entrance to Beauchamp's porch, through the garderobe, also existed by 1890, with doorways of 15th-century design. When the W kitchen wing was demolished in 1931 Barrington's dining room chimney-piece was preserved and is now in the ground-floor room below the 13th-century chamber. Also in the 20th century the two remaining N windows of Beauchamp's parlour, blocked in 1782, have been reopened, a wicket inserted in the false doors of Beauchamp's porch, and two mullioned windows built in the N ground-floor wall of Ward's former hall. The plan has been somewhat simplified for school use.

The Coach-house and Stables

The Coach-house and Stables, associated with the Bishop's Palace, were built to designs by T H Wyatt in 1843 and demolished in 1965 (Fig 25). They were in Old English style with windows having lattice glazing, gables projecting on ogee kneelers, and a weathered chimney-breast and buttresses; the S elevation, facing the Palace, was of ashlar and the others of rubble, some stones with 12th-century carving appearing in the E end wall. The central coach-house was taller than its wings and projected forwards. It had a triple entrance of chamfered four-centred arches with a clock on a gable above, whose bell was housed in a square wooden turret on the N slope of the roof. This had louvred openings with pairs of pointed arches and a pyramidal lead roof with a wrought-iron weather-vane, and formerly stood on the Palace porch (Plate 27). In the E wing there were stables and loose-boxes with a loft over, and to W a cottage and harness rooms.

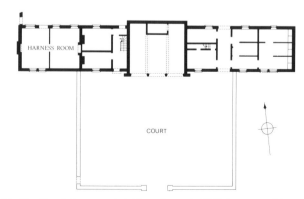

Fig 25 *Coach-house and stables, plan as in 1962 (not to scale)*

Plate 38 *Gatekeeper's Lodge, exterior from SW*

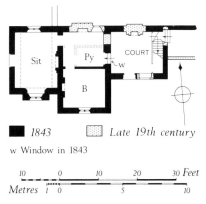

■ *1843*   ▦ *Late 19th century*

w Window in 1843

Fig 26 *Gatekeeper's Lodge*

The Gatekeeper's Lodge

The Gatekeeper's Lodge, N of the Palace, was built in 1843 to the design of T H Wyatt (Plate 38, Fig 26). It is consistent in style with his coach-house (above) and is mainly of ashlar, with brickwork in less conspicuous places. An old photograph shows the windows glazed with leaded octagonal panes [Lovibond, 277], complementing the rounded roof tiles, as shown in the specification drawings [WRO, Bishop's Admin, 28]. Originally the house had only a sitting room, bedroom and pantry, with a court to E, but *c* 1890 the court became the kitchen with a bedroom over it, and the former pantry and passage became a heated room.

Houses in Bishop's Walk

The Organist's House and Song School

The Organist's House and former Song School, now 5 The Close, was formerly a dean and chapter canonry, occupied in 1328 and 1332 by Nicholas Lambert and in 1334 described as near the Palace Gate [Chew 1963, 104]. The choristers were living here in 1455 [Acts, Bergh, 121], but had probably done so from a much earlier date since they had left a previous house (No. 54) by 1347, and in 1629 it was said that they held their 'convenient house with a school' for 'nearly 300 years' [Chancery Procs C2, Ch 1.S.99.22]. Extensive work was done to their buildings in the mid 15th century; Canon Crowton, a former custos of the choristers, gave £6 13s 4d in 1467 for 'repairing and rebuilding' their hall [Robertson 1969, 71] and in 1468 Canon Whitby was owed £23 16s 6½d which he had lent them twelve years earlier for building and repairs [*ibid*, 75–6].

In 1580 the deed appointing John Farrant the elder choirmaster and organist in reversion included an inventory of contents and fittings, which names the hall, buttery, larder, outer larder by the kitchen, kitchen boulting house, parlour, dormitory, Bishop's Chamber, and a chamber 'within' the latter [Everett 10, ff 3–8]. The Parliamentary Survey of 1649 noted a hall, a wainscoted parlour, a kitchen, a large room within the kitchen, a buttery, five chambers, a yard, a woodhouse and a brewhouse. The boys, reduced in numbers from fourteen to eight in 1580, continued to live here until *c* 1620, and from the 1630s the choirmaster has always been the Cathedral organist.

'Repairs' to the choristers' school occur repeatedly in chapter records, but those of 1678 were 'substantial'. The year after John Stevens was appointed organist, something more extensive is implied by a chapter resolution dated 7 August 1747, in which certain canons 'have power to receive proposals, determine upon a plan and agree with workmen for repairing the organist's house'. Until this time no clear distinction was made in documents between the choristers' school and the organist's house. Stevens' successor Robert Parry advertised the house to let 'ready furnished' in 1784 [*SJ*, 6 Sept 1784], but three years later chapter granted him £30 towards 'repairing and fitting up' his house [Acts 1741–96, 28 July 1787].

Joseph Corfe in 1799 was allowed to add a room to the back of his house, measuring 8ft by 20 ft, at his own expense, and two years later the clerk of works was requested to give him some wainscot then in the cloisters for the choristers' schoolroom. In 1878 chapter accepted Mr Adey's plan and estimate for repairs costing £356 5s.

Architectural history

Part of the early medieval canonry remains incorporated in the Song School (Fig 27). The E end, much of the S wall, and the N wall E of a change in alignment are built of rubble containing broken tiles and many carved and moulded stones deriving from Old Sarum; it probably

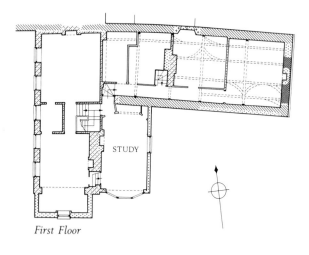

First Floor

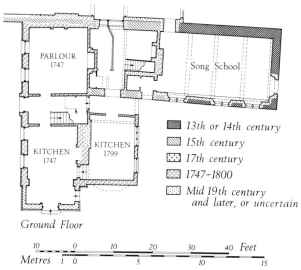

13th or 14th century

15th century

17th century

1747–1800

Mid 19th century
and later, or uncertain

Ground Floor

Fig 27 *No. 5*

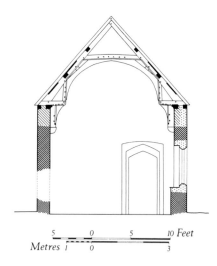

Fig 28 *No. 5, dated section through Song School, looking E, with reconstructed roof truss*

originated in the 13th or 14th century as the storeyed cross-range to an open hall.

In the 15th century the walls were raised, any upper storey being removed, in rubble containing herringbone tile courses (the heightening subsequently faced in brick on S). The building was then divided into single-storey rooms of two bays, as indicated by alternating chamfered and plain false hammer-beam trusses; the E and central rooms remain two-bay but the W room was truncated in the 18th century. The E room is longer and better finished than the others with hollow-chamfered hammer-beams painted red and more elaborate stop-chamfers to the purlins; elsewhere members are generally chamfered, the wall-plates hollow chamfered and the wall-posts have pyramidal stop-chamfers (Fig 28). A chamfered, square-headed stone window in the N wall, now mostly concealed, may survive from the earliest phase.

In the 17th century the building was floored over and a semi-attic storey created with a staircase near the middle, lit on N by a chamfered two-light stone window (now blocked). The present chimney appears to be of 18th-century date and the partitioning of the upper storey is of the late 18th century, perhaps the 'fitting up' of 1787.

The W range was built *c* 1747 as a two-storey residence for the organist, possibly incorporating older work as the N chimney corresponds only approximately with its fire-places. The main elevation (Plate 39) is of brick, with stone used for the eaves modillions and the entrance with its triple key etc. Originally the N room was the parlour and the S the kitchen, the former being fitted with original fielded panelling, wooden cornice and window-seats, and a square-headed recess on E. The kitchen chimney was reversed *c* 1799 when a new kitchen was built by Corfe (to rather larger dimensions than those stipulated by chap-ter); Corfe's addition is of brick in English bond and employs a second-hand ovolo-moulded wood-mullioned window. In the mid 19th century a study was added above the kitchen in stretcher-bond brickwork with a sashed bay-window.

The work performed by Adey *c* 1878 probably included minor alterations to the range of 1747, such as the extension to S and the insertion of plate-glass windows, and also the remodelling of the Song School with cham-fered stone windows and doorways under segmental relieving-arches to suggest its medieval origins, and a partial refacing. At this time or a little later, the E range became a self-contained dwelling, though connected with the organist's at first-floor level. Some early 17th-century oak wainscot frames the chimney recess of the organist's S bedroom; it is possibly part of the consignment intended for the schoolroom in 1801.

Plate 39   *No. 5 from W*

Chapter Office and Deanery

The Chapter Office and Deanery, 6 and 7 The Close respectively, were formed in the 19th century from a 17th-century house (Fig 29). They stand on the site of a canonry belonging to the dean and chapter called Simonsbury Place, named after John Simonsburgh (who was senior canon in 1449 and died in 1454), presumably because he was the last canon to occupy it for any length of time, other residents being noted until 1476; the name remained in use until the late 18th century. The house had been charged with the obits of Robert Strode (alive *c* 1284) and John Langbergh, occupant in 1332 and 1342, who died in 1349. A dilapidations survey of 1455 describes a house with a masonry chapel on the ground floor, entered through a porch with a study over it, a timber-framed long chamber above the parlour, a 'high house' on S, and a kitchen, cellar and stable [Chapter Acts, Bergh 1447–57, 121].

During two centuries of neglect, from the mid 15th to the mid 17th century, the large garden extending to the Close Wall was reappointed, and from 1521 until 1637 the house was a stable for No. 21; in the Parliamentary Survey of 1649 there was a stable for No. 17 to N of the gatehouse and a workshop and timber yard for the Cathedral to S of it.

The present Deanery was built before 1660 (Fig 30); in that year the dean and chapter granted Francis Sambrook a lease in consideration that he had 'lately erected' it at his own expense of about £400, including 'securing' its garden, and he was also granted 'the old piece of building...lying on the south end thereof, being part of the...buildings called Symesbury Place' [Leases, 1636–60, ff 120v–121v]. The appearance of the house has been altered, chiefly by the insertion of sash windows (Plate 40), but the English-bond brickwork with plain quoins, ogee-moulded string course and shaped eaves modillions are original features, also the N chimney with its rusticated square shafts. The upper storey of the rear wall may originally have been timber framed.

The alterations within have been more drastic and the great variety of joinery on the two main floors, much of it 18th-century, suggests repeated changes. A timber-framed dormer on E housed the original upper flight of stairs, showing that the present main staircase is approximately on its original site, and no doubt the large S chimney belonged to the kitchen. A stone chimney-piece with a chamfered Tudor-arched head in the dining room and some miscellaneous oak panelling reset in the S bedroom and elsewhere date from the mid 17th century. The attic rooms have original (blocked) fireplaces and retain one

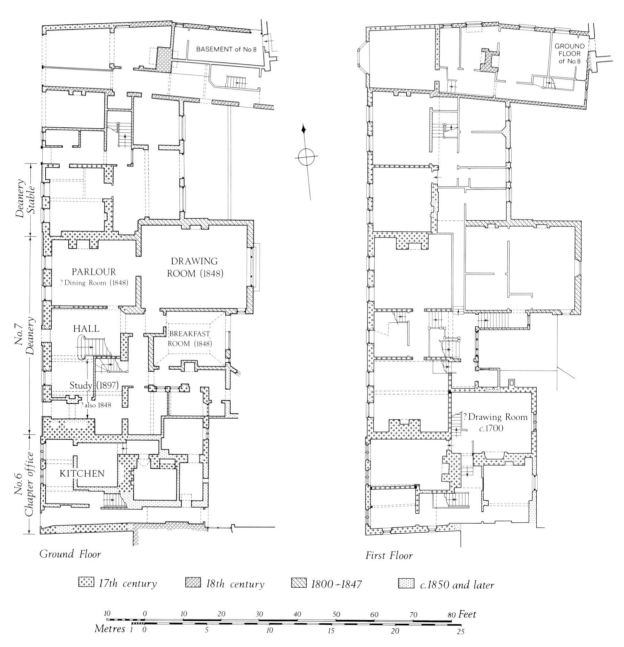

Fig 29 Nos 6 and 7

Plate 40   *No. 7 from SW, with former stables on left*

planked door and a blocked window adjoining the N chimney, with hollow-chamfered stone architrave.

Sambrook rebuilt No. 6 *c* 1661 probably as domestic offices with the principal rooms on the first floor (Fig 30); his lease of 1660 included a covenant to build a new Cathedral 'work-house' elsewhere within six months, giving him vacant possession of the site. The architectural idiosyncracies of windows with hollow-chamfered mullions and rusticated relieving-arches, and steep gables with moulded copings (Plate 41) are closely paralleled at No. 47 Winchester Street [RCHM 1980, Plate 70], built within two years of 1671. There was probably a staircase in the SE corner of the kitchen leading to a first-floor chamber, formerly with two small closets in the SW corner; although structurally these seem to be early insertions, they may be original features and justify the irregular windows of the main elevation. An inner room to E is connected to the same chamber by an original doorway, and a large stone chimney-piece with pulvination and inset central tablet (with later papier mâché ornament) suggests that it was used as a drawing room in the early 18th century. The attic storey retains its original arrangement of three rooms.

W B Brodie, who obtained a back-dated lease in 1817, probably fitted the sash windows and an elegant doorway to the front of No. 7 and added a grand drawing room on E in brick with a slate roof. This dates from *c* 1840. He went bankrupt in 1847, his furniture was sold in 1848 [*SJ*, 8 Jan 1848] and the building was split up. No. 6 became the Diocesan Registry in 1855 and new rooms were added to it on SE, the present entrance and staircase with oak

handrail were built, the ground floor was gutted and a strong-room constructed with a brick vault.

In 1858 F Macdonald requested chapter's agreement to make No. 7 the Probate Registry Office, which it remained

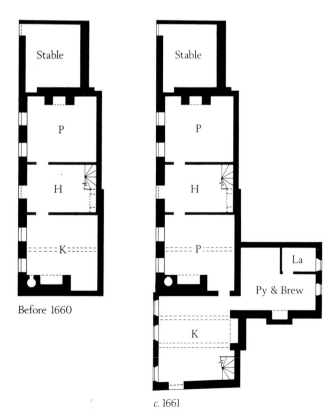

Fig 30   *Nos 6 and 7, reconstructed plans*

Plate 41   *No. 6 from SW*

for at least twenty years [OS 1880]. By 1897 it was again a house, when the S window was made into a door for a Mr Purvis; in 1906 it proved difficult to let, so £513 were allowed for alterations, probably to Crickmay's designs; the main staircase is of this date. In 1922 it became the Deanery.

For the former stables to N, see below.

7A, 7B and 8A The Close

7A, 7B and 8A The Close, former stables etc in Bishop's Walk, are of brick, partly rendered and partly tile hung, of two storeys with tiled roofs. They were built as stables and coach-houses on the ground floor and living accommodation above perhaps mainly for grooms or other servants.

The two bays of building to N of No. 7 (Plate 42, Fig 29) are of 17th-century origin and are named in leases of the 17th and 18th centuries as that house's stables; their appearance is now of the 19th century.

The remainder was the subject of chapter leases from 1530 onwards, described as stables and a plot of land to E; from the early 17th to the mid 19th century it was normally granted to the tenant of No. 9 (who also held No. 8), providing his stabling and coach-house although subletting also occurred. The W build flanking the street is of 17th-century origin and retains its roof, with queen-struts and butt purlins, the wall-plates and purlins projecting with ogee ends at the gable; below, the walls are of brick of various periods and may replace timber-framing. The E build was added after 1880, replacing a projection of different shape [OS 1880].

Plate 42   *Nos 5–9 from W*

The E–W range was added in two phases during the 18th century, that to E the earlier, its upper storey built as an extension to No. 8 and having fittings of the late 17th and mid 18th century, many of them reset.

The buildings have been extended and greatly altered in the 19th and 20th centuries and are now arranged as three dwellings.

8 and 9 The Close

8 and **9** The Close are two houses at the N corner of Bishop's Walk. They originated as the two parts of one house, slightly different in date; from *c* 1700 until the late 19th century the leases ignored the S house, which was sublet by the tenant of No. 9.

A medieval house on the site, of which only some walling at cellar level survives, was charged with the obit of Richard Rupton, vicar, who died *c* 1298. Later occupants included Simon of Kempsey (1328, 1332) and William Notty (1465), vicars, Richard Dunstable, chantry

priest (1530s) and John Ryce, gent, in 1597. The old house, which belonged to the vicars, was noted in the Parliamentary Survey in 1649 but had been replaced by 1671 when a survey of their property described it as 'new built'.

Almost certainly the new house was built by John Holt, who was in possession at the Restoration and died in 1669, when he was succeeded by Richard Holt. In 1675 John Wyndham, the owner of estates at Norrington, renewed a lease then only three years old, suggesting that he add the S wing. Wyndham assigned his lease to Thomas Jervoise in 1696 and in 1701 chapter's demand that the trees in front of Jervoise's and Mr Gauntlett's houses be lopped suggests that it was already divided into two houses as now. Jervoise probably blocked the E windows of No. 8 almost immediately after taking possession, thereby substantially reducing his liability for window tax, which was introduced in the same year.

In the 19th century, No. 9 was adopted as the first

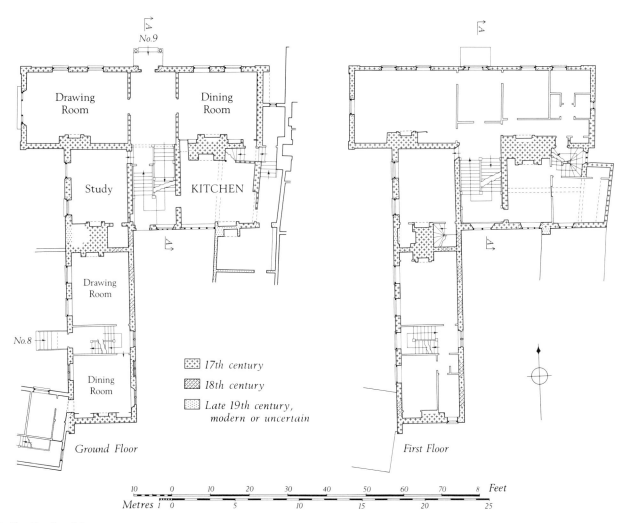

17th century

18th century

Late 19th century, modern or uncertain

Ground Floor

First Floor

Fig 31 *Nos 8 and 9*

home of the Diocesan Training College for Schoolmistresses, which opened in 1841 and remained there until
1845 when the building reverted to being a private house
for T W Gilbert. No. 8 had been 'fitted up for the business
of the Diocesan Societies' in 1841 [*SJ*, 11 Oct 1841] and
later for some decades was the Depository of the Society
for the Propagation of Christian Knowledge.

The 17th-century house

The original build of the house may have comprised only
the drawing room, dining room and kitchen of No. 9 (Fig
31), because the study and its upper chamber are on
different floor levels, with awkwardly contrived doorways,
and their attic is not connected with that to N. The S
build, now No. 8, represents a further phase, with a
straight joint coinciding with a small change in the roof
pitch at the chimney.

In the primary build, the principal rooms on N and W
were raised above cellars and the chamber over the dining
room partly projects above a former passage to E on
multiple corbelling, a brick equivalent of jettying. The
kitchen and its upper chamber are in a lower build with
their floors at mezzanine levels; the first floor at the front
range was probably arranged as two apartments each
consisting of a chamber and a closet (Fig 32).

The hipped roof is lit by ogee-moulded dormer
windows and originally the W eaves cornice with ogee-

Plate 43   *No. 9 from NW*

shaped modillions ending in pyramidal drops continued
on the main elevation (Plate 43). The main staircase is the
principal original fitting (Plate 44, Fig 33), others being
the stout chamfered door-frames in the attics and kitchen
chamber, and an overmantel and moulded oak wainscot
now in the kitchen chamber (Plate 45). A door in the attic
over the study has three softwood planks meeting at ogee-
and V-mouldings.

In the large S extension (No. 8), the basement appears
above ground because of a fall in level at the back of No. 9.
The taller, and therefore the principal storey, is the first
floor and this may have been a single room originally,
perhaps a gallery, with five windows on each side (Plate 46,
Fig 32), all but one of the E ones now blocked. The raised
ground floor was probably always more than one room,
perhaps a private apartment of ante-chamber and bedroom, and the 'basement' floor no doubt provided additional household offices. Externally there are minor
structural differences between the N and S builds but the
eaves cornice is continuous and they both employ chamfered or hollow-chamfered stone-mullioned windows with
recessed frontal rebates. Some reason, perhaps connected
with the symmetry of the new work on a restricted site,
has led to the main elevation being continued slightly
beyond the S gable as a screen wall. Bolection-moulded
oak joinery at No. 9, in the dining room (Plate 47) and the
room above the study, is probably evidence that Wyndham
refitted the house generally *c* 1675.

Later history of the two houses

To convert the S extension into a separate house the
central window of the raised ground floor was made into a
doorway, and a staircase, continuous from basement to
attics, installed between partitions. Bolection-moulded
oak wainscot in the drawing room and scratch-moulded

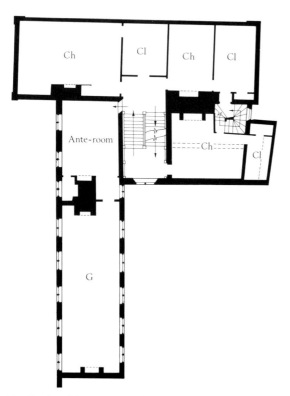

Fig 32   *Nos 8 and 9, reconstructed plans as in* c *1680*

joinery in the dining room were probably placed in position at this time, masking the blocked E windows. The oak staircase (Fig 34) has ball finials and acorn pendants. Other new joinery includes heavy door-frames with bead-moulded edges, and on the first floor two-panel doors with ogee-moulded edges; the attic doors are of pine planks with ogee-moulded lapping edges and wooden latches. Subsequently the house has been extended into the stables to S and some windows converted to sashes.

At No. 9 a staircase to the S attic was built adjoining the chimney *c* 1700. Later improvements for Dr William Hancock (*c* 1746–98), who succeeded Thomas Lord Wyndham of Finglass, included the installation in about 1770 of a rococo ceiling in the dining room, with bearded heads

Plate 44   *No. 9, staircase from entrance hall*

Plate 45   *No. 9, overmantel in kitchen chamber*

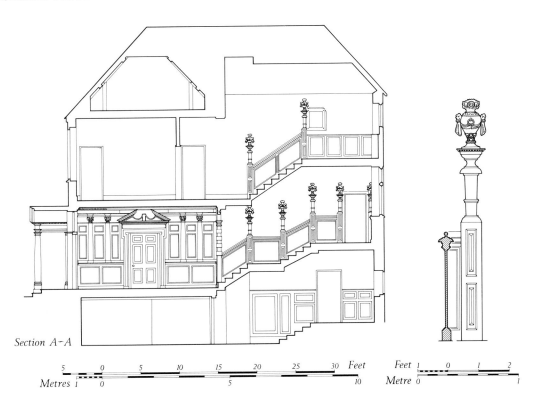

Section A–A

5   0   5   10   15   20   25   30 *Feet*   *Feet* 1   0   1   2

Metres 1   0   5   10   *Metre* 0   1

Fig 33   *No. 9, section with detail of staircase*

Plate 46   *No. 8 from W, showing altered fenestration on upper floor*

Plate 47   *No. 9, chimney-piece in dining room*

Scale: 1 inch = 1 foot

Fig 34   *No. 8, staircase, detail of balustrade*

wearing caps of foliage (Plate 48). He also introduced elegant joinery with fielded and beaded panels, the single and triple sash windows, and built the portico (Plate 43).

Possibly in this period, small plaster panels were transformed to the walls of the staircase at No. 9, with floral arabesques above roundels containing heraldic crests: in one a chained porcupine, and in the other a wyvern. They are of early 17th-century appearance and possibly originated in the King's House, the dwelling of Eleanor Sadler, born St Barbe (wyvern) and cousin to Frances Walsingham who married Sir Philip Sidney (porcupine). Eleanor Sadler's interest in her family genealogy and heraldry is attested by her own memorial in the Cathedral.

A quantity of joinery now in No. 9 is evidently that removed from the Cathedral by Edmund Lush, its surveyor, in 1777. Some panels in the kitchen, together with twelve in the entrance vestibule, retain their pilasters and cornice (Plate 49), bear the names of prebends and were part of the stalls made in 1671 by Alexander Fort to Wren's design [Eltringham 1958]; those in the hall were cleaned and repainted in 1969. The eighteen carved softwood finials on the oak staircase may have the same origin and perhaps survive from the vases and '31 Rich flower doluges' which Fort contracted to carve in deal (Plate 50);

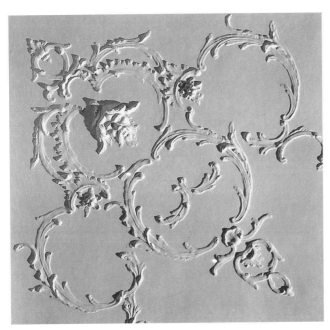

Plate 48 *No. 9, detail of ceiling in dining room*

Plate 49 *No. 9, panelling from Cathedral choir-stalls (1671–2)*

Plate 50 *No. 9, finial, perhaps from Cathedral choir-stalls (1671–2)*

some large oak door-cases to the drawing room and dining room with pulvinated friezes and open pediments also evidently come from elsewhere, possibly the openings in the stone screens which divided the E crossing in the Cathedral from the NE and SE transepts. A description of unknown origin says the panelling was 'painted white, with the panels golden, and groups of garlands or roses and other flowers intertwined round the tops of the stalls; each shall hath the name of its owner in gilt letters or blue writ on it' [*VCH* 1956, 200]. A Mr Fisher noted this panelling *c* 1850 and commented 'in the Singing School [No. 5] was a panel that showed the colouring. I believe the tracery and bottom panel were in imitation of Ven. marble, the top panel deep blue with gold letters and ogee moulding gilded?' [Everett B, 13].

Houses in North Walk

10 The Close

10 The Close is a compact house mainly of 14th-century date and such medieval records as there are show it as a

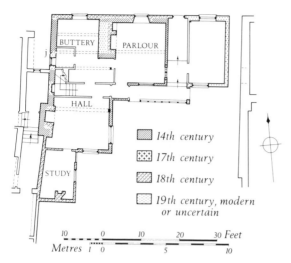

14th century

17th century

18th century

19th century, modern
or uncertain

Fig 35   No. 10

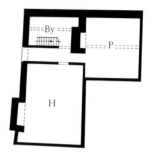

Fig 36   No. 10, reconstructed plan, as built

vicar's dwelling by 1320. By the middle of the 17th century at the latest it belonged to the vicars choral and was the allotted residence of one of their members, who commonly leased it to lay tenants. In 1649 it was listed with a hall, parlour, closet, buttery and four chambers. Richard Trickey, vicar, whose house it was in 1765, was allowed to occupy another for four years on condition that he spent £60 on repairs in two years' time.

The medieval house

The earliest traces of building that can be identified date from the first half of the 14th century, but a change of alignment and building materials in the W wall may be the result of incorporating yet earlier fabric. The house was built partly of rubble and partly of timber-framing, now tile-hung, with the hall range aligned at right angles to the street and entered from W through a stone doorway, of which one chamfered jamb remains (Fig 35, j); ceiling beams on either side probably originated as the heads of partitions forming a screens passage and the position of one E door-post is preserved (Fig 35).

The hall was originally open to the roof, but the chimney is an original feature with the moulded stone base to a former octagonal shaft at eaves level (Figs 36, 37), and a fireback of herringbone tilework and flint. The wall opposite retains a fragment of painted plaster: the ashlaring and curved stalks maroon and the flowerheads scarlet (Plate 51, Fig 38). A wall-plate on E with a stop-splayed scarf-joint probably remains from the 14th-century roof.

In the two-storey N range the buttery has a chamfered ceiling beam and probably contained the staircase. The room over the parlour, presumably the best chamber, was heated by a fireplace with hollow-chamfered stone jambs and broach-stops, probably 15th-century, which super-

sedes a larger one on the same site also with a chamfered timber lintel. The timber-framing of the E wall has been extensively rebuilt, but its plinth, of flint and stone rubble with stone quoins, is medieval.

Later development

In the 16th century an attic floor was inserted over the hall upon a moulded beam support on an inserted post and lit by a window on S with mullion and jambs of oviform section (Fig 39), and a plank-and-muntin partition there probably divides two of the four chambers noted in 1649. In the parlour an ovolo-moulded timber window is witness to early 17th-century repairs.

Trickey's repairs of 1767–8 probably included the general remodelling of the N range, refacing it in brick and raising the roof. The present approach from E dates from this period together with the staircase which is continuous to the attics. The house was refitted generally with fielded panelled joinery, the two first-floor rooms to N receiving the best fittings with sash windows, plaster cornices and wooden chimney-pieces, that to E the more elaborate with ears, pulvination and carved mouldings. He perhaps assembled the miscellaneous 17th-century joinery including panels chip-carved with lunettes in the truncated medieval hall at the same time. Trickey retained the house until his death in 1802, and probably added the single-storey study at the S end, built partly of brick in

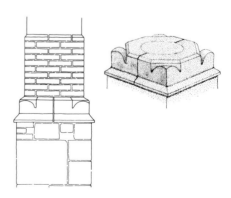

Fig 37   No. 10, hall chimney, details

Plate 51   *No. 10, painted decoration in hall*

Fig 38   *No. 10, reconstruction of painted decoration in hall*

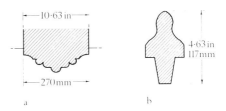

Fig 39   *No. 10, sections of*
a. beam in hall
b. mullion of S window in chamber over hall

irregular bond and partly of tile-hung framing; its cornice and joinery are similar to those elsewhere in the house.

The approach to the entrance was enclosed in a single-storey addition in the 19th century, incorporating an unheated room. The house was extensively repaired in 1978, when the 16th- and 17th-century windows came to light and the medieval painting and fireplaces were revealed.

11 The Close

11 The Close was formerly a house but is now part of Bishop Wordsworth's School. House and garden were amalgamated from four distinct tenements into one comparatively large property between 1547 and 1660. The two W tenements must have been small and were combined probably in the 1580s by Joan Michell who held them both. One belonged to the dean and chapter and had been occupied from the late 15th century until *c* 1548 by the priests serving Bishop Beauchamp's chantry, and thereafter by lay people; the other belonged to the vicars choral. More than half the site of the present buildings and courtyard was formerly a vicars' orchard, 51 ft wide by 138 ft, which was added by Thomas Chafyn between 1649 and 1660. The garden is L-shaped, extending on S of Nos

12–14 to the Close Wall, and the major part of it had formed the canonical garden of No. 7 until after 1547. There are two main periods of construction in the present house, the third quarter of the 17th and the middle of the 18th century, which first enlarged, and then replaced, an older house.

The 17th century

The older range is L-shaped and was built by Thomas Chafyn, who had probably become the tenant only shortly before or in 1649. It was described as 'new' in 1671 and since it stands partly on the site of the vicars' orchard, is not earlier then *c* 1650. But in 1680 a vicars' lease to Chafyn's wife and daughter, Lady Chafyn and Lady Markes (Lady was their Christian name), both widows, refers both to the new buildings and to 'the antient house' on the W part of the site in which they dwell [Vicars' Leases, 1673–1717, 9 Dec 1680]. This suggests that the principal range stood to NW of the new one, with its entrance on to the street, and there are remains of its flint and brick rubble walls with blocked windows in the W wall of the 18th-century house (Fig 40); a quoin stone at the SW corner is inscribed '(16)16H'. In 1649 this house comprised a hall, a wainscoted parlour, a passage room,

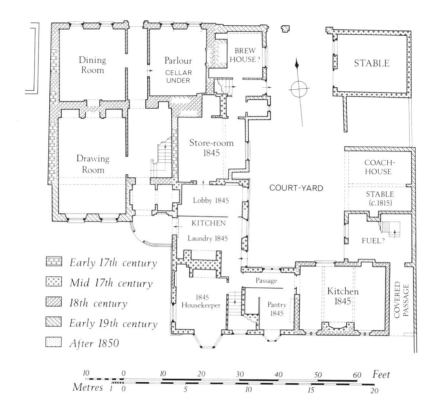

Early 17th century

Mid 17th century

18th century

Early 19th century

After 1850

Fig 40   No. 11

buttery, kitchen and larder, four upper chambers, two garrets and an outhouse.

Chafyn's wing was built at the back to provide new kitchens etc. It is constructed in English-bond brick with a bullnosed plinth and the main elevation to W originally had pairs of casement windows with gauged flat arches, terminating at each end in heavy chamfered quoins banded with plain brickwork; towards the court there are segmental-headed windows, one retaining its wooden mullion with internal ovolo-moulding, and a platband. One gable to S remains, with a blocked segmental-headed window, and the attics are now lit by dormers.

The original room arrangement and the staircase continuous to the attics survive; on the first floor the three rooms are lined with contemporary grooved and moulded oak wainscot, with simple classical cornices of wood (plaster above the kitchen). A chamfered door-frame with ogee stops and a partition on E of the staircase, of moulded plank-and-muntin construction, typify the joinery's stout character.

Thomas Chafyn also built the W garden wall in Flemish-bond brick, with a chamfered plinth and moulded stone coping, described as 'new' in 1660 [D and C Leases, 1636–60, f 137]. Of similar date is the small stable also upon the site of the vicars' orchard. It is gabled, of brick in irregular English and Flemish bond, with an oval light to

the hayloft, and roof with clasped purlins, straight wind-braces, and queen-struts. It now contains 18th-century elm stalls.

The 18th and 19th centuries

Early in the 18th century Chafyn's range was extended to E, perhaps as brewhouse and wash-house with staff bed-rooms above, but it was entirely altered in the late 19th century.

Thomas Chafyn Markes died in 1727 and his widow Frances in 1753. The principal part of the house was rebuilt, probably in the 1750s by their successor, Henry Edwards, and replaces the previous house of which only the W wall remains. The new build is of two storeys with attics although the high parapet gives the appearance of three. The main elevation (Plate 52) is principally in header bond with single courses of black-stained bricks above each platband and the side walls are faced with mathematical tiles in header and stretcher bond (now partly replaced with hung-tiles), the platbands simulated by wooden fasciae. Some fielded panelled joinery remains within, and plaster ceiling cornices on the first floor.

William Boucher, the chapter clerk, occupied the house from 1813 until his death in 1836 and made considerable alterations to the Edwards' addition. He boldly enlarged their S room by pushing out the S wall and raising the ceiling, creating a reception room of some grandeur with double doors and a ceiling frieze in which are medallions of lyres with greyhounds sejant, his crest (Plate 53). The door-case has reeded pilasters and the chimney-piece Egyptian half-columns, supporting entablatures with ribbands, garlands and other neo-classical motifs. He fitted the main entrance with an elegant door-case, renewed the stairs, and introduced marble chimney-pieces and floral and reeded ceiling cornices. His staircase reached only to the first floor and the 18th-century attics were now entered via the S stairs and a roof passage added above Chafyn's kitchens. His creation of the drawing room, and of the NW bedroom as the best one, resulted in suppressing the rooms above them and reconstructing parts of the roof. The drawing room extension and new gate piers are in white brick; a first-floor w.c. projecting into the court and other minor works are mathematical tiled.

Plate 53   *No. 11, drawing room looking N*

Plate 52   *No. 11 from NE*

In 1814 Boucher was allowed by the vicars to rebuild his E boundary wall abutting their hall, which in 1817 was said to be in a straighter alignment than formerly, and this dates his construction of the stable and coach-house, in red brick with leaded casements.

In 1843 the leases were renewed by the Diocesan Training College for Schoolmistresses, which moved here from No. 9 and remained until 1850. The names of rooms in the vicars' part of the house were identified in a lease of 1845 and are marked on Fig 40. Subsequently, the house was occupied by Thomas Davis. At his death it was advertised as 'recently fitted up by Mr Davis, without the least regard to expense' [*SJ*, 19 Aug 1854], and to him may be attributed the 'Tudorisation' of the garden elevations: a timber bay-window of two storeys, geometrical glazing patterns here and elsewhere, and bargeboards. He also rebuilt the S garden wall, which contains stones bearing his initials and the date 1853.

The restoration of the kitchen on S as a superior room (billiards?) with stone mullioned and transomed windows and an early 17th-century moulded stone chimney-piece was made late in the century, perhaps as one of the 'alterations' proposed by E F Pye-Smith in 1894. Since 1947 the house has been occupied by Bishop Wordsworth's School and their new buildings are detached. An account of the house's history has been edited from the research of C R Everett by D H Robertson [*WAM* LII, 307–17].

12 and 13 The Close

12 and 13 The Close, the Vicars' Hall, originated as a medieval canonry, and it is a good example of one that was rebuilt and extended several times within about a century and a half of the foundation of the Close. The only named owner was William de Chadleshunt (archdeacon of Wiltshire in 1304) whose obit was established here in 1319. A century later the house had become the Vicars' Hall; the vicars choral received their charter of incorporation in 1409 [*VCH* 1956, 179] and a reference to their common hall occurs that year, but chapter's grants of this house to newly appointed canons in 1409 and 1412, to

Plate 54   *Nos 12 and 13, Vicars' Hall, from SW*

hold until another house fell vacant, suggest a transitional period in the change of ownership. The charter allowed vicars, who had previously lived in separate houses, to dwell together at the hall and in 1442 chapter passed a statute compelling the vicars of non-resident canons to do so. However, the number of vicars contracted until there were only six, and they ceased to use it as a common residence *c* 1620 [*ibid*, 191]. Under pressure from chapter in 1639 to effect repairs they leased it out, while reserving their muniment room and the occasional use of their hall. In 1649/50 it was described as a mansion house called the Common Hall with the Long House and other buildings, consisting of a hall, a parlour, a large cellar, a kitchen, a larder, six chambers, a coalhouse, stable, woodhouse, and a muniment room over the larder at the N end of the kitchen. The Parliamentary commissioners annulled the lease in 1650 and sold the property to John Dove of Ivychurch, but the vicars reclaimed it at the Restoration and divided it into two houses, granting leases of both to lay people. Until this period the grounds extended to the Close Wall on E, including the site of No. 14, and on W included part of No. 11.

No. 12 has continued to be known as the Vicars' Hall. In 1679 the vicars adopted it as one of their members' houses, it 'being now much better than any of our present dwelling houses'; they exchanged it with Francis Hill for another at No. 19 [Vicars' petn, Acts 1675–96, 51]. From 1797 to 1800 Edmund Benson spent £160 on improvements, but in 1814 he had permission to demolish a 'building adjoining the house, called the Common Hall' [Everett A, 37]; he and his successor leased the house to the Miss Noyes School for boys. From 1707 until *c* 1870 a stable and coach-house stood to NW of the house, leased for many years to the Harrises at Malmesbury House.

No. 13 was held by lay people, who were from 1699 until 1820 members of the Goldwyer family. The property continued in possession of the vicars until 1934, after which it reverted to chapter [*VCH* 1956, 206].

The medieval house until the 17th century

Nothing of the presumed original house of *c* 1220 can now be identified. The present buildings surround a small courtyard, but this arrangement has been arrived at over successive phases. The oldest part of the house is the W range which, together with its SE extension, dates probably from the late 13th century (Plate 54), and was the chamber block to the vanished hall further W; the small SE extension may have housed a chapel. On the ground floor the arrangements have been lost, although a post supporting a chamfered plate towards the N end of the main room ['Cellar', Vicars Lease Book 1699] may be the remains of an original partition, perhaps between buttery and pantry; one E window in the pantry has a shouldered

Plate 55 *No. 12, crown-post in W range*

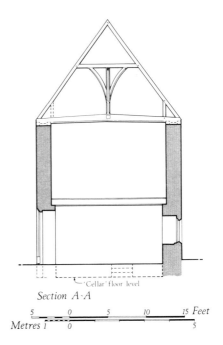

Section A-A

Fig 41 *No. 12, W range*

Plate 56   *No. 12, E window in W range*

lintel, perhaps of 13th-century date. The small room at the N end is also original and is floored at a higher level, reflecting the slope of the site: possibly it was a porter's lodge.

On the first floor a symmetrical pair of apartments, each with a larger chamber entered from external stairs and a smaller one, is suggested by the positions of the fireplaces, windows, partitions and roof-trusses. Above the tie-beams, three crown-posts and a mutilated collar purlin are visible in the attics, which are ceiled at collar level. The S and central partitions remain below tie-beam level but there is no trace of them above, and possibly the roof was boxed in from the start by a ceiling suspended from longitudinal members whose mortices remain in the face of the tie-beams (Plate 55, Fig 41). The asymmetrical placing of the larger side windows within their rooms and of one small light may reveal the position of the original

latrines. One E window of two lights has its jambs and sill restored (Plates 56, 57, Fig 42a); another, larger window, placed centrally in the S gable, is fragmentary (Fig 42b). The S apartment was the larger of the two; the extra E room was possibly a chapel (above Kitchen B, Fig 43) and its roof was originally lower.

In the 14th century the house was greatly extended (Fig 44). A hall was built on W, which no doubt replaced the earlier one on the same site. The main entrance (Plate 58) and part of one window-jamb remain (Fig 45, a and b, Fig 43). The hall was approached by a lean-to passage with a roof supported on an ogee-moulded and hollow-chamfered wall-plate and measured approximately 23 ft wide by 29 ft 6 ins internally. (The width was established by excavation in 1985, and the length by the fact that, at the hall's demolition in 1814, the tenant to W at once applied to rebuild and straighten his boundary wall.) The E gable of the hall blocked the windows of the middle chambers in the older build. A triple doorway, with steep four-centred arches which originally had hoodmoulds (Plate 59), formed a decorative feature at the end of the hall and led into what were probably a parlour on S and service rooms on N with a central passage to a small courtyard across which there was a single-storey kitchen (Kitchen A, Fig 43).

Later in the century, in the SE angle of the court, a chamber was added S of the kitchen, approached by a stone doorway with a two-centred arch now leading to a (later) staircase. The chamber roof, of which the central truss has principals with curved feet, is supported on W by stone corbels projecting from the 'chapel' wall and is framed against the end wall of kitchen A (Plate 60); the chamber is lit from E by another window with shouldered lintel. At about the same time, the fireplace in the S outer chamber of the original W range was rebuilt, with a roll-moulded and coved cornice.

No doubt the acquisition of the house by the vicars led to further changes. They probably added the chimney-piece in the parlour, which retains traces of red paint on its carved foliage and mouldings (Plate 61, Fig 46), and perhaps built the larder to N at this time (drawing room, No. 13) although it has no datable features. The vicars in residence probably took a chamber each, although this allocation is not recorded before 1559 [Frere 1910, III, 33].

The chamber above kitchen A was added in the 16th century in timber-framing, lightly jettied on E, with a clasped-purlin roof with diminished principals and cambered collars. The vicars' muniment room over the larder was built or rebuilt *c* 1605, when W Nowell bequeathed 3s 4d for its 'reparation' [Everett C (i), f 20v]; the thicker walls to N and E may be 14th century but the timber-framing on brick sleeper walls of the whole S wall must be 17th century, together with the clasped-purlin roof lit by

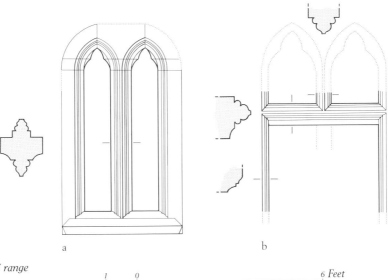

Fig 42   No. 12, windows in W range
a. E wall
b. S wall (mouldings at twice main scale)

1   0   6 Feet

1   0   1 Metre

Plate 57   *Nos 12 and 13, Vicars' Hall, aerial view from SE. Traffic Technology Limited, Skyscan Balloon System*

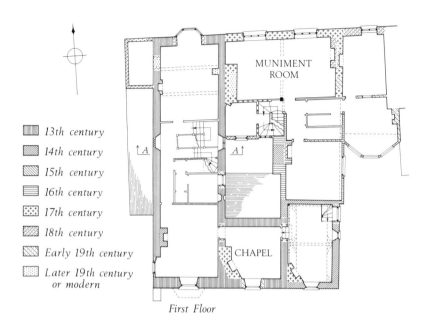

13th century
14th century
15th century
16th century
17th century
18th century
Early 19th century
Later 19th century
  or modern

MUNIMENT
ROOM

A↑   A↑

CHAPEL

First Floor

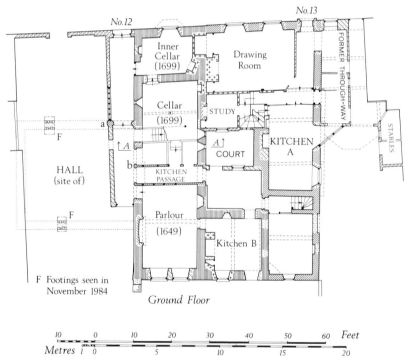

No.12   No.13

Inner
Cellar
(1699)   Drawing
                Room

Cellar
(1699)   STUDY

F   ↑A   A↑
              COURT   KITCHEN
HALL   b⊢   A
(site of)   KITCHEN
             PASSAGE

F

             Parlour
             (1649)   Kitchen B

F Footings seen in
   November 1984   *Ground Floor*

FORMER THROUGH-WAY

STABLES

10   0   10   20   30   40   50   60 *Feet*
Metres 1 0   5   10   15   20

Fig 43 *Nos 12 and 13, Vicars' Hall*

dormer windows (Plate 62) and the transomed timber windows of the muniment room (Fig 47). The timber-framed staircase projecting into the court dates from the same period.

Later history of No. 12 The Close

The separation of No. 12 as a small house some time in the 1660s must have included the formation of a kitchen (B)

(Fig 43) to E of the medieval parlour and the addition of fireplaces across the corners of rooms. Later, in the 18th century, the chamber roof (above kitchen B) was raised, in pine with a haunched king-post truss, and the joinery renewed generally.

At the N end of the W range, the addition of a bay-window above the street and reconstruction of the 14th-century hall passage in brick with a room con-

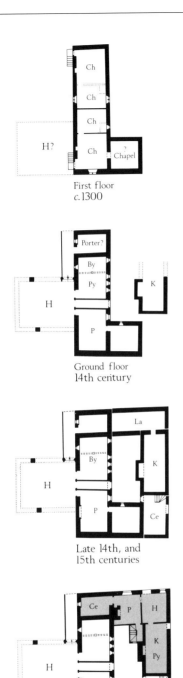

First floor
c.1300

Ground floor
14th century

Late 14th, and
15th centuries

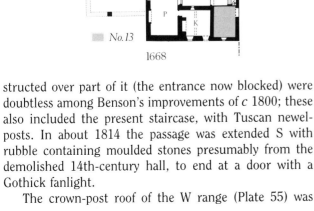

No. 13

1668

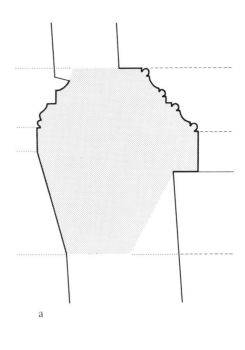

a

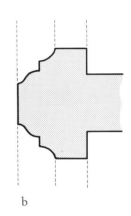

b

Scale: 1 inch = 1 foot

Fig 45 *No. 12, screens passage, doorway sections*
a. hall doorway and window-jamb
b. service doorway

Fig 44 *Nos 12 and 13, Vicars' Hall, reconstructed plans*

structed over part of it (the entrance now blocked) were doubtless among Benson's improvements of *c* 1800; these also included the present staircase, with Tuscan newel-posts. In about 1814 the passage was extended S with rubble containing moulded stones presumably from the demolished 14th-century hall, to end at a door with a Gothick fanlight.

The crown-post roof of the W range (Plate 55) was probably made into attics earlier but their present charac-ter, with arched doorways partly made from old timber, a large oriel window etc, is attributable to Stanley Baker, the last vicar resident in the house. He is reputed to have introduced a number of old fittings *c* 1910, including 17th-century wainscot (perhaps that in the parlour) and a late medieval traceried timber window installed in the entrance passage.

Plate 58   *No. 12, hall doorway and screens passage looking S*

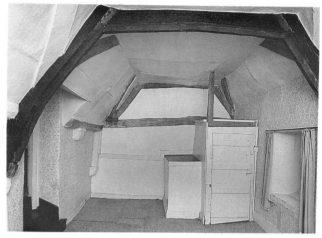

Plate 60   *No. 12, SE chamber looking N*

Plate 61   *No. 12, detail of parlour chimney-piece*

Plate 59   *No. 12, service doorways in screens passage*

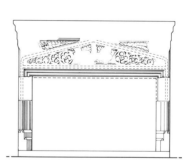

Fig 46   *No. 12, chimney-piece in parlour*

No. 13 The Close

This house was originally L-shaped and was remodelled by 1668 incorporating the vicars' kitchen and larder (Fig 44). The muniment room upstairs was divided into two bed-rooms and the kitchen chimney was enlarged in brick and rubble to support a hearth for the upper chamber there. The present stout front door, with bolection-moulded panels and strap-hinges with fleur-de-lis terminals, is probably of this period but oak wainscot reset in other parts of the house is older.

In 1699 the vicars reclaimed what was then the inner cellar in the NW corner of the building, and gave William

Plate 62   *Nos 12 and 13, Vicars' Hall, from NE*

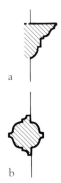

a

b

Scale: 1 inch = 1 foot

Fig 47   *No. 13, sections of window-frame on upper floor*
a. transom
b. mullion

Goldwyer in exchange the N part of the central court abutting his staircase. On this he built a cellar and two upper rooms, at mezzanine levels, served by the older staircase which he adapted. The lower room was probably a study, and is well finished with panelling, a box cornice and a fireplace with bolection-moulded overmantel panel. Fittings of similar character suggest that Goldwyer improved the house generally, reuniting the former muniment room as a first-floor drawing room, fitting the approach with a pair of classical wooden arches at the stair-head, and giving the kitchen chamber a bolection-moulded chimney-piece. The room above the carriageway to NE was added probably at this time.

Some thirty years later the former larder was enlarged as a ground-floor drawing room, the hall reduced and the front door reset. Fielded panelling partly remains and the chimney-piece, with moulded stone panels on its jambs, head and keyblock, abuts a recess panelled as an ornamental cupboard with glazed doors. Outside, the vicars permitted Goldwyer to build a wall around his garden in 1701; to E of the house the wall is of brick with blind arches and a moulded stone coping.

In the mid 19th century, the carriageway to E of the house was enclosed and an extension made to carry an upper sitting room with a large bay-window to S. Alterations made in 1970–1 swept away several fittings described here.

Postscript

During alterations to the SE room in 1984, involving removal of the (apparently 17th-century) upper floor, a blocked recess and the jamb of a doorway, both presumed to be original features, were uncovered in the W wall.

Higher up, a horizontal ashlar weathering course and fragment of lead flashing indicated that this room originally had a pentice roof which was replaced by the existing pitched roof in the 15th century, when a staircase and an upper floor were first inserted, making the ground floor a low cellar. At the extreme S end of this wall were traces of a plastered surface with painted ashlar jointing. The N wall at roof level proved to be of wattle and daub construction, heavily smoke-blackened on the N side which implies that kitchen A originally had an open hearth and the large W masonry stack is an addition, probably of the 15th century.

14 The Close

14 The Close originated as the E part of the garden to the Vicars' Hall, but at the Restoration it was separated as a

Plate 63   *No. 14 from NW*

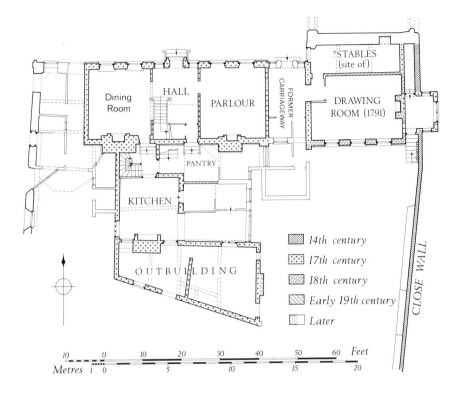

Fig 48 *No. 14*

building plot. It appears that the house was built on it shortly after 1662 by one William Tucker, who had already left by 1670. In 1671 a survey of the vicars' property described it as 'one new built tenement with backside, stable and garden now granted to Mr Edmund Markes and now in the possession of Francis Hill Esq.' [Everett A, 31]. The pattern of tenants changing frequently, many of them living elsewhere and subletting, continued until 1899 when it became the vicarage of St Thomas's Church in substitution for No. 18 and a large drawing room was adopted as the parish room. In 1893 the Church commissioners had conveyed it to the dean and chapter together with the adjoining gate. It is now occupied as a private residence with an independent office in the E part.

The house built in the 1660s was spacious, with a front range of two storeys and attics raised above cellars (Plate 63), a lower kitchen wing, main and secondary staircases; a carriageway led to an outbuilding in a corner of the property (Fig 48). The plan of the first floor reflects that below, with a heated closet above the carriageway serving the adjacent bedroom. Construction is in English-bond brick, the main elevation having a four-brick platband with rounded lower moulding, in the same plane as the first-floor centrepiece which has moulded brickwork framing its window. On S of the main range there was a roofed open area, now enclosed as a pantry, into which the cellar stairs ascend and which provided light to the back stairs. The attics of the front range must always have been lit by

dormer windows, since rebuilt, and original chimney-stacks have brick and tile weatherings.

The original oak joinery survives in part. The lower flight of the front staircase has been replaced at least twice and is now of early 18th-century date, brought recently from No. 84 St Ann's Street [RCHM 1980, Plate 88], but the upper flight is original, with square newel-posts, a close string and turned balusters (Fig 49). In the kitchen and lobby there are heavy plank doors in stout frames, chamfered with ogee stops, and a plank partition with moulded edges flanks the upper stair flight. The back staircase, with square newel-posts, is also original.

Stables were built to E, against the side of St Ann's Gate, where hayloft doors above a window converted from a doorway still exist. The outbuilding to S is of late 17th-century date and was at first unheated; the larger room appears to have contained a staircase. It was built in English-bond brick with much of the first floor timber framed initially, though replaced in brick a century later. The ceiling beams are chamfered with ogee stops, as are those in the kitchen and former stable.

In the early 18th century the front part of the house was generously refitted. Fielded and bolection-moulded panelling, dadoes, shutters and window-seats, wooden cornices, and bolection-moulded chimney-pieces were introduced and on the S wall of the staircase there were two or more round-headed arches with keyblocks and individual projections of the ceiling cornice, now almost

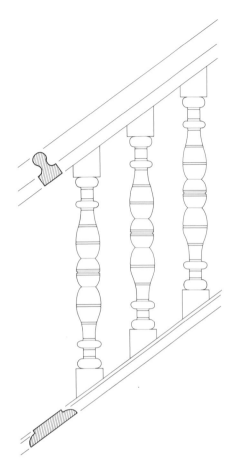

Fig 49   *No. 14, staircase, detail of balustrade*

obliterated. The pedimented door-case of the main entrance was supplied, also handsome doors with pairs of fielded and beaded panels with moulded edges, the front door with five pairs of panels, the ground-floor doors generally of four and the first-floor doors of three. At about the same time a single-storey drawing room was added, partly on the site of the 17th-century stable and somewhat awkwardly beyond the carriageway; it has elegant walls of Flemish-bond brickwork and tall sash windows with gauged flat arches and projecting keystones, but no interior fittings survive.

Towards the middle of the 18th century a small addition, now almost lost among later ones, was made to E of the back stairs; it can have provided no more than a small pantry with a modest bedroom above, whose corner fireplace joins the parlour chimney. In 1791 the tenant, Mary Dalby, made the first of several attempts to sell her lease and the house then comprised 'an entrance hall, two good parlours and two bedrooms over, the same size, ... many other good rooms and offices, excellent cellarage, stall stable, coachhouse etc., fit for the reception of a large family' [*SJ*, 30 May 1791].

Rooms on the first floor were modernised early in the 19th century, and the occupant probably lived chiefly on this storey. The bedroom above the parlour was amalgamated with its closet to E and made into a drawing room with a canted bay-window to S, a plaster ceiling cornice, and new joinery; the larger room in the outbuilding was also fitted as a reception room, a chimney and a triple sash window were built and new joinery installed including a chimney-piece with fluting and lion masks and a fluted chair-rail. Later in the century the offices were expanded to E of the kitchen with staff quarters above. Recent tenants have introduced fittings of 18th-century date, eg a chimney-piece in the former closet.

The 14th-century look-out turret on the Close Wall was rebuilt in ashlar as a gazebo to the house, probably in the 17th century, with a W entrance. It is now mainly 18th century in appearance (Plate 4) with a domical plaster ceiling. Railings (since removed) were added to enhance the walk along the Close Wall, the medieval walkway here projecting on corbels. In the 18th century the vicars leased the turret together with the house.

Malmesbury House, 15 The Close

Malmesbury House, 15 The Close, is a house of post-Reformation date built against the Close Wall, containing magnificent 18th-century plasterwork. The Harris family were tenants from 1660 until 1850, but they sublet it after 1781.

A medieval house on the site had been bequeathed in 1293 by Canon Geoffrey of Milborne to chapter who immediately granted it to Nicholas of Winton, vicar. A century later it had become known as Cole Abbey or Copped Hall, when chapter tried to persuade a canon to adopt it by offering a subsidy of £28 towards its repair and the construction of a hall and chamber; for several years canons who could not avoid occupying it moved elsewhere as quickly as possible and in 1399 chapter agreed to its demolition.

In the 15th and 16th centuries rents were received merely from gardens. By 1583 there was again a house on the site, and the leases of the several gardens were brought together by Willam Blacker, a speculator with several tenancies in the Close. His house was insubstantial and nothing of it is now visible.

From the Restoration until the early 20th century St Ann's Chapel formed part of No. 15, and for a similar period the leases included No. 16.

The 17th century

The property was described twice in the Parliamentary Survey, when Sir George Vaughan at first claimed to have lost his leases. It comprised (in addition to No. 16) two houses 'now held as one entire house' of which the lesser had been reached by the staircase in St Ann's Gate and consisted of the first and attic storeys over the gate and over the larder and buttery of the main house.

The larger, in 1649, had a hall, parlour, kitchen, larder and buttery, a fair dining room above stairs, three chambers and two garrets, a green courtyard in front of the house, two gardens and an orchard. This describes the rear part of the present house which was presumably built by Blacker but rebuilt piecemeal during the 17th century. The phases of the reconstruction are partly identified by their varying inroads on the Close Wall (Figs 50, 51).

The buttery and larder retain some timber-framing on W although the ground floor was replaced in brick on a new alignment in the early 18th century; the upper storey added to the Close Wall is in English-bond brickwork. The hall and kitchen are of the mid 17th century, the S wall in similar brick with mullioned and transomed stone windows with a recessed chamfer and high relieving-arches, and having also an eaves cornice of shaped

modillions with pyramidal pendants added to the larder build. On the E their brickwork is straight jointed with that to either side, and the build to N retains the ovolo-moulded jamb of a former window. A central staircase, which was possibly the principal one, now remains only on the upper storey, with a chamfered newel-post and ball finial. Heavy bolection-moulded panelling in the dining room, with pulvinated entablature, is probably of oak and of late 17th-century date and was evidently intended for a larger room.

The 18th century

In 1703 James Harris (1674–1731) renewed the lease, with a covenant to repair the house, stable and boundary wall on S. In 1705 he again renewed it and received permission to demolish the Close Wall where it bounded his garden and use its stone for his own purposes, replacing it in stone or brick to the same height as before at his own

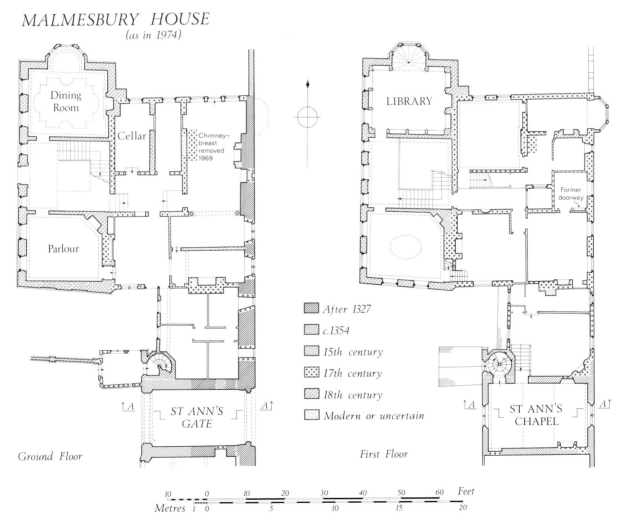

MALMESBURY HOUSE
(as in 1974)

After 1327
c.1354
15th century
17th century
18th century
Modern or uncertain

Ground Floor

First Floor

10   0   10   20   30   40   50   60   Feet
Metres 1 0   5   10   15   20

Fig 50 No. 15, Malmesbury House, with St Ann's Gate

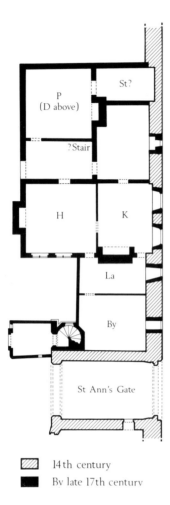

14th century

By late 17th century

Fig 51 *No. 15, Malmesbury House, reconstructed plan*

expense. That this denotes the date and quarry for the construction of his stone range with its handsome W front (Plate 64) is confirmed by chapter's discussion in 1719 of the terms for the next renewal, and of the house's appearance fourteen years previously, before it was 'entirely altered', one canon alleging that it had been 'as good as Mr Lambert's house' (Nos 6 and 7), another that it had not [Hants R O 7M54/274]. In 1707 Harris married Lady Elizabeth Ashley-Cooper, a daughter of the 2nd Earl of Shaftesbury.

The exterior and plan of his new main rooms are little altered although two of the S windows have been blocked; it is no longer clear why the S wall is at an oblique angle. Within, three of the rooms retain their moulded fielded panelling, the parlour having window-seats. Bolection-moulded panelling with fielded centres now in the summerhouse may derive from the library, at first the drawing room. In the parlour chamber, originally the best bedroom, a bolection-moulded oval panel is an original ceiling ornament. The older range was down-graded and

part of the old parlour became a brick-vaulted cellar during the 18th century.

Harris's son James (1708–80) was probably responsible for the restoration of St Ann's Chapel (p 47) which he may have used as a study. The room to N he altered *en suite*, giving it panelling and sash windows with thick glazing-bars, blocking the older stair door and making a new internal flight to the chapel. No doubt he walled up the gateway porch at the same time (Plate 9).

In about 1740 James extensively refitted his father's work. A date before 1743 is suggested by the appearance on the staircase ceilings of the Harris arms, *a chevron ermine between three hedgehogs*, because they neither quarter those of his mother (died 1743) nor impale those of his wife Elizabeth Clarke (married 1745). The stucco and joinery of his lavish redecoration reflect his broad patronage of the arts and mark the heyday of the house [*CL* 19, 26 Oct 1961]. Busts of Ben Jonson, Shakespeare and Milton were introduced on the staircase (Plate 65). The dining room was given a new door-case, and a ceiling decorated with bacchic masks and vine sprays (Plates 66, 67), whereas that in the parlour received oak and mistletoe. A small upper room was transformed by the addition of ceiling ornament, a boldly modelled chimney-piece designed to display porcelain (Plate 68), and an oriel window projecting from the Close Wall, complementing the medieval guard-chamber to S of the gate.

The summerhouse was built in the same period and has similar plasterwork in the pediment (Plate 69); the french windows have diagonal glazing-bars meeting at roundels, and within there is a late 18th-century grate. In 1749 Harris had a sundial painted on the house inscribed 'Life is but a walking shadow'.

Subsequently he made the drawing room into a Gothick library adding a bay-window with leaded gablets (Plate 70); perhaps it was completed in time for a two-night visit by the Duke of York in 1761 [Wheeler 1889, 29]. Inside, the bookcases, doors (one blind), chimney-piece and bay-window are united within a continuous arcade (Plates 71, 72), and the general design has similarities to the former library at Corsham Court of *c* 1759, attributed to Henry Keene [Ladd 1978, 51–2]. However, in view of the family friendship with the composer Handel, it is probably unnecessary to look further than the contemporary Gothick orchestra building (1758) at Vauxhall Gardens as a source for the style of the library [Coke 1984, 75–98]. The shafts, the form of the arches, the canopies, and the crockets are of Gothic inspiration and the dominant shape is the ogee; but much of the detail is classical and the acanthus leaf is a principal motif, upright on the capitals or rolled up as crockets. Above the pillars are urns and busts of Athene and the philosophers Aristotle, Homer, Plato and Socrates. The date of the 'Elizabethan'

Plate 64   *No. 15, Malmesbury House, from W*

Plate 65   *No. 15, Malmesbury House, upper staircase hall, with plaster decoration and busts of Ben Jonson and Shakespeare*

Plate 66   *No. 15, Malmesbury House, door-case in dining room*

Plate 67   *No. 15, Malmesbury House, ceiling in dining room*

Plate 68   *No. 15, Malmesbury House, rococo chimney-piece in NE bedroom*

ribbed ceiling is uncertain. On the ground floor the bay-window, which faces the summerhouse, has the sash equivalent of french windows.

After Elizabeth Harris's death in 1781 her son (created Earl of Malmesbury in 1800) sublet the house to Francis Webb, later described as a 'gentleman in large business, who kept no less than 14 clerks in it' and in 1815 to Webb's daughter Frances Salisbury, but chapter's refusal to allow the occupancy by a boys' school caused an exchange of angry letters in 1864 [Chapter Acts 1797–1870, 7 Dec 1864]. It was assigned to Miss A H Marrian *c* 1887, who employed E Walters to make 'alterations' approved by chapter in 1894. Chapter authorised G R Crickmay to spend £119 on it in 1897. In 1968 Mr J H Cordle acquired the freehold. He restored the main entrance to its original appearance by demolishing a 19th-century porch, altered the partitions in the 17th-century house and introduced a chimney-piece of *c* 1790 to the parlour.

A two-storey stable block NW of the house is of ashlar with a hipped roof and has plain apertures with keystones; it dates from *c* 1705 and was converted as a house *c* 1965. The boundary wall on S of the house was also built as a result of the covenant of 1703, of brick in Flemish bond with moulded stone coping, and pierced by an entrance with chamfered rusticated piers of ashlar; chapter granted £20 towards the cost of the wall in 1705–6.

Plate 69   *No. 15, Malmesbury House, summerhouse*

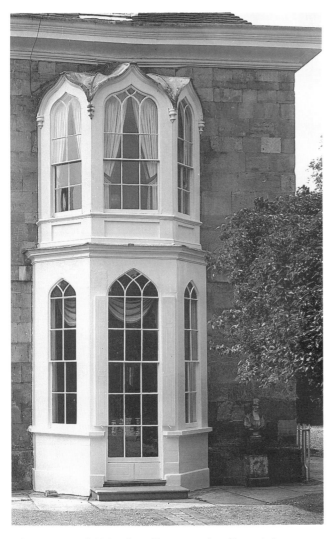

Plate 70   *No. 15, Malmesbury House, exterior of bow-window*

Plate 71   *No. 15, Malmesbury House, the Gothick library*

Plate 72   *No. 15, Malmesbury House, bow-window in library*

16 The Close

16 The Close was granted, from the mid 17th until the late 19th century, to the tenants of No. 15, who took the N part of the garden into their own grounds; the Harris family at first allowed their relations to occupy it, and from 1703 to 1743 it was their dower house. A private tenant purchased the freehold in 1973 and this account describes the house before his alterations.

The oldest part of the house is a small 16th-century timber-framed range, but it succeeds a small canonry whose site was contained by the two existing rubble boundary walls; stone quoins at the S end of the W wall probably remain from the gable-end of a medieval building. Little is known of the canonry, which Henry of Blunsdon may have given to chapter on being appointed dean in 1284; by 1418 it had become a vacant place last occupied by 'Melksham' (? Peter of, alive 1395), and was subsequently in use as gardens.

The present house is founded upon the W boundary wall (Fig 52) which was owned by the vicars choral, and leased by them to the tenants of No. 15, the earliest reference to which, because of the destruction of the vicars' documents, occurs in 1631.

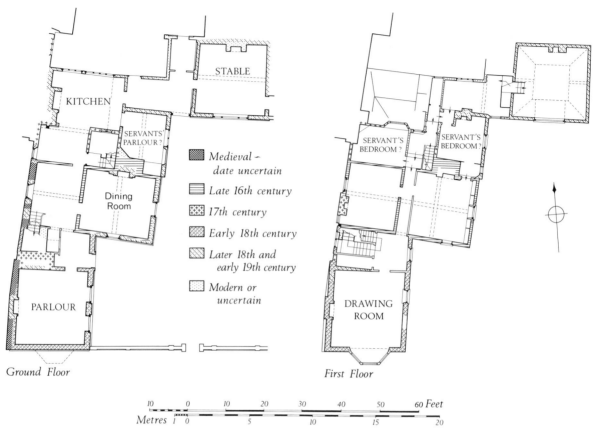

STABLE

KITCHEN

SERVANTS'
PARLOUR?

Dining
Room

PARLOUR

SERVANT'S
BEDROOM?

SERVANT'S
BEDROOM?

DRAWING
ROOM

■ Medieval –
date uncertain

▤ Late 16th century

▦ 17th century

▨ Early 18th century

▧ Later 18th and
early 19th century

▥ Modern or
uncertain

Ground Floor

First Floor

10   0   10   20   30   40   50   60 *Feet*
Metres 1   0   5   10   15   20

Fig 52 *No. 16*

In the Parliamentary Survey, No. 16 was a two-storey building with an attic, the ground floor a shop or little low chamber for servants, and the first floor a chamber with a garret or cock-loft over it, and there was a stable of two bays adjoining. This must in some way refer to the central range which had larger and smaller rooms above one another on each floor including the attics, but slight differences of orientation and roof construction suggest two different dates and the room built against the boundary wall is probably the earlier. The timber-framing is now hung with tiles or rebuilt in brick and the two-flue chimney against the N wall is of flint and stone rubble with stone quoins. The larger of the first-floor chambers has chamfered ceiling beams and is lined with reset oak wainscot of 16th/17th-century date. In the attic the two E bays of the roof have raking struts from tie-beams to principals, pairs of straight wind-braces and collars. The timber-framed wall between the builds has a door of oak planks with hinge-pins, and the W room is remarkable for its floorboards, 18 ins wide.

In the second half of the 17th century a brick extension was built to N (Fig 53), probably as unheated service rooms and an original doorway in their partition and a window with chamfered wooden mullions remain. The

upper storey was a single chamber lined on S with softwood planks and muntins, with an oriel window facing N and a door planked on one face, two-panelled on the other.

Early in the 18th century the house was extensively improved, probably when Joan Harris lived there after the death of Gabriel Ashley in 1702, and the S wing was added containing a parlour with a best bedroom or drawing room above, reached by a new staircase. It encloses the fragment of a wall, seen on W (Plate 73), largely of rough brickwork which is testimony to an earlier building on the site. The new work has Flemish-bond brickwork with decorative use of vitrified headers in the platband and in first-floor window-heads. Original windows are segmental headed below, straight above, and the roof is hipped with moulded plastered eaves. The fittings of the main rooms have gone but the fielded panelling now on three walls of the upper room was reset here probably in the early 19th century. The form of the staircase survives above first half-landing level with its panelled dado, and in the attics there is a partition of fielded planks and moulded muntins. Joan Harris probably also inserted the segmental-arched brick doorway in the medieval wall to E, now blocked, allowing direct access to her son's garden.

Later in the century a new single-storey kitchen was added to N, of brick with lead-glazed windows. In a slightly later phase a small addition to SE of this kitchen was perhaps a servant's parlour and bedroom, and a new back staircase was built in the old buttery. In the same period the 17th-century chimney in the S wing was blocked and dismantled down to ground-floor level and another built in the W wall.

A general restoration of the house was made in about 1820, perhaps by Richard Attwood (subtenant from *c* 1817 until after 1837). The timber-framed range was rebuilt on the ground floor in brick, its upper walls were hung with decorative convex- and concave-ended tiles, and the dining room was enhanced with a glazed door to the garden, a carved wooden chimney-piece with Egyptian motifs (now removed) and a reeded ceiling frieze. Joan Harris's S range received a new main entrance, with reeded architrave and rectangular fanlight, and uniform sash windows were introduced on S and E. The space to W of the dining room became a hall with the lower flight of the stairs given semicircular arches and redirected into it, and the upper drawing room acquired an oriel window with external

Plate 73   *No. 16 from W*

fluted frieze and flat lead roof. The oriel window of the rear bedroom was remodelled with a sash window and Gothic glazing. At the same time the accommodation was extended into a mid 18th-century brick stable NE of the house, which received a large S-facing window and fireplaces on its ground and semi-attic storeys.

17 The Close

No. 17 is a house of early 17th-century date, comparatively unaltered (Plate 74). Boundary walls, largely of medieval flint and stone rubble, determine the irregular shape of the building, straddling the width of the site from E to W. Ranged roughly level with a medieval house on W, it may stand on the site of an earlier house which belonged from the later Middle Ages to the vicars; this was occupied (perhaps mainly) by their members, such as John Wallopp (vicar) in 1442/3, Patrick Ford in 1559 and Richard Ganyett (lay vicar) in 1583.

Ganyett was still alive in 1593 but in 1603 the house was privately tenanted by William Wilkinson, Doctor of Civil Law and theological writer, who died in 1613. This change in the occupant's status may account for the reconstruction, although his successor Richard Haydock had an expressed interest in architecture, his one publication being a translation of J P Lomatius's *Tracte containing the Artes of curious Paintings, Carvinge and Buildinge*, of 1598. Haydock was still the tenant in 1640 and was succeeded by William Hurst and Daubeny Turberville, both of them physicians, as was Haydock. Turberville, who was resident from 1671 or earlier until his death in 1696, was internationally famous as an eye surgeon [*DNB*].

The early 17th century

The house is on two main storeys with substantial semi-attics, and an undercroft in the wing which results in the

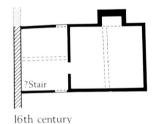

?Stair

16th century

▨▨ Medieval boundary wall

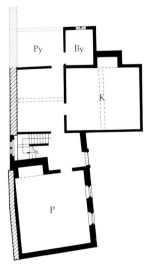

Py   By

K

P

17th and early 18th centuries

Fig 53   *No. 16, reconstructed plans*

Plate 74   *No. 17 from S*

Plate 75   *No. 17 from N*

floors in the W part of the house occurring at intermediate levels (Plate 75). The Parliamentary Survey of 1649/50 lists the house in virtually its original form: 'Mr Dodington... wherein William Hurst...now inhabiteth, consisting of a hall, a parlour wainscotted, a kitchen, buttery, pantry, sellar, dyneing room above staires well wainscotted, five chambers and a garrett; behind the house a colehouse, a shed for wood, and a wash house; little courtyard before the house and a small garden behind'.

Of the reception rooms, the larger was a heated hall and the smaller a parlour, panelled but unheated, and the services occupied the remainder of the ground floor (Figs 54, 55). In the kitchen the main window is notably off-centre and perhaps there was formerly a small internal room to N of the chimney, removed in the 18th century when the shed was added and the doorway made, and the window was then narrowed and given lower lights. Both staircases are original and now have boxed newels.

The largest room is on the first floor, no doubt the original great chamber, magnificent with its panelling, stone chimney-piece, plaster entablature and ribbed ceilings (Plates 76, 77). The panelling had been painted in 1843 [Benson and Hatcher 1843, 900] and has a made-up area on E across a blocked window. The frieze above the chimney-piece includes the crest *a garb supported by two lions*, borne by the Marquess of Exeter and others; it is possible that Wilkinson placed it there to commemorate some connection or act of patronage but perhaps more likely that Haydock invented it to represent a hay-stook as a pun on his name. The ceiling is evidently later than those in the King's House of *c* 1600 and the Old Parsonage, Harnham [RCHM 1980, Plate 93]. There are two chambers on the mezzanine level; that over the buttery is lined with oak panelling having a cymatium cornice supported on brackets carved with quarter-roll and quarter-hollow mouldings, and has an ovolo-moulded and arched stone chimney-piece. The richness of the fittings against the small size of the window (if this is its original width) seems surprising.

On the first floor the principal chambers are identified by their oriel windows (given gables in the 19th century) and were originally of similar size, the W one having an inner chamber and that to E probably two closets. The 'inner chamber' and the small chamber below it are without original heating. The top storey was approached only by the E staircase, and the principal chamber on E resembles that below it in having an oriel window and a closet; the chamber retains its oak panelling with chip-carved frieze and the closet doorway has a Tudor-arch with leaf-carved spandrels.

Originally the side walls and probably the front were of brick in English bond and the back wall is timber framed, but these materials are now heavily renewed, rendered, or

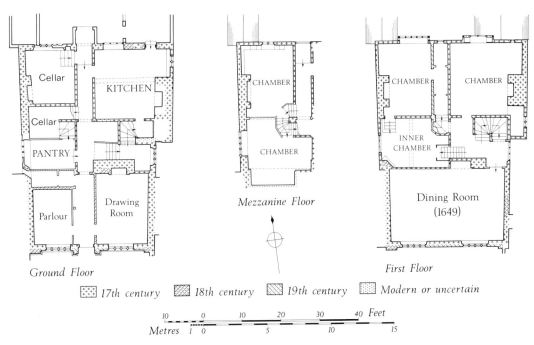

Ground Floor   First Floor

Mezzanine Floor

▦ *17th century*   ▨ *18th century*   ▧ *19th century*   ▦ *Modern or uncertain*

10   0   10   20   30   40 *Feet*

Metres 1   0   5   10   15

Fig 54   *No. 17*

hung with slates or tiles. The main elevation was wholly refaced in the early 19th century with the exception of pilaster buttresses already added; the ovolo-moulded stone windows may be original although they lack hood-moulds and the toothings expected at this date (but compare the contemporary work at the King's House, No. 65). The windows elsewhere are mainly of timber with square mullions set diagonally, although two on N have ovolo-mouldings. The lesser elevations stand on a tall plinth of flint, random bricks and stone rubble including moulded stones, no doubt debris from the older house.

Later history

A general restoration was made of the house in the early 18th century, probably by William Harris who lived here from *c* 1721 and died in 1746. He rearranged the hall and parlour into their present dispositions, the parlour receiving a plain panelled dado and wooden ceiling cornice and the hall becoming a comfortable drawing room lined with fielded panelling and having a box cornice and pedimented stone chimney-piece (Plate 78); wooden archways were also added to N and S of the lower staircase with moulded elliptical heads, keyblocks and cornices. Harris probably

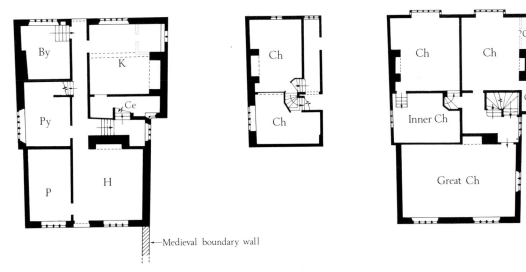

—Medieval boundary wall

Fig 55   *No. 17, reconstructed plans, as built*

Plate 76   *No. 17, chimney-piece in great chamber*

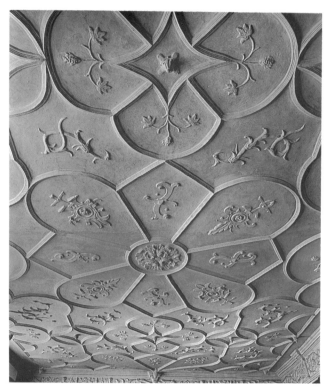

Plate 77   *No. 17, ceiling in great chamber*

also gave the front elevation its hipped roof on a coved cornice and the door its classical stone cornice, now incorporated in the 19th-century 'Elizabethan' door-case. He had chapter's consent to erect railings along his frontage in 1723, and there, with their spear-heads and vase-finialled standards and their stone-coped wall, they remain.

In the second half of the 18th century the leases were renewed by members of the Batt family of New Hall, Bodenham, who sublet to the Earle family. The Earles and their kinsmen the Bensons then acquired and maintained the leases and lived here until 1862; and it was no doubt a member of this family who carefully refaced the front of the house. Subsequently Walter Tower, the architect and legatee of C E Kempe, took it and installed part of his legacy of stained glass there, since removed [Stravidi 1982, 171].

18 The Close

18 The Close was established in 1443 as the subdeanery for John Pedewell (subdean 1442–52). It was then described as having been occupied previously by canons, and was charged with the obits of William of Wokingham, vicar,

Plate 78   *No. 17, chimney-piece in hall*

who was living here in 1301 and may have bequeathed it to chapter, and Canon James of Havant who died in 1349 and was said to have built the house [Edwards 1939, 97].

In 1649 the Parliamentary Survey described the house of Dr Alexander Hyde as having 'at the entry a gatehouse and a chamber over it, a study therein. Then a little yard or court between the gatehouse and dwelling-house, which house consisteth of one little hall benched and wainscoted above the bench 4 foot high, a kitchen, a buttery, a coalhouse, and above the stairs one handsome little dining room wainscoted about to the top, about 10 foot high, three chambers, and another upper room something decayed, all of them being but little rooms'. The following year the subdean had been displaced and James Harris lived here, but residence by the subdean was resumed at the Restoration and continued until 1840 when the Cathedrals Act dispossessed him.

Thomas Naish, subdean from 1694 to 1755, kept a diary [Slatter 1965] and from this and other sources we learn that in 1695 the house was occupied by Frances Hedges; tenancy continued until 1701 when Naish took it over but he left in 1708 to take up a living in Somerset, returning again in 1728. His successors also leased it out and an advertisement of 1842 described it as 'a genteel and comfortable residence' [SJ, 25 Apr 1842]. The gatehouse, which is clearly marked on W Naish's plan of Salisbury in 1716, appears to have survived until 1760 when Subdean Sambre (1759–1801) had permission to take down the 'detached buildings fronting the Close' and sell the materials, on condition that he spend the proceeds on 'repairing and fitting up' his residence [Chapter Acts 1741–96, 14 July 1760].

In 1847 the vicar of St Thomas's Church, the Rev John Greenly, obtained the house and the bishop confirmed it as the vicarage four years later. After his death, a survey in 1863 described the E side as 'modern', the W side mainly 'very old', and the house as rendered, with a roof of slates on E and tiles on W. Among the repairs and alterations proposed, some of them requested by H L Prior, the vicar's new tenant, were the addition of a water closet and coal store in the court and the replacement of a wooden fence with iron railings by Messrs Osmond and Wilson.

Ceasing to be the vicarage c 1899, for most of the 20th century the house has been leased to the Theological College which, in 1937, was allowed to remove a partition from the hall. It has recently acquired the name 'Hooker House' after Richard Hooker, subdean from 1591 to 1595, scholar and author of *Ecclesiastical Polity*, although he is not known to have lived here.

Development of the house

The house built by Havant is doubtless the basis of the present one, and although there are no certain remaining details of the mid 14th century, the bones of a medieval house are clearly detectable within the later alterations (Fig 56). In 1649 the subdean was living mainly on the first floor, with the ground floor given up to the hall, kitchen and offices, and this may have been in part the original arrangement; the hall was originally open to the roof and heated by a central hearth, rediscovered during repairs in 1966.

The remaining functions would have taken place in the long cross-wing, which is mainly two-storeyed and had one comparatively large room on each floor at the rear, probably the kitchen and kitchen chamber. The W wall stands on the boundary, so it is unclear whether the N corner of the house having quoins to the upper floor indicates a continuation of the boundary wall or the former existence of a lean-to or outshut, though in 1649 the boundary here was marked only by a quickset hedge. The lack of axial agreement between hall and cross-wing is doubtless the result of building up to pre-existing boundaries to E and W.

The hall has been very heavily reconstructed, which in itself suggests that it may have been, and possibly still partly remains, timber framed, but a fragment at the E end of the N wall on the ground floor is of coursed flint, stone and tile rubble, the tiles laid in horizontal and diagonal courses. The W elevation is still mainly of the same materials on both storeys and the kitchen retains two

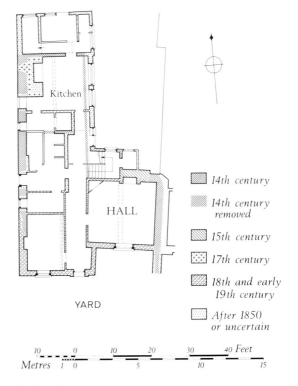

Fig 56 *No. 18*

Plate 79   *No. 18 from S*

original windows with chamfered stone surrounds and sub-rectangular shape, broader than tall, one now blocked, the other retaining its stanchions.

The N and E walls of the W range are of tile-hung timber-framing on the first floor; the E wall is of modern brickwork on the ground floor and the off-centre position of the kitchen's spine beam suggests that a jetty of some 2 ft has been underbuilt. The tiled roof over the kitchen chamber remains and is in two bays with pairs of curved wind-braces; they and the purlins have chamfers with run-out stops, and there is a chamfered wall-plate on E.

A chimney was added to the hall, perhaps in the 15th century. A further phase of alterations dates from closer to 1600 when the hall was floored over on deeply chamfered beams to create a new great chamber, the dining room of 1649; the roof was probably raised at the same time, and the kitchen received its present large chimney. On the first floor other alterations are attested by the door-frame to the SW bedroom which is chamfered with ogee stops, while the roof over the kitchen was ceiled off as an attic. Oak wainscot reset in the mid 18th century as dados etc in various rooms is of two patterns and was probably in the hall and dining room in 1649.

To Subdean Sambre, *c* 1760, may be attributed some refacing of the W wall in brick, a refitting of the main entrance, the hall chimney-piece with its eared stone surround and moulded shelf on consoles, and the staircase behind the hall, with turned newel-posts and balusters. More obvious alterations date from the early 19th century when the top storey was added and the S elevation stuccoed and given uniform sash windows with moulded labels of Tudor style (Plate 79). This work, together with

further reconstruction of the W wall, was probably done at the change of tenancy from Mrs Fuller, widow, tenant in 1806 to the Misses Luxford, tenants of 1820.

The Theological College, 19 The Close

The Theological College, 19 The Close, has as its nucleus a house dating from *c* 1677. A number of sites were brought together partly when the house was built and partly in the 1870s when the college was established. The relatively small house site was dean and chapter property and in 1558 there were two tenements on it, shortly thereafter combined as one; in the late 16th century it was occupied mainly by prebendaries but from 1600 exclusively by lay folk. An increase of rent from 28s 8d to 44s p.a. in 1627 may indicate recent improvements, and the house described in the Parliamentary Survey consisted of a hall, wainscoted parlour, kitchen, buttery, larder, bakehouse and wash-house, and upstairs a wainscoted dining room, five chambers, of which two were wainscoted, a garret and a coal-loft.

In 1674 a lease of this house was obtained by Francis Hill, a prominent lawyer and Deputy Recorder of Salisbury from 1685 to 1693, but he had demolished it by January 1677. In 1679 he renewed his lease and was then living on the site; he also obtained the lease of a vicars' cottage to N, abutting his house, which had been the residence of vicars at least since 1568, and during the 18th and 19th centuries occupied by assignees of Hill and his successors, probably as a staff cottage. He also obtained an orchard and garden belonging to the vicars in 1677, which was to provide the major part of his own garden; it stood to E of the house and extended from street to Close Wall, abutting the subdeanery. This resulted in an L-shaped property, held under three separate leases, so remaining until the 1860s.

Hill's son John sublet the house from *c* 1696 until 1710 when William Hearst took the lease and it remained with his descendants, members of the Hearst and Wyndham families, until 1797. The lease was then sold twice, first to Nicholas Williams, then in 1799 to two Kneller sisters. At their death Charlotte Wyndham bought it in 1828, the advertisement describing it as having a 'handsome entrance hall and two sitting rooms, dining and breakfast, with housekeeper's room, butler's pantry, store-room and an excellent kitchen, with large cellars. The second floor contains a handsome drawing room and three best bedrooms, besides a smaller one for a servant and seven rooms in the attic. Also a small tenement behind the mansion...[and] double coach-house and stables for 5 horses, with brewhouse and all convenient offices' [*SJ*, 18 Aug 1828]. The stable building stood to SE of the house and is marked on city plans from 1716 to 1860.

In 1860 Bishop Kerr Hamilton bought the leases to found a theological college, and the following year acquired part of the large meadow to N, on which the residential buildings now stand. Building, to the designs of William Butterfield, went on in three stages: first the students' lodgings, which are L-shaped and at the rear of the house, begun after September 1873 and completed in April 1875 at a cost of £4775; the second and third stages were licensed in March 1876 and July 1878 and included a library with a chapel above it, consecrated in 1881 (Plate 80) [Thompson 1971, 394].

The house built by Hill is carefully placed (Fig 1, in end-pocket), in one corner of the then site, probably in order to obtain a view through his own gate piers with their pineapple finials down the Bishop's Walk (planted as an avenue by the end of the 17th century) to the Palace, where Bishop Ward had just completed his hall. This positioning had various consequences for the plan (Fig 58), the main one being an elongated layout with rooms in front connected by a passage behind and stairs projecting to N; even the staircase is placed E of centre, with neither its well nor the first flight centred on the hall doorway,

possibly for some reason connected with the older cottage to N. Building up to the W boundary, which meets North Walk at an acute angle, has caused the distorted shape of the W rooms.

Hill's work is of high quality and in general well preserved. The original plan remains intact on the first floor, where all rooms open off the passage and not into one another, and is recognisable on the ground floor despite the dismembering of the hall (Fig 57). Rooms above one another were originally of the same dimensions and the hall was the largest, that above perhaps originally a first-floor drawing room (as in 1828). A cellar beneath the house is now partly filled in but must have contained the kitchens and other offices; the servants' quarters were in the attics, but their fittings and the secondary staircase up to them were destroyed in the late 19th century. The house is in English-bond brick with cellar windows along the front which are chamfered and mullioned whereas the main windows are sashed, a later alteration. The front door was originally in two hinged leaves (Plate 81) and the

Plate 80   *No. 19 from SW, with chapel on right*

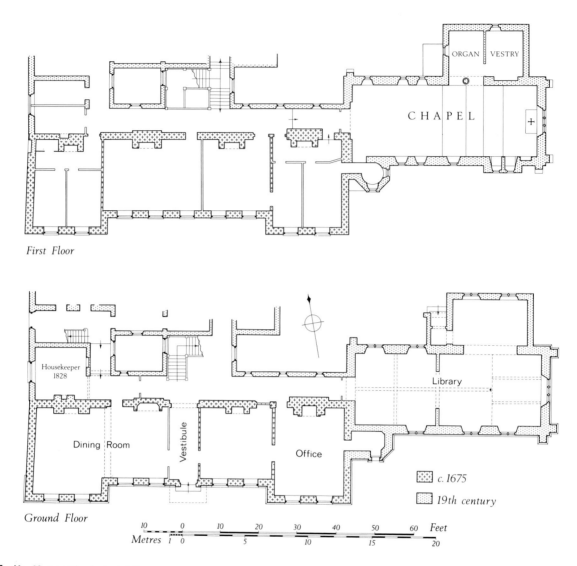

First Floor

Ground Floor

Fig 57   *No. 19, now Theological College*

carved wooden door-hood was added in the early 18th century. The original chimney-stacks have been taken down. Probably all rooms on both the main floors were originally fitted with bolection- or ogee-moulded panelling with elaborate wooden cornices, doors with fielded or bolection-moulded panels, of oak on the ground floor and deal above, in ogee-moulded architraves; fireplace surrounds are also ogee or bolection moulded and of wood (hall), stone (E bedroom) and four different coloured marbles, with chimney-pieces having single or multiple panels, with or without shelves on moulded wooden brackets. The ground-floor panelling (two rooms) is set in three tiers, that on the first floor (three rooms and one with dado only) in two tiers. The most elaborate mouldings occur in the first-floor W room where the chimney is ornamented with panelled pilasters and has a richer cornice than elsewhere in the room, and the door ori-

ginated as two hinged leaves and has an eared architrave. A single-light window on W of the chimney, now blocked, perhaps once lit a small internal closet, its partitions since removed. The staircase is of oak and original except for the pendent finials (Plate 82).

There is now little evidence of 18th-century alterations internally, although one bedroom chimney-piece has brackets and rococo cartouches of papier maché added in the third quarter of the century. More changes were made later, probably *c* 1828 when Charlotte Wyndham acquired the tenure. The housekeeper's room with bedroom above already existed and so apparently did the single-storey extension to E, containing the kitchen. The 'Office', at this time probably the dining room, was entirely refitted, with a grey marble chimney-piece, fluted ceiling frieze, and new chair rail and shutters, and at this time or earlier a window with segmental arch was inserted on E. The lower

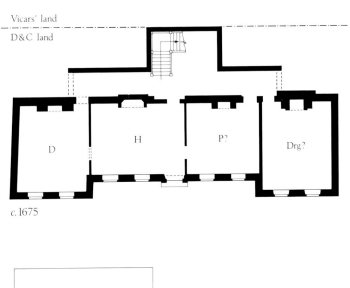

Vicars' land

D&C land

D   H   P?   Drg?

c. 1675

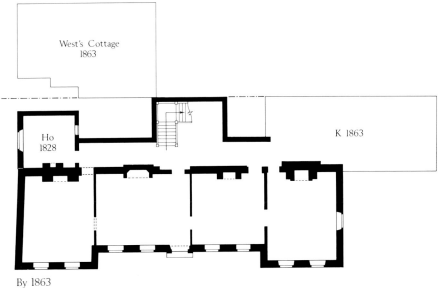

West's Cottage
1863

Ho
1828

K 1863

By 1863

Fig 58 *No. 19, reconstructed plans*

plan on Fig 58 shows the extent of the house in 1863 [outline from D and C Leases 1861–1906, 27 May 1863, plan]. The rear part of the house, including the walls of the passage and staircase, were rebuilt in the 1870s when the college buildings were added. Early 17th-century joinery now reset in the housekeeper's room and elsewhere may derive either from the previous house on the site or from 'West's cottage' demolished *c* 1870 (which had a wain-scoted hall in 1649).

In the garden against the Close Wall (in the former vicars' orchard) is a summerhouse dating from the first half of the 18th century. It is of decayed ashlar on S, in three bays with a central doorway flanked by large sash windows, a coved and moulded stone cornice supported on capitals and a parapet concealing the roof. Within is a blocked fireplace.

Butterfield's flint and brick collegiate range provides

student accommodation on three floors. The two-storey library and chapel range is of flint and stone, with a projecting octagonal staircase carried up as a belfry, and a prominent S oriel window. Inside, the chapel organ is sited in a N alcove behind a double archway with central marble column, and the simple timber roof has, at the chancel end, extra trusses supported on corbels, and decorative bosses. The stained glass E window was installed in 1886 [Wheeler 1901, 20] (Plate 83).

20 The Close

20 The Close is founded upon the gatehouse range of Aula le Stage (Fig 60). In 1718 chapter permitted Canon Coker to lease a piece of his ground, measuring 81 ft by 125 ft, with walls and outbuildings to John Smith, vicar of Bishopstone, on condition that he build a house there within two years (later extended to seven), with rent

Plate 81   *No. 19, main doorway*

Plate 82   *No. 19, staircase*

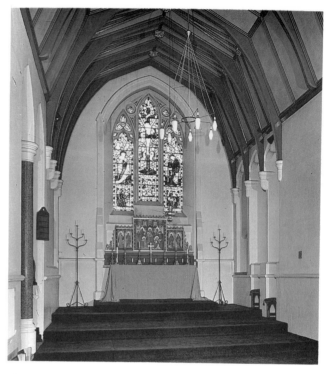

Plate 83   *No. 19, chapel by William Butterfield, consecrated 1881*

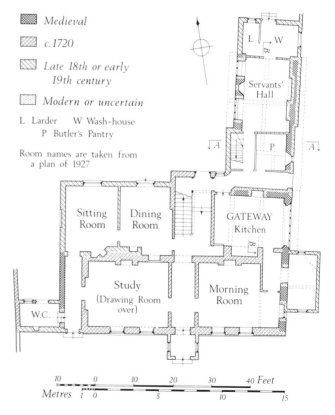

Medieval

c.1720

Late 18th or early
19th century

Modern or uncertain

L Larder   W Wash-house
P Butler's Pantry

Room names are taken from
a plan of 1927

Fig 59   *No. 20*

payable to him and his successors in the canonry. At Smith's death in 1733 Coker granted the house to his son John, who permitted his brother-in-law Arthur Evans (High Sheriff of Wilts in 1755) to live there, probably until his death in 1765. The following year Canon Sherard obtained a lease of ground on E of the house, measuring 8 ft by 16 ft, on which he built a small addition. In 1852 chapter granted a lease to Francis Attwood and in 1861 extended the garden N to the Close Wall, taking in part of what was then a meadow, but had once been the tenement called Crowton's.

The medieval range is of two dates in the 15th century with a structural division between the gateway, which is slightly the earlier, and its N extension; both are timber framed above tile-laced flint rubble, the upper storeys jettied to E and W except on the rear face of the gateway (Fig 61). Formerly the building extended S of the gateway, and in 1586 a room here was an impressively fitted '*garden studdy*', but only part of the E wall now remains. A wall of squared stone with tile-packing in the W part of the 18th-century house was perhaps the end of a second building of medieval date (Fig 59).

The gateway has a stone arch to E, with hollow chamfer, roll and cavetto mouldings, chamfered four-centred rear-arch, and a jetty bressummer moulded with triple hollow chamfers, two fitted with tablet flower (Plate

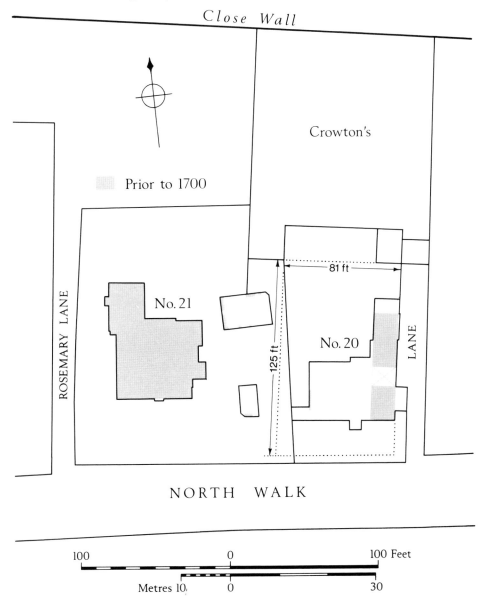

Fig 60 *Nos 20 and 21, Aula le Stage, plan of medieval canonry, showing surviving buildings and fragments earlier than 1700, subdivision with overall dimensions as given in 1718, and additional ground (Crowton's) granted in 1861*

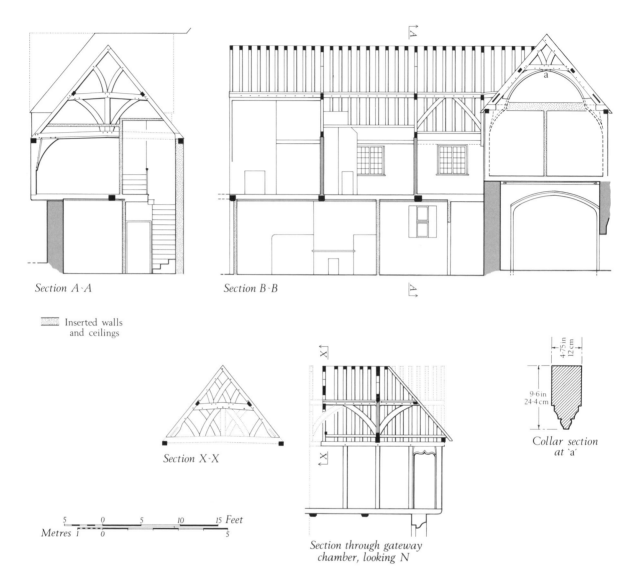

Section A·A

▨ Inserted walls
and ceilings

Section X·X

```
 5      0      5      10      15 Feet
Metres  1      0                        5
```

*Section through gateway
chamber, looking N*

*Collar section
at `a´*

Fig 61   *No. 20, sections of gatehouse range*

Plate 84   *No. 20, gatehouse range from SE*

84); it is spanned by chamfered beams with pyramidal stops. The room to N has chamfered ceiling beams, one of them the trimmer for a staircase (Fig 62), and an original window of one light with a hollow-chamfered, four-centred rear-arch. On the first floor to S the short bay contains the stairs and another small room (Fig 63). The chamber over the gateway is taller with an elaborately braced and cross-braced rear gable (moved inwards in the 18th century) and handsomely finished roof, its central truss having moulded arch-braces which probably rose originally from false hammer-beams; this must have been the 'gatehouse chamber' which contained bedding worthy of bequest in 1558. The position of its original entrance is unknown and the doorway with flattened ogee arch, leading from the N extension, appears to be an insertion into the framing (Fig 61).

Plate 85 *No. 20 from S*

In about 1720 the front range was constructed on two storeys, with cellar and attics, and the older buildings became the kitchen and offices. The new house was probably built with a drawing room (over 'study' in Fig 59) and a dining room ('morning room'), with a passage and servery and bedrooms above each having a dressing room to E. The main staircase led to the first floor and there was a secondary one to the attics, replaced in the 19th century. The thin wall which partly flanks the stairs, and blocked doorways in the 'study' and directly above, suggests that there were originally smaller rooms in the NW angle of the site of the later 'dining room'.

Construction is in English-bond brick with a plinth and plain dressings of stone and a wooden eaves cornice on the main elevation (Plate 85). Original fittings include the main staircase which is of oak with turned balusters three to a tread and ogee-moulded panels on the open string, and the panelling of the morning room, in two heights with a box cornice and a pair of bolection-moulded overmantel panels. A similar overmantel is now in the

gatehouse, and a similar dado rail, cornice and fielded panelling in the lobby on E of the morning room have been removed, perhaps from the study where matching shutters remain. The original doors are probably those with a broad fielded panel between pairs of tall ones, now in the medieval range. The attics of the S range have three rooms separated by chamfered plank partitions.

In about 1740 a handsome chimney-piece was installed in the morning room, having an eared architrave with carved mouldings and voluted cheekpieces with palm fronds. Another, in the bedroom above, is carved with scallops. The addition of *c* 1766 probably contributed a pantry, and allowed the dressing room above to be enlarged and fitted with a fireplace.

A new range, of brick with a hipped slate roof, was built *c* 1830–40 into the NW angle of the house, to provide the present sitting and dining rooms and a large bedroom above (Fig 59). The cast-iron railings with anthemion ornament erected on the street front are also of this date. Some thirty years later the porch was added and plaster cornices and new joinery installed in the principal rooms. The W door of the study is post-1927.

Aula le Stage, 21 The Close

Aula le Stage, 21 The Close, originated in the 13th century as a canonry. It is identifiable in documents after 1316 from the obit of John of Oreby, 13s 4d payable on 7 June, and from 1440 to 1536 the name Aula le Stage, meaning Tower House, was applied to it. The original site was relatively modest for a canonry (Fig 60), and it was effectively filled by the expansion of the house during the 14th and 15th centuries. In the early 16th century chapter enlarged the garden by a grant of Crowton's, the site of a small canonry to NE, which was named after William of Crowton and had probably become redundant at his death in 1477; it was charged with the obit of Peter de Grunvile, who died in 1310. Nothing was built on the site and from the mid 18th to the mid 19th century chapter repossessed it as one half of a large meadow. In 1719 the E part of the curtilage was detached to form a separate residence, now No. 20. No. 21 ceased to be a canonry in 1850, and after being occupied for a while as two dwellings it was thoroughly repaired and converted to three units in 1983, when some walls were entirely stripped of their plaster, and many discoveries about the structural history were made; the plans show it subdivided as in 1972 (Fig 64).

In summary, the house has a nucleus of early 13th-century date, to which a new hall and outbuildings were added by the end of the 14th century. During the 15th century the storeyed accommodation was extended twice. In the Tudor period the house was extensively restored, with ceilings resembling some at Wolsey's Hampton Court Palace, and subsequent documents describe a well-fitted house.

The 13th-century canonry

Of the original house three substantially built ranges survive, of graduated dimension, of which the largest is set at right angles to the others and no doubt contained the parlour and principal chamber (Fig 62a). It can be assumed that there was also a hall, probably detached. The parlour had a latrine in the SE corner lit by a horizontal slit window high up in the wall (Plate 86). The middle range has a second chamber (Plate 87) above a room later called the wardrobe but perhaps originally the wine cellar. Both chambers retain their original roofs, that of the larger (Fig 65, section B–B) having twenty-three couples of scissor-braced rafters of 6 ins by 5 ins scantling and the smaller (Fig 65, section A–A) seventeen couples (the lower 'collars' of the latter being 16th-century additions); they have always been closed in with canted ceilings above moulded cornices (Fig 66a, b), and the gables have never

been plastered inside above this level. These rooms were perhaps originally heated by fireplaces near their present positions and a straight joint remains in the parlour, possibly from a chimney which projected internally but was cut back in the 16th century at the latest. The positions of any stairs to the chambers remain unknown.

The NE range is the smallest and contained a single-storey chapel with a gallery at the W end, which was entered from the lesser chamber through the surviving stone doorway and lit by a single window opposite, rising from close to the gallery floor and the predecessor of that seen by Buckler (Plate 88). The gallery is supported on a moulded wall-plate and beam spanned by joists with individual stop-chamfers (Figs 66c, 67). The vessel of the chapel was lit by single lancets with wide splays and hollow-chamfered heads, of which two remain although blocked, and a triple light to E which was lost when the chapel was curtailed by some 6 ft c 1830; the 13th-century roof and its cornice survive (Figs 66d, 67). A stone doorway with two-centred arch, reset in the E wall, may be the celebrant's entrance removed from S. The chapel remained in use intermittently until the 18th century, as suggested by the Parliamentary Survey of 1649, and a private marriage held in 1692 [Slatter 1965, 26] and the survival of the original windows suggest that it was then relegated to minor uses; it seems not to have been altered radically until c 1830.

A number of broken floor tiles, measuring 11½ ins square with the initials 'J B' in white slip, were found reused beneath the floor on S of the tower in 1983. They are of 13th- or 14th-century date but cannot be associated with any known occupant.

The 14th-century hall and services

In the early or mid 14th century a new hall was added, probably of two bays of which little more than one survives. References in 1586 and 1649 to a screen or screens at the lower (S) end indicate the customary cross-passage there (Fig 62b) with service rooms beyond. The hall roof is well finished with chamfered main members and common rafters individually collared (Fig 65), moulded cornices (Fig 66e) and eaves originally boarded in; smoke-blackening shows that there was an open hearth, but no evidence of this or of a louvre has been found in the remaining bay. The rear-arch of a contemporary window on E is also moulded and the jambs are hollow chamfered with pyramidal stops (Fig 66f), while the jamb of another to S, plain chamfered and with a sill at high level, may be of different date. The sill is at the level of an internal course of disfigured stones which formerly projected. A brattished stone cornice ornamented the extreme N end of the hall, but only the W part, carved with a Paschal lamb and a recumbent boar, remains intact

Fig 62 *Nos 20 and 21, Aula le Stage, reconstructed plans, scale 1 in. to 32 ft*

Ground Floor

a. Early 13th century

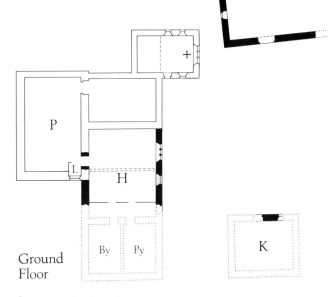

Ground Floor

b. By end of 14th century

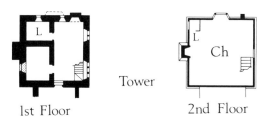

1st Floor   Tower   2nd Floor

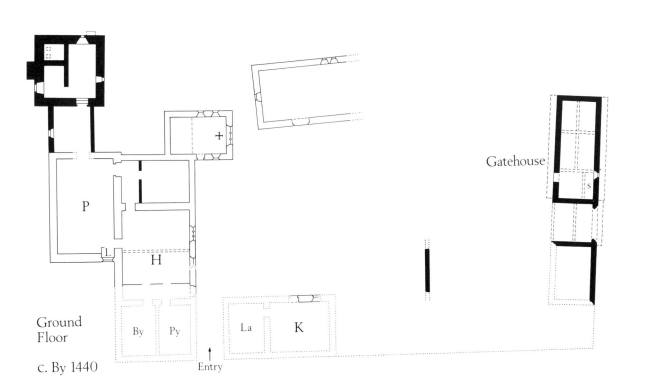

Ground Floor

c. By 1440

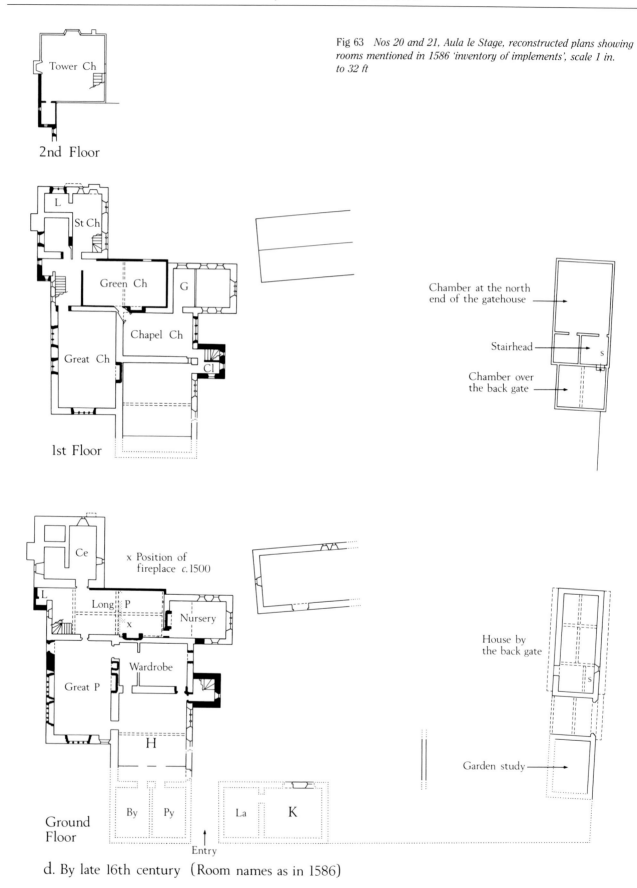

Fig 63 *Nos 20 and 21, Aula le Stage, reconstructed plans showing rooms mentioned in 1586 'inventory of implements', scale 1 in. to 32 ft*

2nd Floor

1st Floor

Chamber at the north
end of the gatehouse

Stairhead

Chamber over
the back gate

x Position of
fireplace *c.*1500

House by
the back gate

Garden study

Ground
Floor

Entry

d. By late 16th century (Room names as in 1586)

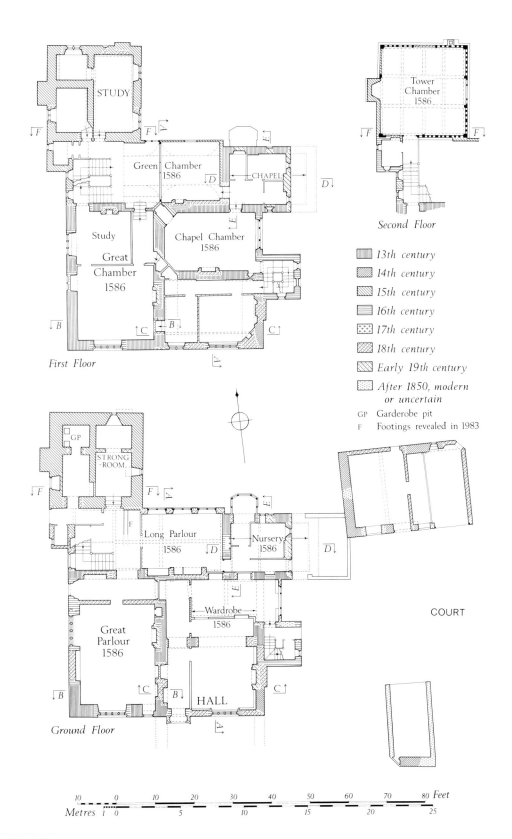

STUDY

Green Chamber
1586

CHAPEL

Tower
Chamber
1586

Second Floor

Study

Great
Chamber
1586

Chapel Chamber
1586

░░░ *13th century*

▨ *14th century*

▧ *15th century*

▤ *16th century*

▦ *17th century*

▨ *18th century*

▨ *Early 19th century*

░ *After 1850, modern
or uncertain*

GP   Garderobe pit

F   Footings revealed in 1983

First Floor

GP

STRONG
-ROOM

Long Parlour
1586

Nursery
1586

COURT

Wardrobe
1586

Great
Parlour
1586

HALL

Ground Floor

10   0   10   20   30   40   50   60   70   80 *Feet*

Metres 1 0   5   10   15   20   25

Fig 64   *No. 21, Aula le Stage*

Plate 86   *No. 21, Aula le Stage, from S*

Plate 87   *No. 21, Aula le Stage, from E, showing truncated hall on left, and gables of the three 13th-century ranges*

(Plate 89). A doorway leading from the hall to the parlour, of which only the stone reveals and lintelled rear-arch survive, was probably inserted at this time. A doorway leading from the parlour to the 'wardrobe', with two-centred arch and ogee moulding with pyramidal stops (but altered), is of late 14th-century appearance. It may be contemporary with a timber partition in the 'wardrobe', which is no longer complete but has three tiers of panels about 2 ft 2 ins wide by 2 ft 11 ins high chamfered towards the room and with signs of a doorway; it is now infilled with brick.

Some fragments remain of medieval outbuildings of uncertain date lying E of the house, together with a gatehouse range which, by the 15th century at latest, occupied the E side of the curtilage and is now part of No. 20 (Figs 60, 62). In 1585 this was the 'back gate'. Carts, or anyone on horseback, would have approached the house from this direction using the lane, which also provided

Section A–A (looking E)

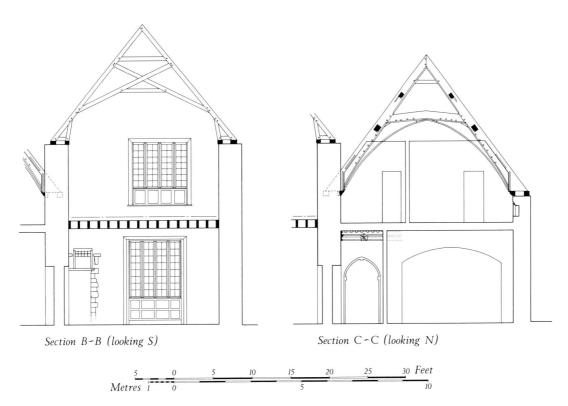

Section B–B (looking S)   *Section C–C (looking N)*

Fig 65 *No. 21, Aula le Stage, sections*
A–A of green chamber, chapel chamber and hall
B–B of great chamber and parlour
C–C of hall

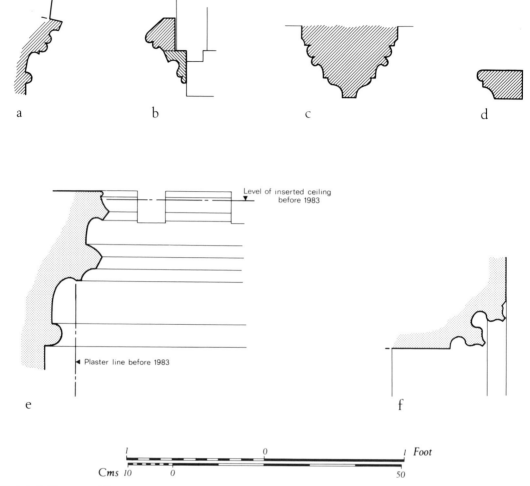

Fig 66   No. 21, Aula le Stage, mouldings

a. cornice of E wall in great chamber
b. cornice of S wall in chapel chamber
c. beam supporting former gallery in chapel

d. N wall-plate of chapel
e. cornice at NW angle of hall
f. rear-arch of E window in hall

access to Crowton's canonry and to the vicars' properties on E. A smaller entry also existed in 1585–6, and presumably earlier, leading into the house between the hall range and the larder and kitchen. A fragment, probably of the kitchen, survives on the S side of the curtilage, of single storey, with the jamb and part of the head of a hollow-chamfered stone doorway and parts of a blocked window adjacent. A further stretch of medieval walling is incorporated in the W wall of No. 20. NE of the house, the ground-floor W end of another outbuilding survives, its original use uncertain, of rubble with a stone doorway on S some 8 ft high, hollow chamfered with a two-centred head, and with square-headed windows in the W and N walls.

The 15th century: enlarged accommodation

In the early 15th century the NW tower was added (Figs 62c, 68, 69, Plate 88), providing a private suite of rooms

Plate 88   No. 21, Aula le Stage, from NE, showing 13th-century chapel on left and early 15th-century tower on right. J Buckler c 1805

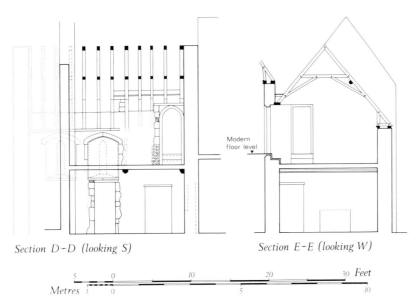

Section D–D (looking S)   Section E–E (looking W)

5   0   10   20   30 Feet
Metres | 0   5   10

Fig 67   No. 21, Aula le Stage, chapel
D–D long-section, with original length restored; E–E cross-section

Plate 89   No. 21, Aula le Stage, hall during restoration, detail of
cornice in NW angle

for the canon on the first floor. Originally the two smaller
rooms opened off the larger which was later a study,
heated by a corbelled-out chimney. The smallest was a
privy chamber, discharging into the basement. The third
chamber has a blocked external doorway dressed only with
tiles, which may have been a temporary one in use during
construction as the others are of stone and hollow chamfered with two-centred heads and broach-stops. All these
rooms have chamfered cornices. The windows may be
largely original, with chamfered edges of differing detail,
and the study has a trefoiled light, while that of the privy
dates from the early 16th century, with hollow-chamfered
and four-centred heads.

The ground floor is barrel vaulted and the floor level
was originally lower than now; the larger room was
possibly a strong-room, with a stout nail-studded door and
original strap-hinges. The N window again has a trefoil
head, while the smaller room has a chamfered slit window
set horizontally.

The lower storeys of the tower are of flint rubble, partly
retaining their render, and faced internally with roughly
banded chalk and flint rubble, but the second floor is
timber framed. It contains a single magnificent room,
much taller than those below, probably the 'certain light
chamber' borrowed by Dean Goldwell in 1463 to draw up a
disciplinary ordinance. There was originally a canted oriel
window some 6 ft wide by 8 ft 10 ins high in the N wall. In
the NW corner there may have been a privy, utilising one
of the two shafts below, but no trace of its framing
survives. In the SE corner the structural vestiges of the
original staircase remain, but its position is anomalous in

that it must have partly masked the three-light window which has the same hollow chamfer and square head as the two chimney-pieces in the tower.

The roof was originally leaded on a heavily timbered ceiling with chamfered tie-beams, purlins, etc. Mortices on the top of the N and S wall-plates must be the remains of a parapet or cresting, but the canon seems to have had no access to his lead-flats, and in the late 18th century they were replaced by a pyramidal structure with purlins braced on to a central post. The impressive timber-framing of the walls keeps much of its rubble infill. The tower was linked to the 13th-century house by a range with a rubble W wall and a timber-framed E one, of which the footings were exposed in 1983.

In 1440 the house was described as needing general repairs throughout and having had its 'implements taken away' [Acts, Hutchins, 14 Oct 1440], such that canons occupied it under protest until 1449. In 1447 chapter ordered the sale of the great furnace for melting lead, which had probably been bought for roofing the tower, the proceeds to be spent on repairs, and in the two years following they twice ordered carpenters and others to rectify the house. One of the areas needing attention was probably the top stage of the tower, where the two original intermediate tie-beams and their arch-braces have been replaced by more massive beams at a higher level, and much of the W framing has been renewed in flint rubble; presumably the lead roof had sagged and pushed out the wall.

A further timber-framed range was added along the N side of the house later in the 15th century, its upper storey supported upon the older buildings to S and E by rounded stone corbels (Fig 65, section A–A, c). On both storeys the timber-framed side wall of the tower-link building was cut away and the new range was extended into it. On the ground floor there was probably a single room spanned by the present intersecting chamfered beams, although its W extent has been reduced since. It was perhaps a with-drawing room for the great parlour. The upper is spanned by two-tier crucks with the remains of arch-braces, which must originally have formed a closed truss even though no traces of the closure survive, because the E bay was a small chamber, perhaps open to the roof, but the W one was ceiled at a lower level and there was a chamfered stone doorway leading into the corner of the 'chapel chamber'. Some decoration on the W wall of the chapel, with wavy lines in red and black, may be 13th century, in which case either the chapel's exterior was ornamented or the framed range had a predecessor; in the 15th century the painting was concealed by a framed wall. Possibly at about the same period two storeys of privy chambers were constructed on SW of the tower, the ground-floor one having a fireplace of which the flue remains.

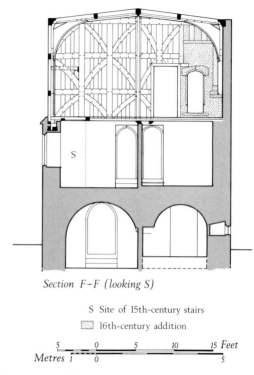

Section F–F (looking S)

S Site of 15th-century stairs
▨ 16th-century addition

	5	0	5	10	15 Feet
Metres 1		0			5

Fig 68   *No. 21, Aula le Stage, section of tower*

16th-century renovations

From the mid 16th to the mid 17th century the curtilage and amenities of the house were at their greatest, with the garden extending N up to the Close Wall; the canons stabled their horses at No. 7 from 1521 until 1637, when stalls were fitted up in the N part of the gatehouse at the Fabric's expense. In this period the canonry was modified in many ways and definition into phases is not entirely possible.

The earliest alterations date from around 1500 when a brick chimney with stone weatherings was constructed with a hearth projecting sideways into the long parlour, a new doorway was constructed in the NE corner of the hall, (Fig 63), and a second floor was added to the privies SW of the tower, faced with flint rubble but constructed largely of bricks measuring 9 by 4¾ by 2 ins; shortly afterwards the party wall between the privies and the tower chamber was rebuilt in rubble with a wave-moulded four-centred stone doorway leading out of the tower (Fig 68).

Some of the work may be contemporary, with several strips of friezes depicting Tudor roses dimidiated with pomegranates (for Henry VIII and Catherine of Aragon) and Italianate motifs, dating from the early or mid 1520s. The panels measure 5½ ins by 18 ins and are of some substance, possibly leather, stamped into a mould (Plate 90). The majority of them are in the long parlour, which may be their original position, as the others are in an early

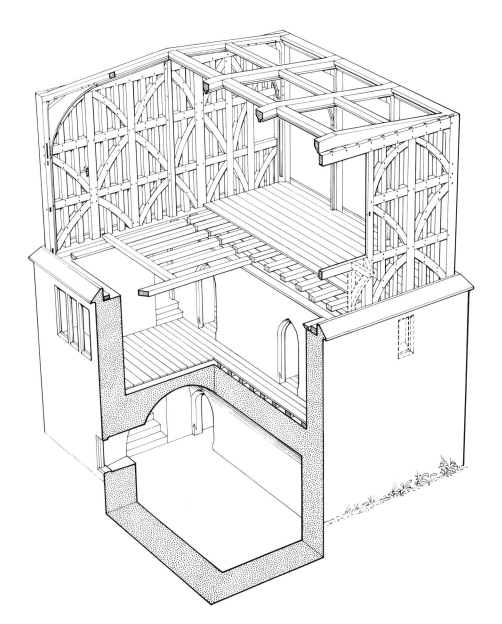

Fig 69   *No. 21, Aula le Stage, cut-away perspective reconstruction of tower*

18th-century study created in the NW corner of the great chamber at the same time as the long parlour was rebuilt.

A more thorough restoration of the house may be attributed to Dr Thomas Benet (1547–58), sometime secretary to Wolsey, supporter of Cromwell, and vicar-general for Bishop Campeggio from 1524 to 1545. He set up his own monument in the Cathedral. The principal rooms were transformed and the great parlour, great chamber and chapel chamber were given handsome windows some 8 ft wide (all now altered or restored), with external hollow-chamfered and cavetto mouldings. Ceilings were inserted with oak ribs forming intersecting geometrical patterns (Plate 91). In the chambers the ribs

Plate 90   *No. 21, Aula le Stage, detail of frieze in long parlour*

Plate 91   *No. 21, Aula le Stage, chapel chamber, ceiling*

fitted a little awkwardly to their canted 13th-century roofs; ribs with simpler mouldings were fixed to an oak boarded ceiling in the long parlour. The great chamber had its floor replaced, probably at a new level, and was given a new doorway from the N stairs, and a brick fireplace. In the great parlour a small stone-lined recess, perhaps of 16th-century date, has its wall towards the fireplace drilled with rows of holes and was no doubt a salt cupboard. The wall opposite in this period had three new windows of equal size with the ribbed ceiling extending into them, but the N one had already been made into a garden door with a window above it in 1586.

A fireplace built in the former chapel suggests a post-Reformation change of use, and the 'long parlour' was reunited, with its chimney set back against the S wall. A stair turret was added on E, lit by windows with four-centred heads and hollow-chamfer, roll and ogee mouldings, or square headed and hollow chamfered; it serviced the chapel chamber via a portal, and a quatrefoil oculus placed there looked down into the hall. The two high level windows on S and E evidently lit the closet referred to in 1586, situated at the top of the staircase. The principal stairs at this date were probably on S of the tower (as in 1586) and the smaller first-floor tower room was made to open off them. Doorways attributed to this period are of stone and chamfered with four-centred heads, some with pyramidal stops, and much use is made of thin bricks measuring 9 by 4½ by 1¾ ins for the construction of hearths and chimneys and the insertion of doorways and windows etc. In his will dated 1558 Dr Benet named the great chamber over the great parlour, the chapel chamber and the gatehouse chamber [*Wilts N and Q* vi, 135].

More substantial information occurs in a dilapidations survey of 1585 and inventory of 1586. In 1585 Canon Procter had sold many of the fittings to a non-resident canon, including wainscot from two and portals from

three rooms, also from the entry by the kitchen and bakehouse; several of these had been installed by Procter, and were renewed within seventeen months by his successor [Everett 1941, 305]. The variety of oak wainscot fitted at one time or another in the house is suggested by the remaining fragments which are mainly 16th century and have chamfered, beaded or moulded edges and plain, linenfold or parchemin panels, as well as flush oak boarding with lapped edges of undetermined date. In several of the principal rooms it was fixed to battens let into the walls, which appear to date from before the 16th century and are possibly original.

The 'inventory of implements' made in 1586 necessarily lists all the wainscot, doors and portals, or interior porches so typical of the period, and incidentally provides a route around the house and gatehouse (Fig 63). Outbuildings are largely omitted, but we know from later descriptions that the area to E was part courtyard, part gardens divided by walling, hence the well-fitted 'garden studdy' in the gatehouse range. The 'dilapidated' granary and dovecot mentioned in 1585 were probably somewhere in the N part of the curtilage. Following is an abbreviated version with modern spelling of the 'Inventory of Implements in Mr Dr Bold's house' [Chapter Act Book 1563–1606, 132–3]. (A fuller version, wrongly dated 13 September 1585, appears in *WAM* xlix, 306–7.)

1586 Sept. 15. Dr Bold's house.
The hall: three screens.
The great parlour: wainscot, one fair portal at the door, with 3 doors and boarded under-foot, the parlour door, the door at the upper end of the parlour, the garden door.
The long parlour: wainscoted and a portal of new wainscot, a door with a hasp and a door towards the nursery.
The nursery: wainscot board round about, with [a] chimney, an old boarded portal.
The wardrobe: the door going into the great parlour and one other going into the court. The door at the upper end of the Hall.
The closet door going into the chapel chamber.
The chapel chamber: sealed with wainscot with 2 portals.
The green chamber: a round portal with a door of wainscot, the chimney, all with wainscot board and a boarded portal and wainscot covers for the window.
The study chamber: wainscot boards round about & a boarded portal.
The door at the head of the stairs going from the great parlour.
The tower chamber: a portal with 2 doors, wainscot boards to the W window.
The great chamber: a portal with 2 doors, sealed with wainscot, 3 cupboards with leaves under the W window.
The cellar.
The buttery; the pantry; the entry by the kitchen; the larder; a pump at the door; the kitchen.

The garden study: a round frame for books with 4 turning desks & double shelves overhead & 2 hanging desks with a chair in the midst.
The chamber over the back gate: old painted cloths.
The stair-head.
The chamber at the N end of the gate house: old painted cloths and sealed with wainscot over the head.
The house by the back gate on the N side.

The 17th to 19th century

In 1637 Dr Matthew Nicholas was appointed to the house and the following year received £24 for dilapidations and permission to 'take down a part of the old buildings behind the screen at the lower end of his hall, also to make a new entrance or passage into his house opposite the church' [Everett C, 27]. This implies that the entry near the kitchen was to be renewed, and possibly moved. Comparison of the 1649 Survey [Everett 1941, 308–9] and that of 1586 reveals little change in the house. In the gatehouse range the N room had become a stable and the garden study had evidently been dismantled.

Canon Priaulx gained possession at the Restoration, and spent £160 on the house before 1670 [Bod Lib, Tanner MS 143, f 259]. His successor Francis Horton was allowed to demolish 'the old bakehouse' in 1675, and by this date a new kitchen must have been established in the former long parlour although the present large fireplace there is of mid 18th-century date. In 1696 he was leasing out the house, a practice continued by Michael Geddes (1699–1713), their tenant being the schoolmistress Ann Deare; graffiti including the dates 1701 and 1709 on the W window-jambs of the great parlour and great chamber are probably relics of her pupils.

Thomas Coker was appointed in 1713 and at once set about refurbishment. Chapter allowed him to 'take down the whole front of his house and to new build the same and make a commodious modern house with proper offices thereto', and to appropriate the trees in front and stone of the Close Wall behind towards the repairs (the latter permit renewed in 1718). The S end of the hall was demolished (Fig 70a) and, in rebuilding it, Coker went to some trouble to preserve an antique appearance, reusing an old doorway and windows and building his new gable some feet higher than the roofline, for symmetry's sake (Plates 86, 87); within the hall an upper storey with two rooms was inserted, reached by the 16th-century stair turret, a chimney was built within the 14th-century window opening, and a new doorway was made into the great parlour. On W a passage into the centre of the house was created and a new main staircase built of oak (Fig 64), the W end of the cruck-built range being cut away to allow its approach to the lower chamber. Coker formed a study in the N part of the great chamber, with a false ceiling

partly constructed of smoke-blackened rafters from the 14th-century hall, and a fireplace with moulded stone architrave and bolection overmantel panel; similar chimney architraves also occur in the green and chapel chambers. The ashlar for refacing the kitchen (long parlour) was doubtless removed from the Close Wall and the upper framing was also largely rebuilt while introducing the windows seen by Buckler (Plate 88).

The outbuildings E of the house appear to have been altered more than once during the 18th century. Naish's map of 1716 shows a long N range linking the surviving outbuildings there with the gatehouse range [RCHM 1980, Plate 16]. In 1758 Canon Sherard was given leave to demolish the medieval kitchen, and in 1766 he altered the N range, demolishing the 'old wash-house', converting the then stable into a coach-house and building a new stable.

A late 18th-century successor, Barfoot Colton (1788–1803), made a further restoration. He turned the old hall into a library with bookcases let into the walls, screening it from the S entrance passage by a partition, and enlarging it into the former wardrobe (Fig 70b); the latter became an entrance hall and was given a slate-roofed brick porch with a hexagonal lantern astride its external doorway. The stairs in the E turret were reconstructed and made to open off this porch through a 16th-century stone doorway brought from elsewhere, and he made a new garden door to the S of the tower. At this time the old chapel was in use as a servants' parlour with a central chimney and a newly added bay window (Plate 88). Colton also inserted a triple sash window in the tower chamber and converted 16th-century ones similarly in the chapel chamber, drawing room and library, and to him may be attributed the widening of two 14th-century doorways on the ground floor, with the addition of imposts and keystones.

The last phase of appreciable modifications was of a mainly antiquarian nature, made by the wealthy poet and antiquary William Lisle Bowles (1829–50). On the S front he built the porch and parapets, restored mullions to the windows, and added window labels generally; he also constructed the internally projecting brick chimneys of the library and drawing room, the latter having a stone chimney-piece with a four-centred arch and coved cornice, and created in the tower cellar an oratory with a late medieval stained glass figure of a kneeling man in a blue habit. However, he curtailed the 13th-century chapel for use as a scullery (although the chapel's identity and its date were still recognised [Dodsworth 1814, 155 n]), removing the inserted central chimney and flooring it over, incorporating a doorway and remains of the lancet windows in a new E wall [Hall 1834]. At the garden entrance Bowles added octagonal ashlar gatepiers with Perpendicular detail and in the garden to E of the house stands a monument of eclectic medieval design in rendered brick and stone which he erected to his predecessor William Coxe [*DNB*], inscribed 'M/GULMI COXE/LITTERIS PER EUROPAM/ILLUSTRIS/W.L.B./SUCCESSOR/HIS   AEDIBUS   CANONICIS/P. MDCCCXXX'.

At Canon Bowles' death in 1850 chapter leased the

house to a Mr Kelsey, with an allowance equivalent to three years' rent for repairs, and at Lady Poore's death in 1869 some £600 was spent on repairs to a specification by T H Wyatt; among their tasks was the truing up of many sagging floors with deal boards.

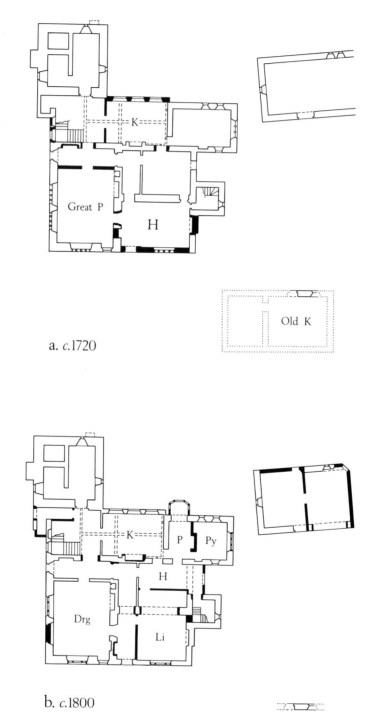

Fig 70   *Nos 20 and 21, Aula le Stage, reconstructed plans, scale 1 in. to 32 ft*

Houses in Rosemary Lane

22 The Close

22 The Close is a cottage in Rosemary Lane, formerly one of two belonging to the vicars and occupied by their members, the earliest identified being John Hobson in 1539–40; its companion has stood to N and was noted from 1649 until 1729. In 1649 No. 22 was the house of James Clarke, comprising a hall, a parlour with wainscoting 5 ft high, a buttery, a kitchen and four chambers. This house was thoroughly rebuilt in the mid 18th century and in 1765 the vicars discussed at a meeting of chapter which of them should occupy 'the new house lately erected in Rosemary Lane' [Acts 1741–96, 20 Nov 1765].

Although now of mainly 18th-century appearance, traces of the older house remain (Fig 71). The medieval building is represented by the ground-floor N wall and is implied by the reconstruction of the E wall at two dates in the 17th century, the earliest fabric being coursed flints with tile lacing courses. The house must have been substantially reconstructed in the early 17th century and the description of 1649 can still be followed; a trimmer joist in the kitchen suggests the position of the 17th-century staircase. Repairs to the masonry in this period include the stone, flint, tile and brick rubble with dressed stone quoins of the N wall and the E chimney, also brickwork in English bond to N of the chimney. Included in the N wall are gobs of fired clay of irregular size but much larger than normal bricks, probably waste material from a brick kiln.

In the 18th century the outer walls were generally rebuilt and probably raised, and a hipped roof built, the main elevation being in English-bond brick with lead-glazed casements but the upper storey of the rear wall tile-hung timber-framing. The house was entirely refitted and the principal internal feature of this period is the staircase, with a latticed balustrade of Chinese style, inserted in the 17th-century hall. Dates from 1770 to 1781

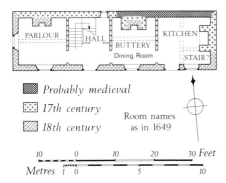

Probably medieval

17th century

18th century

Room names as in 1649

Fig 71   *No. 22*

and initials, mainly G M and W, scratched on the stones and bricks of the N, E and S walls, are of no obvious significance.

The garden wall to S of the house includes a stretch built in flint rubble with lacing courses of tiles set diagonally, of medieval date.

23 The Close

23 The Close is called Loders after a medieval prebendal mansion which stood nearby, if not on the same spot. Loders Place had belonged to a priory of this name near Bridport in Dorset, which was suppressed in 1414, and at that time or later the dean and chapter must have acquired it; by 1443 it had been in ruins for several years and its demolition was ordered in 1446 with a view to salvaging the materials.

From then until 1690 or later the tenement was a garden. The survey of 1649 says it was 120 ft long, 45 ft 6 ins wide at the E end and 57 ft 6 ins wide at the W end; at the entrance was a parcel of land 22 ft square. The dimensions no longer fit because of a small enlargement made in 1712 but the plot is still identifiable; the W wall of the 18th-century house corresponds with the W end of the garden.

In 1683 a lease of the garden was granted to Mr Harvey for forty years, which was transferred in 1705 to Edward Ryder. In 1707 'Mr Ryder's dwelling-house' existed, and that year he acquired land to W for the purpose of building a coach-house and stables. Ryder had probably left the house he built by 1716 and tenants succeeded one another fairly rapidly until 1900, only two families remaining for as long as forty years.

The house was described as 'very much out of repair' in 1763, when it belonged to the Hayters of Mompesson House [Chapter Estate Bk 1, No. 66620, 51]. Sale particulars of 1850 describe it as 'containing an entrance hall, a well-proportioned dining room and drawing room, morning room, 7 family bedrooms, 2 good servants' rooms, a front and back staircase, a large kitchen, servants' hall, back kitchen etc; extensive underground wine, beer and coal cellars etc, spacious yard adjoining with a double coach house, 3 stall stable, large loosebox, harness room, lofts' [*SJ*, 27 July 1850].

The house built by Ryder is in two parts: the front square, of two storeys and attic raised above cellars and incorporating the main staircase, and a lower rear wing housing the kitchen, with a servant's room over and self-contained with its own staircase (Fig 72). Originally the cellar was accessible both from stairs beneath the principal ones and from external ones ascending in the yard by the kitchen door. The very large chimney at the back of the drawing room probably indicates that brewing or washing took place beneath in the best-lit room of the

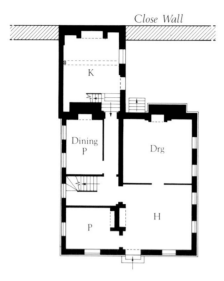

Fig 72　*No. 23, reconstructed plan, c 1705*

cellar. The original position of the front door is uncertain, but presumably was central and led into a hall.

Externally, Ryder's work is of brick in English bond with plain quoins, platband and coved eaves, the roof hipped at the front but twin-gabled to N (Plate 92). Stone is used only for part of the plinth and for cellar windows. The thick-glazed sash windows to S and W are not original although they occupy positions of *c* 1705 on W, but some of the dormer windows, with ogee-moulded cornices, may be original. The E wall was almost entirely rebuilt later in the century, probably at the same time as the plan was rearranged in its present form (Fig 73).

Original fittings on the ground floor include several doors with three pairs of fielded panels and bolection-moulded architraves, and a similar architrave to the stair window. The morning room is fitted with bolection-moulded panelling in two heights under a heavy wooden cornice; it is probably original to the house but supple-

Plate 92　*No. 23 from SW*

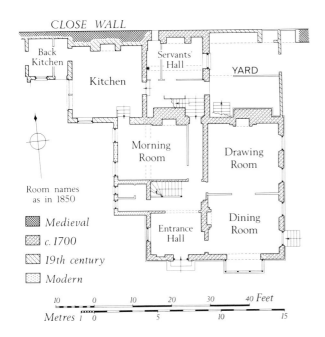

CLOSE WALL

Back Kitchen
Servants' Hall
YARD
Kitchen
Morning Room
Drawing Room
Room names as in 1850
Dining Room
Entrance Hall

▓ Medieval

▒ c. 1700

▨ 19th century

░ Modern

Fig 73   No. 23

mented and partly reset when the room was extended W in 1936. The oak staircase is continuous from the ground floor to the attics, with a close string faced with an ogee-moulded panel, square newel-posts and turned balusters; an archway at its base, with three-centred head and moulded capitals and cornice, is reset and perhaps once spanned the approach from the original hall. On the first floor, the room over the morning room is now partitioned but retains part of its bolection-moulded and fielded panelling with a heavy wooden cornice and a moulded stone fireplace surround. There are original plank and muntin walls and plank doors in the attics. A jowl-headed post supporting the kitchen ceiling beam is of early 17th-century appearance and probably reused.

In the first half of the 19th century a new kitchen was added to NW, later heightened to two storeys, and fittings in the dining room and on the first floor were renewed. In 1899 D J K Macdonald had permission to add a bay-window to a blind wall of his dining room, and possibly he cloaked the S wall in render.

The E wall of the garden is partly medieval and is built of flint with herringbone tile lacing courses.

24 The Close

24 The Close is a three-storey brick house of 18th-century date. It was a vicars' choral property, first recorded in 1649 as a house and orchard, and described in 1677 as an orchard and 'little cottage of two bays of building' [Leases 1673–1717, 24 Sept 1677]. In the Restoration period the lease belonged to the Joyce family of Bagber in Dorset, who also held the adjoining house on S which they appear

to have combined with it; a marked change in ground level across the centre of the property probably defines the junction of the former tenements, no doubt the sites of two of the medieval vicars' dwellings. By the late 17th century it was being sublet, a procedure commonly followed by later tenants until the 1850s, the subtenants being chiefly widows.

In 1721 the house had stood empty for a number of years and shortly afterwards Thomas Haskett took it, subsequent leases crediting him with its construction; in 1731 his lease describes it as a 'messuage lately erected', and chapter's permission to cut down sycamore trees in front of his house in 1728 possibly dates his work. He probably remodelled the old house extensively, but changes of alignment and thick walls which run up within the house, together with variations in floor level, suggest that something of the Joyces' house was kept; Flemish-bond brickwork, especially on the E and N elevations, probably dates from his time, three storeys high on the rear half of the house but two at the front.

A generation later the house was again extensively altered, the S and W elevations being rebuilt in header-bond brickwork, and the whole house raised to three storeys and roofed with three parallel hipped ridges behind a parapet. The joinery is mainly of this period and not of advanced character; the staircase, having slender turned balusters on a close string, with panelled newel-posts and dado rails, is continuous from the ground to the second floor and doors are two-panelled; two bedroom chimney-pieces with moulded wooden brackets have survived and several rooms retain simple moulded cornices. A small cellar was contrived beneath the staircase. No leases between 1731 and 1781 have survived so it is not known for whom this work was done, but in 1787 it was

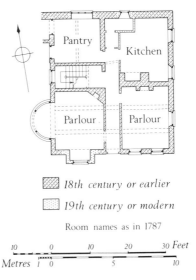

Pantry
Kitchen
Parlour
Parlour

▨ 18th century or earlier

░ 19th century or modern

Room names as in 1787

Fig 74   No. 24

advertised as a 'genteel new built dwelling house consisting of 2 parlours, a kitchen, a brewhouse, pantry and cellar on the ground floor, with dining room, 5 good chambers and a large laundry above stairs' [*SJ*, 24 Sept 1787] (Fig 74).

Among the subsequent alterations, a handsome door with beaded panels leading into the room over the kitchen etc, which is larger and taller than the others, suggests that this room had a more exalted use in the late 18th century than as a laundry and possibly it was at one time a study. In the early 19th century a graceful bow-window with dentilled cornice, convex reeded pilasters and french windows was built for James Foot (tenant 1808–29), since removed, and before 1860 a second bay-window had been added to the same parlour.

In the 20th century the house has been occupied by canons and a clerk of the Cathedral works, and repairs made in the 1950s resulted in extensive refacing of the W elevation. Chancellor Dunlop added a spacious single-storey drawing room to W of the 'parlours' in 1974.

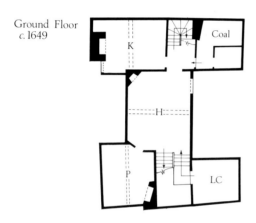

Fig 75   *No. 25, reconstructed plans*

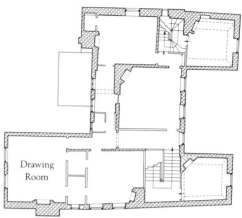

First Floor

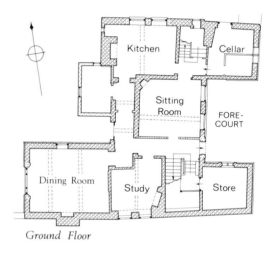

Ground Floor

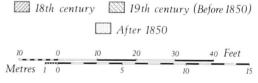

Fig 76   *No. 25*

25 The Close

25 The Close is a house now mainly of early 18th-century appearance but owing much of its form to an earlier one which, with its central hall and 'upper' and 'lower' ends, is sub-medieval in plan (Fig 75). In the early 17th century it had formerly been two tenements, which probably originated as the dwellings of medieval vicars, but they had been combined by 1632 and were described *c* 1649 as 'all those two messuages...consisting of a hall, a kitchen, a parlour, a lodging chamber below ye stairs, a cellar, a coalhouse, and 6 chambers above ye stairs'. These rooms can still be identified.

From 1671 until probably 1709 there were subtenants. Wingfield Brockwell obtained the lease in 1702 and his renewal in 1716 included a piece of land measuring 8 ft by 1 ft on which he had erected a chimney, evidently that of the dining room (Fig 76). The Godolphin School occupied the house from 1784 to 1788 as its first home [*SJ*, 12 July 1784, 23 Feb 1788]. During the 19th century members of the Wickens family lived here, including Elizabeth Wickens, the topographical artist. It was subsequently the Probate Registry, and after its departure chapter paid £150 for 'repairs and alterations' in 1907.

The early 18th century

Brockwell rebuilt the house, which had probably been timber framed, in brick (now mainly pebble-dashed), added the passage behind the hall, and extended the S range westwards. This resulted in two main ranges of two storeys with garrets, and a couple of lower projections to E, of one mezzanine storey above a basement; his main staircase reaches the first floor only, with back stairs to N serving the garrets. On the first floor the four largest rooms, including one that was probably the drawing room, appear to have had closets (Fig 75).

The main elevation is in Flemish bond with a gauged and moulded platband, coved eaves and a hipped roof, and the main entrance was probably central. Within, many of the fittings are Brockwell's, some *ex situ*, while others are later imitation work. His doors are of oak with two pairs of lightly fielded panels or of two plain softwood panels, in ogee-moulded architraves; overmantels generally have a large panel above a low one, and panelled rooms have heavy wooden cornices. The dining room contains bolection-moulded panelling, the central E panels projecting slightly, and a matching doorway. In the parlour, an original door and ceiling cornice, a bolection-moulded stone chimney-piece and matching overmantel and overdoor panels were probably *in situ*, but the walls were mainly lined with 17th-century wainscot brought in more recently (now removed).

The staircases are of oak, the principal one having an ogee-moulded string and spirally turned balusters (Plate 93); that to N has similar strings and newels and slender turned balusters. On the first floor, the approach to the drawing room is spanned by a wooden arch with panelled pilasters and spandrels, and semicircular head with keyblock and cornice. The drawing room and the chambers over the hall and parlour are each partly lined with plain original panelling and in the drawing room there is a bolection-moulded stone chimney-piece. In the roof of the E range, knee-rafters are partly visible and the internal door to the coalhouse is stoutly planked.

Later history

A sash window in the kitchen chamber, with thick glazing bars and small panes, and a widened doorway to the dining

Plate 93   *No. 25, main staircase*

room, with a fielded-panelled oak door, are evidence of 18th-century alterations, and the ceiling plaster of the garret over the drawing room is incised 'IS 1741'. The mezzanine room over the 'lodging chamber' was fitted with a sash window and dentilled chimney-piece c 1800, before which it was unheated.

The front door-case and the french window in the dining room were probably installed for the Wickens, and either they or an early 20th-century tenant fitted the 17th-century oak wainscot, including that in the entrance passage carved with guilloche mouldings, and such neo-Georgian details as the window joinery of the hall chamber. Other 17th-century fittings, including ovolo-moulded window mullions used as struts in the roof and panelled doors in the kitchen chamber and attics, were probably salvaged by Brockwell in rebuilding the house. On 19th-century maps a W extension to the kitchen is shown.

Houses in North Walk

26 The Close

26 The Close was built *c* 1770 as a private house. Formerly there had been on the site a smaller one belonging to the vicars choral and occupied by lay vicars; in 1649 it consisted of a hall, kitchen, little buttery, coalhouse, two chambers and a closet, but of this nothing remains. In 1769 the vicars petitioned chapter, stating that the house, then James Gardiner's, was ruinous and a new one had been provided for him (No. 74); and that John Chaffey, a prebendary and president of the Consistory Court, had proposed to rebuild it 'in handsome manner, which will not be an ornament to the Close but an advantage to all succeeding vicars' [Chapter Acts 1741–96, 25 Nov 1769]. In 1771 the house was 'lately erected' [*ibid*, 19 July 1771].

After Chaffey's death in 1782, the vicars continued to lease it, at first to Edward Moore, vicar of the Close, and then to lay people. In 1818 it was advertised as 'compact, well adapted for a genteel family, [with] a breakfast parlour 13 ft 6 ins by 12 ft 5 ins, Dining room 24 ft by 16 ft 10 ins, and drawing room 24 ft by 16 ft 10 ins, with convenient bed chambers, dressing rooms etc.', together with a stable for three horses and a coach-house [*SJ*, 30 Nov 1818]. It is now occupied by Holmwood School.

Chaffey's house is well preserved and consists of a front range of three storeys above a basement, and a projecting kitchen (Fig 77). The basement, which is entered from opposite the kitchen door, has an open fireplace under the breakfast parlour, probably for washing or brewing. The thin wall at the rear and the apparent lack of an external kitchen door at this period suggest that there may have

Plate 94 *No. 26 from S*

been a lean-to along the back of the dining room originally. On the first floor, the drawing room is accompanied by another parlour, and on the top floor there are two heated bedrooms, each with a dressing room. The kitchen has a housekeeper's room and an attic bedroom above it, of low build, serviced by the secondary staircase.

Construction is in brick, with the projecting courses, chamfered quoins and window keys in stone to S and E (Plate 94); the bricks on S are in header bond, on E in Flemish, while the W elevation is mathematical tiled in header bond and the N is tile hung. The main entrance has a fluted architrave, narrow pilasters with pendent floral garlands, and broken pediment above a wood-glazed fanlight, and the basement area is protected by spiked iron railings. The kitchen is also of brick with a hipped roof. Within, many of the original fittings remain, doors having three pairs of fielded panels and the four principal ground- and first-floor rooms moulded and fluted plaster ceiling cornices, some with dentils; the chimney-piece of the dining room is partly of stone, that of the breakfast parlour of wood, flanked by cupboards surmounted by oval niches and pedestals with floral garlands (Plate 95). On the first floor, the chimney-piece of the drawing room is of white marble flanked by panelled wooden pilasters with Adam-esque swags, that of the parlour stone with dentilled and moulded shelf. The staircase connects all floors continuously and has turned newel-posts with necking bands and square balusters. In the basement, doors are planked and ceiling beams are of pine with beaded arises, while in the kitchen the beams are chamfered with ogee stops.

In the latter part of the 19th century, the family rooms were extended to NE in brick under a slate roof, on two storeys over a basement.

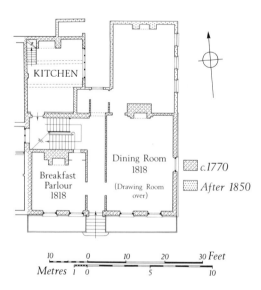

Fig 77 *No. 26*

(Plan labels: KITCHEN; Breakfast Parlour 1818; Dining Room 1818; (Drawing Room over); *c.1770*; *After 1850*)

10   0   10   20   30 Feet
Metres 1   0   5   10

Plate 95 *No. 26, chimney-piece in breakfast parlour*

27 The Close

27 The Close is a small dwelling mainly of two storeys belonging to the vicars choral and formerly occupied by lay vicars (Plate 96, right). In 1649 it was Edmond Tucker's house and contained a hall, parlour, kitchen, buttery and two chambers, but successive rebuilding has altered his house out of recognition. The adjoining property on W also formed part of the house until the Interregnum; in about 1652 William and Dulcibella Paine (Tucker's granddaughter) obtained possession, and spent a 'great sum of money in new building and repairing the premises...as is now very apparent to be seen' [vicars' petition to chapter *c* 1673, Everett L, 11–12]. In about 1660 the older part of the house returned to use by lay vicars while Tucker's descendants obtained leases of their new wing, now No. 28 The Close, which was finally demolished and rebuilt in 1898.

In the latter part of the 18th century the house was sublet and became neglected, so that in 1801 chapter requested the vicars to repair it. They responded by granting a lease to the builder and surveyor John Peniston ('bricklayer') in 1807, and in 1819 he was said to have 'rebuilt' it [Vicars' Leases, Everett A, 38]. Peniston's heirs retained it until 1862 but sublet from 1829, an advertisement in 1836 describing it as 'genteel, consisting of drawing and dining rooms, small parlour, kitchen and offices, four best bedrooms and servants' attics' [*SJ*, 31 Oct 1836]. Chapter minutes of 1937 noted the construction of a new bay-window.

The house is now chiefly Peniston's, with late 19th-century fittings (Fig 78). His work includes the construction of the S wall of brick in header bond, with sash windows, and the single-storey kitchen, of brick with a slate roof. The previous form of the house is suggested in Fig 79. Older elements in the front range are the W chimney, which has 17th- or 18th-century brick shafts

Plate 96 *Nos 27–31 (right to left) from SE*

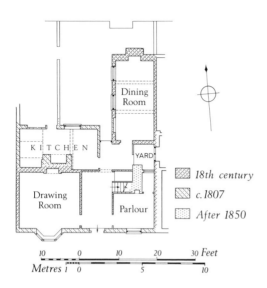

Fig 78   *No. 27*

Plate 97   *No. 29 from SE*

upon a base which may be more ancient, and a late 18th-century chimney-piece in the drawing room, of wood with panelled pilasters and frieze with tablet enriched with ribbands and floral swags. Street-front railings with ball finials are also 18th century.

The E wing escaped Peniston's attention and was probably built by Richard Fortt, resident during the first two decades of the 18th century. Its walls are of poor quality brickwork, now partly rendered and partly tile hung, retaining thick-glazed sash windows, and the ground-floor room has bolection-moulded panelling of deal with an ovolo-moulded and hollow-chamfered cornice; its door has three pairs of fielded panels and the stone chimney-piece has a wooden architrave with pulvinated frieze and heavily moulded cornice, and a single ogee-moulded panel above.

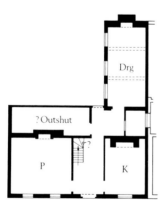

Fig 79   *No. 27, reconstructed plan, before 1807*

29 The Close

29 The Close is a house dating mainly from the latter part of the 14th century, whose interest is belied by the 19th-century details of its main elevation (Plates 96 centre, 97). It probably originated as a minor canonry but is poorly documented and nothing is known of it before 1649, when it belonged to the vicars choral and was the official residence of one of their members, comprising a hall, parlour, kitchen, buttery, woodhouse and three chambers. During the 18th century the vicars appointed to it commonly leased it out. Extensive repairs in 1971 revealed much new evidence while concealing or destroying original features. Originally, an open hall stood to W (Fig 81), but in the 15th century the W part of it was separated off and in 1649 the small dwelling of a lay vicar stood there; it was demolished *c* 1873 by a tenant, A B Middleton.

The medieval house

Despite the truncation of the hall, the original plan is well preserved (Fig 80). In the 14th century the house was entered through a screens passage, dividing the open hall from its storeyed cross-wing, which also had a central passage, leading to the staircase and dividing a comparatively large kitchen with a close-joisted ceiling and a chamfered and hollow-chamfered beam from the front part with a simpler beam which presumably contained the service rooms. In the kitchen there was an open hearth beneath a smoke-bay supported on ceiling beams, and the original external door and a wall-cupboard in the SW corner some 1 ft 6 ins high remain. The upper floor of the cross-wing is divided into two well-finished chambers, both with original fireplaces. The larger was a great chamber (Figs 81, 82), with the stairs leading into it, and there are traces of a window which lit the stairs. A small chamber over the porch was perhaps a study or oratory and it must have been reached either from a passage or gallery over the screens passage, or from stairs within the hall.

Certain architectural details are also well preserved. The porch has an outer arch with double-ogee moulding and convex base-stops (Fig 83), reminiscent of the early rather than the late 14th century and it is possibly the relic of an earlier house, but other doorways at a, b and c on Fig 80 are of the late 14th century with four-centred heads and chamfered jambs with low pyramidal stops. Again, the windows of the porch differ by having two-centred heads and hollow chamfers whereas those in the kitchen are chamfered and square headed, but the wall-recess there has a two-centred arch. One of the porch windows is cut from a single piece of wood. The fireplaces have chamfered stone architraves and each has the remains of a stone shelf with roll and cove mouldings painted red or green.

The timberwork is also of good quality and the main posts of the screens passage wall are triple chamfered to the hall, with double-chamfered ones at the doorway. In the great chamber, the roof is arch braced with many wind-braces and the timbers are chamfered or hollow chamfered (Figs 82, 84) but the private chamber had a more unusual roof with a central truss composed of chamfered and gently curved members forming a scissor-brace (Fig 85). In general, coursed flint rubble including tiles is the principal building material, with stone linings for window-jambs, but a single post and two rails of the timber-framed rear wall of the hall and its screens partitions, with the framing on a rubble plinth 3 ft high, show its mixed construction. Internally, at least part of the wall between front room and stair passage is timber framed with flush panels of oak.

Later history

In the 15th century the open hall was abandoned: in length it was reduced by about half and a floor was inserted to create an upper storey, the roof being raised to gain headroom. The new upper room, which is partly above the screens passage, has an original ceiling of chamfered intersecting beams with step and concave stops and chamfered wall-plates and in the new timber-framed N wall there is a window of three lights with square mullions set diagonally. The roof was always concealed and has clasped purlins, the W truss with a king-strut between tie-beam and collar. A fireplace in the buttery and pantry, with chamfered stone architrave and fireback and jambs constructed with tiles, suggests that this became a parlour.

In the early 17th century the kitchen was enlarged to N, in flint and stone rubble with a new chimney having a brick stack with three weathered offsets, the old hearth was removed and a partition inserted to create the present dining room. This enlargement was extended in brick in the following century, and in the late 18th century an eared wooden chimney-piece was installed in the 'parlour'. Late 17th-century oak panelling, with fielded centres and ogee-moulded edges, is now reset in the entrance hall and on the stairs.

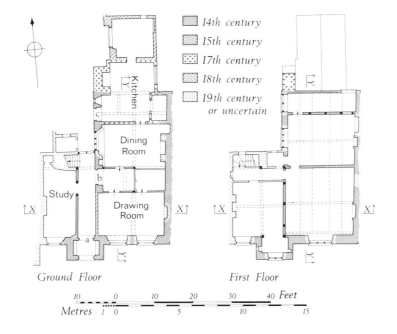

Fig 80   No. 29

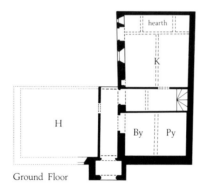

Fig 81   *No. 29, reconstructed plan, as in 14th century*

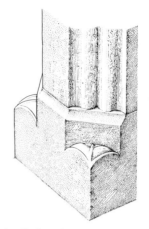

Fig 83   *No. 29, detail of porch entrance arch*

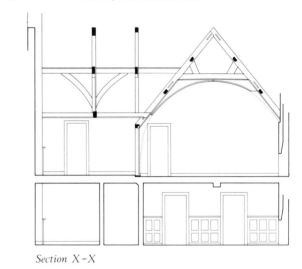

Section X–X

Fig 82   *No. 29, interior view of great chamber*

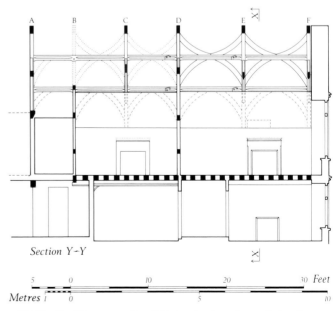

Section Y–Y

Fig 84   *No. 29, cross-section X–X showing truss in great chamber, long-section Y–Y showing roofs of great chamber and private chamber*

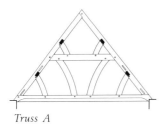

Truss A

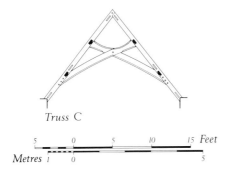

Truss C

Fig 85   No. 29, roof sections:
A Truss, in N gable
C Truss, in private chamber

A minor facelift probably dates from the late 1820s when John Greenly, vicar, obtained the house. The S elevation was stuccoed and Tudorised, with new windows and cement labels, and new stairs were contrived in a small extension (Fig 80), while a cast-iron grate with 'Tudor' details was installed in a bedroom. In 1971 the stairs were replaced on their original site.

31 The Close

31 The Close is a small house which belonged to the vicars choral. It has a substantial medieval nucleus but documents, mainly leases, exist no further back than 1633. In the Parliamentary Survey of 1649/50 the house contained a hall, a parlour, a kitchen, buttery and larder, a dining room above stairs, six chambers and two closets. The vicars granted leases mainly to lay people, some of whom sublet the house, and the longest tenancy was that of several female members of the Wyndham family, from c 1750 until 1836. Their attempt to sell the lease in 1828 included the description: 'on the ground floor an entrance hall, dining parlour, kitchen, pantry and brewhouse; on the 2nd floor a drawing room, 3 best bedrooms and 3 good attic rooms' [SJ, 29 Sept 1828].

The house has two main phases of construction, of which the two parts of the N range are late or submedieval, and the W link and the S range appear to date from the late 17th century (Fig 86). However, it is clear from the Parliamentary Survey that the house was then already of about its present size, and the surviving medieval range set back from the street suggests its origin in the Middle Ages as a courtyard house, which was at least partly timber framed. Two alternative reconstructions of the plan are shown in Fig 87; the main entry was probably through buildings flanking the street, leading to a hall doorway in the position of the present dining room one, but it is possible that the hall and services were in the front range and the parlour etc at the rear. Assuming the former interpretation, there was a hall open to the roof in the N range (Fig 87a), and bays A–C were added to it (Fig 88), probably replacing an earlier range. The N wall retains one timber post at C and this and the new roof were butted against the older hall building. In this position they perhaps housed the service rooms, although they are well finished with a chamfered cornice at the W end and a plank and muntin partition (Fig 86). Of this only part of the former top rail remains exposed; its mouldings are late medieval (Fig 89, a) but it is not certainly *in situ*. The first floor contained two rooms of similar size, but the east one (Fig 88, B–C) was perhaps a first-floor parlour or great chamber and has a well-finished roof with a cornice, wind-braces and purlins all chamfered with run-out stops; the stairs probably led into this room. The W room (private chamber ?) has a chamfer on the lower edge of the purlins only. Roof trusses are closed and have various combinations of curved raking struts from the tie-beam to the collar and from the tie-beam and collar to the principals. Purlins are butted except at the gable (Fig 88, A), where they are clasped.

In the first half of the 16th century the present single-storey hall (or parlour) was built with a new great chamber above it (Fig 88, D–F), and a shorter bay to E which perhaps contained stairs leading to a small room which might have been a chapel. Little remains of the timber-framing; only the head of a post at D remains in the N wall. The former hall retains a central ceiling beam together with a cornice on E and parts of others on N and W with hollow-chamfer and ogee mouldings (Fig 89, b). The great chamber, possibly the 17th-century 'dining room', is spanned by a central truss which formerly had arch-braces to the collar, and purlins chamfered below; the remains of plaster on the slope of the roof are probably original, and the room had its trusses and wind-braces showing below a ceiling at collar level. The roof of the E bay was not plastered in this way, and was wholly open to the first floor. Purlins are clasped at undiminished principals, and closed trusses at D and F (Fig 88) have pairs of curved, raking queen-struts from tie-beam to collar.

The 17th century and later

The street front range (Plate 98) was rebuilt at this period, doubtless to contain a new entrance hall and parlour, with drawing room and principal bedroom above, reached by a staircase behind the hall now remaining between the first and attic floors (Fig 90). The former porch, which has a flat lead roof, projects boldly across the pavement and possibly remains from the older house. Externally, the building is gabled, with a heavy, classically moulded cornice to S, and the roof space is lit mainly by hipped dormer windows with cymatium cornices. Within, the attic storey preserves some 17th-century details, including a window in the N gable with an ovolo-moulded wooden mullion, a chamfered plank and muntin partition in the N range, and further S a stout door-frame with concave stop-chamfers. The SE room has an original hearth. In the N range, a kitchen was created with a new chimney serving both storeys.

In the mid 18th century, the E wall of the N range was rebuilt in brick with sash windows and the original partition removed; similar windows were inserted on the street front. Late in the 18th century the lower flight of the staircase was rebuilt as a projection into the yard, with moulded mahogany handrail and turned newel-posts.

A century later there were more extensive alterations, the porch was stopped up and the front hall/parlour

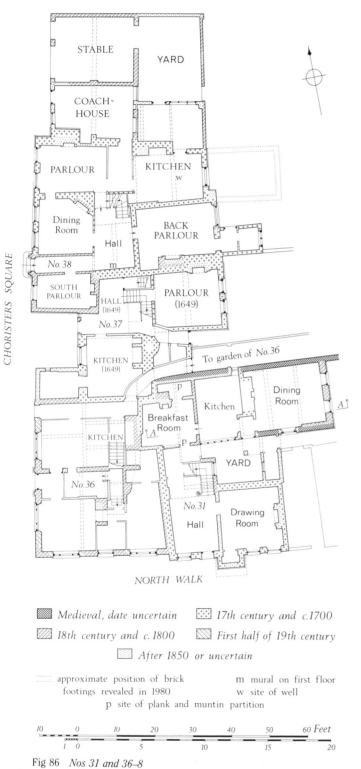

Key to plan:

▨ Medieval, date uncertain   ▦ 17th century and c.1700

▨ 18th century and c.1800   ◩ First half of 19th century

▨ After 1850 or uncertain

⋯⋯ approximate position of brick   m mural on first floor
footings revealed in 1980   w site of well
p site of plank and muntin partition

Fig 86 *Nos 31 and 36–8*

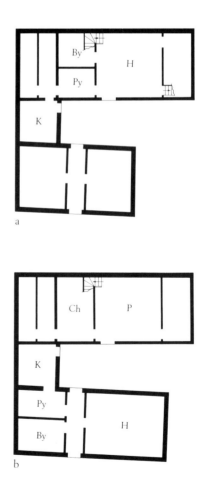

Fig 87 *No. 31, alternative reconstructed plans of medieval house*

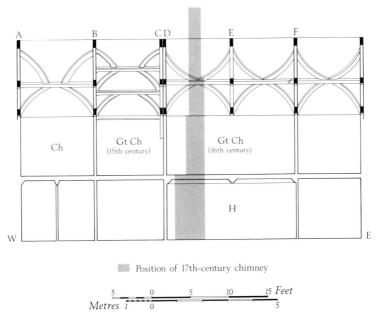

Position of 17th-century chimney

Fig 88   *No. 31, reconstructed long-section of N range*

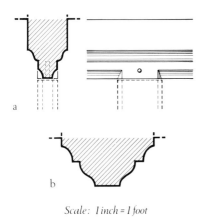

Scale: 1 inch = 1 foot

Fig 89   *No. 31, N range, details of*
a. partition
b. ceiling beam

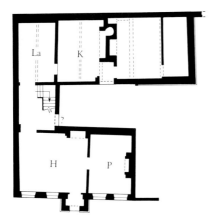

Fig 90   *No. 31, reconstructed plan as in c 1700*

Plate 98   *No. 31 from SE*

partition moved, and the E link between the two main ranges was built (or rebuilt) on two storeys under a slate roof. The house was almost entirely fitted with new joinery of neo-Georgian design, the stairs receiving new balusters.

At an unknown date in the 18th or 19th century a small extension was made to the W end of the N range, enclosing part of a former yard. The chimney in the 'breakfast room' had been built already and was then reorientated (but the earlier arrangement survives upstairs). The exterior of the house is now concealed mainly by render, but also by refacing in brick, in tile-hanging partly with rounded ends, and in mathematical tiles.

32 and 33 The Close

32 and 33 The Close survive from the cluster of cottages and workshops, etc, surrounding the Bell Tower within the Cathedral graveyard, most of which were demolished in 1790.

No. 32 is a house mainly of 18th-century date (Fig 91), but it originated in 1589 with chapter's lease to John Harrison, tailor, of a parcel of ground adjoining the belfry,

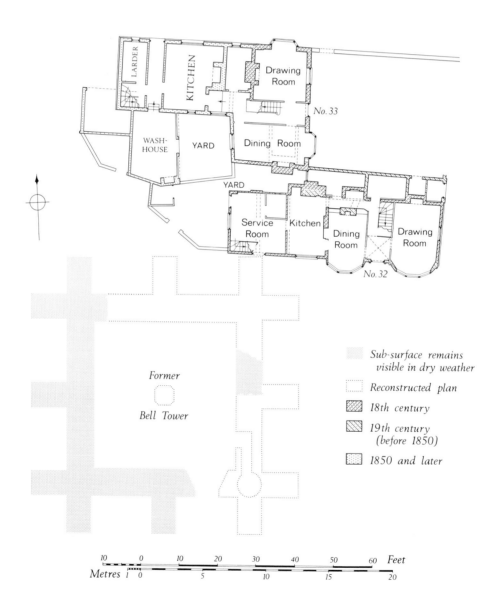

Fig 91 Nos 32 and 33, plan showing site of former Cathedral Bell Tower

Fig 92 *No. 32, reconstructed plan as in c 1775*

and from 1589/90 onwards he paid rent for a house. In the Parliamentary Survey it was described together with a second tenement to S as one building of two storeys with garrets, two rooms on a floor, occupied by Jasper Kelloway, turner, and Hugh Bolter, 'turker' (presumably a maker of turkeywork upholstery).

A succession of tenants and subtenants is chronicled until *c* 1790 when it was adopted as one of the vergers' houses, their former ones elsewhere in the graveyard having been demolished. A valuation in 1788 called it 'the new building now rented by Miss Rothwell' [Everett T, 48]. William Dodsworth, the verger and Cathedral historian, lived here in 1797.

The house is built in brick of two periods, the W part being slightly the earlier. These W rooms are of one storey with semi-attic, incorporating some groove-moulded oak wainscot, perhaps a relic of Harrison's structure. The E part is of two storeys and attic and may perhaps be dated by a glass quarry inscribed 'Abraham Pinhorn Jun. 25 1771' (reset above the scullery); a large chimney at the back of the dining room suggests that the room originated as a kitchen (Fig 92). Some 18th-century two-panelled doors remain on the first floor. Extensive refitting in the early 19th century accompanied the addition of the outshut to N and creation of a passage at the back of the dining room; a plaster vault with anthemion boss in the entrance lobby and the two lead-roofed bow-windows are of this period, though the latter have differing structural details. The house is partly seen in an engraving of before 1790 [Benson and Hatcher 1843, opp p 543] to the right of the belfry.

33 The Close

33 The Close is a small house of 18th- and late 19th-century date (Plate 99, Fig 91). It is known as Ladywell from the fountain of the Virgin Mary which stood nearby in the 15th century. But the history of the present building dates from 1588 when chapter granted Richard Warren a site to N of the Bell Tower, on condition that he build within two years a 'dwelling-house, that is to say a hall, a kitchen and a shop' measuring 34 ft by 16 ft [Everett 10, 9–10], which was described in 1649/50 as a

hall, kitchen, wash-house and four chambers. In 1786 the garden had been enlarged to E and a coach-house and stable yard added to W and S, and the house was divided in two, Mrs Talman's corresponding with the present 18th-century part and Mrs Goldwyer's the remainder. In 1840 the house, restored to single occupancy, comprised a dining room, drawing room and kitchen, three best bedrooms and excellent attics [*SJ*, 21 Sept 1840]. A later tenant, Mr Batt, obtained permission for two bow-windows in 1852, and at his death the W part was rebuilt as a kitchen wing by G R Crickmay in 1891–2.

The principal range to E appears to have been built by Edward Poore, Recorder of the City and one of its Members of Parliament, tenant from *c* 1753 until his death in 1780. The E façade is of mathematical tiles in Flemish and header bond, with sash windows and a central entrance under a segmental hood. The N elevation is of brick with a ground-floor bay-window which is original. Other walls are tile hung, and the roof is half hipped above coved eaves. Inside, the rooms have original joinery, doors of two fielded panels and chimney-pieces with moulded architraves; the stairs, partly rearranged in 1891, have a close string, plain newel-posts and turned balusters, and there is also some 17th-century wainscot with moulded edges reset in the entrance hall. The W part of the S room was rebuilt in 1891, but the position of the chimney and spacing of the ceiling beams suggest that there was originally an outshut or narrow room on this side. Batt must have added the dining room bay-window and that on the first floor to N, showing that his drawing room was above the present one. Crickmay's building is in dark red brick and tile-hanging, of eclectic style.

Plate 99 *No. 33 from E*

Houses in Choristers' Square

34, 35A and 35B The Close

34, 35A and 35B The Close, on S of Choristers' Square, originated as one house. The S elevation stands approximately on the line of the Graveyard Wall but no medieval masonry is seen. A length of medieval flint masonry incorporated in the N wall presumably survives from a building or enclosure which stood outside the graveyard (Fig 93).

A house existed here in 1571 and was granted by chapter in 1585 to Thomas Sharpe, merchant, at an increased quit-rent, which suggests enlargement of the tenure. Another rental increase accompanied the grant to Francis Parry in 1632, including a covenant by him to build a chimney, to project 4 ft from the N wall of his house, and a 'study or other room' which could project to N as far as the staircase and no further [Leases 1608–36, 22 Sep 1632]. The house at that time probably had a simple plan, with the entrance on S (Fig 94). Construction was in part timber framed but changes in wall thickness and an internal thick wall argue for more than one date and building material. Parry's chimney is of flint and other rubble with a square brick stack and his study is timber framed; the stairs today occupy the same site as in 1632. In 1649 the house comprised a hall, parlour, buttery, wash-house, woodhouse and coalhouse, study, four chambers, one closet and three garrets.

In the third quarter of the 17th century an extension with a second staircase was made to W, on two storeys and with attics, all originally heated. The large chimney, which evidently served a kitchen, is set to one side, centred on

the pre-1632 width, and therefore may be older. The N wall is in English-bond brick on a rubble plinth, with a four-brick platband and hollow-chamfered stone windows, but those on the first floor have been suppressed and replaced by a central window, itself blocked (Plate 100). The chimney has a chamfered plinth and weathered brick offsets (enclosed by a later roof) and the roof is of four bays, formerly collared, with butt purlins.

The Parrys relinquished their lease to Roger Pinckney. In 1706 his lease included a small plot of ground which enabled him to build a continuous extension to his kitchen, in Flemish-bond brick with shaped eaves sprockets. Enlarged windows in the kitchen build, early 18th-century panelling and moulded wooden ceiling cornices (now reset on the first floor) and twisted stair balusters (reset in No. 34) are probably further evidence of his improvements. He also obtained possession of the three-stall stable standing at the W end of his garden, built by Sir Thomas Mompesson c 1680; it is marked on 18th-century maps and was demolished c 1807.

During the 18th century two further additions to W were made on a narrower alignment, in brick above an older wall to N. Two-storey bay-windows were added on S, with triple sash frames and lead roofs, together with another on E [seen in the aquatint by F Jukes, 1798, Salisbury Museum].

In 1824 Catherine Moore proposed to spend £285 upon the house and chapter agreed to renew her lease with a repairing covenant. To this period of the 19th century belong the subdivision into two houses, the rendering of the S and other elevations, and the refitting of No. 35, later called 'The Elms' [OS 1880]. The E house was more drastically treated: a porch and upper room were added to

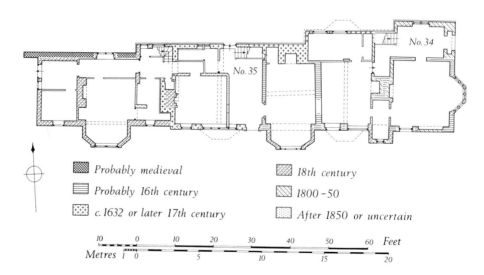

Probably medieval
Probably 16th century
c. 1632 or later 17th century
18th century
1800–50
After 1850 or uncertain

10 0 10 20 30 40 50 60 Feet
Metres 1 0 5 10 15 20

Fig 93   *Nos 34 and 35*

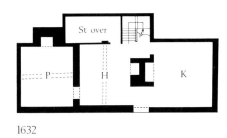

1632

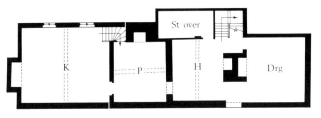

Late 17th century

Fig 94   *Nos 34 and 35, reconstructed plans*

NE and the exterior altered in 'Old English' style, with bargeboards, wooden casement windows, cement labels, Tudor doorway etc (Plate 101). Within, the ceiling of the E room was probably raised and the chimney made smaller. Some two-light hollow-chamfered stone windows that now appear on the N and S elevations are probably 16th century but reset, fragments of 17th-century oak wainscot, some chip-carved with a frieze of lunettes, now occur in various places, and a plaster pendant and cartouches of *c* 1600 have been reset in a first-floor ceiling. The 17th-century staircase in No. 35 was rebuilt with 18th-century balusters said to have been brought from a house in London, *c* 1930, and the house was subdivided *c* 1960.

36 The Close

36 The Close, at the corner of North Walk and Choristers' Square, was built by the Rev John Talman, vicar choral, shortly before 1752. It occupies the site of a small lay vicar's house described in the Parliamentary Survey of 1649 as 'A kitchen, a little buttery, two rooms very mean'. This had become ruinous and Talman built two new houses, one on the site, of which the vicars agreed to grant him a lease in 1752, and a residence for the lay vicar, No. 72 at Harnham Gate. At his death the lease was advertised of a 'new Brick-house ... [with] 3 bed chambers, parlour, kitchen, brewhouse, large garden' [*SJ*, 16 Dec 1765]. Many of the subsequent tenants stayed for only a short time. In 1837 the house had 'undergone material and expensive improvements' during the occupancy of William Housman (1835–7) and his predecessor, Henry Coombes (*c* 1826–35) [*SJ*, 8 May 1837].

Plate 100   *Nos 34 and 35 from NE*

Plate 101   *Nos 34 and 35 from S*

The original site of No. 36 must have been extremely small, but a sizeable corner house was built on it by the simple expedient of encroaching W beyond the original street line. The 'large garden' advertised in 1765 was in fact the E portion of the garden of No. 37, and access to it would have been contrived while the two houses were in Talman's joint occupation, before 1765. Later, in about 1800, when No. 37 was leased to William Arney jointly

with No. 38, a service entry was made at the N end of the house, with a narrow kitchen passage leading to a garden passage, encroaching on No. 37 and running behind No. 31 (Figs 86, 95). A small W extension on two floors was added later in the angle between the two houses.

Talman may have retained an earlier build for his kitchen, which has a thick wall on S and queen-struts in the roof not present elsewhere. His house looks W (Plate

Fig 95   *Nos 36 and 37, sequence of reconstructed plans*

102) and was originally brick faced, with five bays of sash windows with keystones and the present central doorway with stone surround in which Tuscan pilasters support a pedimented entablature [F Jukes, engraving of Cathedral from N, 1798]. The hipped roof projects on coved eaves and is lit by hipped dormer windows. Talman's staircase was probably opposite the entrance and lit by a light-well to E, but his work seems to have been old fashioned and few of his fittings survive; among them are fielded panelled joinery in the first-floor drawing room (above the entrance and SW room), the plain panelled dado and heavy wooden cornice of the bedroom to N, and an archway with keyblock and acanthus enrichment, perhaps originally at the base of the stairs but now reset on the first floor. Probably after Talman's death in 1765 (aged 81) the drawing room ceiling was enriched with rococo cartouches in papier mâché.

If there were two phases of work in the 1820s and 1830s they cannot now be distinguished. The house was stuccoed, ground-floor windows with one exception were converted to triple sash form, and a service entry made to N with reeded pilasters and paterae; joinery was renewed generally and the NW bedroom ceiling received a plaster centrepiece moulded with vine branches. In about 1958 the house was made into flats, partitions were inserted, fireplaces blocked up and new doorways and staircases made, but a tortuous late 19th-century rearrangement of the stairs also partly remains.

37 The Close

37 The Close is a small house mainly of 17th-century date but gutted in the late 19th century. It formed part of the endowment of the vicars choral who leased it to lay people, except for a period between 1650 and the Restoration, when the Parliamentary commissioners sold it to Alexander Hatchett, a London haberdasher.

The Parliamentary Survey of 1649 described it as having a 'hall, a parlour wainscoted, a kitchen, 2 little rooms within the kitchen, 5 chambers, a closet, a garret, a woodhouse' and it was probably then quite new. From

Plate 102 *No. 36 from W*

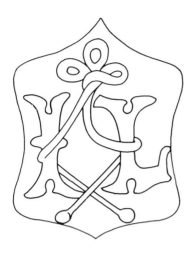

Fig 96   *No. 37, cartouche*

1732 until 1765 it was leased to John Talman, and from 1800 until 1856 or later to members of the Arney family, who also owned leases of the houses to S and N respectively, and this explains how those houses were able to encroach on No. 37.

The front range, aligned N–S on what is probably the original street line, is on two storeys and contains the hall and kitchen, as in 1649 (Figs 86, 95). One bay of the roof with stop-chamfered purlins remains, also part of the kitchen fireplace and its oven, with stone jambs to brickwork and a chamfered bressumer. Behind the kitchen is a range of two lower storeys, mainly of 18th-century appearance, but the stone plinth with chamfered head, returned against the door adjoining the parlour, suggests a 17th-century origin as a kitchen outshut. The parlour, now a study, is raised above the cellar, and has a chamber and attic over it. Its E elevation is gabled and of English-bond brick with irregular stone quoins up to the top of the ground floor. There are chamfered two-light stone windows to the cellars, but other windows have later sash frames.

The main elevation was subsequently heightened and rendered in the 19th century, and the house contains, as well as the late 19th-century staircase, chimney-pieces etc, a number of reset earlier fittings, including 18th-century doors with two fielded panels and 17th-century oak doors with six or eight panels having moulded edges. The parlour also has early 17th-century oak dado panels in three heights with chamfered edges, the upper carved mainly with pairs of roundels which are cusped and contain paterae, including a shield with the monogram IL (Fig 96); the top rail and stiles are carved with guilloche ornament. The initials might be those of John Lowe, who was a counsel to the Cathedral in the early 17th century and gave it a flagon hallmarked 1606.

38 The Close

38 The Close was made into flats in 1980 but was formerly a house and outbuildings facing W on to Choristers' Green. The site originated as three distinct holdings. In 1588 William Rawlins, glazier, contracted to build a shop and hayloft, for which he subsequently paid rent to chapter, on a narrow street-front site measuring 26 ft N–S by 7 ft 3 ins. By the middle of the 17th century, this narrow tenement, which appears to have been an encroachment over the original street line, had been amalgamated, together with the tenement behind it, with a vicars' holding to N. The coach-house and stable at the N end replace a small vicars' house which was occupied by their members until 1725, when it was described as 'altogether beyond repair' [Everett B, 76].

In 1650 the house on the two S sites consisted of a 'hall, kitchen, two other little rooms and a buttery: above stairs 3 chambers, a coal room and 2 garrets'. William Barfoot, clerk of the Cathedral works *c* 1637 to 1666, was living here in 1640 and a wall painting datable before 1658 was probably done for him; he probably enlarged the house, too, since in 1674 the lease was granted to John Stevens 'with all houses and edifices there upon lately erected' [Vicars' Leases 1673–1717, 30 Sept 1674]. A further enlargement was undertaken by Stevens' widow Mary, who petitioned successfully for her house to be assigned its own Cathedral seat in 1692, implying that it had been too small for one at their allocation in 1677. After her marriage to John Gauntlett of Netherhampton the lease continued with the Gauntlett and Wyndham families; a distinguished Wyndham tenant during the 1720s and 1730s was Dr Henry Hele who lived later at Myles Place, No. 68. In 1790, when William Arney obtained the house and displaced the subtenants, an advertisement described it as having two parlours, a drawing room, hall, kitchen, servants' hall, pantry, china and other closets, wash-house, three cellars, seven bedrooms and a laundry, a walled garden, coach-house, and four-stall stable [*SJ*, 14 June 1790].

The plan (Fig 86) ignores the alterations made in 1980.

The 17th century

Much of the fabric dates from the middle and second half of the 17th century but the building sequence is obscure. Distorted shapes occur everywhere in the plan presumably as a result of building against boundaries to N and S which were not parallel, and thick walls are embedded in the house at various points. The oldest part of the building appears to be the present dining room and stair hall, which has a formerly external wall to E. A small chamber over the S part of the hall, measuring 8 ft 6 ins by 10 ft 6 ins, was perhaps a cabinet or study; it has an ovolo- and cyma-moulded plaster cornice and the S wall is occupied

Plate 103 *No. 38, wall painting, hunting scene attributed to Edward Pierce (died 1658)*

by a painting depicting a hunting scene in ochre, red and black (Plate 103, Fig 86, m). Based on an engraving by Antonio Tempesta, it is attributed to Edward Pierce (died 1658) [Croft-Murray 1962, 207]. A nail-studded oak door with ogee-edged panels, later reset in the kitchen, was possibly Barfoot's front door.

The back parlour may have been added next, in English-bond brick with a four-brick platband and gauged window-heads; originally it had a large chimney against the N wall, of which the hearth-support remains in the cellar. The two N rooms appear to be additions of similar date, built against the brick end wall of the hall range (Fig 97). At that time or soon afterwards the W rooms were rebuilt above cellars and the kitchen added, the ceiling beams in the kitchen and cellars all having stop-chamfers with an ogee and V-cut. Above the kitchen, the chamber has an ogee-moulded oak window, and a roof with collar, clasped purlins and diminished principals. A second staircase, of which a chamfered, stone-mullioned window at intermediate level was seen in 1980, existed in the small N room. Much of this work must be attributed to Mary Stevens, *c* 1680–90, including the W façade in English-bond brick (Plate 104), the reconstruction of the main roof with knee-principals and modillion eaves, and the construction of a new main staircase (Fig 98). The asymmetrical placing of the entrance, a feature more usual in the town than in the Close, was no doubt predetermined here, as there, by a cramped site. A small wing was also added at the back of the house; it is of Flemish-bond brick and

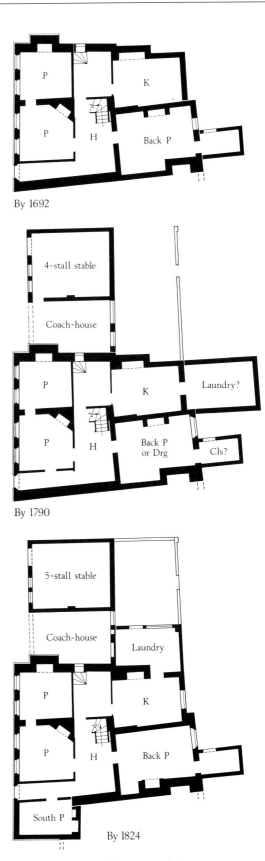

Fig 97 *No. 38, sequence of reconstructed plans*

Plate 104   *No. 38 from SW*

gabled, providing unheated annexes, possibly closets, on
two storeys.

Among the fittings of this period are a door now on E
of the N parlour, with two ogee-moulded panels, a planked
rear face, and hinge-pins in a stout ogee-moulded architrave. Bolection-moulded panelling in the present dining
room has been cut down; it is in three heights with a heavy
wooden cornice, fielded overmantel panels, and an eared
and bolection-moulded door-case with pilasters supporting a pulvinated entablature.

Scale: 1 inch = 1 foot

Fig 98   *No. 38, detail of staircase*

Later history

By 1724 the house was occupied by Dr Henry Hele as
undertenant of Wadham Wyndham, who in that year
acquired the lease of the tenement between it and the
Matrons' College, and by 1732 had built a coach-house and
four-stall stable there. Chimney-pieces of stone or marble
and some fielded panelled joinery in the house indicate
some refurbishment at this period, which may have
included the introduction of sash frames to the W elevation, narrowing the original openings. Early 18th-
century brick footings to E of the kitchen, apparently
incorporating a cellar, were discovered in 1980; this would
have been the third cellar mentioned in 1790, with a large
room above which may have been the laundry.

William Arney considerably remodelled the house
c 1790 and later. A straight joint in the W elevation
indicates where he added the small parlour at the S end,
and so extended the roof and upper room over it as a
first-floor drawing room, which has a bay-window and
dentilled ceiling cornice. This extension encroached upon
the front of No. 37 which was also in his leasehold from
1800. In the back parlour the chimney was moved from N
to S, a marble chimney-piece with fluted frieze and plaque
depicting Pan installed, and the ceiling enriched with a
fluted frieze with paterae. Joinery was renewed generally,
and the staircase partly rebuilt with square balusters. A
bedroom was created over the coach-house which was
remodelled together with the stable, now five-stall, and a
two-storey extension of brick and tile-hung framework,
probably a new laundry, was added to N of the kitchen,
allowing the demolition of its predecessor. The door-case
at the main entrance, with three-quarter columns and an
entablature with Grecian enrichment, is also of this date.

In the early 19th century, perhaps upon Arney's death
in 1824, the N front parlour was refitted and received a
marble chimney-piece with fluted pilasters and square
paterae and a reeded ceiling frieze, and the drawing room
chimney-piece was also renewed in marble.

The Matrons' College, 39–46 The Close

The Matrons' College, 39–46 The Close, is an almshouse
built in 1682 at the private cost of Bishop Seth Ward for
the accommodation of widows of the clergy [*VCH* 1962,
169–70; Eward 1982]. The site in the medieval period had
been partly occupied by the dwelling of the Clown Chantry
priest, but this was confiscated at the Dissolution and sold
to Lawrence Hyde; Ward had to buy the freehold from a
later owner, Thomas Hawles. Other parts of the site
belonged to the vicars choral and one plot was chapter
land, but most of the leases had been aggregated already
by Hawles. In March 1682, Thomas Glover of Harnham
undertook for £1193 12s 8d to remove old buildings and
to erect the new college by 1 November next. The total

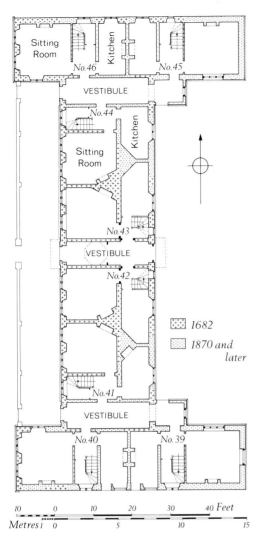

Fig 99   *Nos 39–46, Matrons' College*

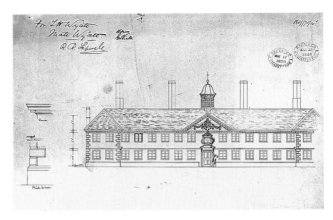

Plate 105   *Nos 39–46, Matrons' College, W elevation. T H Wyatt 1870*

cost of the college to Bishop Ward, including its endowment, was £5123 [Bod Lib Tanner MS 143, f 242]. The detailed contract and specification are preserved and appear to have been closely followed (see Appendix below). Wren's association with Bishop Ward has led to the supposition that he designed the building, but it entirely lacks the refinement of his work and is more likely to have been designed by Glover, who was described on his monument as an architect [Colvin 1978, 348].

In 1870, to improve the widows' accommodation, the number of occupants was reduced from ten to eight and extensive structural changes were made, designed by T H Wyatt (Fig 99, Plate 105). Apart from the W front and the central bays of the main range, which remain largely unchanged, the 17th-century college was virtually replaced by a new building, skilfully designed to blend with the original. Each tenant had a two-storey dwelling with a sitting room and a kitchen on the ground floor, and

with two bedrooms and a bathroom on the first floor.

The original arrangement can be reconstructed with some confidence as consisting of six houses, each with its own staircase, together with two pairs of houses sharing an entrance and staircase (Fig 100); eight of the houses had four rooms each but two adjoining the centre had an extra room over the central passage, in front of or behind the cupola shaft. There were apparently no communal rooms or special provision for a resident overseer. Wyatt's drawings of the college as it existed in 1869 show that minor alterations had already been made, among them the addition of irregularly placed chimneys along the rear to heat the smaller ground-floor rooms, some extension into the roof space, and the joining together of two houses approximately corresponding with Nos 44 and 45.

Externally the building has stone dressings, an ogee-moulded string, and hipped roofs to W (Plate 106) but gables and windows with wooden architraves (renewed by Wyatt) at the rear (Plate 107). On the front the original eared stone doorways with pulvinated friezes remain, but the subsidiary ones were reset by Wyatt and have pediments (not in Glover's contract) containing the arms of Ward in a garter upon a scrolled cartouche. The central doorway has wooden acanthus consoles supporting a pedimental hood, which replaces the 'very handsome frontie...in manner of a shell supported with two carved cantilevers' intended in the contract. No doubt Ward made these changes when he bespoke the central carved stonework, which is also not in the agreement: the first-floor slate tablet in its surround incorporating a cartouche-of-arms (the see impaling Ward), gartered and mitred, the tablet inscribed:

COLLEGIUM HOC MATRONARUM

Do Co Mo

HUMILLIME DEDICAVIT

SETHUS EPISCOPUS SARUM

ANNO DOMINI

MDCLXXXII

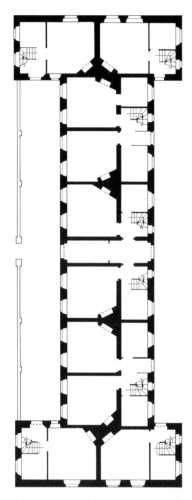

Fig 100 *Nos 39–46, Matrons' College, reconstructed plan, 1682*

Plate 106 *Nos 39–46, Matrons' College from SW*

Plate 107 *Nos 39–46, Matrons' College from NE*

The pediment incorporates a cartouche-of-arms of Charles II flanked by scrolls and backed by a lion skin, now restored (Plate 108). The present chimneys are Wyatt's. The glass in front was to have 'quarreys of diamond fashion' but 'old glass new leaded' at the rear.

Glover's external doors were to be of oak, the internal of deal; the former were replaced *c* 1800 excepting that to E which has two panels with ogee-moulded edges. Interior fittings only survive substantially intact in Nos 42 and 43; they have staircases with ogee-moulded panels on the string and newel-posts with ball finials and acorn pendants, doors mainly panelled on one face and planked on the other, and window-shutters with plain hinged leaves. In addition, an ogee-moulded wooden chimney-piece in the bedroom of No. 42, window-seats having fielded panels with ogee edges in the sitting room of No. 43, and cupboards with plain doors flanking the chimney are probably original.

The lantern or 'cubulo' (*sic*) lights the central vestibule; its octagonal shaft is plastered internally, with cornices at intervals, and a dome. It was to have a vane and crown of wrought iron, gilded.

Some 20 yds E of the college is an early 18th-century wash-house of one storey with walls of Flemish-bond brick and a hipped roof. Its N room is open to the roof and contains a lead pump dated 1713, and the S room is ceiled and has a rebuilt chimney.

Appendix to Matrons' College

8 March 34 Charles II 1682. Agreement between Seth Ward, bishop, and Thomas Glover of Harnham [WRO].

> Thomas Glover shall before 1st November next take down the houses of the Bishop in the Close, which he lately purchased of Thomas Hawles, gent., except the stable which stands on the North East angle of the garden and the wall of the dung mixen by it, and set up a new house on the place where the old stood, to be 120 ft. in front, & break out at each end in form of an H, 12 ft., and to

consist of several rooms:- 20 rooms on the first and lower floor, 10 of which shall be 13 ft. square & 7½ ft. high, with a chimney & 2 windows and one door in each, and 20 rooms in the floor over, of same dimensions, and each of the 10 great rooms shall have a chimney, 2 windows & 1 door, and 1 window and one door in each lesser room. In which said new house, Thomas Glover shall build 8 stair cases of oak near 6 ft. one way, & 4 ft. the other with a single light in each, and also a passage quite through the midst of the house 6 ft. broad & 7½ ft. high, and set up a cubulo in the midst of the building of 7 ft. wide with 8 sides or cants and 13 ft. high to be built of oak, covered with lead and glazed on every side and on top a globe of free stone 20 in. diameter, and that the stem that comes through the globe shall have a vane and crown well wrought in iron work and guilt. The Cubulo will be open quite down into the passage. Out walls of the house to be of hard, well burnt brick, 2½ bricks thick to the ground base, and thence 2½ thick to the middle floor then 1½ brick to the raising piece. The partition walls that run cross the building to be one brick in length from the bottom to top beams, and these partitions that run along the house from North to South shall be a brick & half to middle floor, and one brick to wall plate. Mortar shall be made of 1 quarter of lime to each load of earth. House

Plate 108   *Nos 39–46, Matrons' College, centrepiece of W elevation*

shall be built with a ground base and plinth each 6 in. thick of freestone throughout the front, and with a substantial handsome mundillion cornish suitable to the height of building on all the front and both ends of house. The backside shall be roofed with seven gable ends, covered with a water table of freestone with lead gutters in the six angles of 8 pounds to the foot, and length and breadth for its use with a leaden pipe to each within a foot and halfe of the ground to keep the water from dashing. The foreside of the house shall be roofed with hip rafters after the Italian fashions. The front of the house shall be covered with new tiles, and the back with old tiles, which are sound and not cracked, from the old house, and the hips of the house covered with lead 7 lb. to the foot and a foot broad the whole length of the hips. The 4 coines in the front shall be all of rustic freestone each stone answerable to the 4 courses of bricks in thickness with length and breadth suitable to the thickness. The windows in the front and ends of the house shall be made of free stone 4½ ft. high and 4 ft. wide, with a mullion in the middle of stone, and windows at back shall be made of good oak, three & half inches & 4 inches, the lights equal to those in front. In each room in front of the house shall be set one iron double casement and three iron bars ¾ inch square in each light; to be 3 stone door cases in front of house, handsome & well wrought, and the doorcase in the middle shall be large with a very handsome frontie over it in manner of a shell supported with two carved cantilivers, and over the door cases the cornish shall break in form of a pediment, and be covered with lead of 7 lb. to the foot, and all windows in front shall be glassed with good white glass of quarreys of diamond fashion & the back windows with old glass new leaded.

The doorcases shall be made of good oak handsomely wrought five inches & six inches, and the heighth & breadth suitable to the building and as many as shall be thought fit by the said Lord Bishop or whom he shall appoint to oversee the work. And all the outward doors shall be made of good dry oaken boards, And the inward doors of good deals all glewed and batteened with ledges on the backside, with gimalls, lock & key, iron latch and catch to each door, And the roof and flooring shall be made with good new oak timber or such old oak timber taken down in the old house as shall be found good and sufficient for its place. The beams shall contain eight inches square, the principal rafters at the foot seven inches and at the top six inches square. The purlines shall be eight inches and six inches, the rafters shall be four inches and three and an half. The sumers shall be ten inches square, the joyses two inches and ten inches and the sleepers five inches square, the sealing joyses two inches and six inches. The ten largest low rooms shall be boarded with good smoothed oaken boards and the ten little rooms and little passages shall be paved with the best of the old broad stone taken out of the old house. And that the great passages shall be paved with good new Purbeck Michells and all the upper boarding shall be of good deal board and well wrought, and the partitions between the little rooms shall be made of

good deal board and brace. And that all the side walls and
seilings of both floors shall be plaistered with two coats,
one of good stuff composed of earth, lime & hair, the other
of lime and hair. And all the window boards shall be of
good deal and well wrought throughout the house. And all
the outward timbers as doors, doorcases, cupulo, cornish
and windows shall be very well painted in oil. And the first
floor of the building shall be raised one foot above the level
of the street. And that there shall be a halfe pace of
Purbeck stone set before each fire hearth and capitals of
freestone on the heads of the chimneys. All which said
house of twenty low rooms and twenty upper rooms with
eight staircases, entrance, cupulo and buildings whatsoever
to the old house and premises belonging in manner as is
herein mentioned he the said Thomas Glover for himself,
his executors and administrators and for every of them
doth convenant grant, promise and agree to and with the
said Seth Lord bishop of Sarum his executors
administrators and assigns and every of them at the proper
costs and charges of the said Thomas Glover his executors
and administrators well and sufficiently in workmanlike
manner erect, build and set up the said house and the
other said buildings. And at his and their proper costs and
charges to find and provide good sufficient and fitting
timber, bricks and all other materials whatsoever necessary
for the buildings. And all the workmanship whatsoever
thereof. And with the said good sufficient and fitting
timber brick and other materials to build finish and
complete the said house of building according to the
dimensions aforesaid on or before the said first day of
November. And that the said Thomas Glover doth also for
himself his executors and administrators and for every of
them further convenant, promise, grant and agree to and
with the said Seth Lord Bishop of Sarum his executors,
administrators and assigns that if any of the chimneys
before mentioned to be made in the said house shall smoke
or any other inconveniency or fault shall appear in any or
either of the rooms or buildings so to be built, occasioned
by ill workmanship or want of care in the workmanship,
that then & in such case the said Thomas Glover his
executors and administrators some or one of them shall at
his and their proper costs and charges amend or new made
such default or defect in the chimneys or building
whatsoever the same shall happen to be.

On consideration of which said building the said Seth
Lord bishop of Sarum is to give and allow unto the said
Thomas Glover the said old house so by him to be taken
down and all the materials thereof save only the South
Wall of the house seven foot high from the ground which
shall be left standing for a fence wall [no longer in
existence]. And that from and after the building, finishing
and completing the said house or building in manner
aforesaid and amending the faults if any shall happen to be
therein by the said Thomas Glover his executors assigns or
workmen, the said Seth Lord Bishop of Sarum his
executors or administrators shall pay the said Thomas
Glover his executor or assignee the sum of eleven hundred
ninety and three pounds twelve shillings and eight pence of

lawful money of England in full discharge and satisfaction
of the building materials and all the workmanship thereof.
And it is hereby also agreed by and between the said parties
to these presents that if anything be there omitted and not
set down which was agreed or intended to be done by the
said Thomas Glover touching the building aforesaid that
yet he will do and perform the said as carefully and
effectually as if the same had been here set down and
expressed. And it is farther agreed between the said Seth
Lord Bishop of Sarum and the said Thomas Glover
wherever it is in this indenture said that the materials shall
be good and substantial and the workmanship sound and
handsome or words to the same purpose, that in all such
cases the said Thomas Glover shall use such materialls and
cause the building to be wrought in such form or fashion
as shall be allowed by Thomas Naish clerk of the works [he
was also clerk of the Cathedral works] or such other person
or persons as shall be appointed by the said Lord Bishop to
oversee the said work. In witness thereof the parties to
these presents have interchangably set their hands and
seals the day and year first above written.

On Dorse: Signed, sealed and delivered in the presence
of:- John Reade, Thomas Naish, George Antrobus.

Document labelled: 'My Lord Bishops Articles for
building the Colledge in the Close March 8th. 1681.'

47 The Close

47 The Close is a small house standing a few paces E of the
Matrons' College; it appears to have been created out of
the stable of the Clown Chantry (Fig 101). The ground
leased by Bishop Ward for his college included a vicars'
garden 'upon part of which Thomas Hawles hath lately
built a new stable' [Leases 1673–1717, 7 Mar 1682], and
this he spared from demolition; evidently it had been
erected since the Parliamentary Survey. The timber-
framed stable was enlarged and had its ground floor
rebuilt in brick to form a house, presumably c 1683. In the
19th century it was occupied for a time as two cottages; it
continues to be held by the college's trustees.

The stable must date from the 1650s or 1660s. The
timber-framing is in two equal bays with wall-plates and
tie-beams having straight braces from the main posts, and

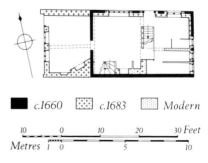

Fig 101   No. 47

the decorative brick nogging of the external walls is original (Fig 102); rebated studs in the W bay indicate the low heads of the original N windows. Butt purlins in the roof are supported by pairs of short, straight wind-braces and all trusses were originally collared.

The bay added when it became a house is partly in English and partly in Flemish bond, with an oval window to N, and to W the elevation has a platband and apertures with gauged heads. The ground floor of the original build is of the same brickwork, mainly bonded continuously. In the 18th century a dormer was built over the W bay in brick and stud to create an attic bedroom.

In its new form as a house, the W bay contained the parlour and best bedroom, both having chamfered ceiling beams with moulded stops (Fig 103). The central room was the hall or kitchen, with a new chimney and staircase continuous to the attics, but the plan is unusual in that the main entrance led into the parlour; the back door is in the E bay, which presumably contained the pantry and larder. The late 17th-century oak joinery and fittings are well preserved and include the stout, ogee-moulded external door-frames and two- and four-light windows to N and W with scratch-moulded mullions and jambs; internal plank doors are similarly moulded with wooden latches,

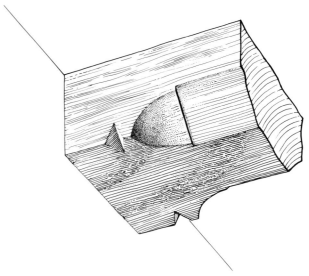

Fig 103   *No. 47, detail of beam stop*

and a partition enclosing the stairs at first-floor level is of matching plank and muntin construction.

48 The Close

48 The Close was, until *c* 1900, the Porter's Lodge to the Close. The office of porter was probably well paid in the 14th century since kings and earls attempted to procure it for their servants [Edwards 1949, 232], William Bever being appointed at the instance of two earls in 1339; he is the earliest porter known and the post was probably created as a result of the decision to wall-in the Close, in 1327. The site of his house is first documented in 1530 and in 1627 it was said to be 'at and over the north gate' [Everett A, 24]. The Close prison was also within the porter's province in the 16th century, perhaps occupying the lower room of the gate. Until the 17th century the lodge abutted the SE corner of the gate but it was then extended some 10 ft W, across the pavement, and a connecting door made into the supposed former prison. Although the property of the dean and chapter, it was omitted from the Parliamentary Survey.

From the 17th century onwards, the porters are often recorded as letting the house and living elsewhere, and among their tenants were Thomas Peniston, who registered a Roman Catholic chapel here in 1797 [*VCH* 1956, 94], and Dean Talbot, whom chapter permitted to live here in 1811 during repairs to his own house. The condition of the Lodge had recently been of some concern to the dean and chapter: on 12 July 1794 a chapter meeting heard that the house had been in serious disrepair for twenty years or more and agreed to 'remedy' it; again, on 7 February 1807, chapter ordered £84 3s 6d to be spent in repairs from their own resources, and in 1811 they allowed Porter Lush £40 towards his expenses already incurred, no doubt in

Fig 102   *No. 47 from NE, showing present appearance, the site being too cramped for photography*

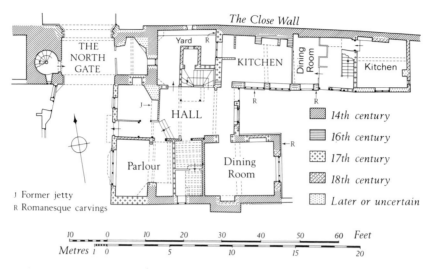

Fig 104   *No. 48, Porter's Lodge*

a. 14th century

c. Early 17th century

b. 16th century

d. Later 17th century

Fig 105   *No. 48, Porter's Lodge, sequence of reconstructed plans*

response to his (undated) petition that he had found the house 'wholly neglected' and spent £180 on putting it into good condition [D and C Muns, Press 5, Box 4]. It was connected to the town police station by a bell in 1886.

The medieval house

The lodge probably dates from the 14th century, although few early details are visible and the anomalous abutment between the two medieval ranges on both storeys argues for more than one building period (Fig 104). The original plan may be interpreted as having a hall and cross-wing (Fig 105a), and the large size and substantial construction of the parlour, with walls mainly of coursed, squared stone, might suggest that the hall was originally larger than at present in keeping with the importance attached to the porter's office; a second bay of equal size would have extended it to the Close Wall and might have contained a chimney. However, it seems unlikely that chapter would have allowed an encroachment on the wall at this early date and the existence of a jettied upper storey, set at a lower level than the parlour ceiling, suggests that the hall was instead unusually small, although well finished with a hollow-chamfered ceiling beam and cornice.

In the cross-range the W part may have contained the kitchen. A pair of later beams probably ceil the original smoke-bay of the hearth, and closely spaced ceiling joists and a trimmer for the staircase also remain; above, the floor has exceptionally wide boards. The E part of the range is roofed independently, and the parlour and great chamber above are heated by an ashlar chimney with three pairs of weathered offsets and a hollow-chamfered drip-course; the chamber walls are of tile-hung timber-framing.

The 16th century and later

Probably in the early 16th century the N range was built against the Close Wall to contain a new kitchen and offices. Another staircase was built in the hall, which partly remains at attic level (Fig 105b) while a new doorway between the chambers over the hall and inner hall (Fig 106) has its mouldings to N, which suggests that the original stairs had been removed. The new building extended to North Gate, where a corbel supported its roof, but now it ends on W at an intermediate truss with diminished principals and seatings for collar-clasped pur-lins and wind-braces.

In the early 17th century a timber-framed service extension was added on E of the kitchen (Fig 105c), and the present staircase was built, with chamfered oak newel-posts, close string and roll-moulded handrail, within walls of brick with stone quoins. A two-storey passage, of timber-framing above rubble, was added behind the hall.

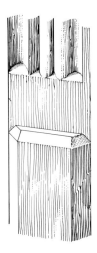

Fig 106 *No. 48, Porter's Lodge, moulding and stop of doorway in S wall of chamber over hall*

Probably a little later new rooms with higher floor levels were added to W, encroaching right up to the E side of the Close gateway (Fig 105d). Walling is rendered but mainly of brick below and timber-framing above, and the attics were lit by gabled dormer windows [Buckler 1809]. The room over the entrance hall, possibly a first-floor drawing room, has a chamfered doorway with ogee stops.

Early in the 18th century the main entrance was handsomely refitted (Plate 6) and the 'dining room' given a white marble chimney-piece, the jambs, shaped head and keystone carved with fielded panels. In the latter part of the century elegant turned stair balusters and doors with two pairs of fielded panels were introduced, also triple-sash windows to E. Lush's work of *c* 1810 probably included the central bay-window on W and a chimney-piece above the dining room with dentilled cornice.

In the 18th century a storehouse was built as a cross-range to E of the kitchen, in weatherboarding above brickwork: the S end was truncated between 1860 and 1879 but the roof retains a tie-beam truss aligned E–W, and it is now converted as a cottage.

Several stones carved with 12th-century ornament, probably from Old Sarum, appear in the walls (Fig 104, R); usually associated in the Close with 14th-century work, these, with the exception of one in the dining room, were probably taken from the Close Wall at a later date. A quantity of early and mid 17th-century fittings also survive *ex situ*, including a nail-studded external door with chamfered cover-strips, and scratch-moulded oak wainscot reset in three first-floor rooms, chip carved with lozenges, pies and gadrooning.

49 The Close – see North Gate.

50, 50A and 51 The Close

50, 50A and 51 The Close are three cottages of two storeys with attics (Fig 107, Plate 109). They originated in the 15th century as two-storey, timber-framed shops and their appearance has been considerably altered, but the documented stages of their history can still be traced in their fabric. Presumably they were built between 1404, when

chapter decreed that 'none shall make fixed shops near the gates or walls of the Close' [Acts 1402–5, 25] and 1431 when chapter passed an act banning the vicars and others from playing ball against the new shops. Bishop Beauchamp condemned the scandal to the canons and vicars of the shops at North Gate in 1454 [Everett G, 29], but chapter seems to have evaded his order that a new use be found for them and the three properties remained shops until about 1730. In the 16th century tenants included merchants, a goldsmith and a joiner; the middle shop was usually the most expensive, being the largest.

In 1608 the three shops and three chambers over them were granted to Hugh Thomas, linen draper, on condition that he repair and enlarge them. This he did and in the Parliamentary Survey of 1649 they were listed as 'three shops, a kitchen, a buttery, three chambers on the first storey and four higher rooms or garrets'. Throughout the 19th century they were arranged as two cottages but they have recently been restored to their original three-unit arrangement.

Nos 50 and 51 were of similar construction, with timber-framed and jettied fronts and rear walls of flint, stone and tile rubble with stone dressings below a timber-framed upper storey, but the differing projection of their jetties shows that they were built separately (Fig 108). The timber framework is now mostly concealed by render and tile-hanging, or replaced in brick. These and the other two shops to S have lost their original plans but the common relationship between the front door and the staircase in buildings refashioned at different periods may perpetuate an original arrangement.

The jetty of No. 50 still projects a little and is tapered to prevent the upper storey from blocking a window in North Gate; two of its principal joists remain, connected

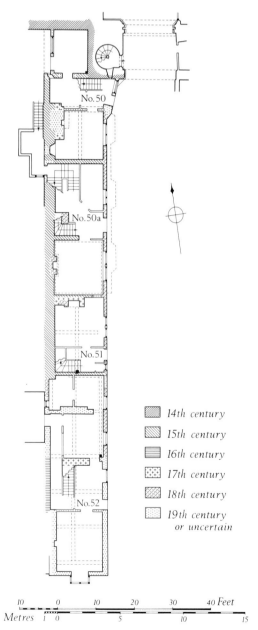

No.50

No.50a

No.51

No.52

▨ 14th century
▧ 15th century
▤ 16th century
▦ 17th century
▨ 18th century
▢ 19th century
    or uncertain

10   0   10   20   30   40 Feet
Metres 1 0   5   10   15

Fig 107 Nos 50–2

Plate 109 Nos 50–2 from SE

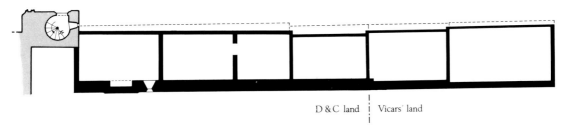

D & C land ¦ Vicars' land

Fig 108   Nos 50–2, reconstructed plan showing range of 15th-century shops near North Gate

by a ceiling beam. The N chimney and blocked window adjacent are original features. From 1608 to 1611 the building was heightened by a semi-attic storey with triple gables and possibly the three oriel windows were added, although now of late 19th-century appearance. In the early part of the 18th century the front was underbuilt in Flemish-bond brick and a cellar dug under the S half, lit from E. The S room was fitted as a parlour, with panelling in two heights and an ogee and ovolo-moulded cornice, and a doorway to S. In the 19th century an extension to N, alongside North Gate, was rebuilt, but it retains elements of timber-framing and is probably of 17th-century date.

In No. 51, a principal jetty-joist is abutted by chamfered ceiling beams and has a mortice for a post, indicating a heavy jetty projection. The first floor was originally a single chamber open to the roof. Its front wall has pairs of long, curved braces supporting the central and corner posts on the jetty-plate but the rear wall is plainer, with rectangular panels, and braces below the mid-rail only. The central roof truss has a cambered tie-beam braced by long curved members on to jowl-posts, all chamfered, raking queen-struts to collars, and clasped purlins with wind-braces.

In the 17th century the S bay was ceiled over at eaves level with a chamfered beam, a gabled dormer window was added on E to light the new attic room, and a large chimney was constructed, mainly of chalk, to heat the main storeys. In about 1730 the jetty was underbuilt in brick, with a double sash window divided by an ogee-moulded wooden 'mullion', the cellar dug, and the stairs built with a close string and small symmetrically turned balusters of late 17th-century design.

52 The Close

52 The Close was formerly two shops belonging to the vicars choral. Both were timber framed and jettied, and the earlier, northern, one probably came into existence between 1404 and 1454 (see Nos 51–2), while the other is probably of 16th-century date. In 1649 they were occupied by lay vicars, the N one having a 'kitchen, a shop, and two rooms over them' and the S one a 'hall, shop, chamber and coal-house'. They were leased in the 19th century to lay folk, Charlotte Lee in 1800 agreeing to make 'improve-

ments' to one of them [Everett A, 37]. The N entrance is now blocked and they are divided horizontally into an office and flat.

The N build is of two bays with chamfered ceiling beams and principal jetty-joists chamfered with step and concave stops; the lower wall-plate is partly exposed and the S post of the original front wall remains (Fig 107). The roof probably covered a single upper room and has curved wind-braces to butt purlins, and a central truss with curved queen-struts to the collar; the N end truss has no in-filling, indicating that it was built after No. 51, and has its tie-beam braced on a pair of long, curved struts. The staircase, with turned newel-posts, dates from *c* 1800 and a twin-gabled dormer window on E with slate-hung cheeks is probably of similar date.

The S build was probably jettied on E originally and mortices show that the transverse beams or principal jetty-joists were directly supported on the posts of the E wall. The first floor was originally arranged as a two-bay room on S of a similar one; the ground floor of this, and possibly the adjoining shop, were probably subdivided also.

Mompesson House, 53 The Close

Mompesson House, 53 The Close, occupies half the N side of Choristers' Square (Fig 1, in end-pocket). The comparatively large site was pieced together in the late 17th century and the house and stable date from 1701, but the intervening service range consists of older buildings, refaced in the mid 18th century (Plates 110, 111).

The main house site was occupied by Robert Ryve, prebendary, before being leased in 1565 to Thomas Sharpe, a Salisbury merchant, for ninety-nine years. Sharpe left before 1587 and little is known until Thomas Mompesson 'of the Close' renewed the lease in 1635 at a specified rent increase from 4d to 8s 4d, and fifteen years later the Parliamentary Survey listed his house as having 'a hall, two parlours, a studdy, a buttery, cellar, kitchen, scullery, a larder and room over it, 7 chambers, 4 garrets, a wood-house and wash-house'.

Confusion between the words 'now' and 'new' in a lease has led to the erroneous supposition that this house had been rebuilt by 1680 [CL, 25 Dec 1958]. In that year

Plate 110   *No. 53, Mompesson House from S*

Thomas's son Sir Thomas, then MP for New Sarum, built a stable near No. 35 (*qv*); he also acquired the leases of the four vicars' choral tenements to E, now the site of the kitchens, stables etc, formerly used for various purposes including that of a mid 17th-century inn called The Eagles. Sir Thomas had either passed the house to his son or was in the act of rebuilding it when he died in June 1701, and the rainwater hoppers are inscribed 'CM 1701'.

Charles Mompesson, also an MP, died in 1714 and the tenancy continued with his wife Elizabeth and her father, William Longueville, and then with her brother Charles Longueville. Much of the fine interior decoration and the harmonious refacing of the service wing appear to date from Charles Longueville's occupancy. After his death in 1750 the property passed to Thomas Hayter of Salisbury, whose descendants remained there for the rest of the 18th century.

From 1802 the house was occupied by members of the Portman family of Bryanston, who sold the lease in 1846 to Captain William Oliver Colt. From before 1860 until 1939 it was held successively by George Barnard Townsend

and his daughters, and from 1946 to 1951 was the bishop's residence, but was found unsuitable. In 1952 the Church commissioners sold the freehold to Denis Martineau, who gave it to the National Trust.

The house of 1701

Externally the appearance of the house of 1701 is well preserved and the iron palisades and gates, which incorporate Charles Mompesson's monogram, are probably part of the original design. The armorial achievement accompanied by military trophies above the entrance is of Mompesson (*a lion rampant charged on the shoulder with a martlet, in chief a mullet for difference*) impaling Longueville (*a fess dancetty ermine between six crosses crosslet fitchy*) and would have been added after Charles Mompesson's marriage in 1703. The rear elevation is of less formal design with its bays arranged asymmetrically, and the levels to W higher than those on E, arising from the extra height of the drawing room. Faced with Flemish-bond brick, it has coved eaves and a number of sash windows with square panes of 18th-century date.

In the original plan a large entrance hall and stairs are flanked by reception rooms, with another drawing room at the head of the stairs (Fig 109). A side passage led from the centre on both floors to the service quarters. There are two cellars, one under the W part of the house for wine, reached from the staircase hall, and a coal cellar beneath the breakfast room, probably dug in 1701.

The rooms on the two principal floors retain many of their original fittings, and they have, or mostly appear to have had, bolection-moulded panelling of deal with heavy wooden cornices, overmantels of one panel or of a large one above a smaller one, and oak doors with four pairs of fielded panels in bolection-moulded surrounds; original shutters, which remain in the study, have lightly fielded panels.

The hall was probably heated originally and had its chimney removed c 1740. The drawing room is both larger on plan and taller than the other ground-floor rooms, which suggests its original importance. In the dining room, the chimney is placed asymmetrically and to S of it there is an archway with an elliptical head and panelled pilasters, probably an original serving alcove. In the study

the panelling is more elaborate than elsewhere, with a richer cornice. The staircase is probably also original (Plate 112).

The Red Room was once a first-floor drawing room (Plate 113), and its doorways into the bedrooms are echoed by false ones there, giving a sense of enfilade. Three of the bedrooms retain their original joinery, also their chimney-pieces, of red and blue marble and bolection-moulded stone; the bedroom to NE, now a bathroom, is said to retain its panelling and chimney-piece behind modern fittings. The NW bedroom was probably the Mompessons' own; it is now entered through a lobby but formerly had a door on S and was furnished with a servant's room and closet, in which plain panelling and the cornice survive.

The garrets are approached by two staircases, that to E arising from the service wing. The rooms are arranged off a central corridor, which is given architectural focus by an elliptical-headed archway at the E end with panelled pilasters and projecting keyblock. The passage retains fielded panelling and doors, and the rooms retain panelling and stone chimney-pieces which, in part, are original.

Plate 111   *No. 53, Mompesson House, former service wing and stables, from SW*

First Floor

17th century
c.1700
18th century
After 1850

Fig 109 *No. 53, Mompesson House*

18th-century and later alterations

In about 1740 ornamental plaster ceiling panels and cornices, and new chimney-pieces and overmantels were installed in the principal rooms, probably designed by Francis Cartwright of Blandford (see p 32). In the entrance hall the ceiling received shaped panels and a central cartouche, and on the staircase the ceiling and wall decoration were formed (Plate 114).

The ceiling cornices of the parlour and dining room resemble that of the hall. The parlour ceiling was enriched with a banded bayleaf garland and the chimney-piece, although moved in by Martineau from elsewhere, matches the room so well that it possibly originated here and has been moved more than once. In the dining room the overmantel was replaced by a carved wooden one with mask and fruit basket and the ceiling enhanced. The

drawing room gained ceiling panels and a plaster cornice with acanthus modillions (Plate 115); its chimney-piece has a marble architrave, with mask, draperies and consoles, and a wooden overmantel with pilasters and an open pediment within which there was formerly an armorial achievement [painting at house, 1857]. In the study the ceiling was divided into panels, with male and female busts between palm-fronds in the four corners. The Red Room was evidently still a drawing room: its cornice was renewed and the ceiling elaborated around an eagle panel in high relief (Plate 116).

Minor alterations dating from about 1800 were probably made when the Portman family took possession. Most of the windows were fitted with new sash frames and shutters and extended down to the floor, and the study was converted into pantries, which it remained until

Plate 112   *No. 53, Mompesson House, staircase*

Plate 114   *No. 53, Mompesson House, upper part of staircase hall*

Plate 113   *No. 53, Mompesson House, Red Room, or upper drawing room*

Plate 115   *No. 53, Mompesson House, ceiling in drawing room*

Martineau's restoration. In the 19th century the dining
room was extended into the passage behind it and plaster
bosses added to the ceiling there.

In the middle or latter part of the century further
ornate detail of 'early Georgian' character, in plaster and
carved wood, was added to the house. This includes at least
the handsome pedimented doorways in the hall (Plate 117)
and the panelled archways opening off the upper and lower
stair halls. Later, panelling and a modillion cornice were
fitted in the dining room extension. In about 1900 the
floor was at the same level throughout the hall [photo at
house] and, surprising as it seems, it suggests that the
floor level almost throughout the ground floor has been
subsequently raised.

Martineau, in the 1950s, replaced Victorian chimney-
pieces with older marble ones in the dining room, library
and Red Room; he also commissioned *trompe l'oeil* panels
by M Battersby for the entrance hall [NMR] and created a
large bedroom in the service range. The National Trust
removed the Battersby panels into storage and fitted new
chimney-pieces in the dining room and Red Room (now
the Green Room) in 1976.

The service range

The E wing incorporates part of the 17th-century tenements. The former kitchen and breakfast room, which
originated in the 16th or 17th century, have a continuous
roof of four bays with clasped purlins and queen-struts.
The kitchen also dates from about 1600, its E wall is built
partly of small bricks in English bond 8½ by 4¼ by 1¾
ins, and one truss of a roof aligned N–S remains, with
cambered tie-beam, two tiers of butt purlins and queen-
struts. It was rebuilt in the late 17th century, the N wall of
purplish brick in Flemish bond with a platband, and a roof
structure aligned E–W, with two tiers of butt purlins set
diagonally.

In about 1700 this wing was remodelled internally –
fielded panelled doors and wainscot suggesting that both
storeys assumed much of their present arrangement then
– and the space between the library and kitchen was
infilled. About the middle of the 18th century it was
refaced on S and extended above a carriageway to the
stables (Plate 111). Many old fittings have been reset in
this range.

The stable and other outbuildings

The stable was converted as a house in the early 1950s
after a period of neglect with many of its windows blocked.
The façade is in Flemish-bond brick with stone dressings
including the chamfered plinth and windows, but the W
return wall is in English bond. The rusticated doorway and
eared opening above, not a window but formerly containing a fielded panelled door to the hayloft, are of mid

Plate 116   *No. 53, Mompesson House, ceiling in Red Room, with*
eagle panel

Plate 117   *No. 53, Mompesson House, 'early Georgian' door-case,*
second half 19th century

18th-century woodwork. The roof is of four bays with tie-beams, collars braced on queen-struts, and butt purlins; the W hip collar has '1701 TTLL 1703' scratched on it.

Behind the stable are ranges of outbuildings, mainly of early 18th-century brick with hipped roofs, whose functions are identified on a plan of 1861. The wash-house is of single storey and the coach-house dates from c 1700, and is partly in English and partly in Flemish bond, with a moulded wooden cornice. The old brewhouse was greatly altered when Martineau made a summerhouse of it, but the English-bond walls and roof resembling that in the stable remain from c 1700.

To N of the house, the 14th-century Close Wall is pierced by a stone doorway of c 1700, with a rectangular window in its entablature; it gives access to a privy, which discharged into the former Close Ditch. Inside, the walls are lined with fielded oak panelling and the seat (which has gone) occupied the length of the N wall.

54 The Close, the Hungerford Chantry

54 The Close, the Hungerford Chantry, is a house mainly of 18th-century date. It is named after the foundation of Lord Robert Hungerford, established in 1472, and served by two priests who lived here until the Reformation. Before then the house had been charged with 12s to the obit of Constantine de Mildevale (alive 1263); possibly he bequeathed it for the benefit of the vicars (who were unable to hold property at that date), because in 1295 chapter granted it to Henry de Middleton, procurator, and his successors in perpetuity [Everett M, 37]. It was appropriated as the choristers' school and residence, probably by Bishop Mortival in 1322 [VCH 1957, 357–8], but they had left by 1347 and subsequent occupants were mainly vicars.

The Crown confiscated the property at the Reformation as an asset of the chantry and sold it in 1550 to Lawrence Hyde. Since the early 17th century the names of the owners and their tenants are well recorded and with a few exceptions they were lay people. From 1752 to 1800 it was occupied by a girls' school run from 1752 by Mrs Stevens and from 1778 by Mrs Ivie [Robertson 1938, 242–3, 254; Everett Q, 33]. The owner, H P Wyndham, then attempted unsuccessfully to sell the freehold, an advertisement of 1802 describing it for the first time as a 'new fronted and sashed house' [SJ, 1 Feb 1802]. His new tenant, Daniel Eyre, agreed to take down a ballroom measuring 44 ft by 21 ft and other 'additional' buildings, and chapter allowed Wyndham to enclose the front court behind a low wall. In 1906 Millicent Jacob conveyed the freehold to chapter.

The house was rebuilt in the early 18th century between the confines of medieval boundary walls to E and W, and Mompesson House (Fig 110). It then consisted of

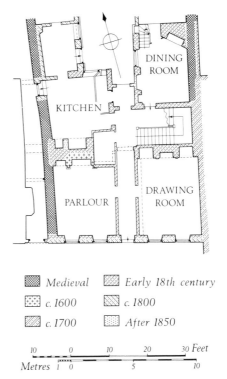

Medieval

c. 1600

c. 1700

Early 18th century

c. 1800

After 1850

Fig 110   No. 54, Hungerford Chantry

the parlour, drawing room and kitchen, three upper rooms on one level, and attics. The principal staircase leads only to the first floor, that to the attics rising to E of the parlour and kitchen chimney. The rear elevations are of brick in irregular bond and tile-hanging with hipped roofs, the tall sash windows being an alteration made later in the century. The parlour fireplace, of stone with a chamfered Tudor-arched head and moulded stop-chamfers, may be evidence that a chimney of c 1600 was incorporated. The principal original fitting is the lower staircase, which is of oak with moulded close strings, plain newel-posts, turned balusters, and broad moulded hand-rails, and in the parlour there is plain panelling on the S wall in four heights with a double cyma cornice.

Shortly afterwards the NE wing was added, on three storeys at lower levels than the others, the top storey reached only from its internal staircase. It is built of poor quality brickwork with two platbands and tile-hung timber framework, and has original casement windows. The doors are of three planks with the centre one recessed, forming a panel with moulded edges; one is inscribed 'HENRY PINCKE 1721' on the top rail, which possibly dates this addition. In the drawing room, a pine chimney-piece with a frieze of acanthus scrollwork and carved centre panel is of the mid 18th century.

In 1801 the S elevation was rebuilt (Plate 118) and the interior extensively refitted, doors having three pairs of fielded panels. The house has numerous reset fittings, including oak wainscot dating from *c* 1600 on three walls of the parlour, of five heights articulated by fluted and cabled pilasters, and with a chip-carved and panelled entablature. On the first floor of the earlier build there is more scratch-moulded wainscot, together with planked and wainscot doors, and the E wall of the chamber over the parlour is built of heavy oak studs and rails with hollow chamfers, evidently medieval. The N staircase is also partly lined with linenfold panelling of mid 16th-century date.

The garden is flanked by walls which partly retain their facing of flints and herringbone tilework. To N the boundary is the Close Wall. Against its N face, two late 17th-century stone doorways with chamfered surrounds and square heads lead to privies, built over the Close Ditch.

55 The Close

55 The Close is a house mainly of 18th-century date, but incorporating an earlier range (Fig 111). In 1618–19 the vicars choral obtained it from chapter in exchange for an orchard abutting No. 21, but its earlier history is obscure. The Parliamentary commissioners in 1649–50 called it a tenement with a hovel, gatehouse and backside, consisting of a hall, a kitchen, a parlour wainscoted, three chambers and 2 garrets, a little cellar, a woodhouse and wash-house, being hovels.

Edward Duke of Winterbourne Stoke took a lease of it in 1661, and at his renewal in 1674 it was described as 'lately new built' [Leases 1673–1717, 16 July 1674]. In 1703 and 1717 Subdean Naish took leases; on both occasions his subtenant was George Mullens, physician, who owned the lease by 1729, and there is little doubt that he grandly rebuilt the house in its present form, probably in the 1720s. He also extended the upper storeys over the narrow passage on E, which leads to the former outbuilding, now No. 55A. After his death in 1738 the property continued until 1865 with his collateral descendants, members of the Bingham and Poore families, and was commonly subtenanted.

The S range is probably partly Duke's work and partly older, the E and W walls being of rubble and orange-red

Plate 118 *Nos 54 and 55 from S*

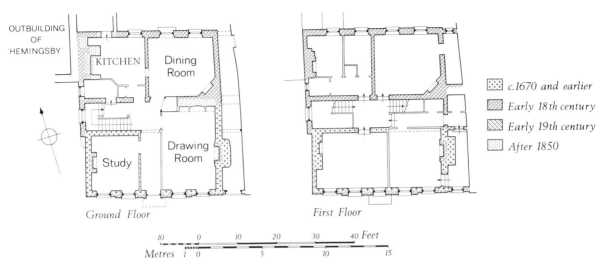

OUTBUILDING
OF
'HEMINGSBY'

KITCHEN | Dining Room

Study | Drawing Room

Ground Floor   *First Floor*

⬚ *c.1670 and earlier*
▨ *Early 18th century*
▨ *Early 19th century*
⬚ *After 1850*

10   0   10   20   30   40 *Feet*
Metres 1 0   5   10   15

Fig 111   *No. 55*

brickwork and the roof having principals with queen-struts. Mullens refaced this build but kept its two-storey and attic arrangement (Plate 118), adding a new and taller range to contain his principal rooms behind. The rooms in the new build generally retain Mullens's fittings. On all three storeys there are fielded panelling, fireplaces with ogee-moulded stone architraves and single overmantel panels, and doors with two to four pairs of panels; windows are mostly fitted with seats and have panelled shutters except on the top floor, where they are plain. The most elaborately fitted is the 'dining room', which has fielded oak panelling (Plate 119) and a door hung on brass hinges with elegantly turned finials. The two first-floor rooms have heavy cornices; that above the dining room was the best bedroom or an upper drawing room with another elaborate chimney-piece and entablature. The principal staircase rises to the first floor and is of oak with an open string, turned balusters three to a tread, and a handrail ramped at columnar newels. At first-floor level it faces a pair of doorways with overdoor panels and heavy cornices, one leading to the upper staircase.

The N elevation has its original combination of thick-glazed sash frames and casements, with the four parallel roof ridges concealed by the parapet (Plate 120). The older rooms were also fitted by Mullens with new window and door joinery but they have been altered subsequently; the 'drawing room' received a new stone chimney-piece but the 18th-century arrangement of the narrow space at the back of the room has been lost.

In about 1800 the S bedrooms had their ceilings raised and a new chimney-piece with dentilled cornice installed; some refacing in brick of the W wall and the insertion of an oculus in the pediment were possibly done at the same time. About thirty years later the study was created by partitioning Mullens's hall and installing a reeded

Plate 119   *No. 55, fielded panelling framing former fireplace in dining room*

Plate 120   *No. 55 from N*

chimney-piece with lion-mask paterae and a chair rail. Probably in the early 19th century the kitchen was extended into a building of one storey above a cellar, but this is now rebuilt and the cellar blocked up. A quantity of moulded oak wainscot, doors and cornices of more than one date in the 17th century is reset almost throughout the house.

55A The Close

55A The Close is a two-storey cottage built in the second half of the 18th century behind No. 55, partly on the site of the Close Wall (Fig 112). Evidently it originated as an ancillary building to No. 55, probably a stable or brew-house. It is of brick in Flemish bond with casement windows, those on the first floor arranged symmetrically on either side of a blind panel. Within, there are cham-fered ceiling beams and a door made of ovolo-moulded planks.

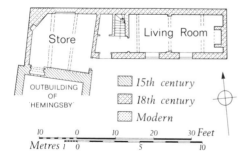

Fig 112   *No. 55A*

'Hemingsby', 56A and B The Close

'Hemingsby', 56A and B The Close, is a former canonry occupying a large plot at the NW corner of the Close. In the Middle Ages it was substantial in size and remained so in 1649 when the medieval house with a central hall, 'lower' end to N and parlour range to S, still existed.

Little of this survives except for a 14th-century porch, and the 15th-century hall (Fig 113). The porch was possibly built by Canon Alexander Hemingby (*sic*) who bequeathed the house to the dean and chapter in 1334, charging it with his obit. The hall was built by Canon Fidion (1457–74, probably William Pheidion, a refugee from Constantinople in 1453), whose name is carved on the woodwork. His prede-cessors included Nicholas Upton, precentor from 1446 to 1457, and one of those responsible for the canonisation of St Osmund in 1457 [*DNB*], and William Loring (*c* 1380–1415), who in 1413 was allowed to charge the house with an additional obit in recognition of his enlargement and thorough repairs, which repeatedly caused chapter to grant Loring privileges from 1387 onwards; but, ironically, noth-ing attributable to him remains.

An inscription in the stained glass of the parlour windows was noted *c* 1700; dated 1525, it recorded Edward Powell's repairs and improvements [BM, Harleian MS 7048, f 314]. In 1547 a lease was granted to Simon Simmonds (vicar of Bray, 1535–51, in the song), but there is no evidence that he lived here. An inventory made of Chancellor White's 'implements' in 1586 names the canon's principal rooms: in the hall wainscot, three tables, five benches, and two side cupboards, in the parlour wainscot, a bench, a portal and a cupboard, in the inner parlour wainscot, in the chamber over the inner parlour wainscot and three doors, in the wardrobe an old press, in the little study wainscot, a turning desk in the midst and a chair, in the upper study two desks, in the 'over chapel' wainscot, and in the middle parlour a wainscot portal.

The Parliamentary Survey of 1649 describes the whole house, as follows:

> One large hall waynescoted about 10 foot high, two Butteryes, a Celler a handsome Kitchin, a wash howse, a Larder, a wood-howse, a Bakehowse, two little colehowses over wch are one wide Roome with an earthen Floare and a little Roome within the same, a great decayed roome anciently a Chappell and a little roome within it, one square lodging roome, and a little roome within it. At the other end of the Hall are two handsom large Parlors waynescoted about, one other little Parlor with a Closet haveing a Chimney within it. Two Chambers waynescotted some eight foot high. Fowre little lodging Chambers. A large Studdy for books and a little waynescoted Studdy within that, two Gardens, and a large Orchard severed by a high stone wall, one plot of ground adjoyneing to the sayd Orchard both wch conteyne per estim : one acre. One

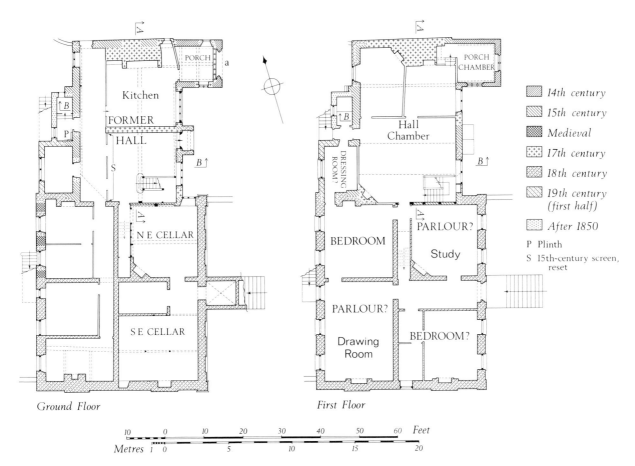

Ground Floor   First Floor

▨	14th century	
◩	15th century	
▩	Medieval	
⋯	17th century	
▨	18th century	
◪	19th century (first half)	
▦	After 1850	
P	Plinth	
S	15th-century screen, reset	

Fig 113   No. 56A and B, Hemingsby

stable one hey loft and a Coach Howse conteyneing five bayes of building.

In 1649 the Parliamentary trustees sold the house to the City, who conveyed it to John Strickland, the presbyterian minister of St Edmund's during the Commonwealth, and probably during his occupation it was greatly altered; the chapel and other rooms at the N end of the hall were pulled down and the hall was divided up. From 1676 for fifty years it was Daniel Whitby's house and in 1683 he admitted being unable to compel his tenant to repair it.

Perhaps in consequence, Joseph Sager in 1727 obtained permission to pull down 'the great parlour, the room called the chappell, the next room to it, the study and the lobby with all the chambers over these rooms, and to build in their stead two parlours, a passage and two bedchambers ... leaving the places under them for cellars and other offices', the work to take no more than 12 months [Acts 1696–1741, f 105].

The house ceased to be a canonry in 1846. Repairs and alterations of an antiquarian nature were made to the hall by Mrs A B Webb and Miss M Ottaway in 1919, and the house became two dwellings in 1950.

The medieval house

The early 14th-century porch was presumably added to an older house to which, with its open archway and moulded ceiling beams (Plate 121, Fig 115), it would have made a splendid entrance. The upper room, which has moulded wall-plates and a two-light window, would have been entered from within the house, and in the late 15th century from above the screens passage. Scratched on the S capital in 15th-century cursive script is 'Hamyn...'.

Fidion's hall doubtless replaces an earlier one and his E wall may incorporate older work though the W wall, with three two-stage ashlar buttresses and a chamfered plinth, is 15th century. Subdivided and with fittings reset, it is still a magnificent room (Figs 114, 116). The roof timbers are smoke blackened and the lower framework of a louvre stands against the N end wall of the hall (Plate 122, Fig 117).

The lower arch-braces of the roof originally sprang from small brackets carved on the cornice, all defaced, but now terminate on larger modern brackets. Of the ashlar-pieces between the cornice and lowest purlins (Fig 118), only one remains, in the S bay, W side, its shields painted

Plate 121   *No. 56A and B, Hemingsby, porch from NE*

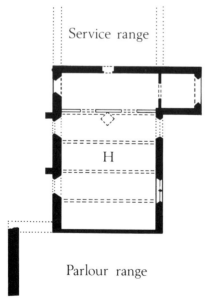

Fig 114   *No. 56A and B, Hemingsby, reconstructed plan of hall in 15th century*

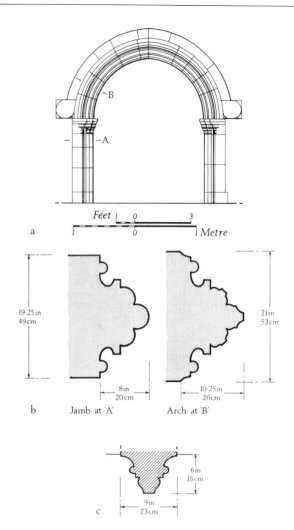

Fig 115   *No. 56A and B, Hemingsby, porch details*
a. doorway
b. mouldings
c. ceiling rib

with 'EPO' and 'IHS' in yellow on black, presumably by Edward Powell in the 16th century (Plate 123). The roof is finely finished with purlins of graduated size; they have roll and hollow-chamfer mouldings, as on the lower arch-braces and the screens partition, while other members are mainly chamfered on their upper faces and hollow chamfered below. Cusping, on all four tiers of wind-braces and repeated on the upper arch-braces, creates a heavily decorative effect, as does the repeated lettering carved on the wall-plates, with the shields and quatrefoils of the ashlar-piece. Traces of red paint occur on many of the timbers.

Much of the screens partition still exists, reset (Fig 113), its doorways, which originally had low four-centred arches and flanking crocketed standards, made narrower and lower (Plates 124, 125), and its presumed cornice remaining in the hall chamber (Figs 117, 118a). On E the outline of a 15th-century window with two-centred arch is partly visible externally (Plate 126), the hall wall-plate serving as a rear-arch, and on W the rear door of the screens passage has become a window (Fig 113).

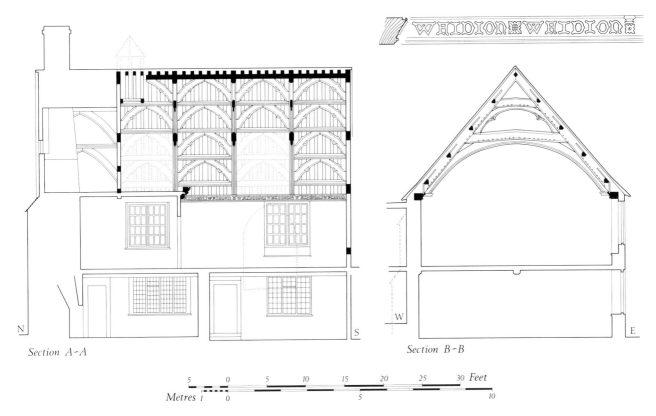

Fig 116   *No. 56A and B, Hemingsby, sections*

The screens bay was also rebuilt in the late 15th century, with an upper storey and a simpler roof. Several features of slightly later date now survive *ex situ*: a heavily moulded doorway may have been salvaged in 1727 and now, together with moulded medieval timbers, forms part of a secondary porch on E of the hall (Plate 127, Fig 119); it has a four-centred rear-arch and retains hinge-pins. Twelve 16th-century Italianate male and female profile busts in roundels, reset as an overmantel in the hall chamber, are said to have been found in the attics of the hall in 1919, and could date from Powell's tenure, as could a quantity of linenfold panelling (Plate 128), possibly named in the 1586 inventory and now reset in several rooms.

The 17th century and later

Shortly after 1649 many alterations were made. The hall was floored over, partly on corbel-stones, to create an upper storey and attics, the whole area being turned into small rooms; the attic windows remain although much of the floor they served was dismantled in the early 20th century. The medieval service rooms to N were demolished and new ones were made; the screens passage was removed and a large chimney built to serve a ground-floor kitchen. The 14th-century porch was walled up, becoming a larder, and a new entrance was made to S,

with an ogee-moulded timber architrave and stops, and a plank door. The first-floor NE room, with a square-set fireplace, has an ogee- and ovolo-moulded plaster cornice and the porch chamber was probably appropriated to it as a closet. In the E wall, flint and stone chequerwork and a four-light wooden window with ovolo and ogee mouldings are of this date, but brickwork and the other windows are early 18th-century alterations.

Plate 122   *No. 56A and B, Hemingsby, louvre in hall roof*

Fig 117   *No. 56A and B, Hemingsby, perspective reconstruction of screens (N) end of hall*

In 1727–8 Archdeacon Sager replaced the parlour wing, but the W wall is partly constructed of medieval flint, stone and tile rubble and suggests the extent of the earlier range. Sager's build has a handsome main elevation (Plate 129), of brick with rusticated stone dressings, unusual in that it consists only of a raised *piano nobile*, with a flight of steps up to the central doorway, and blind openings in the basement and in the high parapet which

hides the parallel ridges of the roof. The other elevations are predominantly of stone rubble with brick dressings, much of the stone probably obtained through Sager's concurrent licence to demolish the W stretch of the Close Wall (see p 40). One of his bedrooms is identified by its brass-bolt mechanism, which allows the E door to be controlled by wires from a bed against the S wall. In the present drawing room, probably originally a parlour, there is a chimney-piece of veined pink and grey marble together with fielded panelled joinery with window-seats, and a heavy wooden cornice which projects above each window. Original fittings in the other rooms include a similar chimney-piece and cornices and plainer joinery.

In the late 18th century the SE bedroom was rejuvenated as a sitting room with an acanthus-moulded cornice,

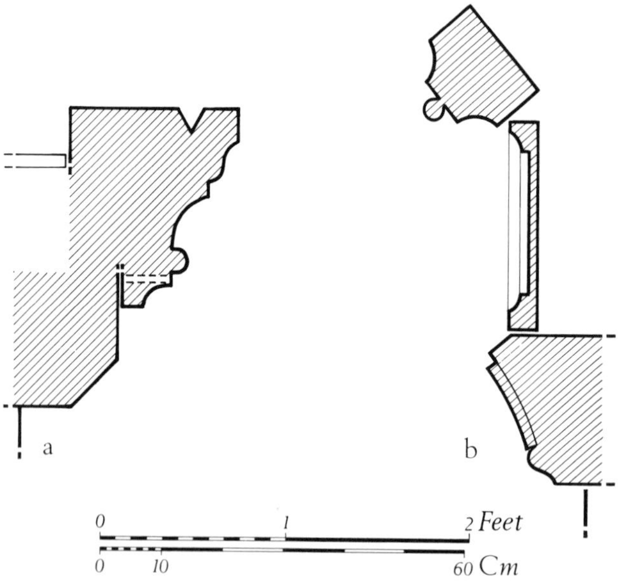

a   b

0   1   2 *Feet*
0   10   60 *Cm*

Fig 118   *No. 56A and B, Hemingsby, sections*
a. screens cornice
b. main cornice with ashlar-piece and moulded purlin

Plate 123   *No. 56A and B, Hemingsby, hall roof, main cornice with lettering, decorated ashlar-piece and moulded purlin (S bay, W side)*

Plate 124   *No. 56A and B, Hemingsby, hall screens, reset*

and a chair rail; internal window-sills were cut away. Small additions on the W side of the hall, in brick under tiled roofs, were made in the early and mid 19th century, and probably in this period a staircase to the basement was built between the bedroom and study, since removed, and a baize door placed at its head. A handsome oak staircase in the former hall, of early 17th-century date, is clearly reset; its joinery is not of local character and it is assumed to have been brought from elsewhere by Mrs Webb.

A single-storey outbuilding to NE of the hall, that is opposite the original butteries etc, is of 15th-century date. It survives to its original extent but has been greatly altered and the small chamfered light in the S gable and chamfered jambs of a doorway in the N wall give little clue to its original use; in 1649 it was probably the stable, loft and coach-house, and the S end still contains stalls for five horses. The walls, again, are heavily laced with herringbone tile courses. The five-bay roof is constructed with

Plate 125   *No. 56A and B, Hemingsby, hall screens, detail of doorway*

Plate 126   *No. 56A and B, Hemingsby, secondary porch from E*

Plate 127 *No. 56A and B, Hemingsby, hall range from E*

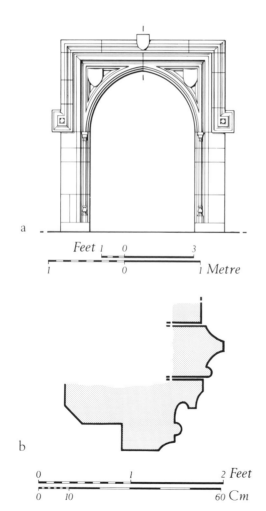

Fig 119 *No. 56A and B, Hemingsby, secondary porch*
a. doorway
b. moulding

Feet 1 0 3

1 0 1 Metre

0 1 2 Feet

0 10 60 Cm

Plate 128 *No. 56A and B, Hemingsby, linenfold panelling reset in study*

vertical studs and pairs of curved raking-struts from tie-beam to cambered collar, and there are pairs of curved wind-braces to clasped purlins.

The boundary wall on S of the gardens has tile-laced stretches that appear to be medieval and are some 9 ft 6 ins high.

The Choristers' Schoolroom, 56 The Close

The Choristers' Schoolroom, 56 The Close, occupies part of the site of William Braybrooke's canonry (No. 57, *qv*), and the Cathedral choristers attended their grammar school at Braybrooke Place from 1559 to 1947. After ten years in the tenure of the Teachers' Training College, it subsequently housed the diocesan and chapter records and has become commonly known as the 'Wren Hall'; since 1980 it has stood empty.

The original school was in the 'fore part' of the house and a latrine 'on the water side' was presumably for its use in 1573. Chapter kept the room in repair and in 1578 contributed to the construction of a study. An entry in the Chapter Acts indicates that the present schoolroom was completed by 7 August 1717 under the supervision of Thomas Naish, Cathedral clerk of works, possibly with the patronage of Sir Stephen Fox, a former chorister [Robertson 1969, 220–3]. A new 'necessary house' was provided in 1721 at a cost of £12 5s 10d.

The schoolroom is at mezzanine level in relation to the small annexe and headmaster's house to S, being raised above a basement (Plate 130, Fig 120). The entrance in the annexe was presumably used by the boys in poor weather, who then ascended into the classroom while the master arrived from his house through the annexe, descending into school. A blocked doorway in the N wall perhaps led to the latrines. The cellar is divided into two parts, the larger entered externally by steps beneath those of the main entrance, the smaller attached to the annexe, both presumably used for storage of fuel etc. The attics were originally an adjunct of the master's house and have a blocked original fireplace, but stairs up to them were placed in the annexe c 1965.

The school is relatively unaltered although the glazing, which was formerly leaded, has been renewed, mainly with

Plate 129   *No. 56A and B, Hemingsby, S range from E*

Plate 130   *No. 56, Choristers' Schoolroom looking W*

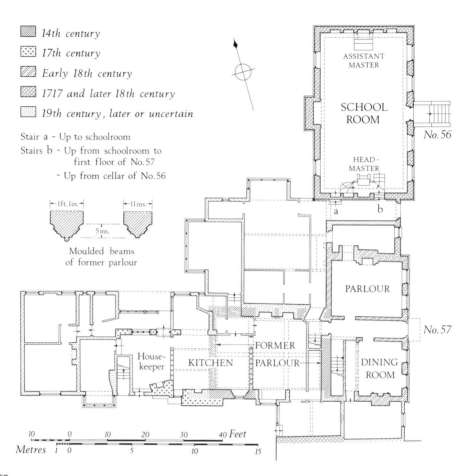

14th century

17th century

Early 18th century

1717 and later 18th century

19th century, later or uncertain

Stair a ~ Up to schoolroom
Stairs b ~ Up from schoolroom to
           first floor of No. 57
        ~ Up from cellar of No. 56

Moulded beams
of former parlour

Fig 120   Nos 56 and 57

Plate 131   No. 56, Choristers' Schoolroom, interior looking N with
assistant master's desk

Plate 132   No. 56, Choristers' Schoolroom, headmaster's desk with
built-in lower seat at S end of schoolroom

horizontally hinged metal frames. The masters' impressive oak seats and softwood desks remain, with a lower seat built into the headmaster's, perhaps for a monitor or for miscreants (Plates 131, 132). The windows are above head height and below them fielded oak panelling incorporates wall-cupboards at the N end, doorways to S, and a bolection-moulded stone chimney-piece; the room is finished with a coved plaster cornice. Above the fireplace formerly hung the wall-clock of *c* 1760 by Hugh Hughes, now at St Nicholas's Hospital [RCHM 1980, 56]. The rear elevation resembles the front, but the coved eaves are of plaster and the plinth of brick instead of stone. Despite its imposing character, conservatism is evident in the use of both English and Flemish bond and in the design of the chimney, with pairs of stone-coped offsets. The first-floor room in the annexe has a dado of miscellaneous 17th- and 18th-century panelling, probably none of it *in situ*.

Details of the whole building are accurately recorded in Macartney *c* 1925, plates 4–8.

Braybrooke, 57 The Close

Braybrooke, 57 The Close, occupies the S part of the site of William Braybrooke's canonry, bequeathed by him to chapter *c* 1329. A dilapidations survey made at the death of Walter Hende tells us that in 1449 the canonry had an 'outer gate', with a hay barn on the N side of it, and a 'long house' aligned E–W which contained hay storage at one end and the horse stable at the other. The kitchen had an oven and was connected to the hall by a passage; the parlour and the principal chamber, which was under the roof, had chimneys, and the chamber over the wine cellar had a chamber annexed to it with a latrine [Acts 1447–57, f 41].

At the deprivation of Canon Harding in 1559 the canonry was split up and the master of the Choristers' School, Christopher Benet, was granted a lease of the house, of which the 'front' part was already called the School House (No. 56) [Everett 9, 19]. His successors continued their tenure until 1947, apparently interrupted by only one brief episode: from 1562 to 1564 it was adopted by Bishop Jewel as the lodging for prebendaries during their term of office at the Cathedral, but the scheme proved ill-founded and was abandoned [*VCH* 1956, 187]. The Parliamentary commissioners noted the house in 1650 as having a hall, a parlour wainscoted, a kitchen, buttery, passage room and two other low rooms without the parlour, four chambers and two studies.

Until 1813 the Choristers' fund was responsible for maintaining their master's house, but its reconstruction early in the late 18th century is undocumented which suggests that it was funded privately, perhaps by the master, Prebendary Hele (1706–56). In 1746 Francis Price, Cathedral clerk of works, was paid £55 towards 'rebuilding'

the house, although nothing significant can be attributed to him.

J W Richards, master from 1850 to 1856, complained in 1850 that 'the house has been frequently and injudiciously added to and altered, while the original portion is extremely old and incapable of repair and improvement' [Everett A (5), f 34v]. But instead of a new house, he obtained 'considerable alterations: houses joined together', although the meaning of the second phrase is unfortunately obscure [*ibid*, f 37v]; an addition on W of the annexe between house and schoolroom appears on the City Health Board Map of 1860 and is probably the second classroom for which Richards asked in 1854 [Robertson 1969, 289]. The boys had boarded intermittently, beginning in the 1760s, but this did not develop fully for another century; in 1895 a sickroom was added, dormitories in 1897 and 1907 and a new 'wing' in 1928. In 1947 the school was moved to the old Bishop's Palace and the house divided into two, the W one now containing two flats. The name 'Braybrooke' has been revived recently.

Architectural development

The present W house originated in the late 14th or early 15th century, probably as a parlour wing lying across the S end of the canonry hall, with the great chamber on the first floor (Figs 120, 121). It is built of rubble, with timber-framed walls to E and W on the upper storey; the N wall is thicker than the S wall, even allowing for 19th-century refacing, probably reflecting the gable-end of the former hall. Both parlour and great chamber were divided

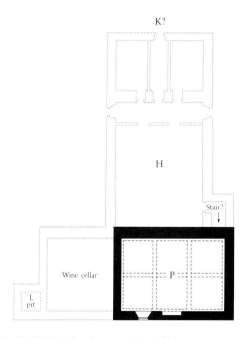

Fig 121   *No. 57, Braybrooke, reconstructed plan*

into three bays by moulded ceiling beams or roof trusses, with a chimney in the centre to S (wholly rebuilt at ground-floor level), and windows to W of it, that remaining at ground-floor level having a two-centred head with tracery lights (now blocked). The chamber roof is built with arch-braced collars, the arch-braces and wall-plates chamfered but the curved wind-braces plain, and the window, which may be of later date, has three lights and a hollow-chamfered moulding and rebate. In 1559 it was probably the canon's hall that became the schoolroom and the 'high' end of his house the schoolmaster's dwelling, eventually arranged with reception rooms at the front and kitchens etc at the rear. A 17th-century schoolmaster rebuilt the latter with a large chimney on S, and other rooms were added to W in brick, stone and flint rubble

with stone quoins, while the E range was renewed shortly before the construction of the schoolroom (completed *c* 1717). It is built of rubble, excepting the Flemish-bond main elevation (Plate 133) which has a door-hood on acanthus brackets and is approached from the street through square ashlar gate piers. The possible original usage of rooms is shown in Fig 120, the awkwardly shaped space W of the dining room being perhaps a pantry or deep cupboards; the drawing room or study lay above the parlour and communicated with the schoolroom.

Original fittings survive mainly in the parlour, where there is panelling with beaded edges, a heavy wooden cornice, and windows with seats. Doors, in stout ovolo-moulded frames, have pairs of panels on the ground floor and two panels on the first floor, with brass rimlocks. The

Plate 133   *No. 57, Braybrooke from E*

staircase is continuous to the attics, with a panelled close string and turned balusters, and a segmental arch of masonry across the base; it now has a landing between flights but originally had winders. The S bedroom was at first equipped with a dressing room above the entrance hall but they were combined under a broad arch in the late 18th century.

The work paid for in 1746 probably occurred in the W build and possibly included the construction of the door and window in the N wall of the housekeeper's room. Later, perhaps about 1800, the secondary staircase was rebuilt in its present position to serve a small addition on S of two storeys and attic. The enlargements of the last hundred years have been made chiefly to the W range and are mainly of brick on the ground floor, tile-hung above, with prominent roofs.

The Wardrobe, 58 The Close

The Wardrobe, 58 The Close, a medieval canonry in the bishop's gift, was presented by Walter Scammel on his promotion to the Deanery in 1277 [Edwards 1939, 67, n 3], but only one grant of it is known, from Bishop Chandler to Alexander Sparawe in 1424. A marginal note on this deed, 'now is called Le Warderobe', is dated 1543

Plate 134   *No. 58, the Wardrobe, from SE. J Buckler c 1805–10*

and implies a recent change of use, perhaps to a household store for the bishop; it seems probable that the house was one of the victims of the 15th-century decline in the numbers of residentiary canons. Bishop Jewel gave it to chapter in 1568 in exchange for the Glass-house.

Chapter divided up the house and granted William Blacker a lease of the great hall, the E and W 'porches', with 'the buildings above them', and the 'houses' to S in 1569, with a repairing covenant; the N range they altered

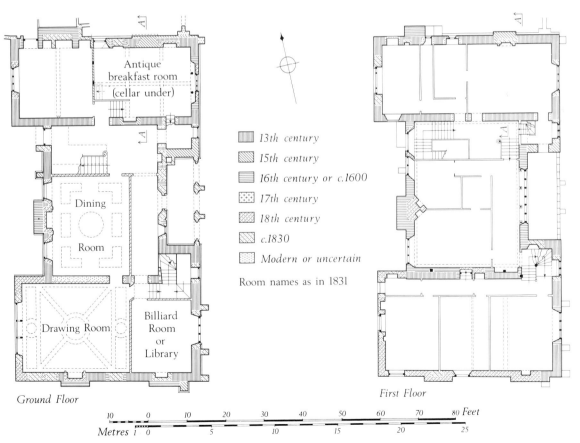

Ground Floor

First Floor

13th century
15th century
16th century or c.1600
17th century
18th century
c.1830
Modern or uncertain

Room names as in 1831

Fig 122   *No. 58, the Wardrobe*

and repaired by direct labour in 1569–70, but in 1576 they granted it also to Blacker. Despite these changes, a chapel chamber still existed in 1586. Substantial alterations, probably made by Blacker's son William, after 1588, must have given the house much of its appearance at the time of the Parliamentary Survey in 1649, when it contained a hall, two parlours, a buttery, cellar, pantry, three larders, a kitchen and coal-loft, a dining room, seven chambers; a gatehouse and three little rooms by it, a stable, woodhouse and four-bay coach-house.

The long tenure of the Coles family began in or before 1659, with four members called William being succeeded by Jane (Coles) Medlycott, who died in 1824. A chapter survey of *c* 1777 notes the 'great alterations and improvements' made by William Coles IV between 1762 and 1776, and that he sublet the 'other' house [Estate Bk 1, no. 66620, ff 50, 51v]. The latter was a gatehouse, named in a lease of 1633; marked on Naish's map in 1716, it was demolished by Jane Medlycott in 1807. A drawing of her house by Buckler *c* 1805–10 (Plate 134) shows the E front, and the stable range on the N side of the forecourt. Mrs Medlycott's trustees sublet the Wardrobe after 1824 and in 1830 chapter instructed them to repair it.

In 1831 the lease was advertised: 'a cloistered entrance, a spacious hall with handsome oak staircase, a corridor with secondary staircase, an antique breakfast room, a fine dining room with enriched ceiling and polished floor, a billiard room or library (unfinished), a superb drawing room communicating with a terrace: 8 bedrooms (with space appropriated for 4 more), 2 dressing-rooms, gallery, butler's pantry and other domestic offices; cellars, w.c., back stairs etc...the house...has been recently repaired and beautified, at an immense expense, and presents one of the purest specimens of Old English Architecture ...'

[*SJ*, 6 June 1831]. Hall ascribed the work to James Lacy in 1834.

After many years as an annexe to the Diocesan Training College (No. 65) and then empty, the Wardrobe was repaired in 1979 as the RHQ and military museum of the Duke of Edinburgh's Royal Regiment. The accompanying plans (Fig 122) do not reflect their alterations.

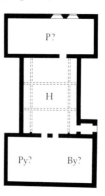

13th century

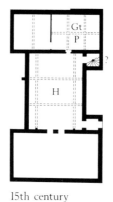

15th century

1649
Ground Floor   First Floor

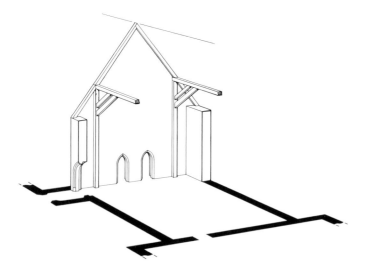

Fig 123 *No. 58, the Wardrobe, perspective reconstruction, service end of hall in 13th century, showing paired braces to roof-plates*

Fig 124 *No. 58, the Wardrobe, sequence of reconstructed plans*

The medieval house

The shell of a substantial house with a hall and two cross-wings remains but there are few features, making dating uncertain. In the hall, the upper parts of a pair of posts about 10 ins square were discovered in the S wall in 1979. They have the mortices for paired braces to roof-plates and one retains its top tenon (Fig 123); a later buttress on W was probably opposite a truss and suggests the division of the hall into three bays (Fig 124). The inward front corners of the posts are rebated, perhaps for decorative boards.

The two cross-wings are probably contemporaneous. The N one included a ground-floor room, probably a parlour, lit by a pair of large windows with chamfered, depressed two-centred heads (Figs 122, 124). Adjoining the S wing was a porch, from which some (mostly very worn) inlaid tiles were removed in 1979 (Fig 125, Plate 135). They measure approximately 5¼ ins square, with four circular indentations on the lower face; they date from the second half of the 13th century and four of the patterns occur also in the Cathedral Muniment Room. No trace remains of the W porch mentioned in 1569 and 1649, E and W possibly being used in error for N and S, and referring to the porch and staircase turrets. The service end appears to have been poorly built as it is now mainly of squared stone, which is presumed to be 16th century, and 18th-century brick.

The N wing was remodelled in the 15th century. The parlour, entered through a stone doorway with elliptical arch of late 14th- to 15th-century date, gained a moulded beamed ceiling (Fig 126b) and the room to W a deeply chamfered ceiling beam. The two upper chambers, which

Fig 125   *No. 58, the Wardrobe, floor tiles from S porch*

Plate 135   *No. 58, the Wardrobe, floor tiles from S porch*

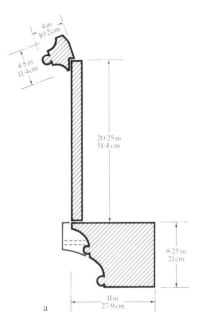

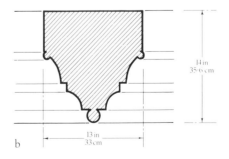

Scale: 1 inch = 1 foot

Fig 126   *No. 58, the Wardrobe, 15th-century mouldings*
a. cornice, ashlar-piece and purlin in great chamber
b. ceiling beam in great parlour

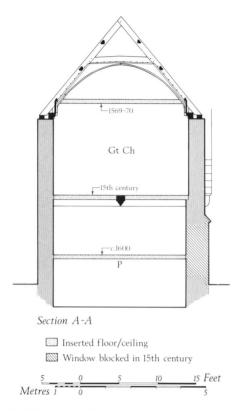

Section A-A

☐ Inserted floor/ceiling

▨ Window blocked in 15th century

Fig 127   *No. 58, the Wardrobe, section of N range*

were probably reached by stairs in the E turret, have arch-braced roofs (Fig 127) separated by a plain truss; their members are mainly moulded or hollow chamfered, without wind-bracing, and the great chamber has a moulded cornice, with boarding (Fig 126a), the smaller chamber a chamfered one. An upper chimney was added on external corbelling, which caused the wall below to be thickened, masking one of the original windows (the arched label of a small window occurs in the E wall of the N range, close to ground level in disturbed masonry; it was presumably found and (incorrectly) reset in the 19th century). A tall narrow window near the corner of the

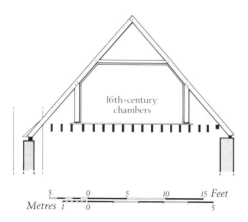

Fig 128   *No. 58, the Wardrobe, section of roof in S range*

great chamber might have lit the latrine which can be expected to have accompanied these chambers.

The 16th and 17th centuries

Blacker's lease of the hall and S range in 1569 almost certainly led him to reroof the cross-wing, building chambers in the roof; here the floor rests on inserted tie-beams and the roof has coupled rafters with posts fixed on top of the floorboards (Fig 128). This work was poorly done and required extensive repairs in the 18th century.

The N wing was probably converted by chapter into a separate dwelling. In 1569–70 a carpenter was employed in removing old stairs and building new ones 'at the east end of the hall', somewhere in the S part of the former parlour. The roof space was also ceiled at eaves level as garrets, of which one partition remains, and the 15th-century arch-braces all removed.

Considerable further improvements accompanied the restoration as one house, probably in part by Blacker in 1576, but more especially by his son *c* 1600. The ground-

Plate 136   *No. 58, the Wardrobe, S staircase, newel-post*

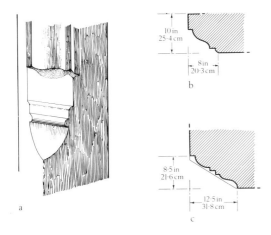

Fig 129   *No. 58, the Wardrobe, mouldings in great chamber*
a. and b. doorway
c. fireplace

plan then became the medieval one reversed, with the main entrance and services to N and reception rooms to S (Fig 124). The placing of the new chimney suggests that the hall still had a screens passage, now on N. The room above was heightened as a new great chamber, measuring 36 ft 6 ins by 27 ft 6 ins, with an exceptionally large E window. This was the dining room in 1649, to which the main approach was probably via the new staircase in the SE turret (Plate 136) and the moulded doorway (Fig 129a, b). In the N wing the W room became a kitchen with a new chimney, and a floor was inserted across the 15th-century parlour, its ceiling beams mutilated to increase the head-room, so providing extra offices to the kitchen with their own external access, above cellarage. The Blackers' work-manship is characterised by ovolo mouldings with an additional ogee on the great chamber chimney-piece (Fig 129c) and certain windows; the sunk chamfer occurs on the principal windows. Brick is used for the chimneys, the great chamber fireplace, and relieving-arches. The new central attics are built mainly with massive timbering, the walls framed to N and S, and roofed with collars, queen-struts and wind-braced butt purlins. The position of the original stairs to the central attic is uncertain and the present ones (Plate 138) cause the blocking of a window high in the S gable.

Plate 137   *No. 58, the Wardrobe, staircase hall, decoration probably of papier mâché*

Plate 138   *No. 58, the Wardrobe, S staircase, attic flight. Similar balusters occur in the neighbouring parish church of St Andrew, Durnford*

Plate 139 *No. 58, the Wardrobe, dining room looking NW*

The 18th and 19th centuries

In the 18th century Blacker's hall was partitioned as an entrance hall, staircase hall (Plate 137) and handsome dining room, and most of his great chamber was made into bedrooms and a passage (Fig 122). This work appears to date from the 1740s and was probably done for William Coles IV, who renewed the leases in 1747, in his father's lifetime. The dining room is especially sumptuous with carved joinery for the chimney-piece and door, and moulded plaster for the wall-panelling and the ceiling with its eagle centrepiece (Plates 139, 140, 141). The further alterations alluded to in the Estate Book in 1762–76 were also made for him and probably included gothicising the sash windows of the staircase hall, and perhaps the extensive reconstruction of the S wing in brick (Plate 142). Other alterations made by members of this family, including the substitution of hipped roofs for gables and the

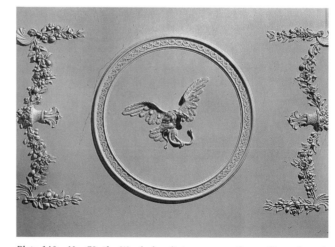

Plate 140 *No. 58, the Wardrobe, dining room ceiling, with eagle and snake*

Plate 141   *No. 58, the Wardrobe, doorway in dining room*

insertion of a central entrance, are partly seen in Buckler's drawing (Plate 134).

In 1830–1 it was mainly the E front (Plate 143) that was converted to the 'Old English' style, with bargeboards (which originally had prominent pendant finials), gables, buttresses and a stuccoed Gothic portico being added, new windows made in wood to match the Elizabethan ones, and the elaborate leaded glazing patterns of that period reproduced. The principal Gothic rooms were the entrance hall, with moulded plaster archways, the NW bedroom, and the library where weak detailing includes tablet-flower in the coved cornice and the figure of a medieval king in the coloured, patterned glass. The 'antique breakfast room' derived its inspiration from the medieval ceiling beams; a little coloured glass was added, and an 18th-century chimney-piece was enhanced with filigree rococo scrolls in papier mâché.

Elsewhere, detail was mainly 'Georgian', evidently a combination of reproduction and old work as in the drawing room, where the polished mahogany doors and the poorly detailed carved mouldings of the triple window and skirting were new. The new central boss of the ceiling and rococo cartouches are probably of *c* 1770 and there is a mid 18th-century chimney-piece. The room above the breakfast room, probably a study, has gilded leaves on a coved cornice and a marble chimney-piece, representing the French taste.

The planning was not greatly altered at this time.

Plate 142   *No. 58, the Wardrobe, from W*

Plate 143   *No. 58, the Wardrobe, from E*

Three bedrooms replaced two in the S range, and a narrow staircase was contrived from the first floor to the breakfast room; some of the household offices in single-storey rooms attached to the kitchen were added now or slightly later. Several rooms were opened up to the exterior, with french windows in the library and drawing room, a Grecian balcony added to the Gothic bedroom, and a balcony above the portico which was accessible from the turret to N and from a doorway cut into Blacker's great chamber window.

In 1979–80 the major part of Blacker's great chamber was reunited by removing the 18th-century partitions, and the transomed four-light window of his hall below was restored. Arch-braces were replaced in the roof of the medieval great chamber in the N wing.

Houses in West Walk

Arundells, 59 The Close

Arundells, 59 The Close, has its origin as a medieval canonry, and the 13th-century cross-wing still forms the nucleus of the present house. Early documentation is poor although this is probably the house charged with the twenty-shilling obit of Henry of Blunsdon, archdeacon of Dorset 1291–7, who died in 1316. Leonard Bilson was the last residentiary canon to live here and he was deprived in 1562, presumably for practising magic [Jones 1879, 424], after which the house was leased by chapter to secular tenants, from 1562 to 1606 first John and then Henry Hooper. 'Mr Hooper's Chapel' was repaired in 1579.

In 1609 the lease was taken by Sir Richard Mompesson who so improved the house that the renewal premium was raised from £20 to £80 in 1637. In 1625, when the succession to the lease was fought over in a court action, it was stated that the previous tenant (Sir Gyles Wroughton) held it 'before it was so fair built as now it is' [PRO Ex Depo C 21 Davy v Parry]; some of Mompesson's work is still evident. The lease then passed through Thomas Davy, Lady Mompesson's son by a previous marriage, to the Davy family, with whom it remained until 1690, and in 1714 was granted to William Pinsent of Urchfont.

The Parliamentary Survey of 1650 listed a wainscoted hall and parlour, a kitchen, buttery, cellar, two larders, bakehouse and poultry room, and upstairs a handsome wainscoted dining room, a gallery, a little chapel, twelve lodging chambers, one closet and two garrets; there was a gatehouse with a handsome lodging chamber above the gate, and next to it a building of four bays containing coach-house, stable and hayloft and coalhouse, with a further four bays of building described as 'decayed rooms'. In 1637 a long ruinous extension behind the house towards the garden consisted of a mealhouse of three rooms, 37 ft 7 ins by 8 ft 8 ins and a 'back house' of three rooms, 40 ft by 22 ft 2 ins, all of which Davy was allowed to demolish if he applied the materials to 'repairing the rest'. Whether or not this had been done by 1650 is unclear.

Much of the appearance of the present house is manifestly the result of expenditure by John Wyndham, who owned the lease from 1718 to 1750. A survey by J Lyons dated 1745 gives the plan, elevations and garden layout begun c 1720 (Plate 144, frontispiece); this was presumably the John Lyons who made an engraved survey of St Thomas's Church in the same year [RCHM 1980, 24]. Of Wyndham's garden buildings, the summerhouse still exists; it stands on a plot of ground overlooking the junction of the rivers Avon and Nadder. This he leased in 1719 from the North Canonry, to the garden of which it subsequently reverted.

The name of the house derives from James Everard Arundell, a son of the 6th Lord Arundell, who married Wyndham's daughter in 1752 and was the tenant until 1803; for some years he accommodated Jesuit priests here [VCH 1956, 93].

Following the tenure of Mr and Mrs Thomas Jervoise, from 1821 to 1836 Arundells housed the Goldolphin School and from 1839 to 1844 it was a boys' school under F N Bracher, with sixteen boarders. An advertisement of 1835 lists a dining room, drawing room and breakfast parlour, four best bedrooms, three dressing rooms, four servants' bedrooms, butler's pantry, housekeeper's room and other offices, a double coach-house and six-stalled stable [SJ, 14 Sept 1835]. After a period of decay, when demolition was considered, the house was renovated for R Hawkings in 1964.

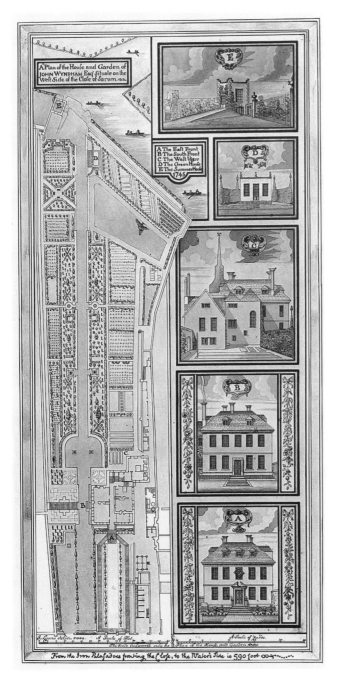

Plate 144   No. 59, Arundells, survey by J Lyons 1745 of house and garden layout designed c 1720

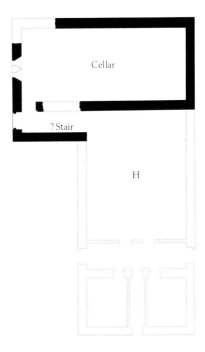

Fig 130   No. 59, Arundells, reconstructed plan of medieval house

The 13th-century house

A clearly identifiable remnant of the 13th-century house is the major part of the present N range, in which there was originally a tall floor above a lesser ground storey, probably the canon's apartment above cellarage. The alignment and position close to the N boundary suggest that it was originally the N cross-wing to a main hall range, the extent and layout of which is entirely conjectural (Fig 130). Smoke-blackened rafters from an open hall have been reused as joists in the parlour and drawing room floors, where other former roof timbers originated as passing or scissor-braces with halved junctions. It is tempting to suggest that these timbers came from the large building measuring 40 ft by 22 ft 2 ins which Davy was given leave to demolish in 1637, but the descriptive term 'back houses' would imply that this was not part of the main range. It is possible, but other evidence is entirely absent, that it was a detached hall sited well back,

comparable with the probable early house measuring 42 ft by 21 ft at Pynnok's Inn in the High St, which was already ruinous in 1385 [RCHM 1980, 67].

The restored W window (Plate 146) of the first-floor room has tracery chamfered externally and hollow chamfered within, with a two-centred rear-arch exposed briefly in 1964, and the roof, now half hipped, retains five pairs of 13th-century rafters of uniform scantling, individually collared without longitudinal bracing. The W wall has part of a blocked doorway probably also of 13th-century date, with hollow-chamfered depressed arch and plain jambs, which provided access to a small extension perhaps containing a staircase.

Sir Richard Mompesson

Although Mompesson's work of *c* 1610 was extensively refashioned in the early 18th century, its broad lines can still be visualised. He must have demolished the 13th-

Plate 145 *No. 59, Arundells, from E*

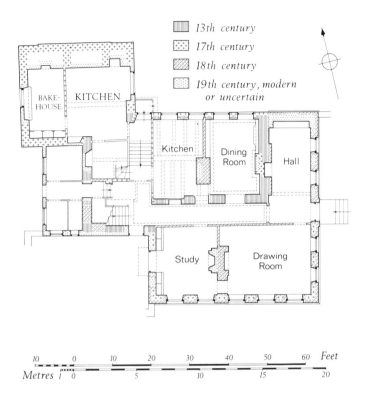

13th century
17th century
18th century
19th century, modern
or uncertain

BAKE-HOUSE   KITCHEN

Kitchen   Dining Room   Hall

Study   Drawing Room

10   0   10   20   30   40   50   60   Feet
Metres 1   0   5   10   15   20

Fig 131   *No. 59, Arundells*

century hall and service rooms, constructed the present S range as his new hall and parlour, and added on new kitchens at the NW corner; these are at intermediate level to the 13th-century cross-wing, where he made the ground-floor ceiling yet lower; his staircases connecting the two builds still exist (Fig 131). An adjustment in the original cross-wing allowed an extra storey to be inserted there and this helped to provide the large number of lodging chambers listed in 1650. The kitchen and bake-house remain comparatively little altered, although their brick chimneys were taken down in 1964 (Plate 146). The upper storey contained a best bedroom and inner chamber in 1745, well fitted with cupboards (Fig 132), and this arrangement, which survives, is probably the original one. Fittings include blocked windows with chamfered wooden mullions and a ceiling beam and door architrave

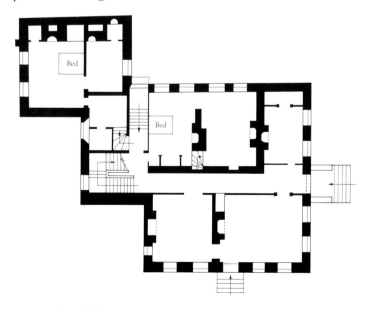

Bed

Bed

Fig 132   *No. 59, Arundells, plan redrawn from 1745 survey*

Plate 146   *No. 59, Arundells, from SW*

chamfered with ogee stops. In the S range, which was originally gabled to E and W, only Mompesson's roof survives with collars, queen-struts and two tiers of butt purlins, the upper wind-braced. 17th-century oak wainscot remains in several parts of the house but probably none in its original position.

In the late 17th century much of the N wall was refaced in stone, flint and brick rubble; a lead rainwater-head there, probably *ex situ*, is inscribed 'W P P 1699' and doubtless refers to William Pinsent.

From the 18th century to the present day

John Wyndham's refurbishment was comprehensive. He refaced the E, S and part of the W elevations in stone (Plate 145), no doubt obtained from the Close Wall adjacent, which was standing in April 1719 but is not referred to afterwards. A uniform hipped roof on an eaves cornice was obtained by raising the eaves of Mompesson's roof on the S range and building a structure with knee-principals above the N range; in this period the N elevation had a plaster cornice, probably of coved form, since removed. The central window on S was then a

garden door with rusticated stonework (Plate 144, B), and the approach to the house was improved by ashlar gate piers with fielded panels and heavy iron gates with scrolled panels [Macartney *c* 1925, plate 56].

The drawing room and parlour and the rooms above

Plate 147   *No. 59, Arundells, drawing room looking NE*

and to N were handsomely fitted with bolection-moulded and fielded-panelled joinery below heavily moulded cornices (Plate 147); the drawing room and parlour doors have face-hinges with turned finials and cover-plates of brass. A new main staircase was built in oak, lit from W by a round-arched window (Plates 144 (C), 148), and the plan drawn in 1745 shows the house as altered by Wyndham; the kitchen wing to NW is given at upper mezzanine level and here and in a room nearby the positions of beds are marked (Fig 132, Plate 144).

In the 19th century the house was fitted with plate glass and the cornice on S was altered; the attics were refitted *c* 1840 largely as servants' quarters. A stuccoed drawing room or ballroom was added on SW between 1860 and 1879 (Plate 146) but the site is now a terrace.

In 1964 the floor level of the present kitchen and dining room, which must have been raised since 1745, was restored to its 17th-century level and corresponding alterations made to the windows here and in the cellar. The general renovation included the demolition of the Victorian drawing room and the elimination of the central valley of the roof. A recent renovation has included the reopening of a doorway from the ground-floor corridor to the dining room.

Plate 148   *No. 59, Arundells, staircase*

The stable and other structures

A stable to NE of the house has rubble walls incorporating brick and a roof with diagonally set butt purlins, suggesting a 17th-century origin. A handsome external cornice was added, probably by Wyndham.

To W of the house, the main boundary walls to N and S are partly of medieval date, up to 8 ft high; they are coped with tiles and incorporate layers of tiles set diagonally, alternating with courses of flint and stone. Minor walls of brick, stone and flint are of 17th- to 18th-century date, and appear on the 1745 survey.

The North Canonry, 60 The Close

The North Canonry, 60 The Close, is a 16th-century house fashioned mainly within the shell of a very large 13th-century one, with several later phases of development (Fig 133, in end-pocket, Plate 149). Until the 18th century there were four ranges around a courtyard, the W one perhaps incomplete, and the principal rooms appear always to have been in the E part of the house, facing the Cathedral. In 1430 chapter granted the house to Canon Whitemer on condition that he repair a chamber above the entrance gate and an inner chamber called 'Faus Chamber', in return for which he was excused three years' payment of an obit; but the house is poorly documented until 1547 when Canon Robert Okyng, archdeacon of Sarum and Doctor of Law, was granted this house and another, possibly to enable him to reconstruct it. At this time a substantial house was made still larger but Okyng had to renounce it following the accession of Mary, to Chancellor William Geoffrey and he in turn, at the end of her reign, was succeeded by Thomas Lancaster, treasurer from 1560 to 1584, archbishop of Armagh from 1568 to 1584. An inventory made in 1586 during Canon Colcell's tenure listed the fittings in what was substantially the present house.

Residents in the early 17th century were Chancellor Thomas Hyde (*c* 1600–18?) and Canon Osborne, who was evicted under the Commonwealth in favour of John Conant, presbyterian minister at St Thomas's; in 1649 Parliament sold the house to the City after including it in its Survey. Alterations in the second half of the century display the initials 'R H' (Plate 150), which belong to none of the known residents at that period, and possibly refer to an unnamed successor of Conant's or a relation of one of the Restoration canons Anthony Hawles (1660–4) or Dr Thomas Hyde, precentor (1664–6), who may have occupied part of the house. Thomas Hyde was eighth of the twelve sons of Laurence Hyde of Heale House, whose second son and heir, Sir Robert Hyde (1596–1665), was a noted Royalist [Benson and Hatcher 1843, 390–3, 445–6]. Recorder of Salisbury from 1635 to 1640, and reinstated in that office in 1660, Robert became Chief Justice of

Common Pleas in 1663, in which year he gave a pair of altar candlesticks to the Cathedral, and his monument, set up by his wife after his sudden death in 1665, is in the S transept. It may be that the initials R H on his brother Thomas's house refer in some way to Robert. Later residents included Chancellor Drake (1666–81) and Treasurer Ward (1681–90), the bishop's nephew.

Naish's map of 1716 [RCHM 1980, Plate 16] shows the house with its courtyard plan little altered. In 1739 John Bampton (1725–51) [*DNB*] was allowed to demolish much of the S part of his house, including the whole of the S and W ranges. He also reconstructed the area to S of the 16th-century great parlour as three reception rooms with attic rooms over, and built new kitchens etc, reducing the size of the house considerably. Further destruction was authorised for Canon Gilbert (1751–77), the bishop's brother, in 1751, when the house was described as very large with many decayed and superfluous buildings, Mr (Francis) Price being his 'undertaker'. A drawing made of the house from E by Bray *c* 1800 (Plate 151) shows Bampton's S range with its lower roofline, shortly before Canon Hume (1803–34) elegantly remodelled the principal reception rooms. An antiquarian restoration made by Sir Gilbert Scott [Cole 1980, 222] for Canon Swayne (1874–95) partly reversed his work (Plate 152) and was

Plate 150   *No. 60, North Canonry, gateway from E, showing 17th-century window above with initials R H*

Plate 149   *No. 60, North Canonry, aerial view from W. Traffic Technology Limited, Skyscan Balloon System*

Plate 151   *No. 60, North Canonry, from E. Bray* c *1800*

described in 1876 as 'extensive and judicious' [Stevens 1876]. This phase is commemorated in a well-carved 'W. GOODWOOD 1875' on an attic window-jamb. The house ceased to be a canonry in 1940 [*VCH* 1962, 76] and the name 'North Canonry' has not been traced before the present century.

The medieval house

The house was so transformed in the 16th century that few earlier details remain and any reconstruction of its medieval arrangement must be tentative (Fig 134). However, by the 13th century, the main range with two principal floors above a sunken basement seems to have occupied the full frontage of the tenement, with the gateway in its present position leading into the courtyard. Two first-floor chambers near the middle are of equal width and were perhaps the inner chambers of a pair of apartments, while further accommodation existed in a cross-range to N where there was a passage and staircase alongside one or more chambers. The hall is unlikely to have been in the S part of the E range in its 16th-century position (Fig 135); 13th-century walling and doorways indicate that there was a cellar under this area, and if the hall were at ground level with an open hearth it is more likely to have been in a return range to W, or possibly in the vanished range W of the courtyard.

The floor above the undercroft N of the gateway is original, but elsewhere levels have been altered (Fig 136): in the S part, the middle storey has been increased at the expense both of the cellars and of the first floor, where the W window in inner chamber 2 formerly descended to the present floor level, but painted decoration on the gable of that window shows that the roof remains at approximately its primary level. The ground floor was originally about 7 to 8 ft high and the first floor some 12 to 13 ft at the eaves. On the ground floor there was probably a parlour with inner chambers, and it may be that a small window high up in the corner of one of them lit a privy.

Plate 152   *No. 60, North Canonry, from E*

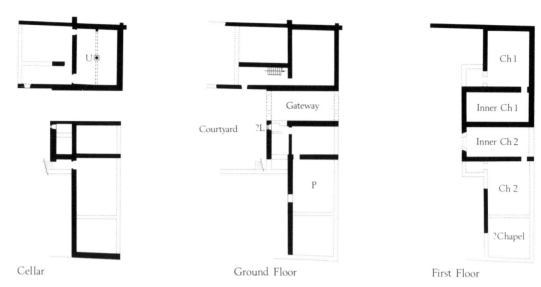

Fig 134   *No. 60, North Canonry, reconstructed plans of 13th-century house, scale 1 in. to 48 ft*

Fragments of painted plaster (now concealed) are all that are known to indicate the original decoration of the two principal floors; in chamber 1 there is said to have been a dado with ochre colouring below a double band in red and red-line ashlaring; inner chamber 2 has red-line ashlaring forming rectangles 6½ by 10 ins below red *rinceaux* ascending a window-jamb, and the N passage has a frieze of *rinceaux* with a wavy line border and ashlaring in red (Plate 153).

At basement level there are original doorways, two with pyramidal stop-chamfers, suggesting that the main approach to the S cellar was from the courtyard and down steps to an internal porch. The N undercroft is partly buttressed as though it were originally vaulted, but no other signs of this remain, and the stone column probably supports its original beam with joists lodged on top of it (Plate 154); the wall-plates are deeply chamfered with splayed and tabled scarf-joints with a secret tongue, and the wall-plate on E with its heavy stop-chamfers at the corbels resembles those of the Cathedral nave triforia, roofed before 1266.

Alterations made in the later Middle Ages are visible only in the basement, where a lower ceiling was inserted in the internal porch, close joisted with extra-wide floor-boards, truncating the W doorway.

The W part of the N courtyard range may have been built in the 14th century, with horizontally set sub-rectangular windows. It may always have been single storey but has been considerably altered and is now a disused stable.

The 16th century

In the mid 16th-century reconstruction the central and N parts of the E range were established in much their present form, with floors at their existing levels (Fig 136), and the hall sited in the S part, but any reconstruction is necessarily tentative (Fig 135). The 1586 inventory names the hall with a boarded floor, the buttery, the cellar, the great parlour with wainscot and a portal, the little study within the great parlour, the gallery over the buttery, the parlour at the upper end of the hall now a study with wainscot, a portal and a chimney, the kitchen and kitchen loft, and the inner and outer larder. Above, there was a chapel, the great chamber, the middle chamber over the gate with a chimney, two doors and shuttered windows, Mr Colcell's bedchamber wainscoted with shuttered windows, a portal and two doors, the inner chamber and the higher study. Elsewhere (presumably on the ground floor N of the gate) there was a stove chamber and stove house, both wainscoted with a portal, the inner chamber, the lower parlour with a portal having two doors, another inner chamber, a cupboard in the wall in the entry, and the stair foot on the right of the gate coming in, also a seven-stall stable, the saddle house and (presumably in the W range) two chambers at the end of the gallery with wainscot overhead.

While the main rooms in the E range are clearly identifiable, the service end of the house is now totally altered. The kitchen, buttery and larders were certainly in the S range at ground level, while the cellar was under the hall; the gallery must have been on the first floor of the S range, leading no doubt to chambers in a two-storey part of the W range. The carriageway or 'entry' existed in its present form and its 'cupboard' of 1586 was a hoist to the middle chamber, ascending to a 'little cupboard by the chimney' there; this small but unusual luxury was complemented by the very exceptional steam-bathing chambers of the N range, and by the provision of two water

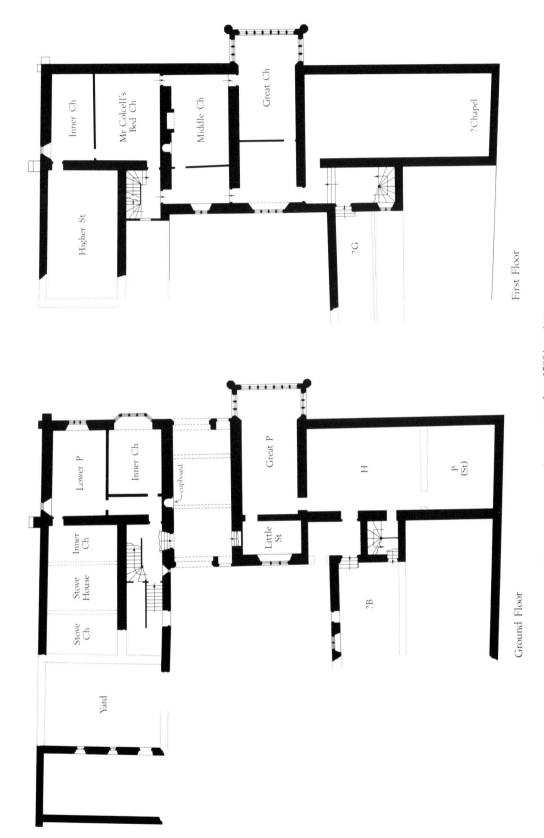

First Floor

Ground Floor

Fig 135   *No. 60, North Canonry, reconstructed plans of 16th-century house with room names from 1586 inventory*

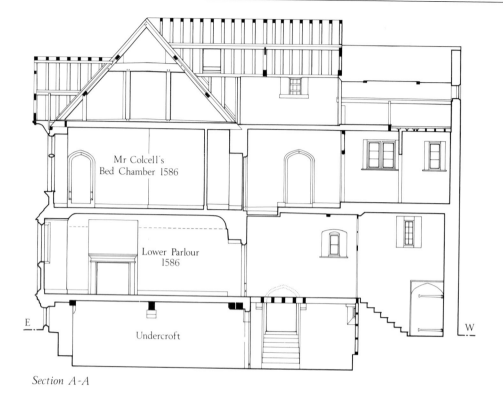

Section A-A

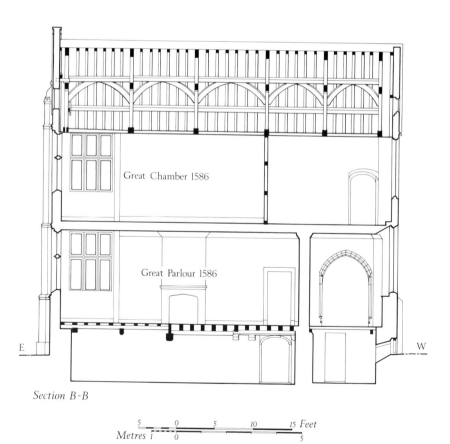

Section B-B

Fig 136   *No. 60, North Canonry, sections through N range and main cross-range*

Plate 153   *No. 60, North Canonry, wall painting on N wall of passage in N range*

Plate 154   *No. 60, North Canonry, undercroft under N range looking SE*

pumps. There was one in or near the kitchen, and one of brass in the inner chamber of the stovehouse.

Both the present staircases are of 16th-century date. The N one was created in a part of the 13th-century passage (which was heightened in stone-dressed rubble and timber framing) to serve the N part of the house and the attics of the main range. These are fitted with oak floorboards and were lit by jettied dormer windows on E, but have an awkward approach and, like the great attic, can hardly have been used for more than storage. The roofs above the great and N chambers are characterised by their terminal trusses being placed some 1 ft away from the gables, perhaps as a precaution against rot. The principal ranges are constructed with wind-braced butt purlins and collars braced on stout queen-struts, while the lateral roofs over the W gables have clasped purlins and diminished principals.

The S staircase was probably the principal one, with an octagonal newel-post and a plank and muntin partition with hollow-chamfered mouldings at its base. This partition divided the cellar flight leading to the brewhouse from the main staircase. The great chamber and both floors of the main range N of the gateway were all subdivided into outer and inner rooms by framed partitions with large panels.

Many stone doorways remain, mostly with four-centred arches and moulded stop-chamfers with broached bases (Fig 137) and arched or timber-lintelled rear-arches. The two E windows with hollow-chamfered and roll-moulded four-centred lights might pre-date Okyng, but attributable to him is the magnificent ashlar bay-window with its polygonal angle buttresses and curious cellar light, apparently shaped more for ventilation than for vision. At this period the undercroft and S basement were

reached by doorways opposite each other in the carriageway.

Much of the joinery described in 1586 is lost although several stout doors remain on their original hinges, including those of the gateway which are nail studded and framed, each with five bevelled panels. Other doors are mainly planked, but one, of three by two linenfold panels, now reset in the pantry, is 16th century and 'the cupboard under the window going (from the Inner Chamber) into the Higher Study' remains built into the wall, lined with oak boards and having doors with chamfered panels.

Bricks (measuring 9 x 4 x 1½–1¾ ins) occur frequently, being used to build the chimneys on either side of the Middle Chamber (seen at attic level), the hoist etc.

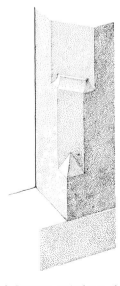

Fig 137   *No. 60, North Canonry, typical stop-chamfer of 16th-century doorways*

The 17th to 19th century

The evidence of 17th-century alterations is comparatively modest. The 13th-century N passage was heightened by a storey against the quoins of the 16th-century staircase to give first-floor and attic rooms, with chamfered windows matching the 16th-century ones, and these new rooms were perhaps included in the summary survey made by Parliament in 1649: 'this house has for its entrance a great gate and contains a large hall, a kitchen, a low gallery and a high gallery 80 ft by 9 ft, 2 larders, 2 woodhouses, a pantry wainscoted, 3 cellars, 2 wainscoted parlours, a buttery, 12 chambers whereof 4 are wainscoted, 8 other rooms beside garrets, and a stable of 6 bays.'

In the latter part of the 17th century finely moulded windows and a cornice were added below the jettied dormers of the main elevation, combining a classical element with the antiquarian gesture of initialled shields (Plate 150). Some refitting is also suggested by a number of panelled doors with chamfered edges or bolection mouldings and chamfered oak wainscot in Mr Colcell's chamber, but all are *ex situ* and their context has been swept away.

By the early 18th century Canon Okyng's house must have seemed both very large and hopelessly old fashioned, and in 1738 Bampton's first request to make alterations referred to the buildings on the S side as 'entirely useless and inconvenient' and 'gone to decay' [Acts 1696–1741, 262]. From this and the proposal of the following year we learn that the S part of the E range then consisted of the hall, a lumber room adjoining it and a passage from the gatehouse, and in the S range there was a kitchen, a brewhouse, a drying loft and a long passage, which led to the W range containing a garden parlour and two lumber rooms, with other rooms over them.

Bampton's first intention was to turn the gateway into his hall, with doors into the parlours on either side, and to build a new kitchen behind it. His second proposal, which was put into effect, allowed him to build on the site of the old hall three new rooms 20 ft long and 12 ft high: a hall 16 ft wide, a parlour 18 ft wide and a withdrawing room 12 ft wide. Among his surviving fittings are the scallop-moulded plaster cornice in the hall, and probably the eared chimney architrave reset in the present drawing room. Elsewhere a passage was built past Mr Colcell's chamber, and his inner chamber was given a chimney and a moulded stone fireplace. Bampton's demolition of most of the S range allowed him to build new kitchens etc of single storey (Fig 133, in end-pocket), and a joint in the S wall beneath the W casement window marks the abutment of undisturbed medieval work. Chimneys of this period have brick stacks above pitched stone weatherings.

The truncation of the stable and N range in rubble-faced brick is perhaps attributable to Canon Gilbert,

c 1751. The former was curtailed on S and its 16th-century doorway reset and widened, while the 'coach house' became a two-storey building by filling in the cellar and inserting an upper floor at a new level lit from N. About the middle of the 19th century it was again altered for single-storey use as a coach-house with a four-centred stone arch, and the roof was lowered and the windows blocked. In much of the 18th-century work moulded stone can be detected in the rubble and a few older stone windows are evidently reset, eg the 14th-century ones in the N wall of the coach-house and S wall of the stable.

In the early 19th century Canon Hume combined Canon Bampton's parlour and drawing room and gave the new room handsome door-cases and window furniture with convex reeded architraves and beaded panelled joinery, and a plaster cornice with deeply undercut leaves; this was linked by double doors to the library, where the 18th-century triple fenestration was adapted to take a pair of bookcases with friezes of chaste paterae, and the chimney-piece appears to be a contemporary essay in the Early Georgian style. On the first floor a number of the 16th-century stone door-cases were genteelly encased in joinery, and the large mullioned windows of the 16th-century great parlour and chamber were given sash frames [Hall 1834, Plate XXVI], but reinstated by Scott who restored the windows generally, both in their stonework and lattice glazing.

Scott made various changes. In the carriageway he remodelled the minor gateways, E and W, adding a new mullioned window above each. Inside, he cut back the S wall beneath an arched stone corbel table as an eye-catcher and invented the present main doorway, with '*Nisi Dominus aedificet Domum in vanum Laborant qui aedificant*' ('Unless God shall be the foundation, those who build the House are labouring in vain') carved in Gothic letters above a reset 14th-century moulded stone archway. It leads towards the stairs which were altered to their present form. This approach replaces the main entrance on W supposedly in use since the 16th century, around which there was a large excrescence by 1860 [Bothams 1860], presumably an entrance vestibule etc; the latter was then reduced to the present sanitary offices, faced with flint, and the roll-moulded stones of a two-centred arch were incorporated in the N wall. The W parlour and chamber were extensively rebuilt at the same time, although the N wall appears to be medieval with areas of herringbone tilework, and the 17th-century roof survives. Elsewhere, the 18th-century rooms had their sash windows replaced by wooden ones with mullions and transoms and the attics above were heightened into a semi-storey with three dormer windows which replaced the four small dormers visible in Bray's drawing, *c* 1800 (Plate 151). On the other side of the gate, 'medieval' bargeboards were added to the three 16th-century cross-gables (Plate 152). No doubt it was Scott who removed the cloak of render from the exterior generally. An elaborate stone chimney-piece in the dining room, in 14th-century style with corbelled candle brackets, is presumably also his work.

The summerhouse

At the bottom of the garden a summerhouse (Plate 144 (E)) is built of brick with dressings of stone and simulated ones of plaster. It consists of a basement lit by oval windows of gauged brick and a main chamber with a chimney which was added during the 18th century, its shaft sitting on an iron bracket. There is a flat lead roof reached by external stairs. Designed *c* 1720 for the garden of Arundells (*qv*) to whom the plot of land was leased out, it reverted to the North Canonry probably soon after 1800. Nearby stands the surviving W stretch of the Close Wall (see p 44).

The Old Deanery, 62 The Close

The Old Deanery, 62 The Close, is directly opposite the W end of the Cathedral and its site is the most prominent, and one of the largest, on the W side of the Close. Robert of Wykehampton, dean from 1258 to 1274, gave the house to chapter as the Deanery in 1277 during his reign as bishop [Everett 1944, 425], but it is not unlikely that his three predecessors as dean had lived in the same place. Except during the Commonwealth, when it was occupied

by the city recorder William Stephens, it remained the Deanery until 1922.

In the Middle Ages, periods when deans were resident, as from 1220 to 1297 and 1382 to 1431, coincide with the main phases of construction, or alteration, and alternate with periods of non-residence, 1297 to 1382 and 1463 to 1563. In his formal deed of gift Wykehampton made no claim to have built the house, and for reasons connected with the initial distribution of building plots in the Close (p 11) its site was probably one of the first to be developed, *c* 1220. Wykehampton may have constructed the hall, the roof of which is unlikely to be earlier than his decanate, but there are two layers of paintings on the gable-wall of which at least one must be evidence of the earlier hall. When he left, the Deanery probably comprised the present large open hall with service rooms continuously roofed to N, and a cross-range with a chapel projecting from it to S.

This house was considerably enlarged in the late 14th or early 15th century, probably for the vigorous and reforming dean Thomas Montacute who entered residence in 1390, with new private rooms at one end and service rooms at the other. Most of these buildings survived until recently and are listed in a very valuable inventory of 1440 (p 212), together with outbuildings which no longer exist. It is said that Henry VI stayed here in 1457 [Wheeler 1889, 11]. Further work is documented in 1571 for Dean Piers (1571–7) when five timbers were dragged out of the house, and in 1621–2 when bricks were carried away. The

Plate 155   *No. 62, the Old Deanery, from NE. J Buckler 1805*

Plate 156   *No. 62, the Old Deanery, from E, in 1949*

naming of the chamber over the services as the 'king's chamber' in an inventory of 1586 may imply a visit from one of the early Tudor monarchs.

In 1649 the Parliamentary Survey summarised the house as having one large hall, three kitchens, a bakehouse, three cellars, six other small low rooms for several offices, a large dining room 60 by 24 ft, wainscoted with a portal, a lesser dining room also wainscoted, eight chambers, two of them wainscoted, six other mean rooms, two garrets, also a stable and coach-house of four bays, and along the street a handsome stone wall with a fair gate therein [Drinkwater 1964, 59]. The Deanery at this time had already been requisitioned by Parliament, who in 1646 ordered the slighting of Longford Castle and the removal there of the state's belongings [Waylen 1892, 374]. Dean Bailey (1635–67) returned at the Restoration, and it was probably he who restored the house at a cost of £475 in 1670 [*VCH* 1956, 194].

In the 18th century, Dean Clarke (1728–57) 'lived much at Cambridge' and perhaps neglected the house [Jones 1881, 324]. Upon the appointment of his successor Dr Thomas Greene (1757–80) the *Salisbury Journal* announced his intention to 'rebuild the Deanery in a magnificent manner' [*SJ*, 21 March 1757]. Chapter allowed him to pull down two rooms one above another at the W end of the great dining room, and a 'garden wall' on W, and to extend the W side of the hall. Described as 'artistic and finical' [*VCH* 1956, 199] Greene is the man most likely to have gothicised the E elevation as seen in Buckler's drawing of 1805 (Plate 155).

Greene's works were largely destroyed by Charles Talbot (1809–23) who had permission in 1810 to demolish the E wing, measuring 40 by 18 ft, the presumed 13th-century chapel, and in 1811 to inhabit the Porter's Lodge during the 'repair'. The 'great' internal changes of this period resulted in 'two large reception rooms [which] are fine, and command two unrivalled views, but much else in the house has been sacrificed for this arrangement' [*CL*, 2 Aug 1913]. His successor as dean, H N Pearson (1823–46), applied the same expensive principle to the garden and in 1845 demolished the next house to S, compensating chapter for its loss, and absorbing the garden which extended down to the Avon. The house was so close to the Deanery that a document of 1228 allowed the dean to erect ladders in its court for purposes of maintenance. It was one of the smaller canonries until the mid 16th century; but despite its narrow site, the 1649 survey lists extensive accommodation there and its heyday was probably the early 17th century, with Sir Lawrence Hyde and Sir Anthony Ashley-Cooper (later 1st Earl of Shaftesbury) as residents. Chapter records generally refer to it as the 'little house south of the Deanery'.

The Diocesan Training College annexed the buildings to their premises at the King's House in 1922, and in 1938 commissioned from C Williams-Ellis a new residential wing, which remained unbuilt in 1939. In 1948 the architect Curtis Green proposed to enlarge the college and pull down the Deanery, the significance of which then went largely unrecognised (Plate 156), and in 1950 erected a building in the garden to E, thus breaking the visual link between Deanery and Cathedral. Destruction was finally averted after the NE wing had been demolished, and from 1960 to 1963 the 13th-century buildings were restored by the removal of floors and partitions, when many discoveries were made. The 13th-century roof was dismantled so that missing members could be reinstated and the hall became the college assembly hall.

The Deanery is described and the plans drawn as it appeared in 1950 (Fig 138) with additional information recovered in 1960–3. This account and the plans differ in

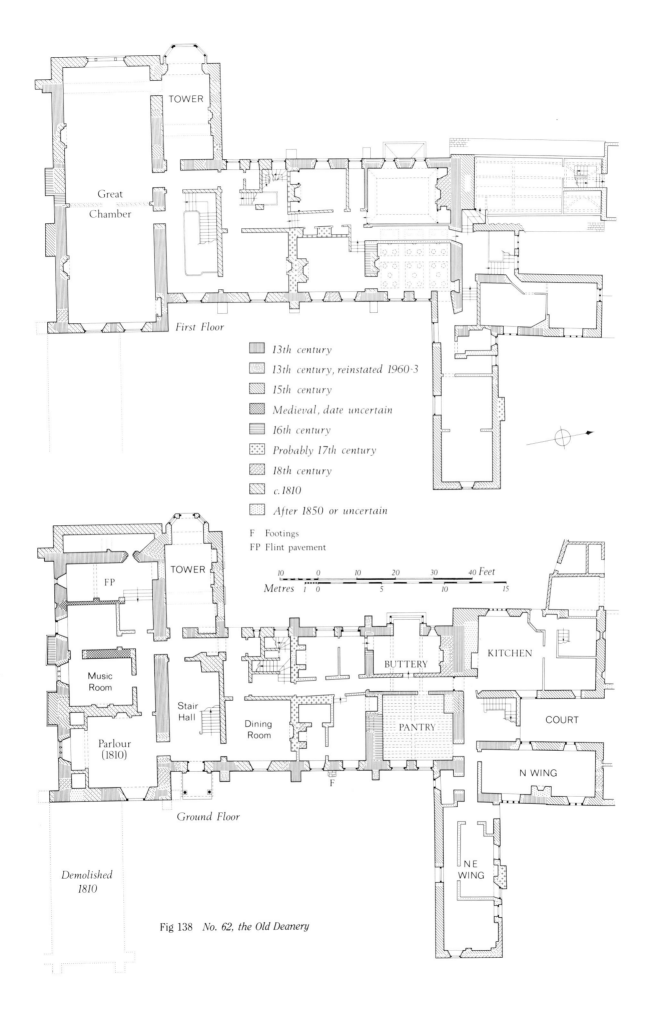

TOWER

Great
Chamber

First Floor

13th century

13th century, reinstated 1960-3

15th century

Medieval, date uncertain

16th century

Probably 17th century

18th century

c. 1810

After 1850 or uncertain

F   Footings
FP Flint pavement

10   0   10   20   30   40 *Feet*

Metres   1   0   5   10   15

FP

TOWER

KITCHEN

Music
Room

Stair
Hall

Dining
Room

BUTTERY

PANTRY

COURT

N WING

Parlour
(1810)

F

Ground Floor

NE
WING

Demolished
1810

Fig 138   *No. 62, the Old Deanery*

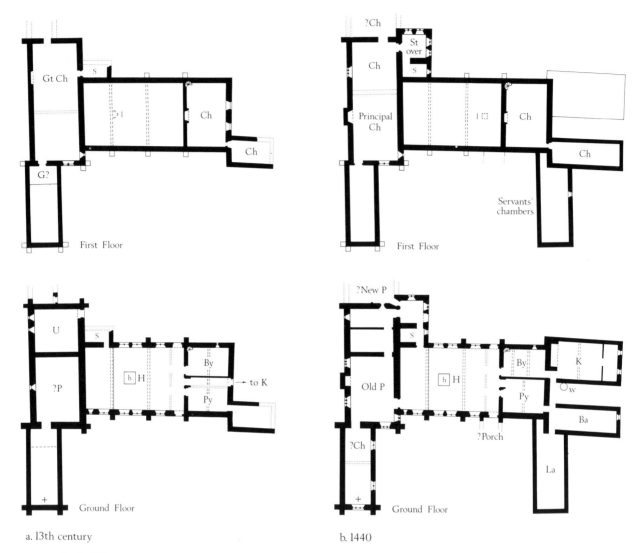

a. 13th century   b. 1440

Fig 139   *No. 62, the Old Deanery, reconstructed plans, scale 1 in. to 48 ft*

several respects from those of N Drinkwater [Drinkwater 1964], but the destruction of evidence has made a complete reassessment impossible.

The original house

The 13th-century Deanery had an open hall with opposed external doorways at the N end, a hearth near the centre, with louvre almost above it (Figs 139a, 140), and a dais at the S end with painted plaster decoration on the gable wall above it. In the cross-range at the S end, the upper rooms were no doubt divided into great and inner chambers. The building to E seen in Buckler's drawing (Plate 155) appears from its corner buttresses and the offsetting of the great chamber window to have been original, and was probably the chapel; at the W end there may have been a small extension, of which the sole survival is a door-jamb at ground-floor level.

The services comprised the buttery and pantry and presumably extended into the NE arm. Their hall doorways flanked a central arch which presumably led to a kitchen, probably the detached building with a floor of tiles on edge discovered in 1961 some 50 ft N of the pantry [Drinkwater 1964, 55–6].

In the hall, the roof was probably the best preserved feature in 1960, its timbers soot blackened over red paint. The upper part of the roof consists of twenty-nine trusses, each having a pair of rafters and two collars measuring 5½ ins square. Except in the main trusses, where there are tie-beams, these upper trusses rest directly on longitudinal plates, scarf jointed. At the two principal trusses (Fig 141) the lower collar is supported by a chamfered crown-post and two braces, one of which halves across the post and the other is tenoned into it. The crown-post is tenoned into the collar above and is abutted by a braced collar

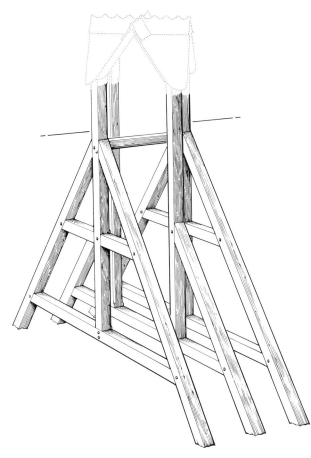

Fig 140   *No. 62, the Old Deanery, hall roof, original louvre*

.... Suggested original
          height of buttresses

———— Original timbers

▨▨▨▨ Timbers installed
          in 1963

A. Collar purlin

B. Brace to collar purlin

C. Plate

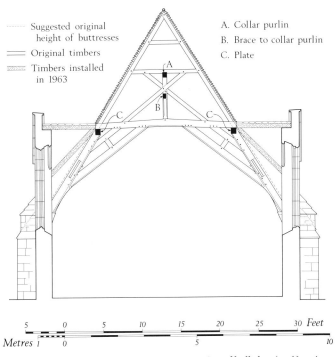

| 5 | 0 | 5 | 10 | 15 | 20 | 25 | 30 *Feet* |

Metres 1   0   5   10

Fig 141   *No. 62, the Old Deanery, cross-section of hall showing N main truss, as restored*

Plate 157   *No. 62, the Old Deanery, hall interior looking N, after restoration*

purlin; this had been removed and dismembered but parts were discovered reused within the roof in 1960. The main trusses have stout principals on stone corbels, with double braces to the tie-beam and longitudinal braces to the plates. Against the N wall the ends of the plates are supported vertically by wall-posts on stone corbels, with longitudinal braces from post to plate, lateral ones from post to tie-beam, and dragon braces from tie-beams to plate (Plate 157).

At the S end of the hall, painted decoration presumably followed the underside of the roof and its border lies parallel with the former creasing-stones for the joint between the hall roof and the N wall of the cross-range (Plate 158). The painting is in two layers, neither of them later than the mid 13th century; the older is in red with 9-in squares containing curling stems and four-petal flowers at the intersections and the later consists of red ashlaring forming rectangles 11 by 6 ins abutting an inclined frieze of scrollwork in red and cream with black outlining.

The hall buttresses now extend in two stages well above eaves level but were probably originally lower and corresponded with the single-stage buttress shown elsewhere in Buckler's view, the coincident coursing of buttress and wall occurring only in the lower 7 ft 6 ins. Few details of the original fenestration survived in 1960; the hall was restored with single windows in the central and S bays, but it may be that originally they were double, as in the accompanying drawings (Figs 139, 142). One window in the N bay on E retained much of its two-centred opening with double hollow-chamfered mouldings and the greater part of the gabled dormer above it. In the S bay, the sill of one narrower window remains some 7 ins higher than the others. The dais is an original feature, occupying the whole of the short S bay where the floor of pounded

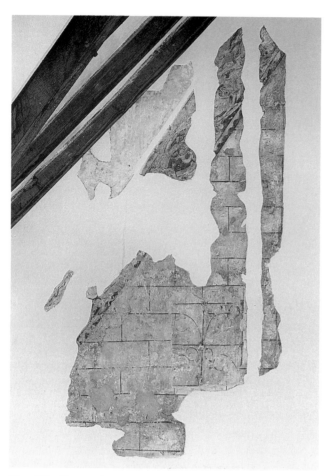

Plate 158   *No. 62, the Old Deanery, painted decoration on S gable of hall*

chalk is 1 ft 2 ins higher than elsewhere. The central hearth of clay tiles was also found in 1960 and was seen to have been rebuilt twice in the same position. Doorways in the hall have tall broach-stops, the external ones having a quarter-hollow moulding and two-centred heads, those to the services chamfered with low arches. Scarf-joints are employed both in the plates of the hall roof and in the pantry ceiling beam (Fig 143).

In the service end of the house the buttery is lit by an original chamfered slit window and the pantry has an original ceiling, but the E partition of the kitchen passage, if it existed, has gone without trace. The upper room was a large chamber, probably heated on S, entered from a staircase within the services and communicating with an inner chamber through a two-centred stone doorway. Of the roof of this chamber, the S truss with two collars remains, continuous with the hall roof, the low eaves suggesting that the main windows were originally in the N gable or perhaps in small gables to E and W.

At the S end Buckler drew buttresses on the cross-range and chapel, where the roofs may have been similar to the hall, although the chapel was possibly vaulted. The undercroft of the cross-range was entered through an external doorway with depressed two-centred head and lit by chamfered slit windows; a stout wall defining a square room in the W part is possibly original. The W end has remained until recently very little altered, poorly lit, with a floor of knapped cobbles at the original level, and at least part of the remainder may have been a parlour. The upper storey was entered through a narrow doorway (Plate 159),

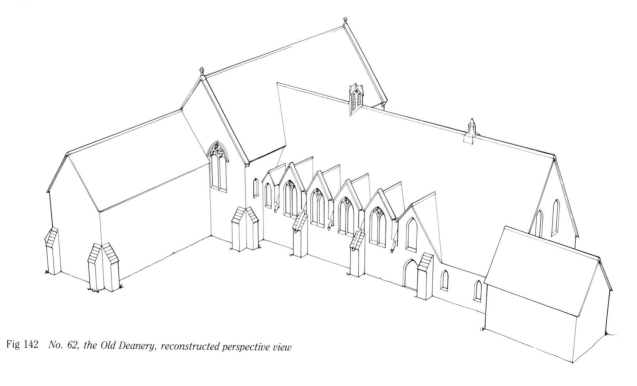

Fig 142   *No. 62, the Old Deanery, reconstructed perspective view*

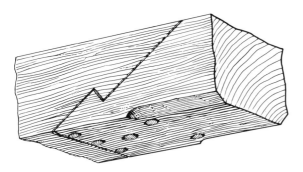

Fig 143 *No. 62, the Old Deanery, scarf-joint in pantry ceiling beam*

approached by a projecting staircase, of which the N wall is incorporated in later masonry. The E chamber was lit until Dean Talbot's day by a large E window with bar tracery under a gable crowned with a stone finial, and a trefoil-headed window on the N return wall, which came to light in 1960. The chapel probably had a private gallery, of which one stone door-jamb remains.

Objects dating from the 13th century discovered *ex situ* include fragments of encaustic tile [Drinkwater 1964, Plate XXXIII d], four of the five identifiable patterns occurring also in the Cathedral Muniment Room; a male head and a stiff-leaf corner respond-capital retaining traces of red paint [*ibid*, Plate XXXII], all of the middle or second half of the century; the capital probably derived either from vaulting or the corner of a decorative feature such as a window embrasure. Walling of this period is in coursed flint rubble containing a scatter of broken roof tiles, with stone dressings, and in the S wall there are put-log holes lined with stones or tiles.

The late medieval expansion

The inventory of 1440 describes a larger house than the identifiable 13th-century remains, with extensive outbuildings [printed in full in Drinkwater 1964, 56–8]. It names the hall, principal chamber, the chamber adjoining, the little chamber adjoining, the *Capella Bassa*, the chamber next to the Oratory, the old parlour, the chamber adjoining, the tower or wardrobe, the chamber at the end of the hall over the pantry and buttery, the next chamber; the kitchen, the larder beyond the bakehouse, four upper chambers for servants, a lower chamber; the steward's chamber near the gate, the porter's chamber, the chamber over the gate; the stable and chamber adjoining; the entrance leading to the kitchen; the new parlour. The new rooms appear to be the chamber one away from the principal chamber and the tower or wardrobe, together with the larder, bakehouse, four upper and one lower chambers. The 'new parlour', containing new benches, was possibly in an addition at the W end, demolished in 1757, of which only a stone doorway on the ground floor of the tower, with steep four-centred arch, remains.

The addition of the tower caused the approach from hall to great chamber, including the dais doorway, to be rebuilt (Fig 139b). The tower originally had a parapet of which the gargoyles, demi-figures holding jars under their right arms, remain. It was unheated, a chimney above the SW corner shown by Buckler being presumably an addition of the 17th or 18th century (Plate 160); its well-fenestrated upper rooms measured approximately 12 ft square and the top floor was perhaps originally a study. The associated doorways have four-centred heads with hollow chamfers and broach-stops.

The 'old parlour' appears, from its position in the inventory, to have occupied the E half of the undercroft, and was fitted with new windows in the 15th century; these broadly resemble the tower windows and originally

Plate 159 *No. 62, the Old Deanery, original doorway to great chamber*

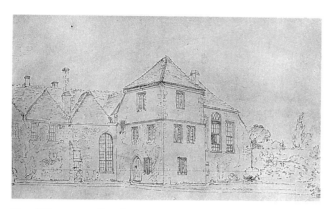

Plate 160   *No. 62, the Old Deanery, from NW. J Buckler 1805*

they had labels (Figs 144, 145). Presumably the eastern-most of the S chimneys was added to heat this room and part of its chimney-piece survives (Plate 161). Another 15th-century chimney-piece was recorded by W Twopeny as 'formerly in the Deanery' in 1833 and possibly orig-inated in the great chamber (Plate 162). The associated doorways, however, from hall to parlour and from tower to great chamber (Plate 163, Fig 146) are more probably of the late 15th or early 16th century, when the first floor of

the tower can have been little more than an ante-room to the great chamber. In the chapel Buckler's drawing shows the lower storey with cusped windows resembling the 15th-century ones elsewhere, and it may have been at least partly floored over and divided up, but the phrase '*capella bassa*' implies that the chapel still operated on two levels.

The service rooms were also improved and a new kitchen built *c* 1400. This was single storeyed and consis-ted of a large room for cooking, and a smaller inner room, the roof of which is better finished with curved and chamfered wind-braces; it was perhaps the cook's cham-ber. The kitchen is entered through a hollow-chamfered wooden doorway with an original door of two planks, counterplanked, with circular studs and fish-tailed hinges. Inside, the remainder of the S wall is filled by a huge fireplace with a chamfered segmental arch. The roof rests on tie-beams and stone corbels and has butt purlins with the common rafters tenoned into them. A parallel range, which might have been the bakehouse in 1440, is of similar date; both have timber-framed N gables and hollow-chamfered windows with two-centred heads. A similar window existed on the upper floor of the NE wing, possibly servants' chambers above the larder in 1440. A

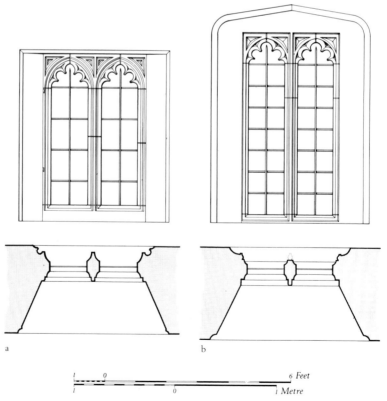

Fig 144   *No. 62, the Old Deanery, windows in*
a. tower
b. parlour

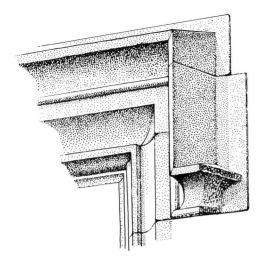

Fig 145 *No. 62, the Old Deanery, hoodmould of parlour window*

Plate 161 *No. 62, the Old Deanery, fireplace in parlour*

stone-rubble-lined well outside the new kitchen door may be that named in 1440.

In the 14th or 15th century a second louvre was built at the lower end of the hall (Fig 147) and the original one closed in with new rafters, which became smoke blackened; masonry footings discovered on E of the hall in 1960 were interpreted as those of a porch, added at an unknown date [Drinkwater 1964, 53].

The building materials of this period are flint rubble with courses of tiles laid diagonally, notably in the S chimney where they occur in horizontal, diagonal and herringbone courses, and in the tower as regular lacing-courses.

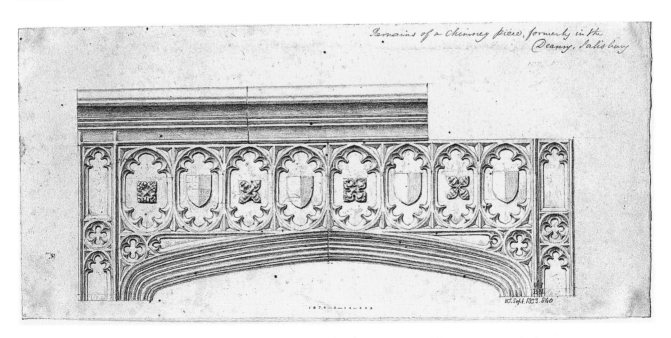

Plate 162 *No. 62, the Old Deanery, fireplace probably once in the great chamber. W Twopeny 1833. BM S&D 1933 Vol IV b. 27*

Restorations in the 16th and 17th centuries

The inventory made of the canonries in 1586 lists relatively few contents in the Deanery and beyond telling us that the hall, the little parlour and the three principal upper chambers had seven portals between them, six of them the gift of Dean Bridges (1578–1604), it adds little to our knowledge of the house [*ibid*, 58]. The upper floor of the cross-wing was then a single room called the great

Scale: 1 inch = 1 foot

Fig 146   *No. 62, the Old Deanery, moulding of doorway from tower to great chamber*

Plate 163   *No. 62, the Old Deanery, doorway from tower to great chamber*

chamber, known in 1649 as the 'large dining room' when it measured 60 ft by 24 ft, and was heated by a new chimney placed as near centrally as the 15th-century parlour windows would allow (Fig 138).

In the mid 16th century, extensive alterations were also made above the 13th-century buttery and pantry, when the original large chamber there was heightened under a transverse roof of uniform-scantling timbers. It was then divided into a larger room with a heavy beamed ceiling and a smaller one whose floor was raised to its

present level, and the roof space was made into attics with a stone window in the E gable. The W wall was largely refaced at this time in squared stone rubble. A new chimney was built to heat the larger room, whose base blocked the 13th-century pantry door; the fireplace suggests a date before rather than after 1563, when Dean Bradbridge returned to residence (Fig 148).

In the late 16th or early 17th century the hall trusses were renovated with timbers and lath and plaster so as to form round arches with central pendants, part of the N one remaining until 1960. Not long afterwards a stone wall was built below this truss converting it into a partition, and the N bay of the hall was floored over, creating low rooms on the ground floor; a stone doorway into the W one remains. No doubt the main entrance was moved S and a new staircase built within the reduced hall.

In their survey, the only feature of the Deanery praised by the Parliamentary commissioners was the front wall with its classical gateway, of which the piers are ornamented with square-cut rustication in vertical strips (Plate 164). They must then have been very new and may be attributed to Dean Bailey.

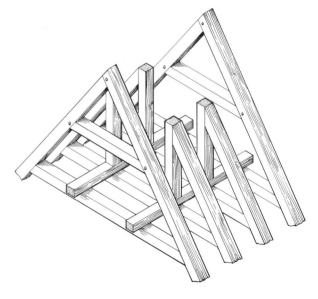

Fig 147   *No. 62, the Old Deanery, hall roof, secondary louvre*

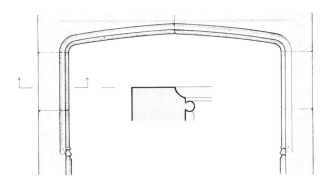

Fig 148   *No. 62, the Old Deanery, fireplace in chamber above pantry, with detail of moulding*

From 1700 to the present

Probably in the decanate of John Younger (1705–28) the walls of the whole of the original hall were raised and the lower rafters removed. This allowed a higher ceiling in the two remaining bays of the open hall, where a round-arched window was inserted on W, and taller bedrooms in the floored bay where sash windows and fielded panelled joinery with bold, ovolo-moulded architraves were installed. The bedroom ceiling above the medieval buttery was also extended into the attic, with a deep cove and a moulded plaster cornice. At the same time, a new attic storey was added to the whole area of the original hall, with hipped dormers built on each side of the ridge to give headroom, and the general alteration of gables to hips was done in this period.

Dean Greene's alterations of *c* 1757 chiefly involved gothicising the E elevation as depicted by Buckler (Plate 155), with stucco detail added to features partly of earlier date. A possible architect was James Essex, to whom chapter paid 2 guineas in 1758, this small sum suggesting that it took advantage of his presence in Salisbury on other business. Essex, an early practitioner in Gothick, restored Ely Cathedral from 1757 to 1762, of which Greene was a prebendary [Jones 1881, 324], and they had a mutual friend in Rev W Cole of Cambridge, for whom Essex worked [Colvin 1978, 299]. The half-hipped gables facing E were then joined up as a continuous parapet and the building rendered. The quatrefoil windows on E lighting the attics, of which no trace was discovered in 1961, might have been 13th-century roundels *ex situ*. The E half of the NE arm was also rebuilt, and the only Gothick details to survive until 1950 were its E window and the two posts from the porch, each of four clustered shafts with bell capitals and roll-moulded bases, reset in the original pantry. On the W side, the rooms added to the cross-wing in the 15th century were demolished and a Palladian window with Gothick glazing bars inserted. Until this period alterations had been faced in stone rubble but now rendered brickwork was employed.

Plate 164   *No. 62, the Old Deanery, gateway from W*

The piecemeal nature of the alterations up to this time allowed Britton to comment that the Deanery 'still retains an air of antiquity, being but very partially modernised' [Britton 1801, 47]; but Dean Talbot's modifications of *c* 1810 were more extensive. Externally, he removed the Gothick detail and introduced sash windows generally, and he destroyed two of the original buttresses and heightened the third. The main entrance was again moved S, and the remaining bays of the original hall floored and divided, chiefly into circulation space, with no less than three staircases to the first floor, and a fireplace in the passage behind the main stairs (Fig 138). The 17th-century stairs to the top floor of the tower were removed and the link between tower and hall was enlarged, the tower rooms having their 15th-century windows blocked, new ones built on W, and fireplaces inserted. The cross-wing was heavily altered, a new W wall being built and the old demolished at first-floor level. The eaves were raised some 7 ft, in order to create two noble upper rooms originally divided by central double doors, the W room having a chimney-piece of heavily reeded marble with corner roundels. On the lower floor a music room and parlour were formed, their new chimney having its flues raking across to enter the S stack. In the parlour an alcove on S has a ceiling of intersecting ribs and small squares, framed by a four-centred arch, and the 15th-century window had its mouldings cut back and was filled with miscellaneous fragments of stained and painted glass. Joinery of this period has beaded panels and the main entrance was equipped with two pairs of double doors; the chimney-pieces were renewed throughout the house in marble, stone or wood with corner roundels. Alterations were done mainly in rubble with stone or white brick dressings.

Dean Boyle borrowed £700 from Queen Anne's Bounty to make alterations in 1881, and to him may be attributed some general repairs including the uniform reconstruction of all chimney-stacks in brick and improved fenestration in the kitchen quarters. He may also have added the bay-window of the tower and renewed the E fireplace of the great chamber.

From 1960 to 1963 post-medieval features and the second louvre truss were removed from the hall, the buttresses were restored to their 18th-century height and the roof was rebuilt with the lower rafters, which had all been removed, at a shallower pitch than the upper ones. The remaining original window was reinstated with bifurcating tracery and others were built beneath gables. The central hearth was uncovered and a louvre constructed upon the remains of the original one. The tower similarly had its medieval features exposed. The Training College was closed in 1977 and the two ends of the building were converted to flats in 1981.

Appendix to the Deanery
Survey 1440, Chapter Act Book, Hutchins, f 27
Translated from the Latin. Words in quotes are in English in the original.

Implements belonging to and being in the house of Mr. Dean.
In the hall,
First, a long table, seven ells long, and made in three pieces, one ell wide.
Item, another table for the middle of the hall, six ells long and one ell wide.
Item, another table five and a half ells long and three and a half quarters wide.
Item, seven large and small benches for the principal table.
Item, four movable tables with four forms for them.
Item, an English cupboard, with English furnishings.
Item, two forms for the middle table.
In the principal chamber,
Item, a wooden bed.
Item, a chair of Sarum make.
Item, a new cupboard.
Item, a most beautiful table, four ells long and one and a half ells wide.
Item, a pair of trestles for the said table, curiously made.
Item, another table for the same room, five ells long and three quarters wide.
Item, two new forms each four and a half ells long.
Item, two other smaller forms.
Item, a pair of trestles for the aforesaid table.
In the chamber adjoining the principal chamber,
Item, a wooden frame for a bed.
Item, a chair of Sarum make.

Item, a new cupboard.
Item, three forms.
In the little chamber adjoining,
Item, a wooden bed and a small cupboard.
In the lower chapel,
First, an old image of the Blessed Virgin, gilded.
Item, another image of the Blessed Virgin, of alabaster, holding her dead Son to her breast.
Item, a great bell, to ring at the mass.
Item, two old benches with reading desks of equal length.
In the chamber next to the oratory, a wooden bed.
The old parlour is benched around,
and in the chamber adjoining is a wooden bed.
In the tower or wardrobe,
Item, three trestles with a table made of two pieces.
In the chamber at the end of the hall, viz. over the pantry and buttery,
Item, a wooden bed.
Item, a cupboard.
Item, a long form, five ells long.
Item, a wooden bench.
Item, a chair of Sarum make.
In the next chamber
Item, a wooden bed.
Item, a board for a press and two trestles.
In the buttery, two stands for beer.
Item, a hamper for keeping drinking cups.
Item, an old chest.
Item, two 'shelfes'.
Item, an iron bucket with a short chain arranged at the well with a wooden pole for the well,
and in the pantry, three 'bynnys' for keeping bread, a table for chopping.
Item, three 'shelfes', a form about two ells long.
Item, a square 'bynne' for keeping cut bread,
and in the kitchen, three large dressers and a small one.
Item, a table for baking, with trestles.
Item, a brass cauldron,
and in the larder, beyond the bakehouse, a great 'trowe' for salting meat.
Item, one 'vate', broken.
Item, one dresser,
and in the bakehouse, two casks, two 'trowes'.
Item, a 'moldyngbord'.
Item, two 'vattys' made from one cask.
Item, in four upper chambers for servants, four wooden beds.
Item, in a lower chamber, one wooden bed.
Item, in the steward's chamber near the gate, one wooden bed.
Item, in the porter's chamber, one wooden bed.
Item, in the chamber over the gate, three wooden beds.
In the stable are 'mangers Rekkys and plankes and postes' beneath, and one cask.
In the chamber adjoining, a wooden bed.
Item, in the entrance leading to the kitchen, two stone mortars.
Item, in the new parlour, two new benches.

63 The Close

63 The Close is a late 18th-century house and its E façade, which directly abuts West Walk, is part of a unified composition with No. 64 (Plate 165). The back part, however, is older and its history can be traced from the 13th century and the establishment on it and three adjoining tenements of the obit of Simon Micham (chancellor 1274–88 and dean).

Between 1395 and 1545 the chaplains of John Chandler's and Lord (Walter) Hungerford's chantries lived here, partly concurrently, together with the beadle in the mid 15th century. After the Reformation chapter leased it mainly to lay folk. In 1605 John Poncherdon took it and the house passed through his descendants, members of the Roberts, Hearst and Wyndham families until they relinquished their lease in 1785. From 1895 until 1977 it formed part of the Diocesan College at No. 65; it has now been made into flats.

In 1448 the chantry house was described as having high chambers and ones below, with chimneys. Of this period only a party wall with No. 64 at ground and cellar levels remains (Fig 149). The 17th-century arrangement with a parlour above the cellar, and hall and kitchen in line may well perpetuate something of the medieval arrangement, that is unless the medieval house had no hall (Fig 150). The party wall at cellar level is of flint and stone rubble banded with herringbone courses of tiles and contains the jambs of a chamfered stone doorway leading from S to N, which suggests that the properties were at one time divided differently, although abutting one another on N and S.

The Parliamentary Survey of 1649 named a hall, parlour, kitchen, woodhouse, two butteries and coalhouse, four little chambers, a gallery and another mean room. The W end of the house was rebuilt shortly after the middle of the century, in purplish brick with a platband, as a kitchen with a chamber and attic over it, the large chimney having a brick weathering. The original windows

Plate 165 *Nos 63 and 64 from SE*

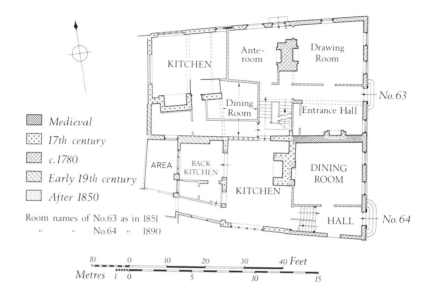

Medieval

17th century

c.1780

Early 19th century

After 1850

Room names of No.63 as in 1851
    "   "   No.64 "   1890

Fig 149   *Nos 63 and 64*

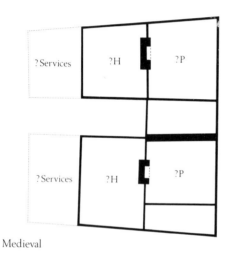

Medieval

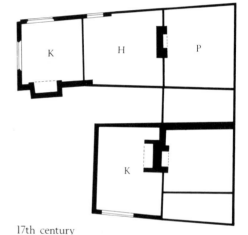

17th century

Fig 150   *Nos 63 and 64, reconstructed plans*

are of wood with ovolo-moulded mullions, one transomed on the first floor, and a scratch-moulded wainscot door remains *ex situ*.

Three chimney-pieces suggest improvement in the early 18th century, perhaps following the tenancy of Mary Roberts (1687–1725); two stone ones are now reset on the 18th-century top floor and the third with an elaborate bolection-moulded architrave of wood is now in the kitchen chamber.

The house was advertised in 1785 as a 'new genteel brick built dwelling' [*SJ*, 29 Aug 1785], the front range having been totally rebuilt (the lease of 1800 described it as 'rebuilt' since the last renewal) in tandem with No. 64 (*qv*); its main elevation has wooden keyblocks to the windows and a plinth of white brick with stone dressings, and the rear elevation is partly of tile-hung timber-framing (remaining on the first floor). Within, many

fittings of this period remain, including plaster ceiling cornices, chimney-pieces and panelled joinery on the ground and first floors, and the staircase has a close string and rounded handrail ramped at columnar newel-posts.

Two later descriptions show the rooms differently used. In 1851 the reception rooms were all on the ground floor; above, the chambers over the entrance hall and drawing room were a large dressing room and bedroom. By 1896 the hall and drawing room had become sitting rooms, and a first-floor room had recently been in use as a small drawing room. In 1903 a science room was built in the yard, when the house was part of the Training College.

64 The Close, the Audley Chantry

64 The Close, the Audley Chantry, was reconstructed *c* 1780 together with No. 63 (Plate 165). It also was charged with Micham's obit and from 1290 until the late 14th

century was occupied by vicars and afterwards by chantry chaplains, expecially those of Henry Bluntesden's chantry.

In 1548 it housed Richard Turnbull, lately the priest of Bishop Audley's chantry; evidently it had belonged to the chantry and was forfeit to the Crown in 1545, remaining freehold until sold by Canon Edward Steward to chapter in 1915, although an annual rent of 6s 8d remained payable to chapter, presumably a relic of Micham's obit. The Crown leased it to Robert Paddon in 1577, without fine on condition that he repair it, and in 1610 sold it to Francis Philips. From the mid 17th century until 1796 its ownership followed the tenancy of No. 63. In 1690 it was called The Chantry [Everett 1936, 385] and in 1790 Audley House.

An 'old chapel' existed in 1324 to W, and in 1444 an earth partition wall in the W high chamber needed repair. The medieval house may therefore have had a front parlour raised above a cellar, a hall (if any), and a chamber over the services (Fig 150). The rear part of the house was rebuilt in the middle of the 17th century as a kitchen with a chamber and attic over it, perhaps taking advantage of a pre-existing chimney (Fig 149). The exterior is of brick with a platband and bullnosed plinth, and the purlins project from the W gable.

The front rooms were rebuilt before 1785, probably as a result of a lease made in 1777 between H P Wyndham and William Lush, builder, and son of Edmund Lush, Cathedral clerk of works. The fittings are similar to those in No. 63, with the addition of a three-centred classical arch across the base of the staircase, and on the first floor the rooms were arranged as a large bedroom with a dressing room over the entrance hall.

In 1890 Mrs Trollope sold the house to Canon Steward of the Diocesan Training College (No. 65) having built the back kitchen and fitted the house with plate glass windows (since removed); the first-floor front rooms were then in use as a large and small drawing room. It was later adapted as the Cookery School, with dormitories and bed-sitting rooms etc.

The King's House, 65 The Close

The King's House, 65 The Close, formerly called Sherborne Place, occupies a large plot of ground to S of the Old Deanery. The present mansion is of the 15th to 17th centuries and is named after King James I, who occupied it when visiting Salisbury in 1610 and 1613, although the title was not adopted until c 1780. Before 1539, when the abbey was abolished, it had been the abbot of Sherborne's prebendal residence in Salisbury. The buildings and 'court of the abbot of Sherborne', as they are named in late 13th-century documents, have been replaced by a 15th-century house, the major part of which survives, consisting of a single range with porch at the front and stairs at

the rear, and a minor range to N (Fig 151).

In 1559 chapter leased Sherborne Place to John Hooper of New Sarum, and in 1564 to Hugh Powell of Great Durnford, one of the bishop's registrars; he also rented a pasture to S, the site of a canonry bearing Nicholas de la Wyle's obit. The Crown disputed chapter's ownership until as late as 1575, granting leases first to George White and then to Lord Cheney, presumably claiming that the freehold had belonged to the abbey. In 1572 chapter granted Powell leave to sublet part of the tenancy in consideration of his expenditure on lawsuits maintaining its rights, and on repairs and new buildings, and he may well have floored over the abbot's hall. Powell died in 1587 and in 1599 the lease was granted to Thomas Sadler, who three years earlier had married Powell's widow Eleanor (her memorial is in the Cathedral). The lease records that Sadler had already spent 200 marks on repairs and improvements, and gave him the right of a future renewal at a fixed rent, suggesting that he intended further expenditure.

Probably soon afterwards Sadler erected the brick-built cross-wing to N of the 15th-century range, containing a great parlour, a handsome staircase, and two magnificent first-floor rooms; doubtless these were used for the king's accommodation. A lease of 1615 refers to Sadler's recent construction on the tenement to S, which by this time had effectively been united with the main one, of a kitchen, brewhouse and bakehouse with lodgings and chambers upstairs, and between 1615 and 1621 he added a large stable with a hayloft and chamber over it on the E part of this site, adjoining the road. Sadler, who had been knighted in 1623, died in 1634 and the tenancy passed to his son, also Thomas. His house is recorded in the Parliamentary Survey of 1649. It consisted of a 'handsome large hall, 4 butteries, 4 kitchens, 2 pantries, a scouring room, larder, 2 woodhouses, a parlour 16 ft square wainscoted 10 ft high, a large parlour 40 ft by 23 ft wainscoted 11 ft high, a little hall and bottle room: above stairs a fair large dining room, 12 chambers, 3 garrets, 3 other cocklofts, a gatehouse and chamber over it, 3 staircases and a stable and hayloft containing 4 bays of building'. The court before the house had a high stone wall handsomely railed and the garden at the rear held a banqueting house of one room.

Following the death of Thomas Sadler II in 1658 and his widow Mary in 1659, the tenancy passed to her cousin Mary Miller, whose repairs to the W end of Sir Thomas's cross-wing carry the date 1661 on the keystone of a relieving-arch. She remained in the house until her death in 1698, probably dividing it between several undertenants. For most of the 18th century the lease was held by members of the Beach family of Keevil, under whom the mansion continued to be occupied in separate parts. In 1791 the lease was offered for sale in six lots and bought by

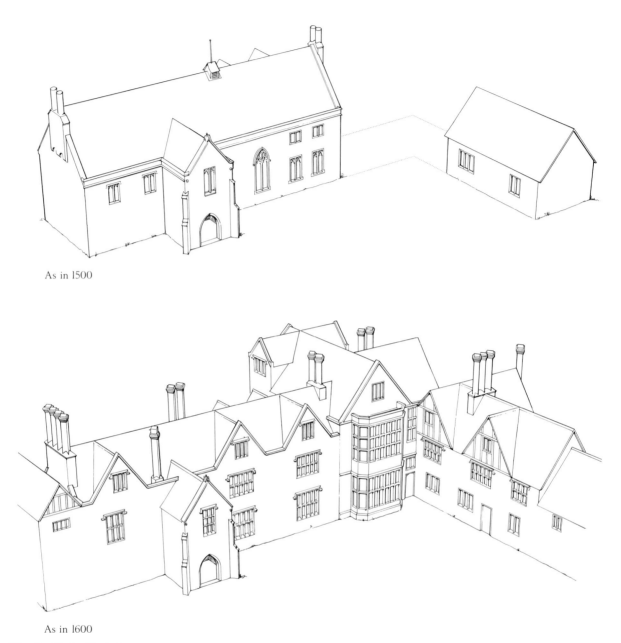

As in 1500

As in 1600

Fig 151 *No. 65, the King's House, reconstructed perspective views*

Thomas Atkinson, builder, who was no doubt attracted by the advertisement stating that 'so large a spot of ground in such a situation is not often to be purchased' [*SJ*, 17 Oct 1791]. A scheme to demolish the old house and build a street of 'residences for genteel families', thirty houses in all, was announced the following year [*SJ*, 11 June 1792] but not proceeded with.

In the early 19th century the house was again occupied by a single tenant, General Slade, who was in residence by 1803. He demolished some parts and rebuilt others, a 'house and gateway' being taken down in 1804 [*SJ*, 2 July 1804]. Some of his alterations are seen in John Buckler's

drawings dated 1804 and 1807 (Plates 166, 167). Advertisements in the *Salisbury Journal* at various dates from 1816 to 1839 offer the lease, at first for short periods, later for sale, Slade's furniture being auctioned in 1836 [*SJ*, 14 Mar 1836]. In 1816 the house had on the ground floor an entrance hall, eating room and a drawing room opening into a conservatory and grapery, and on the first floor a library and fifteen bedrooms, with fourteen more for servants; there was also a kitchen, scullery, brewhouse, tepid or cold bath-house, stables for eight horses, coach-house for three carriages, cow house, piggery etc [*SJ*, 15 Apr 1816]. This was partly the result of 'great alterations in

Plate 166   *No. 65, the King's House, from E. J Buckler 1804*

the last 3 or 4 years', and in 1828 'many thousand pounds' had been spent in the 'last few years' [*SJ*, 15 Dec 1828].

By 1836 the house was again in dual occupancy and from 1836 to 1848 the Godolphin School was held in the N part under Miss Bazley. In 1849 the Diocesan Board of Education obtained and demolished the subchantry, a medieval dwelling which adjoined the King's House to N

[Harding 1897, 95–9], and can be partly seen in Plate 168. In 1851, a building by T H Wyatt having replaced the subchantry, the Diocesan Training College for Schoolmistresses moved to the King's House. In 1873 chapter gave £50 towards new dormitories, and the college acquired the small houses to NE (Nos 63 and 64) in 1890 and 1895. A wing designed by E Doran Webb, built in 1898–9 to W of

Plate 167   *No. 65, the King's House, from E. J Buckler c 1807*

Plate 168   *No. 65, the King's House, from SW. J Buckler* c *1804*

Wyatt's building, added dining rooms for the pupils and
governesses, a chapel, and a classroom with a dormitory
over it, and other additions have been made during the
present century. In 1979, following the closure of the
college (latterly the College of Sarum St Michael), the
King's House was acquired by the Salisbury and South
Wiltshire Museum. For a general history of the house and
references to sources, see Everett 1936.

The abbot's house

The first phase of construction is characterised by flint
rubble including herringbone tile courses, with the principal dressings mainly in Ham Hill stone. This is significant
because this stone was rarely if ever used in Salisbury
before the 19th century but was commonly used at
Sherborne during the 15th century, and it is safe to infer
that those parts of the house in which Ham Hill stone
occurs were built during the abbey's ownership. A further
structural parallel with Sherborne in this period lies in the
roof, where all trusses have or originally had collars with
pairs of curved upper struts (Fig 152), as in the former W
range of the abbey cloister [RCHM 1952, Plate 201]. The
possibility that Abbot Saunders (1459–75) rebuilt the
house, and temporarily occupied No. 71, is discussed on
p 242.

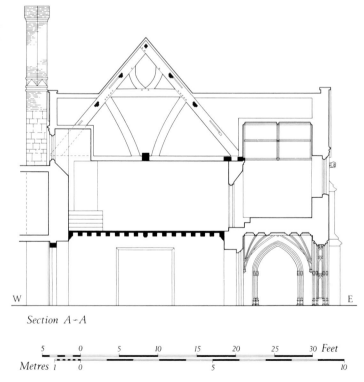

Section A – A

Fig 152   *No. 65, the King's House, cross-section through porch and
screens passage*

The original house comprised a great hall with a parlour to N, and chamber over it reached by a stair on W. To S of the hall a porch with an upper chamber protects the entry to the screens passage, with a service room and kitchen adjacent and tall chambers over them, one probably the great chamber (Fig 153). The original roof survives, although mutilated mainly in the late 16th century, and the trusses are numbered I–VIIII. It has diagonally set ridge-pieces and hollow-chamfered butt purlins; the open trusses all had moulded arch-braces to the collars.

The hall was open to the roof and was lit by tall windows with arched heads, of which one on W was seen by Buckler (Plate 168) and the outer jambs and springings of the two on E partly remain. The hall roof is distin-

guished by its upper wind-braces, which alone remain; they are chamfered and cinquefoil cusped (Figs 152, 154). At its centre, a pair of truncated rafters are trimmed to provide the seating for a louvre (Fig 155), now gone, the ridge-piece is pierced for the iron shaft of a revolving wind-vane, and a yoke below has a socket for the shaft-base. The reconstruction of the louvre is in doubt, as its framing lacks almost any evidence of seatings, with only flat areas on top of the flanking rafters, and vertical pegs. The open hearth was probably not much used because the abbot would have visited the house only occasionally, and there is little sign of soot on the roof timbers.

In the parlour two window-jambs of Ham Hill stone remain on either side of the present E window and in the chamber above there is a moulded stone chimney-piece

Fig 153 *No. 65, the King's House, reconstructed plans, as in 1500*

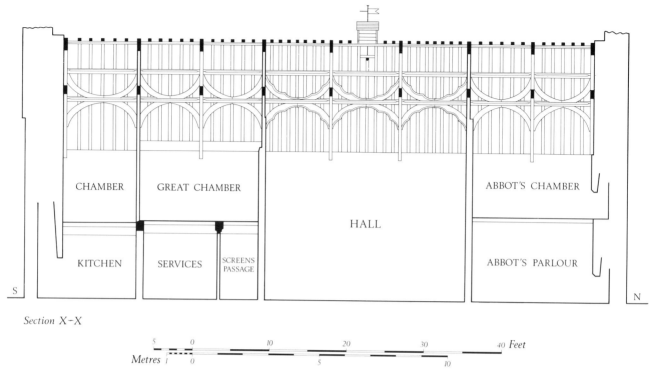

Section X–X

Fig 154   *No. 65, the King's House, reconstructed long-section*

and fireback of stone, flint and tile rubble. The staircase leading to it appears to have been rearranged in the latter part of the 17th century and now has a wooden newel-post carved with an acorn finial. The stair window seen by Buckler was possibly not original, and was replaced by one at a different level in the mid 19th century.

At the 'lower' end of the house, the main entrance leads into a screens passsage which is sited under the great chamber and has a moulded stone doorway at either end; that to E retains its two-centred arch and nail-studded door with hollow-chamfered cover-strips, small wicket leaf

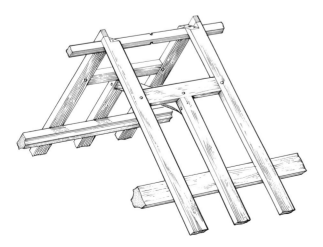

Fig 155   *No. 65, the King's House, detail of louvre in hall roof*

and original strap-hinges (Plate 169). The passage ceiling is also original, with moulded cornices and central beam. Mortices for the posts of the S wall suggest by their spacing that there was a single service room with a central doorway, and a kitchen beyond it reached by a passage placed to one side.

The ceiling of the service room has heavy joisting, as in the screens adjacent, and part of a cornice to N which formerly continued, at least on W; an area on the E side where the ceiling has been rebuilt is probably the position of the original stairs. In the kitchen the cornice remains on S and E. Ceiling timbers in both these rooms have relatively heavy chamfers, up to 6 ins deep, lightly hollowed. One of the many openings in the walls here may be an original kitchen door, and the room probably also contained stairs to its upper chamber. In the great chamber the roof was handsomely finished with ashlar boards at the eaves.

The porch seems to have been added slightly later, to create a grand entrance with its moulded archway (Fig 156), fan vault (Plate 169) and grotesque animals projecting forwards from the coved stone eaves. The vault, which is of Ham Hill stone, resembles those added after 1437 to Sherborne Abbey, especially that in the Wykeham Chapel [RCHM 1952, 203], and structural details date it to the last quarter of the 15th century [Leedy 1980, 198–9] and the abbacy of Peter Ramsam (1475–1504). The small upper chamber has a moulded, two-centred doorway, and

Plate 169   *No. 65, the King's House, porch interior, showing fan vault and earlier doorway*

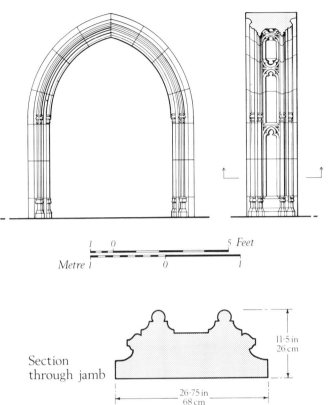

Fig 156   *No. 65, the King's House, entrance arch of porch, with details of jambs and mouldings*

a semicircular wagon ceiling with moulded oak ribs rising from oak wall-plates with shield-shaped brackets.

That the porch may not be an original part of the house is indicated by the preservation, in the chamber, of a section of the main coved stone cornice, which was presumably intended to be external, and was removed from the remainder of the E elevation in the 16th century. Also, whereas the hall etc is faced with alternating layers of flint and stone rubble and occasional courses of tiles laid diagonally, the porch has mainly flint rubble, coursed, with put-log holes dressed with stones and tiles to N and E. The use of mouldings is also slightly different. In stone the double ogee occurs on the screens passage doors and the abbot's chamber fireplace, but is replaced by the ogee and hollow chamfer on the vaulting ribs and upper doorway of the porch (Fig 157). However, in timber, ogee and hollow-chamfered mouldings occur together on the arch-braces of the main roof, the cornices and beam of the screens passage, and on the ceiling ribs of the porch chamber; the hall windows also are disposed symmetrically in relation to the porch and possibly it was merely built separately or replaced an earlier, lower porch which had initially been kept (as happened at Hemingsby in the same period).

The NE building was perhaps detached originally. Its position at the 'upper' end of the house and its hollow-chamfered and ogee-moulded windows of Ham Hill stone suggest that it had a domestic purpose (perhaps as lodgings) and dates from the main building phase. The upper storey now appears to be a late 16th-century addition; it contains a miniature window with a two-centred head, carved from a single block of Chilmark stone, which presumably dates from the 14th or 15th century and was placed here later.

In about 1500 a small addition was made in squared stone rubble against the N staircase, containing inner

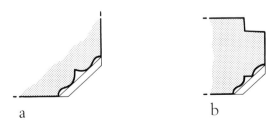

Fig 157   *No. 65, the King's House, porch mouldings*
a. ribs of vault
b. screens passage doors

rooms off the parlour and abbot's chamber. Their original windows, of Ham Hill stone with hollow-chamfered lights in an ogee-moulded architrave, are shown by Buckler *in situ*.

The 16th and early 17th century

In the third quarter of the 16th century Hugh Powell remodelled the hall, dividing it horizontally into a great parlour and great chamber, and mutilating the lower part of the roof to gain headroom. He raised the E wall by half a storey, but on W his great chamber was lit by semi-dormer windows piercing the original eaves, while cross-gables on E light attics created in the remaining roof space (Plate 170). The rooms were served by an ashlar chimney capped by broaching and square shafts of brick, and the brick fireplace in the great parlour has a herringbone fireback and a Tudor arch with ovolo and ogee stone mouldings. His new windows are hollow chamfered with mullions, transoms and labels and include that on E to the abbot's chamber. Two similar windows (one heavily restored) occur on the upper floor of the NE range, which he rebuilt and probably extended to W, perhaps as guest accommodation; its W wall, exposed briefly in 1983, is of coursed flints and survives from some medieval range. In the older build the roof has clasped purlins, diminished principals and queen-struts, and Powell perhaps inserted the S doorway.

Plate 171   *No. 65, the King's House, ribbed plaster ceiling in great chamber*

Of Sadler's ambitious enlargement of the house begun *c* 1598 only a part survived the later subdivision and demolition. His new cross-wing to N of the original house contains three magnificent rooms lit by huge windows, the upper rooms having splendid ceilings (Plate 171). Until the 19th century this range had its own narrow external doorway in the NE angle (Fig 151). The wing is in brickwork, ornamented on E with developed lozenge

Plate 170   *No. 65, the King's House, from E*

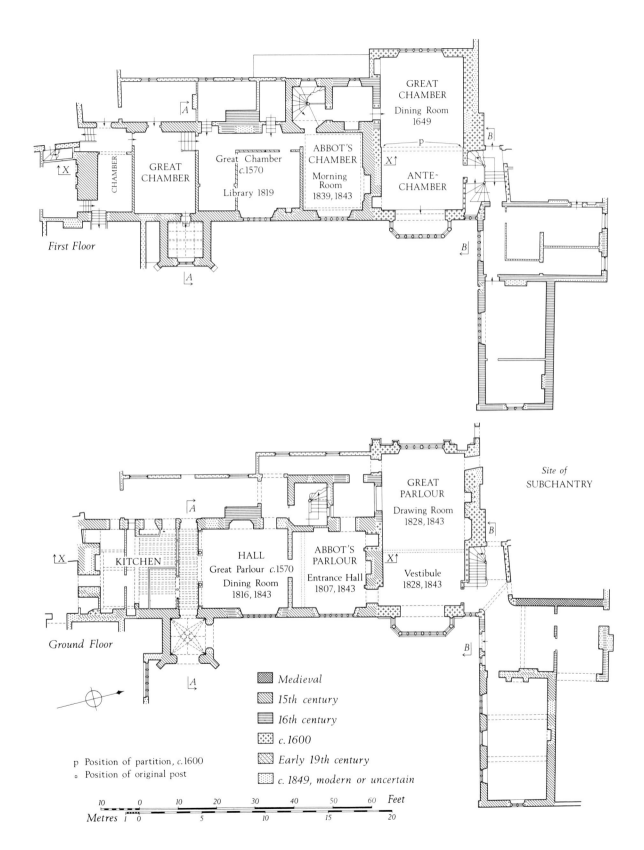

First Floor

CHAMBER

GREAT
CHAMBER

Great Chamber *c.*1570

Library 1819

ABBOT'S
CHAMBER

Morning
Room
1839, 1843

GREAT
CHAMBER

Dining Room
1649

ANTE-
CHAMBER

Ground Floor

KITCHEN

HALL
Great Parlour *c.*1570
Dining Room
1816, 1843

ABBOT'S
PARLOUR

Entrance Hall
1807, 1843

GREAT
PARLOUR

Drawing Room
1828, 1843

Vestibule
1828, 1843

Site of
SUBCHANTRY

p Position of partition, *c.*1600
▫ Position of original post

☒ *Medieval*

▨ *15th century*

▤ *16th century*

▦ *c.*1600

▧ *Early 19th century*

▩ *c. 1849, modern or uncertain*

Feet
10   0   10   20   30   40   50   60

Metres   0   5   10   15   20

Fig 158   *No. 65, the King's House, or Sherborne Place*

diapering, and with Chilmark stone dressings replaced here and there in Bath stone. The windows are ovolo moulded with king mullions having a recessed frontal rebate and with a pair of moulded cornices on the E elevation. Buttresses on W were added in the 19th century. The staircase rises at NE between timber-framed partitions on three sides (Figs 158, 159), which are tile-hung where exposed on the upper storeys, and contain an ovolo-moulded timber window at attic level to N; the curious angle of the N wall was probably conditioned by the former subchantry which stood to NW. In the N wall of the great parlour is a stone chimney-piece resembling that built by Powell in the hall but with bulbous stops; it was found *c* 1965 during repairs, partly *in situ* and partly dismembered behind plaster. At attic level, a pair of stout timber doorways on the staircases are chamfered with moulded stops (Fig 160).

The abbot's chamber was improved in harmony with the new rooms, receiving its plaster panel above the fireplace, frieze of strapwork, cartouches and carnations, and decorated ribbed ceiling (Plate 172). The middle light of the window has a crowned and gartered shield-of-arms: France and England quarterly, quartering Scotland and Wales, with a label of three points, no doubt for James I's eldest son, Henry, Prince of Wales.

Fig 160 *No. 65, the King's House, detail of attic doorway, N staircase*

A further extension, presumably made by Sadler to E of the great wing, is visible in Buckler's drawing of 1804 but had been demolished by 1807. Its former W doorway (now a window) has an ovolo-moulded square-headed architrave with bulbous stops.

From 1650 to the present

The house was subsequently converted to tenements, but the vestiges of these were almost entirely obliterated by General Slade in the early 19th century, when he restored the house to single occupation. He renovated the exterior in medieval-Tudor style and the interior with neo-classical detail, removing single and triple sash windows on E and a doorway with Gothick fanlight on W, seen in Buckler's earlier drawings, and added buttresses to the abbot's house. Slade made the abbot's parlour his entrance hall, used part of the great parlour of *c* 1600 as his drawing room, and his dining room and library occupied the two storeys of the original hall (Fig 158). A few fittings of his day survive including some beaded panelled joinery, the reeded mouldings of his dining room window, and in his entrance hall the reeded white marble chimney-piece flanked by segmental-headed arches. When Slade demolished the E extension of the NE wing, he made its E doorways into windows and gave the lower one 'medieval' headstops.

Between 1824 and 1839 the dining room appears to have been enlarged by some 4 ft, by replacing the S wall with the present Roman Ionic colonnade and extending the room into the original screens passage. From 1839 to 1843 the abbot's chamber was a morning room.

Certain alterations of an antiquarian nature were made to the original house, probably by Wyatt *c* 1850. Among them are the addition of a second archway on the N side of

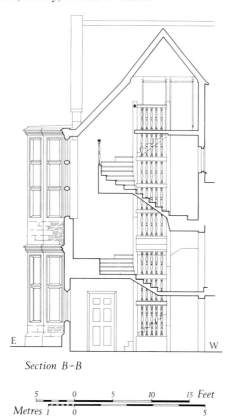

Section B-B

Fig 159 *No. 65, the King's House, section through N staircase with side elevation of bay-window*

the porch, the removal of Slade's buttresses and main entrance, and the restoration of the windows in the original hall to Elizabethan form. The medieval hall-parlour partition was also moved some 3 ft 6 ins to S. The NE range was partly heightened to three storeys in chequered stone and flintwork, and miscellaneous oak wainscot was assembled in the rooms of this wing perhaps at this time.

Large extensions were made in 1849 and later, to N and S, linked by a corridor along the back of the abbot's house. Wyatt's building on the site of the subchantry to N (not shown on plan) has a N elevation in stone-dressed brickwork, with a Gothic arcade in brick, mullioned windows and dormered attics. Webb's additions of 1898 face S across the back of the original house and are of ashlar-dressed rubble, the classroom and dormitory building in Jacobean style with a canted bay-window of nine lights, and the chapel late Gothic, with cusped round-arched side windows and an octagonal turret of Tudor design. The 20th-century contributions are mainly neo-Georgian, and the student accommodation they provided has recently been made into flats.

Plate 172   No. 65, the King's House, fireplace and plaster decoration in abbot's chamber

66, 67 and 68A The Close

66, 67 and 68A The Close form part of a group of former coach-houses, stables etc built in or before 1800 (Fig 161). Their tenancy was advertised in 1838 as three brick-built stables, loose-box, double coach-house, outbuildings, stable-yard etc and walled garden, having a fine view of the Cathedral, 'particularly adapted as the site for a superior dwelling house' and with sufficient building materials present to erect it [SJ, 7 May 1838], a scheme not pursued.

Nos 66 and 67 probably originated as outbuildings to the King's House. They were converted into cottages following a decision by chapter in December 1892, at an estimated cost of £280, and were to be let the following August at 5s 6d per week. Chapter was to spend a further £70 to £80 on 'alterations' to No. 66 in May 1916, possibly demolishing a N room [OS 1880]. No. 66 was formerly of one storey with mid 18th-century brickwork and ruled pointing, and has a window with a gauged head. Built of brick probably in the late 18th century, No. 67 originated as an outbuilding or stable with an upper storey, hipped roof and dentilled eaves, but the windows and fittings date from 1893.

No. 68A was built by Sir Lawrence Hyde, tenant of a former house on S of the Old Deanery (see p 202), to whom chapter leased a plot of ground 37 ft by 29 ft in 1631, measurements which correspond to the present structure's length, allowing a plot of ground in front. It was described as adjacent to a stable recently erected by Sir Thomas Sadler at the King's House, and in 1649 in the Parliamentary Survey as a stable and coach-house of four bays of building. 17th-century deep red brickwork in English bond partly remains on E and perhaps on N at ground level while above, tile-hanging and jowl-posts on S and 19th-century brickwork on E show that the upper storey was timber framed. Plain ceiling beams below and tie-beams above are probably original and there is a blocked window in the W wall. It was in use as a stable for No. 68 until the mid 20th century, when conversion to a house took in the coach-house to W.

The buildings adjoining on W were at least in part the outbuildings to No. 68. The small E stable and former coach-house are of mid 18th-century date and were sandwiched between existing buildings to E and W. They are two-storeyed and of brick-dressed clunch below and of brick above, with original doorways and lead-glazed casement windows, a dummy 'window' over the W entrance being a recessed panel of vitrified bricks. The N windows are of oak. The coach-house has been gutted but a staircase in the stable is of 18th-century date and led to an upper room with two S windows. The roof is original with collars and queen-struts and diagonally set butt purlins of oak. A large flue and the remains of ovens date from a secondary use as a wash-house or brewhouse.

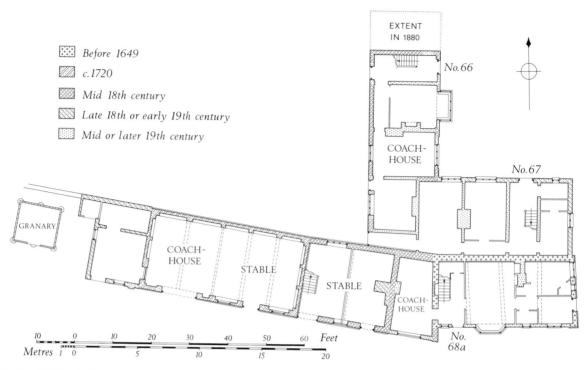

Fig 161 *Nos 66, 67 and 68A*

The W stable and coach-house date from probably soon after the construction of No. 68, c 1720, and their bricklaying is of a better standard than that of the house. They are of two storeys with ashlar quoins, original windows have segmental heads of alternate red and vitrified bricks and leaded casements, and the stable door is united with a hayloft entrance above it. Within, ceiling beams are chamfered with concave stops. The roof has cranked tie-beams and queen-posts with the lower purlins butted and the upper ones clasped. It is hipped on W and originally had a hipped gable on E. In the stable the floor is of brick and in the coach-house of flint. A fireplace added at the W end of the first floor, probably in the 18th century, has been largely removed; it served a poorly lit area.

A small addition at the W end was perhaps a groom's room with a hayloft wholly within the hipped roof space; a chimney added on the S face must have served an obliterated fireplace. It is built of brick, chalk and stone rubble.

The W building is a granary with weatherboarded walls and half-hipped roof, on staddle-stones. It is probably named in an advertisement of No. 68 in 1778 [*SJ*, 14 Dec 1778].

Myles Place, 68 The Close

Myles Place, 68 The Close, is a four-storey mansion which was begun in 1718 by Willam Swanton (town clerk, 1704),

and was held by lay occupants throughout the 18th century. The site was a vacant plot of land named Myles Place or Close after the last known occupant of a medieval canonry which once stood there. In 1559–60 rent was paid for a dwelling 'lately inhabited by Master Miles of Wells' [Communar's A/c, 117], and it was subsequently held by canons as a meadow or pasture.

On 19 June 1718 the ground was leased to Swanton 'for him to build a house on ' [Acts 1696–1714] which must have been finished when he left his previous dwelling at 9 The Close before September 1722. The Swantons were prominent in the legal profession, but their genealogy is obscured by the numerous members of the family to be christened William. One William Swanton (died 1681) was appointed Recorder of Salisbury in 1668. Another William Swanton later built Myles Place, and probably it was the same William Swanton who resigned as deputy recorder in 1742. His wife Anne, daughter of Francis Hill, deputy recorder from 1685 to 1693 (see 19 The Close, p 110), had died in 1714 [Cathedral, N transept, floor slab], and perhaps by 1718 Swanton was intending to share his house with his brother – heraldic details in the new house (see below) indicate an alliance with the Pyles of Over Wallop. His brother, Francis Swanton of Over Wallop (1661–1721), who was appointed deputy recorder in 1712 and was MP for New Sarum from 1714 to 1721, certainly had some connection with the Pyles, inheriting land in 1713 from Edmund Pyle [Benson and Hatcher 1843, 502 and 507,

708 and 711]. William Swanton remained at 68 The Close until *c* 1740 and it seems that the lavish decoration of this rather grandiose house was done for him, but in two phases: the original fitting-up of the house when first built *c* 1720, and a partial refurbishment *c* 1740 with elaborate plasterwork in a style then at the height of local fashion.

By 1744, Henry Hele, Doctor of Physick, later one of the first pair of supervisory physicians to Salisbury General Infirmary [RCHM 1980, 52; Salisbury 1966, 16] had obtained the lease, and remained at Myles Place until his death in 1778, when it passed into the hands of the Mitchell and Jacob families, the latter the descendants of Dr John Jacob, Hele's colleague at the hospital.

The house is a tall rectangular block of seven bays, the front elevation of ashlar, the rear of Flemish-bond brick with stone dressings. The basement, only partly underground, serves as a podium to giant Doric pilasters and the attic floor rises above a Doric entablature. In the main elevation, the three central bays are projected slightly, adding to the Baroque mass of the building (Plate 173). The ashlar, where original, is smooth on the main architectural elements but combed elsewhere. Framing the entrance, Corinthian pilasters support a pediment within which is a shield-of-arms of Swanton with inescutcheon of Pyle, with swags and helmet. The thick glazing bars may be original and on the garden front (Plate 174) those of the

Plate 173   *No. 68, Myles Place, from E*

Plate 174   *No. 68, Myles Place, from W*

door meet at roundels, carved with paterae on the interior. Tile-hanging now conceals the S elevation. The roof is designed with low hipped ridges forming two rectangular wells. The front garden is separated from West Walk by a low brick wall surmounted by a wrought-iron railing with panels of iron scrollwork at intervals, supported by square piers of rubbed brickwork banded with ashlar, with ball finials. The central gate is more elaborate, with scrolled standards and overthrow.

The principal rooms are on the raised ground floor, approached both front and back by a central doorway reached by a flight of steps (Figs 162, 163). A side entrance at ground level to N served the original kitchen and offices. In the principal rooms, several on the ground floor are fitted with window-seats, and original chimney-pieces of veined white, grey or pink marble with matching hearth slabs. Doors have pairs of fielded panels, four on the ground floor, mainly three on the first floor, and are of oak or painted. The library extends the full depth of the house and may have been planned to be a saloon, but was fitted with bookshelves and magnificent oak joinery (Plate 175); the door-cases have architraves with carved mouldings and the panels are ogee and ovolo moulded. In the withdrawing room the panelling (as elsewhere) is painted and has beaded fields, and the corner chimney-piece is original with large and small wooden overmantel panels. In the dining room and hall the door and window joinery have ogee-edged panels which may be original. The W part of the first floor appears to have been a private apartment, with a well-appointed drawing room and a bedroom to S having its E door fitted with a remote-control mechanism originally operated from the bed.

The hall rises through two storeys and the balustrade of the oak staircase continues as a gallery with square,

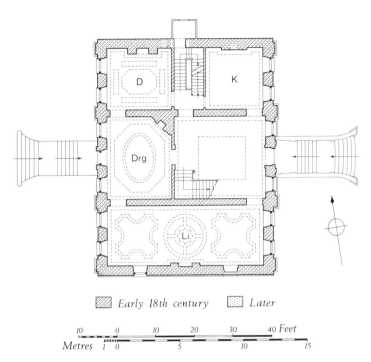

Early 18th century   Later

```
10      0      10      20      30      40 Feet
Metres  1  0              5              10              15
```

Fig 162   *No. 68, Myles Place*

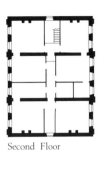

Second Floor

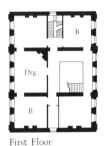

First Floor

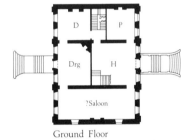

Ground Floor

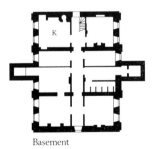

Basement

Fig 163   *No. 68, Myles Place, reconstructed plans of all four floors, as built, scale 1 in. to 48 ft*

panelled posts around three sides on the first floor (Plate 176); the spandrels are carved with arabesques and the treads inlaid with a band of walnut. On the lower landing, marquetry represents the arms of Swanton, *a fess gules between three mill-rinds sable*, with an inescutcheon of Pyle, *a saltire raguly between four passion-nails gules*, surrounded by rays and accompanied by stars and small shields each charged with 'a gryphon's head erased', presumably Swanton's crest (Plate 177).

The original back staircase serves all storeys. It is painted and has a close string and balusters of the same pattern as the front stairs. In the basement, a central stone-paved passage extends between a pair of classical plaster arches with segmental heads and keystones. There is a moulded stone chimney-piece in the SE room, and plain shutters throughout the storey. The attic floor similarly has a central passage and classical archways. The NE room has an original marble chimney-piece, and the moulded plaster cornice at the head of the stairs was probably added *c* 1740. The doors are two-panelled and the shutters have plain panels.

The baroque plasterwork

Two handsome wooden doorways lead W out of the staircase hall at ground- and first-floor levels, the lower one Doric with a pediment (Plate 176), the upper one having a rusticated architrave with a pulvinated entablature, and they project as if to allow for panelling. The lower one, which carries Swanton's presumed crest, fits awkwardly with the foot of the stairs and rudely disrupts the original panelling in the drawing room behind, but the upper one is harmonious with the plaster panelling in the upper drawing room; if the crest belongs to the doorway, this suggests that it was Swanton rather than his successor who in *c* 1740 introduced the stucco decorations, with magnificent ceilings in the ground-floor drawing room (a mask surrounded by rays set in a garland of laurel), the library (Plate 178), dining room (rococo cartouches in the

Plate 175   *No. 68, Myles Place, chimney-piece and panelling in library*

Plate 177   *No. 68, Myles Place, staircase marquetry inlaid in first-floor landing*

Plate 176   *No. 68, Myles Place, staircase hall showing inserted doorway*

Plate 178   *No. 68, Myles Place, ceiling in library*

narrow panels) and the upper staircase hall (which collapsed in 1968). The plaster cornices also date mainly from this phase and have classical mouldings, some with enrichment; they occur in the lower hall, the dining room, parlour and three of the first-floor rooms. In the ground- and first-floor drawing rooms and the upper staircase hall they are coved, with individually moulded acanthus leaves. The panelling is also of plaster and has waterleaf mouldings (dining room and SW bedroom), fielded panels (parlour) and egg and dart mouldings (first-floor drawing room and NE bedroom); in the ground-floor rooms it accompanies wooden chair rails.

Further alterations were made after J H Jacob acquired the tenancy in about 1790. The panelling in the main hall was partly replaced by plaster, incised with fine lines to represent ashlar, and a small room was added at ground-floor level in the early 19th century, presumably as a w.c. It had rendered walls and stands on Roman Doric columns of wood at 'basement' level.

The Walton Canonry, 69 The Close

The Walton Canonry, 69 The Close, was built *c* 1720, probably by Canon Francis Eyre to replace an older house of which nothing now remains (Plate 179). The medieval ownership of the canonry remains unresolved but it probably belonged to the bishop. In 1313 Henry de la Wyle (chancellor 1313–29) gave it to Simon of Ghent 'canon', presumably Bishop Ghent (1297–1315), and his successors. Chapter surveyed its dilapidations in a survey dated 5 November 1443, naming its hall, a parlour adjacent with a privy, the chapel, a chamber above the passage towards the kitchen, the principal chamber over the main entrance, and another adjoining it with buildings leading from it to the principal gate; there was also a bakehouse and larder, a stable, strawhouse, longhouse for fuel, dovecote and poultry house. A similar report in 1585 and an inventory of 1586 together provide an informative view of the house: the hall had a window on its W side, a screen, and an upper end with a boarded dais; there were three parlours including the great parlour with an E window and the little W parlour, and a buttery, a little chamber opening into the yard, a larder and a cellar (possibly the same as the larder or buttery). There was a back door to the kitchen and two other 'entry' doors as well as a garden door, a loft over the kitchen, the great chamber and its roof, a woodyard and stable. The great gate had pentices towards the street and the court, and a staircase on S led to its upper chamber, where the chimney needed brick workmanship. Chapter received its rent and assigned canons to it at least from the last quarter of the 16th century.

In 1649 Parliament had dispossessed Canon Edward Thornborough and granted the house to a layman, but sold it that year to the City. In the Survey the house was recorded as having a strong stone wall with a handsome gate leading through a green court to the house, with a handsome hall, a parlour, a kitchen, bakehouse, coalhouse, pantry and cellar, six chambers, four other rooms, a cockloft, stable and two woodhouses. It was recovered at the Restoration and from 1698 to 1719 belonged to Canon Isaac Walton, a son of the celebrated writer, who obtained permission in 1717 to demolish a part of the canonry which had been occupied by a Mrs Hedges. Over the entrance of the present canonry (Plate 180) are displayed the arms of Eyre (*on a chevron three quatrefoils*) impaling Hyde (*a chevron between three lozenges*) for Walton's successor Francis Eyre (1719–38) who had married Anne, daughter of Bishop Alexander Hyde.

Either Hugh Wynn (1739–54) or William Dodwell (1754–85) added the wings; these were built with a quantity of moulded stones and may replace some part of the medieval house which had been retained in the early 18th century, Naish's map of 1716 showing that house on approximately the same site and alignment as the present

Plate 179 *No. 69, Walton Canonry, from E*

one [RCHM 1980, Plate 16]. Considerable refurbishment of the interior probably dates from the occupancy of Robert Price (1785–1823). Since the death of Archdeacon Lear (1862–1914) the house has had private tenants, among them Rex Whistler in 1938.

The early 18th century

The central block of the house is attributed to Canon Eyre although it was possibly built or begun by Canon Walton. Its main elevation is of seven bays, framed by two giant pilasters of stone on a brick plinth. The façade is brick faced with stone dressings but the other elevations are mainly of brick-dressed rubble including some banded brick and stonework. A high parapet on all sides conceals the roof of four parallel ridges.

Plate 180 *No. 69, Walton Canonry, pediment with armorial cartouche*

The original plan placed the offices and service accommodation in the basement, which is at ground level, with the original kitchen under the 'dining room'. The raised ground floor (Fig 164) contained the reception rooms with a garden door (originally in a lobby), formed with sash windows and a low door beneath. Above is a shell hood, set rather high, and perhaps an addition. A small room beside the staircase was originally a study with built-in cupboards beside the chimney, one filled with pigeon-holes for documents; it opens into a closet beneath the upper landing of the stairs, with a window which was blocked when the N wing was added. On the upper floor, bedrooms lead off a central passage: the two on E were served by unheated dressing rooms occupying the middle three bays of the house, and the central and N rooms on the garden front, both heated, were connected as a principal suite, the larger room in the centre being the drawing room.

The joinery of this period survives only fragmentarily and is of painted deal, some of it clearly reset. Original doors on both the main floors have three pairs of fielded panels in ogee-moulded architraves and the staircase has turned balusters, partly vase-shaped, three to a tread. Fielded panelling survives as a dado in the library and on the stairs, and upper panels exist in four of the first-floor rooms, although no room has a full complement of panelling; wooden cornices with two orders of cymae remain in the dining room and the two E bedrooms, and the NW bedroom has a stone chimney-piece with fielded panels carved on the jambs, arched head and keystone. In the basement, doors and shutters are planked except in a room at the SW corner, which has a panelled dado and shutters, moulded wooden chimney-piece and boarded floor.

The front garden is separated from West Walk by a stone-coped brick wall with ashlar piers carved in two heights with fielded panels and coved caps; they support a gate and side panels with richly scrolled wrought ironwork and a wrought-iron arch which supports a lantern.

Later history

Certain details in the house may be of slightly later date and were perhaps added in the 1730s or 1740s. These include the plaster panelling in two heights with a coved cornice in the entrance hall (the W wall altered later), and elaborately moulded cornices each with a corona in the NW and SW bedrooms.

The wings on plan have their extremities canted slightly forward but are not a perfect pair, the N one being smaller. It originated as a single-storey addition, perhaps a stable, in Flemish-bond brick, but was enlarged in poor quality brickwork and rubble when the S wing was added. Both were self-contained with staircases and had external doors and door to the main house at the lower level. They are on two storeys with attics and probably held service

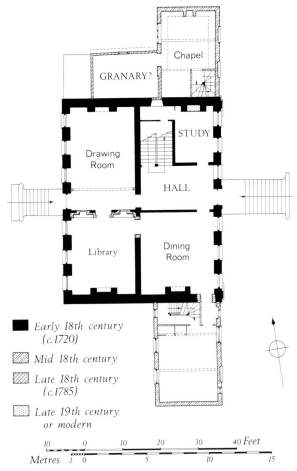

Fig 164   No. 69, Walton Canonry

rooms and servants' quarters, originally unheated except for the lower room on S which was a wash-house or brewhouse; there was probably no connecting doorway between the room above the 'dining room' until the 19th century, when a chimney was also built for the N chamber (now a chapel).

The library was created in the late 18th century with bookcases let into the N wall and a new plaster ceiling cornice, doors with beaded panels, and a chimney-piece with wooden pilasters and cabled frieze with ears of wheat. In the drawing room the ceiling has a fluted frieze containing ears of wheat and plaques depicting harvest motifs. The neo-classical chimney-piece has foliate ornament, and the window joinery beaded panels. The dining room also has a late 18th-century chimney-piece and doors, and the first-floor drawing room was refitted with a coved plaster cornice, chair rail with ogee-moulded panel and chimney-piece with fluted frieze.

A small addition was made against the W side of the N wing at a similar time, on three storeys with tile-hung timber-framed walls above a brick basement, the top floor oversailing. The 'ground-floor' room is poorly lit and had a large opening in the floor adjacent to one in the side wall of the N wing, and possibly it was designed for use as a granary. Its second floor connects with the main staircase at upper landing level, and reused sash windows with thick glazing bars, possibly those removed from the drawing room in this period, and a cast-iron fireplace of *c* 1840, suggest that it was then a bedroom.

17th-century oak wainscot was introduced into the study and dining room, perhaps by William Macdonald (1832–62), and in the dining room it was then painted (recent cleaning having revealed imitation-work in pine). On the first floor, in three of the four rooms in which it occurs, it is curiously mixed with early 18th-century panelling, some of which is evidently *ex situ*, and possibly the latter was partly or wholly moved from ground-floor rooms in the late 18th or early 19th century.

In the 19th century Venetian shutters were added to the garden façade and the drawing room was enlarged into the lobby on S. The chapel in the N wing was created

c 1960 for Bishop Pike of Sherborne, by removing the ceiling of the upper floor and exposing the roof.

The Leadenhall, 70 The Close

The Leadenhall, 70 The Close, was one of the original canonries built *c* 1220. The present building appears to be partly of *c* 1720 and partly of the early 19th century but the rendered wall surfaces doubtless conceal older masonry (Plate 181).

A document of 1232 states that Elias de Dereham, a canon famous for his advice on architectural matters, erected the house as a model for other canonical houses and bequeathed it, in the bishop's collation, to succeeding canons for the endowment of his own obit. Like the Old Deanery (No. 62), Elias's canonry comprised a hall with service rooms at the N end and a cross-range to S containing one or more magnificently decorated upper rooms (Fig 165); the latter partly remained in 1915. The distinctive name, which was in use by 1305, implies that

Plate 181 *No. 70, the Leadenhall from E*

Fig 165   *No. 70, the Leadenhall, reconstructed interior view of great chamber*

this was then the only house in the Close with a lead-roofed hall.

An inventory of 1440 mentions only the hall, chapel and pantry. A fuller survey made in 1586 lists a large house which had a hall with a portal, a wainscoted parlour with a dais, a kitchen and its chimney, a larder, buttery, cellar, and a chapel with a timber partition and wainscoted roof; also an old study at the upper end of the great chamber, containing a bed, an inner chamber over the parlour, and a wainscoted chamber next to the court. A gallery by the

garden appears in a second inventory made that year.

The house went through various vicissitudes in the 17th century, though it is not easy to see how they affected it. Thomas Mason was 'burnt out' of his house and prebendship in 1643 [Everett A, 10 and F, 4] and Dr Faithfull Tate, the presbyterian minister of the Cathedral, replaced him here some time before January 1648 but left Salisbury within a year or two. In 1649 Parliament sold the house to the City and listed it as comprising a handsome gate into a green court, and a hall, a kitchen, a coalhouse, a bakehouse, four cellars, a cloistered walk, a buttery, two wainscoted parlours, a large dining room measuring 40 ft by 20 ft with wainscot 10 ft high, a chapel, six chambers, three passage rooms, a closet, a loft over the bakehouse, and a stable. From 1660 to 1665, when he became bishop, it was the house of Alexander Hyde, Dean of Winchester, who spent £300 on repairs; he maintained the chapel which was used for a marriage in 1664.

In 1718 the Cathedral treasurer, Edward Talbot, had leave from chapter to pull down the old house and rebuild it, on condition that the new house had at least four rooms to each floor and a façade 50 ft in length. He was considering the expenditure of £800 above the value of the materials salvaged and requested that his successor repay a proportion of the cost if he should leave within twenty years. His work can be identified now only with difficulty.

Nathaniel Hume (1772–99) leased the house to private tenants for at least part of his term. His successor was the son of Bishop Douglas, the wealthy Chancellor William Douglas (1799–1819), who so transformed the house as almost to obliterate its earlier history, with Gothic detail on the exterior and neo-classical within. His death was followed by an impressive sale of household goods, including 6000 bottles of wine and sixty to seventy paintings attributed to Raphael, Poussin, Reynolds, Rembrandt, Canaletto and others [SJ, 14 June 1819]. His successor Archdeacon John Fisher (1819–32), the friend of John

Constable and nephew of Bishop Fisher, complained of 'Douglas's great dinners' and was not surprised when his 'rubbish', ie his old masters, sold for a mere £600. Constable came to stay in the house several times, and the first of his large canvases, *The White Horse* (New York, Frick Collection), was bought by Fisher to hang over the chimney-piece in the drawing room. The famous views of the Cathedral were painted from sketches made on these visits, which include one made from the watermeadows with the river, the Leadenhall and its garden in the foreground (London, National Gallery). Fisher made no alterations to the house which he had permission to sublet from time to time, presumably when in residence at Osmington, his Dorset living, where Constable was also a visitor, painting views of Weymouth Bay [Beckett 1952, *passim*].

Permission to take down the SE wing was given by chapter in 1857, and repeated at intervals until 1915. A discrepancy between Buckler's drawing of *c* 1810 (Plate 182) and the OS map of 1880 (Fig 1, in end-pocket) suggests that limited demolition took place, but the main part was spared until 1915; then, when the later extensions and internal features had been removed, it was photographed and summarily measured before being pulled down, the 13th-century windows and doorway being saved for re-erection in new walls approximately on the same site. An account of the house with photographs

Plate 182   *No. 70, the Leadenhall from E. J Buckler c 1810*

Plate 183 *No. 70, the Leadenhall, SE wing in 1915, from NE showing gable with oculi*

Plate 185 *No. 70, the Leadenhall, SE wing in 1915, from S showing two-light window with quatrefoil*

Plate 184 *No. 70, the Leadenhall, SE wing in 1915, from N showing undercroft doorway*

Plate 186 *No. 70, the Leadenhall, SE wing in 1915, from W showing roof, tie-beam and painted decoration*

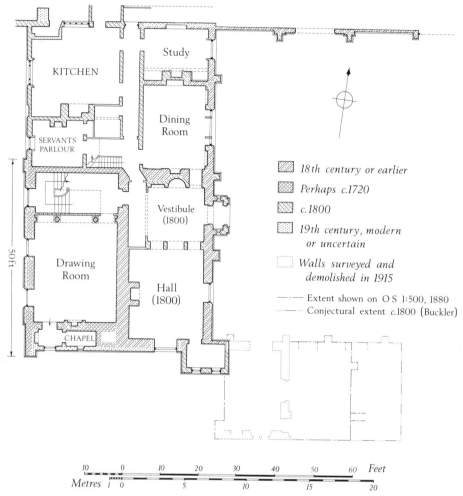

KITCHEN

Study

Dining
Room

SERVANTS
PARLOUR

Vestibule
(1800)

50 ft

Drawing
Room

Hall
(1800)

CHAPEL

▨ *18th century or earlier*

▨ *Perhaps c.1720*

▨ *c.1800*

▨ *19th century, modern*
    or uncertain

      Walls surveyed and
      demolished in 1915

—— Extent shown on O S 1:500, 1880
——— *Conjectural extent c.1800 (Buckler)*

10   0   10   20   30   40   50   60   *Feet*
Metres 1   0   5   10   15   20

Fig 166   *No. 70, the Leadenhall*

and drawings was published in 1917 [Wordsworth 1917]. It remained a canonry until 1947 when it became a girls' school.

Elias de Dereham's house

Of the medieval house, all that survived recognisably into the present century was the E end of the cross-wing, the first floor measuring internally 20 ft wide by 14 ft 6 ins [Wordsworth 1917, 437]. There can be little doubt that this room belonged to Elias's house and was one of his principal private chambers. The photographs taken in 1915 are informative (Plates 183–6); they show a building with a low undercroft and tall upper chamber, with a floor evidently at its original level. Elaborate painted decoration framed windows to E and S and a doorway at the SE corner, and continued on the gable. The roof had timbers of uniform scantling, with tie-beams, braced collars, ashlar-pieces and a moulded cornice; it may have been original, although the internal stone hoodmould of the gable window was cut across by the collar, which was

either an anomaly in the original design, or the result of alteration. The first-floor doorway in the E wall led into an extension to SE, probably the chapel.

This range extended across the S end of the 'leaden hall', which stood on the site of the present N–S range, and the undercroft N doorway (Plate 183, Fig 166) appears to have been external originally, as at the Deanery. The ogee-moulded jamb of a doorway shows that in the 14th or 15th century the upper chamber was reached from a two-storey adjunct against its N wall, which may have been no more than a lean-to containing a staircase from the hall (Fig 167).

Later history

The house as it now exists has developed by a series of piecemeal adaptations and although no medieval features certainly remain, the true history is effectively obscured by Canon Douglas's uniform coating of stucco. His stucco is of exceptional quality, being incised in imitation of ashlar, each 'block' having imitation mason's tooling marks. The area of the hall and vestibule in the E range now appears the oldest part and a buttress on E, thicker than the others, perhaps remains from the medieval hall, being merely altered *c* 1800. The dining room of 1649 would have fitted the dimensions of the upper storey, an area now divided into two rooms by a thin partition; the attics of this range are 17th century with a butt-purlin roof and ogee-moulded dormer windows.

Treasurer Talbot, *c* 1720, probably built the S part of the W range and apparently extended it with blind walling at either end to produce the façade 50 ft long mentioned in his chapter permit (Fig 166). The drawing room is taller than the other ground-floor rooms, probably an original feature, but no original decoration survives. The elegant oak staircase to N, with turned balusters and open string, carved on the tread-ends with fielded panels, is undoubtedly Talbot's work but the cramped position and signs of alteration indicate that it has been moved from elsewhere in the house, probably *c* 1800. He may also have built the 'dining room', which has a roof of lower pitch and thinner walls than the hall and vestibule; part of a formerly external plinth remains on its N end wall and chimney. There is a coved cornice along the E elevation, now covered in stucco, which may also have been added by Talbot.

Canon Douglas evidently built the kitchen range, which has a mansard roof, together with the single-storey

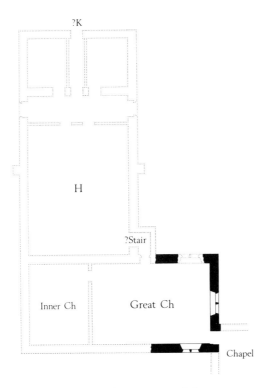

Fig 167 *No. 70, the Leadenhall, reconstructed plan*

pantry, larder etc to N (not shown on Fig 166), and rebuilt the roof of Talbot's range, probably to make his first-floor rooms taller. To the existing buildings he added buttresses and a porch in Gothic style on the main elevation, and gave labels to the windows (Plate 182). Within, he removed nearly all the earlier features on the two main storeys, and introduced marble chimney-pieces, beaded panelled joinery and plaster ceiling cornices, either with deep friezes and anthemion ornament etc or with small-scale mouldings and motifs. A feature of his work is the use of dummy doors to effect symmetry, perhaps imitating Sir Robert Taylor at the Palace. In the drawing room he introduced an Ionic colonnade with fluted columns and richly detailed entablature, the cornice continued round the room. The room above, which was a library when Constable painted the view from the window, was also grandly decorated.

Stained glass in the porch windows ornamented with flowerheads within the letter C possibly dates from the tenure of Liscombe Clarke (1832–41), and he may also have been responsible for the rounded arches and recesses which occur in the hall and dining room.

His successor W K Hamilton (subsequently bishop from 1854 to 1869) probably rebuilt the narrow bay S of the drawing room, although a photograph taken looking down the blocked area to E indicates that the S and W walls are of various dates [by G L Steer, copy in NMR]. He made the ground floor a small chapel, with an arched stone light, pitch-pine ceiling and 17th-century oak wainscot on the walls; its lobby window has shutters sliding horizontally into the wall. Both windows to the upper rooms have cast-iron balconies.

In June 1898 the house was uninhabitable because of extensive repairs for Canon Bankes (1898–1915), when the E attic was refitted as servants' accommodation.

The forecourt and other structures

The forecourt is separated from West Walk by a low wall with railings, flanking buttresses and cement-rendered Gothic piers, erected probably by Canon Douglas. They stand to either side of a pair of gates for carriages with side gates for pedestrians, in which the uprights have the form of arrows with barbed heads and feathered tangs. A central lantern is supported above the carriageway by a thin archway and by square hollow standards with panels of rich scrollwork, all of cast iron.

To N of the forecourt is an 18th-century brick wall with an entrance to the stable yard of gauged brick with a segmental arch and stone imposts and key, but refaced on S by Canon Douglas with cement rendering and the arch given mouldings, a four-centred head and buttresses (Plate 182). An early 19th-century row of Tuscan shafts, at first on one side and then on the other of this wall, supports a slate roof and provides a pair of elegant covered areas, one facing S and one N.

Further N a pair of early 19th-century square buildings flank the main stable yard entrance from West Walk. Of single storey and of white brick, with slate roofs projecting on cornices with Grecian mouldings, one appears to have been a lodge and the other a coach-house.

70A The Close

70A The Close was built in the 18th century as the stable and coach-house, with hay loft, to the Walton Canonry. It was formerly symmetrical, with two-light casement windows set in brick walls, but has been greatly altered, as a dwelling.

The South Canonry, 71 The Close

The South Canonry, 71 The Close, lies secluded in trees at the SW corner of the Close and is now the Bishop's House. It dates mainly from 1890, which is ironical as it is one of the most fully documented canonries and was a choice preferment throughout the 14th and 15th centuries, when it was normally occupied by Cathedral dignitaries.

The original house may have been built by Stephen of Tisbury, archdeacon of Wilts from c 1226 to c 1244, but no more than a piece of wall with a single doorway in it remains from his tenure (Plate 187). It was described in about 1275 as one of 'two places with the buildings then lately built' which Tisbury's executors had sold to Chancellor Hecham. Chancellor Henry de la Wyle bequeathed it to chapter for the establishment of his obit in 1329; this may have led to the assumption in the 16th century that Wyle had built it.

The medieval house was a large one, though only a fragment of it survives, together with a range of outbuildings. A survey of 1402 refers to the hall, which had a high chamber above a storehouse and small chambers at the N end, the kitchen, bakehouse and brewhouse with an oven, 'high' and 'low' chambers forming one bay, the chapel above a little chamber, the great chamber to N of the chapel with a privy and little chamber adjoining and another chamber on S of the chapel, also other offices and outbuildings. A further survey in 1427 places the great chamber at the S end of the hall and implies that it was at the W end of a cross-range.

Two surveys and an inventory made in 1586 make no mention of the chapel but describe a hall with a 'fotepace' (dais?) at the upper end of an oriel window sealed with wainscot, the great parlour sealed with wainscot on two sides, a bench at the 'upper end' and old painted cloths, a little parlour with a W window, a timber staircase and a study; there was a kitchen, larder, buttery, pantry, and a little room within the store chamber. Above, there was a little chamber over the porch, and the great chamber,

perhaps identical with the chamber over the little parlour which had a portal and adjoined a closet. Elsewhere, the house had a backhouse and a gallery next the court, evidently a pentice.

In the 1630s Dr Seward is said to have lived here in the greatest luxury [*VCH* 1956, 190]. In 1649 there were listed a hall, three parlours wainscoted, three kitchens, three larders, one buttery, a chapel, nine chambers great and small, four other little upper rooms and three garrets, also a stable and gatehouse at the entrance. Parliament leased the house in 1648 to one John Trenchard, who pulled much of it down and sold the materials. At the Restoration, Bishop Henchman ordered that canonries must be

Plate 187   *No. 71, South Canonry, 13th-century doorway in 'cellar'*

Fig 168   *No. 71, South Canonry, plans after G R Crickmay*
a. c *1875*
b. c *1895*

Plate 188   *No. 71, South Canonry, from E*

inspected annually and repaired, but specifically excluded this building from his statute. In 1665 Thomas Hill was elected a canon resident on condition that he build a new house within fourteen months, chapter contributing £160 to the cost. Hill had spent £315 on the house by 1670 and in 1672 his successor Richard Hill (1671–95) was also building, having laid out £200 'and yet supposeth it to be far short of what it was before' [D and C Muns, box 'Dean and Chapter']. Part of their work can probably be identified on the plan of *c* 1875 as the 'housekeeper's room' and 'kitchen' (Fig 168a), where the size of the chimney suggests a 17th-century date.

Canon Richard Eyre (1710–45) was allowed to add new offices and take down the gatehouse in 1711 and his successor, Canon Moss (1746–86), had permission to demolish and rebuild the back parlour, hall and cellar in

1749 and to 'carry up' a new staircase and make unspecified alterations, chapter donating timber. The present E front dates from this time (Plate 188) and resembles the Organist's House, No. 5, where Moss had been one of the supervisory canons two years earlier. In 1760 he added a small room and chamber over it on the site of the cellar (which he was to replace elsewhere in the house), and no doubt he built the brick vault in the present cellar (Fig 169). A further enlargement was authorised for Dr Thomas Eyre (1798–1812) in 1798, of offices measuring 21 ft 8 ins square, probably the 'servants' hall' etc on the plan of *c* 1875 (Fig 168a).

In 1890 the major part of this house was demolished by Canon Bernard (1889–1910), and with the aid of £1000 borrowed from Queen Anne's Bounty it was rebuilt to the designs of G R Crickmay (Fig 168b). Bishop Anderson chose it as his residence in 1951.

Architectural history

The early 13th-century doorway is now an isolated feature and the reason for the curious alignment of the wall in which it stands is no longer clear (Plate 187, Fig 169). It occurs at the N end of the fragmentary 15th-century range, which formed part of the 'upper' end of the house, and lay to S of the hall. The roof shows that the remaining part of the medieval building contained a two-bay room above the present chapel, continuous with rooms to N and S, evidently part of the reconstruction and enlargement of the original house portrayed in the 16th- and 17th-century surveys. The two large rooms above one another are of sufficient height and quality of finish to suggest that they were a principal chamber above a new parlour or withdrawing room but they cannot be identified in the 1427 survey and may post-date it.

In the present chapel, ceiling beams moulded with two hollows and a roll intersect at a central boss carved with a shield charged *per chevron, argent and sable, three elephants' heads erazed, counter changed*, probably for Saunders (Plate 189); no medieval canon of this name is known other than a 15th-century abbot of Sherborne and the arms remain an enigma. (A painted shield in the vault of the central crossing at the Cathedral has similar charges and is tentatively ascribed to Abbot Saunders of Sherborne (1459–75). This is approximately the time at which the abbot's residence, No. 65, was entirely rebuilt and it is conceivable that he made use of No. 71 during the reconstruction.) The 15th-century fireplace (Plate 190) had its stack demolished in 1890. In the upper chamber there is an eaves cornice with roll and coved mouldings carved on the wall-plates etc, and it is spanned by a truss with a cambered collar, originally open to the room; at either end are closed trusses with central struts and pairs of curved V-struts from tie-beam to collar and pairs of

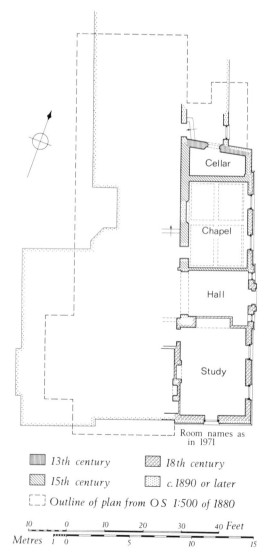

Cellar

Chapel

Hall

Study

Room names as in 1971

▦ *13th century*   ▨ *18th century*

▧ *15th century*   ▩ *c.1890 or later*

⌐_⌐ *Outline of plan from O S 1:500 of 1880*

10   0   10   20   30   40 *Feet*

Metres 1   0   5   10   15

Fig 169 *No. 71, South Canonry*

Plate 189 *No. 71, South Canonry, ceiling boss with shield in present chapel*

Plate 190 *No. 71, South Canonry, fireplace in present chapel*

curved upper struts to the principals, with purlins clasped by cambered collars, and pairs of wind-braces.

The only room to survive intact from Moss's renovation of 1749 is the SE 'sitting room', now the study, with its ceiling formed into panels by classical mouldings around cherubs' busts in low profile representing the four seasons, and a chimney-piece with an eared surround, pulvinated frieze, and heavily carved mouldings. The main elevation of 1749 remains substantially unaltered although the roof was rebuilt at the S end in 1890, and no doubt that of the pediment was changed then.

Crickmay's work is in brick with sparse detail in an omnibus Jacobean to Georgian manner but his principal ground-floor rooms have been altered out of recognition. The main bedroom, at the head of the stairs in the SW corner, is now the chief survival with a square oriel window projecting on wooden brackets and a ribbed ceiling with a broad diapered cornice. The bedrooms over the 'hall' and 'dining room' both have 17th- or 18th-century wainscot in them, reset at an unknown date.

The present entrance to the South Canonry is through gate piers of brick and stone with ball finials, dating probably from 1711.

71A The Close

At the entrance and flanking the street is a building measuring 75 ft by 18 ft 6 ins, described as stables in 1649, now converted as a house. Only the E wall and the roof survive from the Middle Ages but possibly the other walls were timber framed. A horizontal junction some two thirds of the way up the E wall, which retains much of its external plaster, divides the coursed flint rubble of the lower storey from the tile-laced rubble above, and clearly the building was constructed upon a boundary wall, perhaps of 13th-century date. A large archway at the N end blocked with brick may remain from the gatehouse referred to when it was taken down in 1711, and the medieval boundary wall continues to N of it. Ceiling beams within indicate that there were always two storeys, perhaps a steward's room below and staff accommodation above. The roof is continuous with tie-beams supporting lower curved struts, collars, clasped purlins and pairs of curved wind-braces, probably 15th-century.

The W wall of the stable was rebuilt in Flemish-bond brick with two-light casement windows in the 18th century and the N wall, of flint rubble with brick lacing courses, is of similar date.

Houses at Harnham Gate

72 The Close

72 The Close was built *c* 1754 as a lay vicar's residence by the Rev John Talman, who obtained in exchange the site of a ruinous vicars' dwelling (No. 36). The house he agreed to build was to consist of a kitchen, parlour, wash-house, brewhouse, two chambers over the parlour and kitchen and two garrets [Vicars' Lease Book 1718–1800, 4 Oct 1753]. The original dimensions of the site were much greater on N than on S, resulting in the oblique SW wall, but nothing appears in this position on Naish's map and the anomaly is unexplained.

The house is mainly of brick, with an area of squared rubble below a tile-hung gable on the W wall (Plate 191, right). The plan probably followed the specification but the S lean-to was rebuilt in brick in the 19th century (Fig 10, p 49). In 1887 Robert Adey, the verger then living there, spent £69 on repairs and adding the bay-windows, and in 1925 a bedroom and bathroom were built on S in brick and tile-hanging under a flat lead roof to a design by Robert Messenger.

73 The Close

73 The Close is a small house built by William Lambert, gunsmith (Plate 191, centre). Chapter granted him a lease of the site to erect a dwelling in 1713 and in 1721 it was 'lately built' [D and C Leases, 1710–22, 25 March]. Formerly the Close Pound had stood there and in 1703 three gentlemen of the Close had obtained the place to build a kennel for their hounds.

The house is built of brick, except at the E end where the Close Wall is incorporated, with tile-hung gables. Originally it probably comprised only the main build of two storeys with attics but lean-to additions have been made on S (Fig 10, p 49). The exterior has changed little since Buckler's watercolour of 1803, two upper windows being already blocked and the others having leaded glazing (Plate 17, p 51).

The principal features of the interior remain, including the staircase with close string and wavy-splat balusters, and in the roof one pair of straight wind-braces. A moulded stone chimney-piece perhaps indicates that the best bedroom was originally that above the kitchen.

74 The Close

74 The Close is an 18th-century house (Plate 191, left) occupying a narrow space between the Close Wall to N and W and a brick garden wall to S and, although entered from within the Close, lies mainly outside it (Fig 10, p 49). It was built c 1769 by Prebendary John Chaffey as a dwelling for one of the lay vicars, whose former house (No. 26) Chaffey received in exchange (compare the similar circumstances at Nos 36 and 72 in c 1754). The site was previously part of the garden of 4 De Vaux Road and belonged to chapter, whose lease to the vicars of August 1770 described the house as newly erected.

The walls are now partly rendered, but where they rise above the pre-existing walls to N and S they are of Flemish-bond brick. The fenestration of the W wall dates from after Buckler's drawing of 1803 (Plate 17, p 51). Two rooms above one another in the SE angle were built recently and the house has been modernised internally and the roof renewed. Within the roof space is seen one of the 14th-century gargoyles of Harnham Gate (Plate 15, p 50).

Plate 191 *Nos 72–4 from NW*

Bibliography

Abbreviations

Ant J	*Antiquaries Journal*	NMR	National Monuments Record
Arch J	*Archaeological Journal*	OS	*Ordnance Survey*
BL	British Library	PRO	Public Record Office
BM	British Museum	RCHM	Royal Commission on the Historical Monuments of England
Bod Lib	Bodleian Library		
CBA	Council for British Archaeology	SJ	*Salisbury Journal*
CL	*Country Life*	VCH	*Victoria History of the Counties of England*
DNB	*Dictionary of National Biography*	WAM	*Wiltshire Archaeological and Natural History Magazine*
Hants RO	Hampshire Record Office		
HKW	*History of the King's Works*	Wilts N and Q	*Wiltshire Notes and Queries*
HMC	Royal Commission on Historical Manuscripts	Wilts Rec Soc	Wiltshire Record Society
JBAA	*Journal of the British Archaeological Association*	WRO	Wiltshire Record Office

ALCOCK, N W. 1981. *Cruck Construction*. CBA Research Report 42, London.

ALCOCK, N W and BARLEY, M W. 1972. 'Medieval roofs with base-crucks and short principals'. *Ant J* LII, 132–67.

AUBREY, J. 1969. *The Natural History of Wiltshire*. Compiled 1656–91, published 1847, reprinted by David and Charles, Newton Abbot.

BECKETT, R B. 1952. *John Constable and the Fishers*. London: Routledge and Kegan Paul.

BENSON, R and HATCHER, H. 1843. *The History of Old and New Sarum* (constituting Vol VI of Colt Hoare, R, *The Modern History of South Wiltshire*). London: printed by and for John Bowyer Nichols and Son.

BERESFORD, M. 1959. 'Six new towns of the bishops of Winchester 1200–55'. *Medieval Archaeology* III, 187–215.

1967. *New Towns of the Middle Ages*. Lutterworth Press.

BRITTON, J. 1801. *The Beauties of Wiltshire* I.

BRODIE, W B (pub). 1848. *The Salisbury Guide*. Salisbury: Brodie.

BROOKE, C N L. 1957. *A History of St. Paul's Cathedral*, ed W R Matthews and W M Atkins, Chapter i. London.

BUCKLER, J. Drawings in BL and Devizes Museum. 1803–11.

CAL PAPAL LETTERS. *Calendar of Entries in the Papal Registers relating to Great Britain and Ireland*. London: PRO.

CAMDEN MISCELLANY 1936. XVI Hammond, *A Relation of a Short Survey of the Western Counties*, 1635.

CARTER, J. 1803. 'Pursuits of architectural innovation'. *Gentleman's Magazine* LXII, 515–17; LXIII, 642–4; LXIV, 735–7; LXV, 1020–3; LXVI, 1122–4.

CASSAN, S H. 1824. *Lives of the Bishops of Salisbury*. Salisbury.

CHANDLER, J. 1983. *Endless Street. A History of Salisbury and its People*. Salisbury: Hobnob Press.

CHAPTER ACTS. See note on ms sources, Editor's Preface, p ix.

CHENEY, C R (ed). 1961. *Handbook of Dates*. Royal Historical Society.

1967. *Hubert Walter*. Manchester University Press.

CHERRY, B and PEVSNER, N. 1975. *The Buildings of England, Wiltshire*, 2nd edn. Harmondsworth.

CHEW, H M (ed). 1963. *Hemingsby's Register*. Wilts Rec Soc XVIII. Devizes.

COLE, D. 1980. *The Work of Sir Gilbert Scott*. London.

COLVIN, H M. 1978. *A Biographical Dictionary of British Architects 1600–1840*, 2nd edn. London: John Murray.

COKE, D. 1984. 'Vauxhall Gardens' in *Rococo, Art and Design in Hogarth's England* (exhibition catalogue, V&A Museum). London.

COOK, G H. 1948. *Medieval Chantries and Chantry Chapels*. London: Phoenix House.

COULSON, C. 1982. 'Hierarchism in conventual crenellation'. *Medieval Archaeology* XXVI, 69–100.

CROFT-MURRAY, E. 1962. *Decorative Painting in England 1537–1837*.

CROOK, J M. 1981. *William Burges and the High Victorian Dream*. London.

DODSWORTH, W. 1814. *An Historical Account of the Episcopal See and the Cathedral Church of Sarum, or Salisbury*. Salisbury.

DRINKWATER, N. 1964. 'The Old Deanery, Salisbury'. *Ant J* XLIV, 41–59.

EAMES, E S. 1958. 'A tile pavement from the Queen's Chamber, Clarendon Palace dated 1250–2'. *JBAA* (1957–8), 95–106.

EDWARDS, K. 1939. 'Houses of Salisbury Close in the 14th century'. *JBAA 3 ser* IV, 55–115.

1949. *The English Secular Cathedrals in the Middle Ages*.

Manchester University Press. 2nd edn 1967.

ELTRINGHAM, G J. 1958. 'Alexander Fort and Salisbury Cathedral'. *WAM* LVII, 56–63.

EVERETT, C R. Notebooks, numbered A, B, C; 1, 2, 3, etc: see note on ms sources, Editor's Preface, p ix.

1936. 'The prebendal mansion of Sherborne Monastery'. *WAM* XLVII, 379–441.

1941. 'Aula le Stage'. *WAM* XLIX, 288–312.

1943. 'An episcopal visitation of ... 1607'. *WAM* L, 170–87.

1944. 'Notes on the Decanal and other houses in the Close of Sarum'. *WAM* L, 425–45.

EWARD, S M. 1982. 'Seth Ward's widows'. *Spire*, 15–20.

1983. 'Vistas and vandals'. *Spire*, 15–19.

FAULKNER, P A. 1958. 'Domestic planning from the 12th to the 14th centuries'. *Arch J* CXV, 150–83.

FIRTH, C H. 1894. *The Memoirs of Edmund Ludlow, 1625–72,* I. Oxford.

FLETCHER, J M J. 1938. 'Bishop Richard Beauchamp, 1450–1481'. *WAM* XLVIII, 161–73.

1938. 'Humphrey Henchman D.D., Bishop of Salisbury, 1660–1663'. *WAM* XLVIII, 301–12.

1939. 'Elias de Dereham'. *WAM* XLVIII, 488–98.

1940. 'Seth Ward, Bishop of Salisbury, 1667–1689'. *WAM* XLIX, 1–16.

FRERE, W H. 1910. *Visitation Articles and Injunctions of the Period of the Reformation.* Alcuin Club Collections XIV–XVI. London.

GOUGH, R. 1796. *Sepulchral Monuments of Great Britain,* II. London.

GREIG, J (ed). 1925. *The Farington Diary* by Joseph Farington V (1808–9). London.

HALL, P. 1834. *Picturesque Memorials of Salisbury.* Salisbury.

HARDING, J. 1897. 'The ancient sub-chantry house formerly in the Close'. *WAM* XXIX, 95–9.

HARVEY, J. 1984. *English Medieval Architects,* a biographical dictionary down to 1550. Gloucester, supplement 1987.

HILL, R M T. 1982. *Oliver Sutton, Bishop of Lincoln 1280–99.* Lincoln Cathedral Library publications.

HKW 1963. *The History of the King's Works,* ed H M Colvin. Vols I and II, *The Middle Ages.*

1973. Vol VI, 1782–1851.

1975. Vol III, 1485–1660, Part I.

1976. Vol V, 1660–1782.

1982. Vol IV, 1485–1660, Part II.

HMC 1901. *Various Collections* I. Royal Commission on Historical Manuscripts.

HUSSEY, C. 1955. *English Country Houses, Early Georgian 1715–60.* London.

JACOB, E F. 1947. 'The medieval chapter of Salisbury Cathedral'. *WAM* LI, 479–95.

JAMES, T B and ROBINSON, A M. 1988. *Clarendon Palace.* Society of Antiquaries.

JONES, S R. 1974. *Four Minster Houses.* Friends of Lincoln Cathedral.

JONES, W H Rich-. 1879. *Fasti Ecclesiae Sarisberiensis,* Part I. Salisbury and London.

1881. (ed) *Fasti Ecclesiae Sarisberiensis,* Part II. Salisbury and London.

1883. (ed). *Register of St Osmund,* Vol I. Rolls Series LXXVIII. HMSO.

1884. (ed). *Register of St Osmund,* Vol II. Rolls Series LXXVIII. HMSO.

1891. (ed). *Sarum Charters and Documents.* Rolls Series XCVII. HMSO.

KIDSON, P, MURRAY, P and THOMPSON, P. 1965. *A History of English Architecture.* Harmondsworth.

LADD, F J. 1978. *Architects at Corsham Court.* Bradford on Avon.

LATHAM, R and MATTHEWS, W (eds). 1976. *The Diary of Samuel Pepys* IX, 1668–9.

LEEDY, W C. 1980. *Fan Vaulting.*

LOBEL, M D. 1969. *Historic Towns* I. Lovell Johns: Cook, Hammond & Kell Organization.

LONG, C E. 1859. *The Diary of Richard Symonds, 1644.* Camden Soc LXXIV.

LOVIBOND, J L. Collection of 289 photographs of Salisbury, dating from c 1850–1900, assembled by J L Lovibond, now kept by the Town Clerk. Copies in NMR.

MACARTNEY, M E. c 1925. *The Practical Exemplas of Architecture,* Series iii.

MAGALOTTI, Count Lorenzo. 1821. *Travels of Cosmo the Third through England.* London.

MAJOR, K. 1974. *Minster Yard.* Lincoln Minster Pamphlets, 2nd ser 7.

MALDEN, A R. 1893–4. 'Survey of the Close in 1649'. *Transactions of the Salisbury Field Club* I (1893), 95–9, 132–8, 167–71; II (1894), 81–7.

1912. 'The burial places of the Bishops of Salisbury'. *WAM* XXXVII, 339–52.

MOORMAN, J R H. 1945. *Church Life in England in the 13th Century.* Cambridge.

NEVILL, E R. 1911. 'Salisbury in 1455'. *WAM* XXXVII, 66–91.

OVERFIELD, H V. 1942. 'Ancient masons' marks'. *WAM* LII, 65–9.

PANTIN, W A. 1955. *The English Church in the 14th Century.* Cambridge.

1957. 'Medieval priests' houses in south-west England'. *Medieval Archaeology* I, 118–46.

PEACOCK, E. 1889. 'Licence to crenellate'. *WAM* XXIV, 127–9.

PLATT, C. 1978. *Medieval England.* London.

POOLE, A L. 1955. *From Domesday Book to Magna Carta, 1087–1216.* Oxford History of England, 2nd edn.

POWICKE, M. 1962. *The Thirteenth Century 1216–1307.* Oxford History of England, 2nd edn.

PRICE, F. 1753. *A Series of Particular and Useful Observations made with Great Diligence and Care upon that admir-*

able Structure, the Cathedral-Church of Salisbury. London: R Baldwin.

RADY, J, TATTON-BROWN, T and BOWEN, J A. 1991. 'The Archbishop's Palace, Canterbury: excavations and building recording works from 1981 to 1986. *JBAA* CXLIV, 1–60.

RCHM 1952. *Dorset, Vol I, West Dorset.* HMSO.

1970. *Dorset, Vol III, Central Dorset.* HMSO.

1972. *Dorset, Vol IV, North Dorset.* HMSO.

1975. *Dorset, Vol V, East Dorset.* HMSO.

1980. *City of Salisbury, Vol I, Ancient and Historical Monuments.* HMSO.

1981. *York, Vol V, The Central Area.* HMSO.

1987. *Churches of South-East Wiltshire.* HMSO.

REEVE, J A. 1891. 'Notes on the architectural history of the Palace'. *WAM* XXV, 181–91.

REEVES, J and BONNEY, H M. 1981. 'No. 15 Minster Street, Salisbury'. *WAM* LXXVI, 99–104.

RIGOLD, S E. 1966. 'Two camerae of the military orders'. *Arch J* CXXII, 86–121.

ROBERTSON, D. 1938. *Sarum Close.* Reprinted 1969.

SALISBURY 200. 1966. *Salisbury 200: the Bicentenary of Salisbury Infirmary 1766–1966.* Salisbury General Hospital.

SALZMAN, L F. 1967. *Building in England down to 1540,* 2nd edn. Oxford.

SANDELL, R E. 1976. 'Two medieval bishops and their wanderings'. *Hatcher Review* I, 19–25.

SHORTT, H de S. 1970. *The Hungerford and Beauchamp Chantry Chapels.* Friends of Salisbury Cathedral Publications.

SLATTER, D. 1965. *The Diary of Thomas Naish.* Devizes: Wilts Rec Soc XX.

Spire. Annual Reports of the Friends of Salisbury Cathedral, 1964–.

SPRING, R. 1987. *Salisbury Cathedral.* New Bell's Cathedral Guides, Unwin Hyman.

STALLEY, R A. 1971. 'A 12th-century patron of architecture'. *JBAA* 3 ser XXXIV, 62–83.

STRAVIDI, M. 1982. 'Charles Eames Kempe and the work of his firm (1868–1934) in stained glass'. *Hatcher Review* XIV, 171–8.

STEVENS, E. 1876. Salisbury Meeting of the Wiltshire Archaeology and Natural History Society, 25 August 1876.

STREET, F. 1915. 'The relations of the bishops and citizens of Salisbury between 1225 and 1612'. *WAM* XXXIX, 185–257, 319–67.

TATTON-BROWN, T. 1982. 'The Great Hall of the Archbishop's Palace'. *Medieval Art and Architecture at Canterbury,* 112–19. British Archaeological Association.

TAYLOR, R. 1982. 'Knee principal roofs'. *Vernacular Architecture* 13, 34–5.

THOMPSON, A H. 1925. *The Cathedral Churches of England.* London.

1941. 'Master Elias of Dereham and the King's Works'. *Arch J* XCVIII, 1–35.

THOMPSON, P. 1971. *William Butterfield.*

THORNTON, P. 1979. *Seventeenth-Century Interior Decoration in England, France and Holland.* London.

TORRANCE, W J. 1978. *The Story of Saint Osmund, Bishop of Salisbury.* Friends of Salisbury Cathedral Publications.

TOULMIN SMITH, L. 1964. *The Itinerary of John Leland 1535–43* I. London.

VCH 1911. *A History of Hampshire* IV. London.

1973. *A History of Hampshire* III. London.

1956. *A History of Wiltshire* III. London.

1957. *A History of Wiltshire* V. London.

1959. *A History of Wiltshire* IV. London.

1962. *A History of Wiltshire* VI. London.

1970. *A History of Dorset* III. London.

1975. *A History of Dorset* V. London.

WAYLEN, J. 1892. 'The Falstone Day-Book'. *WAM* XXVI, 343–91.

WEEKES, E L. 1915. *Some Studies in the Topography of the Cathedral Close, Exeter.* Exeter.

WHEELER, W A. 1889. *Sarum Chronology.* Salisbury.

1901. *Supplemental Sarum Chronology 1881–1900.* Salisbury.

Wilts. Inq. p.m. *Abstracts of Wilts. Inq. p.m. 1327–77* (Index Library xlviii).

WOOD, M. 1965. *The English Medieval House.* London: Phoenix House.

WORDSWORTH, C. 1891. 'The Bishop's Palace at Salisbury'. *WAM* XXV, 165–81.

1915. and Macleane, D (eds). *Statuta et Consuetudines Ecclesiae Cathedralis Beatae Mariae Virginis Sarisberiensis.* London.

1917. 'Elias de Derham's Leadenhall in Salisbury Close 1226–1915'. *WAM* XXXIX, 433–44.

WREN SOC, 1941. Vol XVIII. Oxford.

Index

32a–b, 100b, Plate 67;
Mompesson House, 32a–b,
164a–b, Plates 114–116; Myles
Place, 32a, 229b–231a, Plate 178;
No. 9 The Close, 81b–82b,
Plate 48; Wardrobe, 32b, 186a,
Plate 140
TIMBER
15th century: Bishop's Palace, 10b,
63b, Plate 31, Fig 22; Wardrobe,
183b, 185b, Fig 126
16th century, 24a, 25a; Aula le
Stage, 24a, 25a, 118a, 127a–128a,
Plate 91
cellars, medieval and 16th century,
16a–b, 18b, 24b
Chaddesley, Richard de, 40a
Chadleshunt, William de, archdeacon of
Wiltshire, 88b
Chaffey, John, prebendary and president
of Consistory Court, 33a, 136a,
244b
Chafyn, Lady, 85b
Chafyn, Thomas, 27b, 85a, 85b–86b
chambers, principal see great chambers
chancellor, office of, 1a, 11a–b
Chandler, John, chantry of, 213a
Chandler, John, Bishop of Salisbury,
181a
chantries and chantry priests, 10a–b,
13a, 23a, 79a–b, 152b
HOUSES OF CHANTRY PRIESTS, x,
10a, 13a, 18b, 85a, 167a, 213a,
215a
chapels
MEDIEVAL, 15b–16a; Aula le Stage,
16a, 27a, 28a, 118b, Plate 88,
Figs 66–7; Deanery (Old), 16a,
201b, 202a, 204a, 206b, 207a,
208b, 212b; St Ann's Gate, 47a,
47b, 48b–49b, 100b
16TH-17TH CENTURY, 24b, 25a, 25b,
27b, 28a; Bishop's Palace, 27b,
55a, 64a–b
18TH CENTURY: Bishop's Palace, 70a,
71b; Porter's Lodge, 157b
19TH CENTURY, 34b, 35b;
Theological College, 35a–b, 111a,
113b, Plate 80, Plate 83
Chapter Office (6 The Close), 27b, 29b,
75a–78b, Plates 41–2, Figs 29–30
Chedworth, John, x
Cheney, Lord, 215b
Cheney, Sir John, 10a–b
Chichele, Henry, Archbishop of
Canterbury, 14a
Chichester
BISHOPS OF see Poore, Richard
CLOSE, 11a
Chilmark stone, 18b, 38b, 44b, 221b,
224a
chimney-pieces see fireplaces, chimney-
pieces and overmantels

chimneys
MEDIEVAL, 15a, 18a, 19b–20a, 84a,
184a, Fig 37
16TH–17TH CENTURY, 24a, 24b, 25b,
210b
choristers (see also Choristers' School),
11a
Choristers' School (Cathedral School,
Choir School)
AT BISHOP'S PALACE, 35b, 53b, 58a
AT BRAYBROOKE (see also
Choristers' Schoolroom), 23b,
179a–b, 180a–b
AT NO. 5 THE CLOSE (Song School),
73a–74b
AT NO. 54 THE CLOSE, 11a, 73b,
167a
Choristers' Schoolroom (56 The Close),
29b, 176b–179a, Plates 130–2,
Fig 120
Choristers' Square, houses in,
146a–188a
Clarendon, Earls of see Hyde
Clarendon Palace (Wilts), 5a, 7a, 8b, 9a
FLOOR TILES FROM, 21b–22a
Clarke, Dean, 202a
Clarke, Elizabeth, wife of James Harris,
100b, 102a
Clarke, James, 131a
Clarke, Liscombe, 239b
clerks of works see Cathedral, clerks of
works
clockmakers: Hughes, Hugh, 179a
clocks, 18th century, 179a
Close
HISTORY AND FOUNDATION, 1a–9b
LANDSCAPING, 18th century, 34a–b
OCCUPANTS
medieval, 9b–13a
16th-17th century, 22b–24a, 28a–b
18th century, 30a–31a, 34b
19th century, 35a
houses in (see also Bishop's Palace):
NO. 5 THE CLOSE see Organist's
House and Song School
NO. 6 THE CLOSE see Chapter Office
NO. 7 THE CLOSE see Deanery;
Simonsbury Place
NOS 7A, 7B AND 8A THE CLOSE,
78b–79a, Plate 42, Fig 29
NO. 8 THE CLOSE, 29a, 78b,
79a–83b, Plate 42, Plate 46,
Figs 31–2
staircase, 29a, 80b, 81b, Fig 34
NO. 9 THE CLOSE, 28a, 29a, 29b,
31a, 78b, 79a–83b, 226b, Plates
42–3, Plate 45, Figs 31–3
dining room, ceiling and chimney-
piece, 80b, 81b–82b, Plate 47,
Plate 48
staircase, 28a, 80b, 82b, Plate 44,
Plate 50, Fig 33
as Training College for

Schoolmistresses, 35a, 80a
woodwork from Cathedral choir-
stalls, 82b–83b, Plates 49–50
NO. 10 THE CLOSE, 18a, 26a, 33a,
83b–85a, Plate 51, Figs 35–9
fireplace, ?15th century, 19b–20a,
84a
hall, 15a, 18a, 84a, 84b, Fig 39;
chimney, 18a, 19b–20a, 84a,
Fig 37; painted decoration, 21b,
84a, Plate 51, Fig 38; tiled
fireback, 20a, 84a
moulded timber window, 16th
century, 24b, 84b, Fig 39
timber-framing, 14th century, 20a,
84a
NO. 11 THE CLOSE, 27b, 35b,
85a–88b, 89a, Plates 52–3, Fig 40
house of chantry priests on site of,
10a, 13a, 85a
mathematical tiles, 33b, 86b, 87a
NO. 12 THE CLOSE see Vicars' Hall
NO. 13 THE CLOSE (see also Vicars'
Hall), 28b, 43a, 88b–92a,
94b–96b, Plate 54, Plate 57,
Plate 62, Figs 43–4, Fig 47
bay window, 33b, 96a
NO. 14 THE CLOSE, 27b, 33b,
96b–98b, Plate 63, Figs 48–9
Close Wall at, 42a, 98b
staircase, 29a, 97b, Fig 49
NO. 15 THE CLOSE see Copped Hall;
Malmesbury House
NO. 16 THE CLOSE, 14a, 24b, 26a,
33b, 103b–105b, Plate 73, Figs
52–3
floorboards, ?medieval, 20b, 104a
NO. 17 THE CLOSE, 25b–26a, 27a,
28b, 75b, 105b–108a, Plates 74–8,
Figs 54–5
Close Wall at, 43b
great chamber, 25b, 26a, 106b,
Plate 76, Plate 77
hall, chimney-piece, 107b, Plate 78
panelling, 17th century, 25b, 26a,
106b
NO. 18 THE CLOSE see Subdeanery,
former
NO. 19 THE CLOSE see Theological
College
NO. 20 THE CLOSE, 30a, 113b–118a,
Plates 84–5, Figs 59–63, Fig 70
gatehouse range of Aula le Stage,
14b, 17b, 30a, 113b, 115a–116b,
122b, 126b, 129a, Plate 84,
Figs 61–3; garden study, 25a,
115b, 128b, 129a; in inventory
(1586), 128b, 129a; roof of
chamber over gateway, 21b, 116b,
Fig 61; timber-framing, 15th
century, 20a, 20b, 115b
staircase, 18th century, 32b, 117a
NO. 21 THE CLOSE see Aula le Stage